D1535486

WITHDRAWN

The Tragedies of
EURIPIDES

The Tragedies of
EURIPIDES

T. B. L. WEBSTER

METHUEN & CO LTD
11 NEW FETTER LANE · LONDON EC4

First published in 1967 by
Methuen & Co Ltd
11 New Fetter Lane London EC4
© *1967 by T. B. L. Webster*
Printed in Great Britain by
W. & J. Mackay & Co Ltd
Chatham, Kent

DISTRIBUTED IN THE USA BY BARNES & NOBLE INC

Contents

Acknowledgements

My wife read my manuscript and Mr. E. W. Handley read my proofs. I am deeply indebted to both of them, but for the errors which remain I am responsible. I am also very grateful to Professor A. D. Trendall for letting me see the proofs of his *The Red-Figured Vases of Lucania, Campania and Sicily* (abbreviated below as *LCS*), which has enabled me to make my appendix on illustrations more correct. My debt to my wife is far more complicated than I can assess, since we talked to each other about Euripides on and off for more than twenty years. Now I can only dedicate this book to her memory.

T. B. L. WEBSTER

I

Introduction

More is preserved of Euripides than of either of the other two great Greek tragic poets. As far as I know, no book in English has given anything like a full account of the lost tragedies since Gilbert Murray added an 'Appendix on lost Plays' to *The Athenian Drama*, III *Euripides* in 1906. That brilliant and sympathetic account deserves to be far better known than it is, and anticipated a number of later conjectures. But much has been discovered since 1906; Professor Page's very useful first volume of *Greek Literary Papyri* (Loeb) in 1940 gave papyrus fragments of eleven plays, all published since 1906, and more papyri and book fragments have been published since 1940.

This book is written in the belief that an attempt to describe all the tragedies of Euripides might be useful to students of ancient drama, both those who know Greek and the much larger number who study ancient drama in translation. For all the surviving plays they have now the admirable translations edited by Richmond Lattimore and David Grene for the University of Chicago Press. The longer papyrus fragments are translated in Professor Page's volume. For the fragments quoted by ancient authors I have provided either translations or briefer paraphrases. Reconstructing lost plays is a dangerous business, and I have therefore thought it essential to give all the evidence (or at least to refer to places where the evidence can be found). Where the argument inevitably involves quotation of Greek, I have tried to make clear the points at issue.

The material is much greater for Euripides than for either of the other two tragic poets. The preserved plays of Euripides take three volumes of the Oxford Classical texts; the preserved plays of Sophocles and Aeschylus take one each. Papyrus fragments exist of fifteen tragedies by Euripides and of perhaps seven by Sophocles and of perhaps ten by Aeschylus (many of these are short, corrupt, and doubtful, so that exact figures for Sophocles and Aeschylus cannot be given). The fragments quoted from ancient authors are published in Nauck's *Tragicorum Graecorum Fragmenta*[2]: Aeschylus occupies 123 pages, Sophocles 124, but Euripides 344, to which must be added the 17 pages of Professor Snell's supplement to the reprint of 1964.

Two other things differentiate the Euripidean material. The seven preserved plays of Aeschylus and of Sophocles are the Byzantine selection. For Euripides we have in addition to the nine plays of the Byzantine selection eight tragedies from a collected edition in alphabetical order, so that we have not only more plays but also plays which have survived by chance. These are the *Helen, Heraclidae, Hercules, Electra, Supplices, Ion, Iphigenia in Tauris, Iphigenia in Aulis.*

Another reason for a study like this is that we have far more chronological information about Euripides' plays than we have about the plays of the other two, so that his plays can be studied in chronological order. In the first place the Hypothesis or Argument affixed to the *Alcestis, Medea,* and *Iphigenia in Aulis* fix their dates and the dates of the plays produced with them; we also have reliable information for the *Peliades, Hippolytus, Erechtheus,* for the *Trojan Women* and the plays produced with it, for the *Helen* and *Andromeda,* for the *Orestes,* and for the *Archelaos*;[1] the *Phoenissae* is firmly dated between 412 and 408 B.C. Secondly, quotation (usually parodied) in dated comedies gives a bottom date for fifteen plays which have no other external evidence to date them.

An extremely valuable internal criterion was exploited by T. Zielinski in *Tragodoumenon libri tres,* Krakau, 1925. The iambic trimeter of spoken dialogue contains six naturally long syllables; any of the first five long syllables may be resolved into two short syllables. Zielinski showed that Euripides used this permission in well under 10% of the trimeters of the plays dated 438, 431, and 428 B.C.; the proportion rose to 16.6% for the long fragments of the *Erechtheus* dated 422 B.C.; 21.2% in the *Trojan Women* of 415 B.C.; 27.4% for the *Helen* in 412 B.C.; 25.8% for the *Phoenissae* (411–09 B.C.); 39.4% for the *Orestes* in 408 B.C.; 34.7% for the *Iphigenia in Aulis* and 37.6% for the *Bacchae,* which are both posthumous. Given these fixed points in what seems to be a remarkably steady progression, it was possible to give approximate dates for the other preserved plays by the same criterion. It is obviously

[1] I have adopted the convention of using the Latin form for the titles of preserved plays and the Greek form for the titles of lost plays.

a less certain indication for the chronology of lost plays, where the number of iambic lines preserved may be small. But there are various indications that the grouping so constructed may be reliable although the order of the plays within the groups must remain conjectural. In the first place Zielinski formulated ten laws which Euripides normally observed in his iambics down to 428 B.C., but then progressively infringed; these infringements, where they appear in the fragments, can be used for dating in addition to the brute count of resolved syllables.[2] Secondly, the dated lost plays agree very well with the dated surviving plays: the fragments of plays dated 455, 438, 431, 412, 407 and posthumous show exactly what one could expect; although *Alexandros* and *Palamedes* in 415 and *Antiope* (411–09 B.C.) have fewer resolutions than they should, they are well ahead of the early plays and *Alexandros* has some good infringements of Zielinski's laws. The five undated plays quoted by Aristophanes in 425 B.C. in the *Acharnians* are all put by their resolution figures in the earliest group, as one would expect. Thirdly, no surviving play before the *Trojan Women* of 415 B.C. has trochaic tetrameters: the three examples in the fragments all belong to plays which are also late on their iambic resolutions, *Meleager*, *Oidipous*, *Archelaos*. A parallel regular development can be shown in lyric monodies and lyric dialogues: this criterion too confirms the sequence of preserved plays constructed on the resolutions in the iambic trimeter; the lyric fragments of lost plays are, however, few and from this point of view unrevealing. (I have sketched this metrical development here simply as an aid to establishing chronology; it does, of course, also reveal a change in the poet's intentions, which must be examined later.)

The following table is based on Zielinski but has been brought up to date by including new evidence which has become known since 1925. Preserved plays of Euripides are in italic type.

I. SEVERE STYLE (30 TRAGEDIES): 455–428 B.C.

Certain dates

455 Peliades 4%
441 First victory
438 Cretan Women 9%, Alkmaion in Psophis 7.5%, Telephos 8.7% (*Alcestis* 5.1% – 17th play)

[2] For a very clear statement of the principles involved, particularly in the later plays cf. A. M. Dale, *Euripides Helen*, xxiiff.

431   *Medea* 6.5%, Philoktetes 6%, Diktys 6%, (Theristai)
428   *Hippolytus II*, 5.6%

Dates with external evidence	*Metrical dates*
Likymnios 0% (before Kratinos, *Archilochoi*, 448)	Alkmene 4%
Aigeus 8.5% (soon after 450, see below, p. 77)	Danae 4%
Heraclidae 5.9% (before *Knights*, 424)	Kretes 0%
Hippolytus I, 5.4%, before 428 (*Hippolytus II*)	Oinomaos 0%
Ino 4% (before *Acharnians*, 425)	Chrysippos 0%
Stheneboia, 8.4% (before *Wasps* 422)	Alope 7%
Bellerophon, 8% (before *Ach.*)	Protesilaos 0%
Phoinix 2.5% (before *Ach.*)	Skyrioi 0%
Oineus 0% (before *Ach.*)	(Kadmos)
Thyestes 7% (before *Ach.*)	
Theseus 3% (before *Wasps* 422)	
Peleus 0% (before *Clouds*, second edition 421–417)	
Phrixos A (prologue)	

II. SEMI-SEVERE STYLE 427–417? (11 TRAGEDIES):

Certain dates

422   Erechtheus 17.4% (see however p. 130)

Dates with external evidence	*Metrical dates*
Hecuba 14.7%, before *Clouds* 423	*Andromache* 12%
Kresphontes 16.6%, before *Georgoi* 424	*Supplices* 14.2%
Melanippe Sophe 16.6%	
Aiolos 10%, before *Clouds* 423	
Electra 17% (421–415)	
Ixion 14% (death of Protagoras)	
Phrixos B 9% (prologue)	
Melanippe Desmotis 19.2% (before Eupolis, *Demes*, 412)	

III. FREE STYLE 416?–409 (16 TRAGEDIES):

Certain dates

415   Alexandros 17.3%, Palamedes 13%, *Troades* 21.2% (Sisyphos)
412   Andromeda 23.6%
     Helen 27.5%

Dates with external evidence	*Metrical dates*
Phoenissae 25.8% (411–409 B.C.)	*Hercules Furens* 21.5%
Hypsipyle 28.3% (411–409 B.C.)	*Iphigenia in Tauris* 23.4%
Antiope 17.4% (411–409 B.C.)	*Ion* 25.8%
Pleisthenes 25%, before *Birds* 414	Antigone 18%
Meleager 26.6%, before *Birds* 414	Phaethon 23.3%
	Polyidos 26.5%

IV. FREEST STYLE 408–6 (9 TRAGEDIES):

Certain dates

408   *Orestes* 39.4%
407   Archelaos 30.5%
Posthumous: Alkmaion in Corinth 62%, *Iphigenia in Aulis* 34.7%, Bacchae 37.6%.

Metrical dates

Auge 42.5%
Oidipous 40%
Temenidai 30%
Temenos 31%

The number of tragedies certainly by Euripides which were known in antiquity and of which either complete versions or fragments have come down to us is sixty-six, which seems to agree with the twenty-two productions given to Euripides by the Souda lexikon. Three tragedies and a satyr-play were produced on each occasion at the City Dionysia. We know from the Hypothesis of the *Alcestis* that the *Alcestis* took the place of a satyr-play in 438 B.C.; of the normal satyr-plays the *Cyclops* survives and we know the titles of *Autolykos, Bousiris, Eurystheus, Skeiron, Syleus,* as well as the *Theristai* of 431 B.C. and the *Sisyphos* of 415 B.C. No satyr-play is recorded for the posthumous production. We know therefore the titles of satyr-plays or pro-satyr plays in nine productions and that there was no Euripidean satyr-play in the last production. We have therefore lost all trace of the satyr-plays of twelve productions: probably some Euripidean satyr-play titles had been lost (for 431 B.C. the title *Theristai* survived but the text was lost) but it is possible that for some productions some other poet provided the satyr play (Demetrios, the poet of the satyr-play celebrated by the Pronomos vase[3] at the end of the fifth century, is unknown as a tragic poet but may have been the contemporary comic poet).

Two other problems remain before the sixty-six tragedies can be accepted without reservation as representing the content of twenty-two productions. No words need be wasted on the *Peirithous*, *Rhadamanthys*, and *Tennes*, which were recognized as spurious in antiquity. The preserved *Rhesus* (which would bring the number to sixty-seven) was also doubted but has been stoutly defended by Professor Ritchie.[4] Quite apart from the absence of all serious thought such as characterizes even the earliest Euripides, the metrical technique excludes Euripides since it is incredible that Euripides should unite in one play iambic trimeters of his earliest manner (before 428), trochaic tetrameters (which we only know from 415 and after), and an anapaestic dialogue for which the only parallel is the posthumous *Iphigenia in Aulis*. The younger Euripides writing in the early fourth century may be the easiest conjecture to account for all the difficulties.

The other problem concerns the *Andromache* and the *Archelaos*. If the *Andromache* was produced in Argos, as some have argued, it may not have been included in the number of productions; the same argument[5] has been used to exclude the *Archelaos*, which we know to have been produced in Macedonia. The easy answer is that what the Souda lexikon says is that Euripides produced 'in 22 years altogether' and does not say where he produced. The case for *Temenos*, *Temenidai*, *Archelaos* belonging together is so good that they certainly cannot be excluded from the list of productions.[6] The information about the *Andromache* is given by the scholiast in a note inspired by Andromache's attack on the Spartans in l. 445.[7] 'Euripides abuses the Spartans because of the war. The Spartans had broken their truce with the Athenians, as Philochoros records. But the play cannot be certainly dated. For it was not produced at Athens. Kallimachos says it carried the name of Demokrates.' All

[3] Cf. my 'Monuments illustrating Tragedy and Satyr play', *B.I.C.S.*, Supplement no. 14, 1962, 48 (second edition, 1967).

[4] W. Ritchie, *The Authenticity of the Rhesus of Euripides*, Cambridge, 1964. See the review of E. D. M. Fraenkel, *Gnomon*, 37, 1965, 228.

[5] E.g. by Van Looy, *Zes Verloren Tragedies van Euripides*, Brussels, 1964, 5 (quoted hereafter as *Zes Tragedies*).

[6] See below, p. 252.

[7] Bibliographical note: Callimachus fr. 451, Pfeiffer; Wilamowitz, *Analecta Euripidea*, 148; D. L. Page in *Greek Poetry and Life*, 206ff.; A. Lesky, *Tragische Dichtung der Hellenen*, 172.

sorts of explanations have been proposed: Demokrates has been emended into Menekrates (a contemporary actor) or Timokrates (an Argive musician who according to the ancient *Life* wrote songs for Euripides) or has been identified with a tragic poet of Sikyon. Professor Page argued for production in Argos on the grounds that Andromache's unique elegiac monody was in the tradition of Argive elegiac laments. Wilamowitz suggested that the play was produced in Athens but under the name of Demokrates.[8] This seems to me more probable and in that case it belonged to a normal Athenian production. If it was produced elsewhere, the conditions may have been the same and the Souda lexikon may have reckoned the three plays produced together as one production.

If twenty-two productions is adopted as a working hypothesis, we can immediately date ten of them: Euripides produced in 455, 441, 438, 431, 428, 415, 412, 408, 407 (in Macedonia), and posthumously. The *Alcestis*, which was produced instead of a satyr-play as the fourth play in 438 B.C., is also said in the Hypothesis to have been the seventeenth play in order of composition. Probably it was really the twentieth, and by the time this numeration was established three of the earliest plays (satyr-plays) had been lost.[9] Then the production of 438 B.C. was the fifth production. It looks as if the production list, down to and including 428, ran I 455 B.C., II undated, III 441 B.C., IV undated, V 438 B.C., VI undated, VII 431 B.C., VIII undated, IX 428 B.C. At the other end productions XX–XXII are dated 408, 407, and posthumous, and the nine tragedies of Zielinski's Group IV, Freest Style, can be allotted to them. For Zielinski's Group III, Free Style, a production before 415 B.C. is needed for the *Meleager* and *Pleisthenes* since both were quoted in Aristophanes' *Birds* in 414 B.C.; 415 B.C. is occupied by the Trojan trilogy; a production between 415 and 412 B.C. is needed for *Iphigenia in Tauris, Hercules Furens*, and another play; 412 B.C. is fixed for *Andromeda, Helen*, and another play; and the scholiast to Aristophanes' *Frogs* 53 attests another production between 412 and 408 B.C. This Group,

[8] The *Life* of Satyros records that Kleon prosecuted Euripides for impiety (39, x), and production under another name might have been necessary at such a moment. Impiety was according to Aristotle (*Rhet.*, 1416a23) used as an argument against Euripides in an exchange suit. And a late teacher of Rhetoric imagined an accusation of impiety against Euripides after the *Hercules Furens* (*P. Oxy.* 2400) but this all adds up to little certain information.

[9] A. M. Dale, *Euripides Alcestis*, V.

therefore, covers Productions XV–XIX, fifteen tragedies and runs from at latest 416 B.C. to at latest 409 B.C. Group II, Semi-Severe style, runs from at earliest 427 to at latest 417 B.C. and covers Productions X–XIV, fifteen tragedies.

The detailed allocation of plays to productions will be discussed in connexion with the individual plays. The principles which guided Euripides in putting plays together seem to have changed between Group I and Group III, and one factor may have been a change in the rules of the competition.[10] In the time of Aeschylus each poet probably had a separate day in which to produce his three tragedies and satyr-play. With the institution of the actors' competition about 450 B.C. the rules were probably changed, and each of the three competing poets produced one tragedy each day so that variety in plays was more telling than an interconnected story. I believe that some time not long before the Trojan trilogy of 415 B.C. the rules were changed again: from now on each poet, instead of having all his plays acted by one company (leading actor, two assistants, and mutes), had the services of all three companies so that he again produced all his three tragedies on a single day but each was acted by a different company; this made it possible for the poet once more to relate the three tragedies to each other in some pattern which he expected the audience to appreciate. The application of these principles and the consideration of the various other factors which may determine the placing of a particular play makes it possible to construct a calendar of Euripidean production. I would not claim that such a calendar is more than a working hypothesis, but it is the easiest method of examining the whole of Euripides' production and tracing his development, if there is a development to be traced.

I have adopted Zielinski's groups (with the slight alterations indicated above in discussing Productions) as my chapter headings. I do not mean thereby to imply that the boundaries between them have any significance other than metrical. Metrically each boundary marks a considerable step forward to freer versification. The highest figure for a preserved play in Group I is 6.5%, the lowest in Group II 12%; the highest in Group II is 17%; the lowest in Group III is 21.2%; the highest in Group III is 27.5%; the lowest reliable figure in Group IV is 37.6%.[11]

[10] Cf. *Hermathena*, 100, 1965, 21.

[11] The 34.6% of the *Iphigenia in Aulis* includes extensive rewriting, and no one after Euripides copied the free late Euripidean iambics.

It is arguable, I think, that in each case a new conception of plot and characters *precedes* a step forward in versification.

Within each chapter I have studied together the three plays produced in a single year whenever possible. But in Groups I and II much of the grouping is necessarily conjectural. There except for 455 (where two plays are known), 438, and 431 B.C., it seemed better to arrange the plays under their different kinds and examine each kind together. Because I wanted to discuss the whole production of Euripides, I had to include the preserved plays, but I had no reason to treat them in great detail because that is admirably done in other books on Euripides, in the commentaries on individual plays, and in books on Greek tragedy and histories of Greek literature. My discussions of the surviving tragedies are summary, eclectic, and only refer to modern literature for particular points.[12] I have given an outline of what happens in each play, but my chief concerns have been first to emphasize the points of connexion between surviving plays and lost plays and secondly to point out those sides of Euripides' art for which the lost plays give us least evidence – the whole complex fabric of spoken, recitative, and sung which constitutes a Greek tragedy, the structure of the whole and the relation of its parts to each other, and the function and texture of the choruses.

For the lost plays we have a number of different kinds of evidence. This evidence will of course be discussed in detail for each play but it may be useful to enumerate the chief kinds here.[13] They can be classified as summaries, papyrus fragments, book fragments, translations, and illustrations. The Hypotheses at the beginning of the surviving plays at best give the background of the story, the story, the date, the other plays produced at the same time and the other competitors. They derive from collections of Hypotheses made at various dates; some at least go back to the fourth century B.C.[14] (I have sometimes wondered whether the original Hypothesis was provided by the poet himself and whether this was what he read to the archon when the archon chose the three tragic poets to compete at the festival in his year.) A papyrus roll of Euripidean hypotheses (*P. Oxy.* 2455-6 of the second century A.D.) was

[12] Very good commented bibliography is given by A. Lesky, *Tragische Dichtung der Hellenen*.

[13] A very good bibliography of the lost plays is given by H. van Looy, *L'Antiquité Classique*, 32, 1963, 162ff., 607ff. I have therefore under the particular plays only quoted bibliography when important for my argument.

[14] G. Zuntz, *Political Plays of Euripides*, Manchester, 1955, 129ff.

published in 1962, and though in an extremely bad state of preservation provides a considerable amount of information on some lost plays. This was arranged alphabetically by titles but there were other collections arranged by the stories of the plays: the individual plays were arranged in the chronological order of the story.[15] The Hypotheses were used by later rhetoricians and mythographers, and we often only know their rehandling. The mythographers in particular have to be used with great caution because they do not usually quote their sources and they may weave their story together out of different sources.

Papyrus fragments of plays vary greatly in length and in state of preservation. The optimum is the *Hypsipyle*, where considerable fragments are preserved from different portions of the play and can be placed either by the numbers attached to each hundredth line or by the physical constitution of their fibres. But even a small papyrus fragment is a chance selection of lines from a complete text, and almost always implies something about what has gone before or what is coming after, so that it almost always gives us more knowledge than is contained in the actual preserved words. The vast majority of book fragments come from anthologies from which someone has excerpted self-contained moral pronouncements from two to four lines long, and in most cases we only know in addition the name of the play. There are of course a certain number of quotations made by ancient authors (as distinct from anthologists) and they occasionally tell us a little more, sometimes the name of the speaker and very occasionally the situation in which the words were spoken.

Greek tragedies were translated by Roman tragedians.[16] Except for the late Seneca, who practically only concerns us in the *First Hippolytos*, they also only survive in book fragments. We very seldom have external evidence as to which Greek tragic poet they are translating and we depend on a lucky coincidence for knowledge. Like the Greek book fragments, too many of their fragments are self-contained and tell us nothing, but the Roman habit of quoting tragedy to illustrate a rare word is in practice more revealing than the Greek habit of excerpting moral sentiments. Cicero also deserves our gratitude for giving a good deal of context and sometimes the name of a speaker.

Greek tragedy was often illustrated on Greek vases and sometimes

[15] Cf. below on the *Peliades*, p. 33.
[16] My references are all to the third edition of O. Ribbeck.

soon after the time of its production. The relevant vases were collected by L. Séchan in *Études sur la Tragédie Grecque*, Paris, 1926, 233ff., with illustrations and a full and useful discussion of the plays. A certain amount of new vase material has been added since 1926, and most of the vases have been attributed more precisely to painters or schools. I have given the recent bibliography of the vases which I have used in an appendix.[17] For some plays the so-called Homeric bowls, which derive from Alexandrian originals of the third century B.C., Hellenistic Etruscan ash-chests, and Pompeian paintings provide information.

From these sources the attempt can be made to reconstruct lost plays. The attempt is worth making both because it gives more information about Euripides and because it may give us a clearer view of the surviving plays. It is reasonable to want to know something about the *Peliades* which was produced only three years after Aeschylus' *Oresteia*, or about the very strange *Oidipous* from the end of Euripides' life. Our view of Hippolytus in the surviving play is, I think, materially altered by seeing how he appeared in the earlier lost play, and our appreciation of the *Trojan Women* is enhanced by knowing how some of the characters conducted themselves in earlier stages of the same story represented in the *Alexandros* and *Palamedes*, which belong to the same production.

Of course all reconstructions are conjectural. The guides, which are at the same time controls, are two. The first is the assumption, which is suggested by the existing plays, that Euripides did change in the course of half a century. The early *Medea* is very unlike the late *Phoenissae*, and we shall suspect that something is wrong if the reconstruction of the *Alkmaion in Psophis* of 438 B.C. looks like the reconstruction of the posthumous *Alkmaion in Corinth*. The other guide and control is the traditional character of Greek tragedy. The poet is producing for a festival. He has to use a chorus; he has only three actors (but he may employ mutes); no scene can have more than four speakers (including the leader of the chorus), and if he wants an actor on stage to come on in another role, he must either send him off in the middle of the scene or have a choral interlude. He cannot change scenery in the course of the play and in fact he has only a palace set and a country set at his disposal. Each set has a single door, a roof, and side-entrances up the parodoi. His stage-machinery is limited to the *ekkyklema* which can be rolled out through the central door and the *mechane* which can swing an actor on

[17] See below, p. 297.

to the stage from behind the stage-building or suspend him above the roof. Certain types of scene suited these conditions: prologue speeches in which a character gives the background for the poet's new treatment of the legend, debates in which two characters (sometimes before a third) put their divergent points of view with no holds barred, and messenger speeches. These are all recognizable in fragments, and the anthologists often chose the sentiments with which messengers finished their speeches as well as the sentiments thrown off in debates. The surviving debates, Medeia and Jason or Theseus and Hippolytos, show how tangential these sentiments can be, not so much because the speeches are rhetorical (though they are) but because an angry Greek says anything and everything that comes into his mind; this is a warning not to try and interpret the sentiments quoted by the anthologist with too narrow a reference to the matter in hand.

The tragic poet must have had to work fast. Euripides produced three tragedies and a satyr-play twenty-two times in fifty years and over the last period from 415 to 406 he only had two years without a production. The archon took office late in June. He had to choose the three poets to compete, and then he had to appoint them their chief actors, who engaged their own two assistants, and their choregos, who engaged the chorus and the flute-player. The poet had to train the actors and the chorus in time for the production in late March. It would be fascinating to know the details of the calendar but on any reckoning the schedule must have been tight. Quite apart from the restrictions of theatre and cast, the poet must have tended to think his chosen story into shapes which had proved successful before, whether in his own plays or in the plays of his rivals. These echoes can sometimes be detected in the lost plays, and sometimes a scene or a theme in a lost play can be shown to antedate its echo in a surviving play.

Aeschylus was the grand old man of tragedy when Euripides was growing up: Euripides was born either in 484, the year of Aeschylus' first victory, or four years later. This means that he would have seen Aeschylean tragedies at least from the time of the *Persae*; and after Aeschylus' death his tragedies were revived.[18] The *Life of Aeschylus*

[18] On revivals cf. most recently R. Cantarella, *Rendiconti Lincei*, 20, 1965, 363. In general for a very interesting comparison of Aeschylus and Euripides see J. de Romilly, *L'Évolution du Pathétique*, 1961, particularly 52 'luring scenes', 58 suppliant scenes, 118 Klytemnestra and Medeia.

gives Aeschylus thirteen victories, but the Souda lexikon gives him twenty-eight. This may mean that fifteen victories were won with Aeschylean tragedies after his death in 456 and before the regular institution of the competition for old tragedies in 386 B.C. Four of these may have been the victories which Euphorion is said to have won with tragedies that his father had not yet produced; the rest were won by other poets (or actors?). Dikaiopolis' expectations in the *Acharnians* mean that Aeschylus was revived in 426; his disappointment was due to a change in the order of the festival, not to the dropping of Aeschylus. A few years later was the revival of the *Oresteia*, which caused Aristophanes' allusion to the *Choephoroi* in the *Second Clouds* and sparked off Euripides' *Electra*. The suggestion that our *Septem* is a version revised for production under the influence of the Sophoclean *Antigone* is perhaps the easiest way of accounting for the discordant ending. Here again the revival may have moved Euripides to write his very different *Phoenissae* and *Oidipous*.

The *Electra* and the *Phoenissae* allow us to formulate crudely what Euripides did in his later period. He stripped away the Aeschylean divine machinery, and rethought the story as a situation in which ordinary people are involved – members of a family including connexions by marriage, friends, and retainers, all contributing their individual actions or reactions to the general situation of which the essential action is the murder of a mother by a son in the *Electra* and the double fratricide in the *Phoenissae*.

Euripides could use Aeschylus in two ways. He could take a story which Aeschylus had already dramatized and remodel it from his own point of view, or he could borrow a type of character, a situation, or a dramatic effect from an Aeschylean play and insert it into a play on a different theme. Here he is simply borrowing something which he regarded as effective; the first use also implies criticism of Aeschylus' treatment of the story.

That Euripides was partly at least inspired by the Aeschylean Klytemnestra to write his plays about bad women seems to me likely. She was both a murderess like Medeia and an adulteress like Stheneboia and her fellows. The parallel between the unhappy women of Aeschylus and the unhappy women of Euripides is not so clear. But Laodameia and Hekabe clearly belong to a tradition which goes back to Atossa in the *Persians* and Europe in the *Carians*, and the conduct of the Danaids could have given him the idea of the suffering woman who turns into a murderess like Alkmene in the *Heraclidae*. And Aeschylus had already brought a pregnant Semele on the stage in the *Semele* (356M), which may have inspired Euripides' much more realistic treatment of Deidameia in the *Skyrioi*. Aeschylus' *Iphigeneia* must have contained the sacrifice of Iphigeneia, which he describes so movingly in the *Agamemnon*, and this may be the ancestor of Euripides' scenes of heroic self-sacrifice. More remotely Prometheus' defiance of Zeus has an echo in the Euripidean Bellerophon's flight to heaven.

What I have called above the traditional forms of Greek tragedy were in a large measure the creation of Aeschylus, and in a number of instances we can point to a particular shaping of these traditional forms by Aeschylus which was later taken over by Euripides. In Aeschylus' *Hiketides*, probably produced in 463 B.C., the daughters of Danaos took refuge on an altar and so set the pattern for many altar scenes in Euripides. (In the *Danaides*, if not already in the *Aigyptioi*, Hypermnestra separated herself from the chorus of her sisters, and this may have been the model for Alkestis and her sisters in Euripides' early *Peliades*.) The agonized decision of Pelasgos to accept the Suppliants is the ancestor of speeches of decision in Euripides; the most obvious example is Medeia's decision to kill her children.

The *Oresteia*, which was first produced only three years before Euripides' first production contains many 'pre-echoes'. The watchman of the *Agamemnon* and the nurse of the *Choephoroi* are realistic figures like the faithful and unfaithful retainers in Euripides, but Euripides gives his retainers a new independence of action which sometimes affects the course of the story. Klytemnestra's welcome to Agamemnon is a superb luring of the victim to his doom, which Euripides takes over and uses quite differently in the *Hecuba* and *Electra*. The *Choephoroi* has the earliest recognition that we know and it is followed by an intrigue – a sequence which Euripides used again in the *Kresphontes* and frequently afterwards: it has the first surviving mad scene, enacted and not told in a messenger speech (in the *Xantriai*, and perhaps in the *Toxotides*, Aeschylus brought Lyssa, a personification of madness, on the stage like Euripides in the *Hercules*). In the *Eumenides*, the change of scene (from Delphi to Athens) was marked by the chorus leaving the orchestra, as perhaps in the Euripidean *Andromeda*; there was a trial scene before judge and jury, which Euripides adapted to the simpler form of a debate

INTRODUCTION   15

before a single judge (the earliest which we can detect is the dispute
between Telephos and Menelaos before Agamemnon in the *Telephos*
of 438 B.C.); and the subsidiary chorus introduced at the end foreshadows the subsidiary chorus of boys in the Euripidean *Supplices*.
(Further examples of borrowing will be discussed below where they
are relevant.)

The relation between Sophocles and Euripides is much more difficult to define. In later years some clear instances can be shown in which
each poet stoutly maintained his own position against the other. The
Euripidean *Electra*, which with its country-setting, its pathetic Klytemnestra, its bitterly repentant Elektra and Orestes, brought the Aeschylean *Choephoroi* down to the level of everyday and ended with an open
criticism of Apollo, was answered some five years later by the Sophoclean *Electra*, which focused the whole action on Elektra herself, black-
washing Klytemnestra and minimizing Orestes' part so as to make
Apollo's command tolerable. Euripides answered five years later with a
neurotic wreck in the *Orestes*. The three Philoktetes plays have a much
wider spread of time, and Sophocles was not answering Euripides' play
of 431 when he wrote his *Philoktetes* in 409; similarly Euripides was not
answering Sophocles when he wrote his very different *Antigone* in
414(?). But the Oidipous of the *Oedipus Coloneus* may reasonably be
seen as a restatement of the fierce unbroken hero of the *Oedipus Rex*,
who passionately protests his innocence, thwarts his enemies including
his own son, helps his benefactor, and in the end is marvellously translated so that in some sense the gods are justified. This is an answer to
Euripides' picture of the Theban family in the *Phoenissae* with the wise,
resigned Iokaste, the sympathetic Polyneikes, the odious Eteokles,
and the broken, pathetic old Oidipous, and to the strange *Oidipous*, of
which at least we know that Oidipous did not blind himself but was
blinded by the retainers of Laios and that Iokaste remained loyal to him
through everything.

Earlier in the century one other sequence has been plausibly suggested:[19] Euripides' *First Hippolytos*, in which Phaidra shamelessly
approached Hippolytos herself, Sophocles' *Phaidra*, and Euripides'
Second Hippolytos. Sophocles seems to have made excuses for his
Phaidra, but they were excuses which Euripides could not accept. His
second Phaidra still acts against her conscience even if she lacks the

[19] See below, p. 74, for details.

shamelessness of the first Phaidra. In the same period (the late thirties and the early twenties) Sophocles' *Tereus* and Euripides' *Medea* both centred on women who murdered their children and Sophocles' *Trachiniae* on a woman who murdered her husband. Both the Sophoclean heroines were cruelly provoked; Prokne was roundly condemned for exceeding human bounds, but Deianeira in the *Trachiniae*, like the Sophoclean Phaidra and his Oidipous, could claim ignorance, whereas Medeia, like the second Euripidean Phaidra, is terribly aware that she is doing wrong.

For the earlier period of Sophocles we are largely in the dark. If the institution of the actor competition about 450 B.C. both put an end to the poet acting in his own plays and to the production of connected trilogies,[20] we can be fairly certain that the *Thamyras*, in which Sophocles himself played the hero, had a remote formal echo in Amphion's song in the *Antiope*, and that in the *Mysians* (the second play of the *Telepheia*) Auge was saved at the last moment from murdering her unrecognized son Telephos: this was reported in a messenger speech, but Euripides some thirty years later put a similar scene on the stage in the *Kresphontes*.[21] The two preserved plays of Sophocles which can be fairly certainly dated in the neighbourhood of 440 B.C., the *Ajax* and *Antigone*, both deal essentially with the problem of a great individual at variance with authority. As resisters, Ajax and Antigone have some likeness to the Aeschylean Prometheus: both choose certain death rather than abandon their ideals. There is no real analogy for them in Euripides: Bellerophon and Pentheus resist, but they resist the gods, not men, and they do not expect death; Makaria and the others who accept self-sacrifice choose death, but in modern phraseology they are heroines, not martyrs. If, as seems possible, the *Ajax* and *Antigone* in some sense reflected Sophocles' reaction to the political situation of the forties, Euripides either did not react in the same way or did not dramatize his reaction.

Sophocles started to produce thirteen years before Euripides, but from 455 till Euripides left Athens after the Dionysia of 408 they were producing together in Athens and together accounted for something like a third of the total number of tragedies produced at the City festival. They were producing in the same theatre for the same festival under the

[20] *Hermathena*, 100, 1965, 21ff.
[21] See below, p. 131. Other examples of echoes are given under individual plays.

same strict conditions: only three actors, a chorus, a minimum of scenery. Inevitably they borrowed effects from each other on far more occasions than we can detect. Unless some criterion can be discovered for dating the lost plays of Sophocles, our knowledge of this interaction will remain hopelessly imprecise, particularly on such questions as to which was responsible for changes in choral technique and for the development of lyric dialogues and monodies. But their approach to tragedy was essentially different, as Sophocles himself said. What he meant by calling Euripides' characters 'the sort of people that are' is fairly clear even from the fragments of Euripides' earliest play, the *Peliades*. Sophocles' own characters, 'the sort of people that ought to be drawn', had perhaps to conform to a double standard: major characters must exemplify (usually by breaking it) the rule that mortals should have mortal thoughts, and minor characters must be shaped to display facets of major characters. The period when they were nearest together in spite of these differences was the period when Euripides was writing plays in which a small number of major characters dominated and directed the action, before he had multiplied characters to an extent where they could no longer direct or dominate but only influence the action. Our evidence for Sophocles is insufficient at all stages, but in the three late surviving plays, *Electra*, *Philoctetes*, *Oedipus Coloneus*, the chief characters still dominate the action even if they do not still direct it.

One other name should be mentioned here, the lyric poet Timotheos of Miletos. Both Plutarch (*Mor.* 795d) and Satyros' *Life of Euripides* (39, xxii) tell the story of Euripides comforting him after a defeat. Satyros gives the fuller version: Timotheos was considering suicide, but Euripides made fun of his audience and comforted him because he saw in him a great musician; he further helped him by writing the prologue of the *Persae*, and success with this restored Timotheos' opinion of himself. The victory with the *Persae,* as Paul Maas[22] saw, must have been won in Athens and must have been the victory won over the ageing

---

[22] On Timotheos see Wilamowitz, *Timotheos die Perser*, 1903. The latest text is D. L. Page, *Poetae Melici Graeci*, nos. 788–791. Wilamowitz' late dating of the *Persae* has been dealt with by S. E. Bassett, *C.P.*, 26, 1931, 153; P. Maas, *R.E.*, VI A 2, 1232. Timotheos was born between 462 and 446 B.C. (*Marmor Parium* and *Souda*). He may also have written tragedy (the *Telepheia* inscription, *I.G.* II², 3091, and the Themison inscription, *Hesperia*, 22, 1953, 192). The preserved hexameter opening of the *Persae*, *P.M.G.*, no. 788, may be by Euripides or may belong to a new opening by Pylades. On Phrynis see A. W. Pickard-Cambridge, *Dithyramb*² etc., 43f.

Phrynis. Phrynis was still the rage in 423 (Ar. *Nub.* 970) but had won a Panathenaic victory in 446, and his teacher was famous at the time of the Persian wars. Paul Maas put the *Persae* between 420 and 415 B.C. Timotheos had supplanted Phrynis by the time that Pherekrates wrote his *Cheiron.*[23] Pherekrates describes Timotheos' music as 'twisting ant-tracks', a phrase which Aristophanes uses in 411 B.C. to describe the music of the young tragic poet Agathon (*Thesm.* 100). This both gives a good bottom date for Timotheos' triumph and shows that his musical style affected tragedy as well as choral lyric.

For Euripides himself Bassett made the essential point that the long polymetric narrative of the attempted murder of Helen sung by the frightened Phrygian in the *Orestes* (1369ff.) not only recalls the *Persae* in manner and metre but also in one line echoes its words: *Or.* 1397 Ἀσιάδι φωνᾷ, βασιλέων echoes *Persae* (Page, *P.M.G.,* no. 791, 147) Ἀσιάδι φωνᾷ διάτορον, Wilamowitz[24] had seen the connexion in metre, but his late dating of the *Persae* obscured the relationship. A minor point which again suggests that Euripides was aware of a debt to Timotheos is his reference to the lyre as Asiatic. In the whole of tragedy the lyre is only called 'Asiatic' or 'the Asiatic (instrument)' in the *Erechtheus* which was produced in 422, in the *Hypsipyle* produced probably in 410, and in the *Cyclops,* which may have been produced in 408.[25] Timotheos came from Miletos, and to call the lyre Asiatic was a compliment to him: Euripides paid it first probably at the time when he most needed consoling.

Some 240 lines of the *Persae* survive, the end of the narrative of Salamis and a tailpiece in which Timotheos speaks of his defeat at Sparta and his new music. The preserved narrative connects together four laments in direct speech, one by a swimming Persian, one by Persians huddled together on the shore, one by a Phrygian captured by a Greek, and one by Xerxes himself. The style varies from extreme artificiality to extreme realism. The metre of the 39-line tailpiece is alternating glyconics and pherecrateans with a rather more elaborate

[23] I. Düring, *Eranos,* 43, 1945, 179; Schmid-Stählin, 4, 101.

[24] *Griechische Verskunst,* 333, cf. 340, 356, connexion with *Phoen.*

[25] *Erechtheus* fr. 370N² imitated by Aristophanes, *Thesm.* 120 (who puts it in the mouth of Agathon); *Hyps.,* fr. 64, 101 (Bond); *Cycl.* 443. On the dating see A. M. Dale, *Wiener-Studien,* 69, 1956, 106, Schmid-Stählin, 3, 533 n. 2; A. D. Trendall, *Frühitaliotische Vasenmalerei,* 24; *LCS,* 27.

aeolic ending. But the narrative itself is written in short lines, mostly single-short dimeters, often syncopated and more often iambic than trochaic; occasionally double-short lines are inserted, aeolic, dactylic, or choriambic; and there are a few obvious runs of identical lines: 90–3, choriambic dimeters; 116–20, cretics; 130–133, dactyls; 144–147, iambic dimeters; 164–167 trochaic dimeters. The monody of the Phrygian in the Orestes is not unlike, but it has a large admixture of dochmiacs, particularly in the second section (1382ff.), and anapaests,[26] particularly in the third section (1404), because these metres are traditional in dramatic monodies; a great deal of the rest is in single-short dimeters, sometimes iambic, sometimes trochaic, often syncopated. The insertions of double-short are mostly anapaestic, but three times choriambic and once dactylic. The runs of identical lines are much more numerous in proportion to the length of the narrative: 1403–6, anapaests; 1419–24 cretics; 1437–40 bacchiac; 1444–1446 iambic dimeters; 1485–7 anapaests; 1490–2 dochmiacs. Thus Euripides patterns his lyric narrative more than Timotheos, and he also cuts it into six sections by the iambic trimeters spoken by the chorus, but the influence is clear.

As Timotheos shows no sign of strophic correspondence, we naturally look to the astrophic songs of Euripides to detect his influence. Epodes added to strophes and antistrophes, whether sung by the chorus or by an actor, are of course old, but from the time of the Trojan Women (551–67) Euripides frequently composes long epodes; for instance, the epode of the parodos in the posthumous Iphigenia in Aulis (206–230) runs to twenty-five lines. The new style[27] is however most obvious in monodies and lyric dialogues. The earliest preserved example is the recognition dialogue of the Iphigenia in Tauris (827–99), the dominant metre is dochmaic (normal and dragged) but there are insertions of iambics, cretics, and anapaests; the whole structure is punctuated by the spoken trimeters of Orestes. The recognition duets of the next production, Helen (625–97) and Ion (1437–1509) in 412 are even more varied, particularly the Ion where the dochmiacs have yielded a great deal of ground to 'associable metres'.[28] The still later Hypsipyle

[26] Timotheos does probably have a run of anapaestic dimeters in P.M.G., no. 800.
[27] On the new style in stasima see W. Kranz, Stasimon, 235ff.
[28] On the Helen see A. M. Dale Euripides Helen, 104ff. and on 'associable metres' see her Lyric Metres of Greek Drama, 198.

(between 412 and 408 B.C.) had apparently eighty-three lines of recognition duet,[29] and the preserved part shows dochmiacs interspersed with iambics, cretics, anapaests, dactyls, and trochaics. But all the recognition duets have a pattern element in the spoken trimeters of one of the partners. The *Phoenissae*, probably produced in the same year, has four great passages of polymetric astrophic song: the dialogue of Antigone and the old man (103–192), the monody of Iokaste (301–354), and the two lyric dialogues of Antigone and Oidipous (1455–1580, 1710–1758. After the *Orestes* Iphigeneia has two long polymetric monodies in the *Iphigenia in Aulis* (1279–1335, 1475–1509). If Maas' dating of Timotheos' *Persae* before 415 is right, it looks as if Euripides waited until the new music was well established before he took it over into tragedy first for recognition duets and then for monodies. Nothing can be said of the music, but metrically Euripides never goes so far as Timotheos. Even with his increasing use of resolution in aeolo-choriambic metres the shape of the lines is clearer, partly because metrical pause coincides with word end more often, partly because he uses more and longer runs of metrically identical lines and other pattern elements. But the new music clearly gives a new range of expression for his characters in his last two periods.

Aeschylus fought at Marathon and Sophocles held administrative offices, but very little is known of Euripides' life.[30] His father is said to have started him off as an athlete; then he became a painter, then he turned to tragedy. The father who misinterprets an oracle is too common a figure to encourage belief in the story that Euripides became an athlete in the hope of victories. In view of his vivid visual imagination one would like to believe that he was a painter. Most ancient authorities put in a school period with Archelaos, Anaxagoras, Protagoras, Prodikos, and Sokrates before he turned to tragedy: of the list of teachers only Anaxagoras was certainly older than Euripides; Prodikos and Sokrates were certainly younger. The school period is obviously a deduction from later educational practice. The Souda lexikon varies this by saying that Euripides turned to tragedy because he saw the

[29] Fr. 64, 70–152.
[30] The ancient sources are the *Life* of Satyros (G. Arrighetti, *Studi Class. e Or.*, 13, 1965), the *Life* attached to the manuscripts (reprinted by Arrighetti and in the Budé, vol. I), Aulus Gellius *N.A.*, xv, 20, the Souda Lexikon. A very good assessment is given by P. T. Stevens, *J.H.S.*, 86, 1956, 87.

dangers which Anaxagoras ran for his beliefs; if his source took into account the date of the *Peliades*, it must also, like Professor Davison,[31] have placed Anaxagoras' trial in 456/5. But why tragedy should be safer than philosophy is not apparent.

These are not Euripides' teachers but they may have had some effect on his thought. Archelaos is too dim a figure for his influence to be detected. For Anaxagoras' influence ancient authorities quote Hippolytos' appeal to mother earth (601), the generation of living things from earth and aither and their return to earth and aither (*Chrysippos*, $859N^2$), the separation of earth and heaven and the generation of living things from them (*Melanippe Sophe*, $484N^2$), Hekabe's prayer to Zeus as 'necessity of nature or mind of men' in the *Trojan Women* (886), the golden clod or golden rock of the sun in the *Phaethon* ($783N^2$) and the *Orestes* (982), and the source of the Nile in the *Helen* (3) and *Archelaos* ($228N^2$).[32] Certainly these references show that Euripides knew the theories of Anaxagoras. Most of them are passing allusions. The fragment from the *Chrysippos*[33] is probably a consolation; we do not know that Anaxagoras developed his cosmogony in this direction but it is compatible with his statement that 'coming to be is a mingling and passing away a separation' (B17). Melanippe is using Anaxagoras' cosmogony to show that miracles are impossible and therefore that babies discovered in a cowshed cannot be monstrous births of the royal cattle.[34] Melanippe gives her mother Hippo as her authority: Euripides modernizes her wisdom by putting it in Anaxagorean form. For the *Trojan Women* (884ff.) Satyros quotes 'whether necessity of nature or mind of men' as Anaxagorean; the rather confused ancient commentator on the passage takes 'mind of men' as 'the mind which goes through everything' and attributes this conception to Anaxagoras. Here in a moment of astonishment, when she thinks Helen is to be punished, Hekabe says really 'whatever is the explanation of the universe, there appears to be a principle of justice at work'. But we have no evidence that Anaxagoras extended his cosmogony to include Ethics. Euripides here uses modern philosophy to express Hekabe's

[31] *C.Q.*, 3, 1953, 41f.
[32] The other passages quoted come from the spurious *Peirithoos* either certainly ($593N^2$) or probably ($912, 964N^2$).
[33] Cf. below, p. 111.
[34] Cf. below, p. 148.

deep emotion. Later when Hekabe tears Helen to pieces, she says 'your mind seeing Paris became Kypris', i.e. sexual passion. We do not know that Anaxagoras so rationalized Aphrodite, but he said that what we call Iris is the reflection of the sun in the clouds (B19). Hekabe's explanation of Aphrodite is consistent with Anaxagoras' equation of Zeus with universal mind and so with disparate human minds.

Prodikos, who was younger than Euripides but was well-known in Athens by 423 B.C. (Aristophanes, *Clouds*), said that men originally called beneficial natural phenomena gods so that bread was believed to be Demeter and wine Dionysos (Diels-Kranz B5); Euripides is clearly quoting him in the *Bacchae* (275f.) when Teiresias speaks of Demeter nourishing men with dry things and Dionysos discovering the liquid draft of the grape. (It is possible that Satyros in his *Life* connected Euripides' injunctions to young men to win fame by toil with Prodikos' parable of Herakles' choice of Virtue rather than Vice;[35] but in fact such passages are found from the earliest to the latest plays and need no other source than the established view of a hero.)

The *Life* prefixed to our manuscripts of Euripides adds Protagoras as one of Euripides' teachers. He is not mentioned by the Souda or Aulus Gellius; possibly the section in Satyros (39, ii–iii) about tyrants and bad politicians quoted Protagoras, but the passage in which an authority was probably named is lost. We have, however, the tradition recorded by Diogenes Laertius (IX, 54) that Protagoras read his book *On the Gods* in Euripides' house. It is true that other traditions give other places, but at least this is independent evidence for a belief in a connexion between Protagoras and Euripides. The thought and the chronology of Protagoras have been much discussed.[36] Protagoras seems to have set up as a public teacher in Athens soon after 460, left Athens for Thourioi 444/3, was back in Athens by 443, was certainly in Athens in 422/1, and was probably accused and condemned soon after. His teaching embraced theology, physics, ethics, politics, and rhetoric. His statement that there are two opposed arguments on every subject (Diels-Kranz B 6a) is quoted by Euripides in the early *Phoinix* (fr. 812N²) and in the late *Antiope* (fr. 189N²), and probably the debates in all Euripidean plays

[35] Arrighetti, *op. cit.*, III.
[36] See particularly W. Nestle, *Platon Protagoras*, 1931, 11ff.; J. S. Morrison, C.Q., 35, 1941, 1ff.; J. A. Davison, C.Q., 3, 1953, 41ff.

show something of Protagoras' technique of argument. If, as J. S. Morrison suggests, the Persian political debate in Herodotos (III, 8off.) owes much to Protagoras, then the Euripidean political debates which remind us of these chapters of Herodotos may well derive from Protagoras rather than Herodotos; Theseus' debate with the Theban herald in the *Suppliants* (403ff.) is the most obvious case.[37] and Theseus' account of the growth of civilization (*Suppliants* 195ff.) has naturally been compared with the myth of Plato's *Protagoras*. The earlier part of Plato's myth is closely paralleled in Herodotos (III, 108) and therefore it seems probable that, as the style suggests, Plato is truthfully reporting Protagoras. In the same play Adrastos asserts that courage can be taught, and this with a number of passages (e.g. *Phoinix* fr. 811N²) in Euripides agrees with Protagoras' view that virtue can be taught at least to the right people (Diels-Kranz, B 3a). Nestle saw an echo of Protagoras' relativism (Diels-Kranz, B1) in the *Aiolos* (22N²): 'What is base if it does not seem so to those who practise it?' and later in the *Phoenissae* (499ff.), where Eteokles says that men give the same names to their ideals but the objects that they actually pursue differ widely. Iokaste's answer that proportional balance is an ideal in politics as well as a fact in nature (535ff.) uses the idea of balance on which Protagoras builds the economy of the natural world.

The opening sentence of *On the Gods* (Diels-Kranz, B 4), which Protagoras is said to have read in Euripides' house, states his inability to know either that the gods exist or do not exist or of what form they are. But he cannot have stopped there. Nestle has suggested that the positive side is given in the myth of Plato's dialogue and Protagoras' later exposition of it: 'man alone of living things believes in the gods and worships them' (322A) and 'the laws were invented by old and good lawgivers' (326D). Law is too narrow a translation for the Greek *nomos*, which includes customs such as religious belief, and 'believes in' is in fact the verb derived from *nomos*. Protagoras may then have said that knowledge about the gods is impossible, but belief in the gods is a human characteristic and the whole fabric of ethical and political conduct which is supported by such a belief should be respected as the work of ancient and good lawgivers. Euripides, as Nestle saw, comes very near to this in the *Hecuba*, when Hekabe appeals to Agamemnon

[37] See below, pp. 125. Arrighetti 116ff. on Satyros 39, ii–iii, quotes also *Hec.* 254; *Or.* 902; frs. 362, 626, 644, 738, 784N².

as King to punish Polymestor, who has murdered his guest, her son
Polydoros (798ff.): 'I am a slave and weak, it is true. But the gods are
strong, and the Nomos, which is their master. For by Nomos we
believe in the gods and determine right and wrong in our lives. If you
allow this Nomos to be destroyed and no penalty is paid by those who
kill guests or rob sanctuaries, there is no balance in human affairs.' We
may not know that gods exist, but the same Nomos includes belief in
them and standards of right and wrong, and on upholding this Nomos
depends 'the balance in human affairs', which Iokaste later compared
to the balance in nature (*Phoen.* 535ff.). A less striking passage, which
also comes very near to Protagoras' 'invented by old and good lawgivers', is Teiresias' retort to Pentheus (*Bacch.* 200ff.): 'Our wisdom is
nothing in the eyes of the gods. But our ancestral traditions which are
as old as time, will not be destroyed by the cleverest human argument.' We cannot know about the gods; but Protagoras would say
that their existence and their forethought was a reasonable deduction
from human religious observances and the principles which appear to
obtain in the natural world.

The two cross-references to Protagoras in Herodotos come in
passages which were probably composed in Athens between 448 and
442 B.C. If Nestle is right in seeing an allusion to *On the Gods* when
Kreon in Sophocles' *Antigone* (1043) says that he knows well that no
man can pollute the gods, that too would be dated before 442 B.C. Even
if the book was composed so early, it was still well known in 421 when
Eupolis (146K) speaks of Protagoras talking nonsense about the heavens
and eating the fruits of the earth, so that when Pythodoros secured his
condemnation for impiety he was not flogging a dead horse. The
allusions to Protagoras which have been detected in Euripides (apart
from his use of debates, which goes back at least to the *Telephos* in
438 B.C. and probably earlier) start with the *Phoinix*, in the first period,
continue with the *Hecuba* and *Suppliants*, which can be dated between
428 and 423, probably nearer the later date, and then run through the
later plays, long after Protagoras' death. The *Suppliants* is the most
important. In other cases, even in Hekabe's appeal to Agamemnon, we
can say that Euripides is modernizing, that he is giving a heroic character the sort of ideas which a contemporary Athenian would quote in
such a situation, but Theseus in the *Suppliants* is surely Euripides' ideal
ruler, and Theseus both when he speaks of politics and when he speaks

of divine providence seems to quote Protagoras, and he approves Adrastos when Adrastos gives Protagoras' theory of education. The Theseus again is surely speaking with the mouth of Euripides when he insists on Herakles, who is sitting muffled among the dead bodies of his wife and children, uncovering his head (*H.F.*, 1232): 'you are a mortal and you cannot pollute what is divine'. And this also may be a quotation of Protagoras. As Nestle pointed out, the difference we have seen between Sophocles and Euripides is beautifully demonstrated by the fact that Sophocles makes Kreon at his most impious hold the same view that Theseus quotes when he is nursing Herakles back to sanity.

The other thinker whom all our sources connect with Euripides is Socrates. Aulus Gellius and the Souda lexikon send Euripides to lectures on moral philosophy by Socrates. Satyros (39, i) accounts for Euripides' unpopularity by his admiration for Socrates: in the *Danae* Euripides made Socrates alone exempt from the universal desire for money. The reference is clearly to fr. 325N^2: 'No man born is above money, or if there is one I do not see who he is.' This is rather like the interpretation of Oiax' lament for Palamedes (588N^2) as a reference to the death of Socrates (although it was written sixteen years before Socrates died). It is curious that no ancient authority, as far as we know, found a reference to Socrates in Medeia's words to Kreon (*Med.*, 300f.): 'if the city thinks you superior to those who have a reputation for wisdom, you will not be popular'. Satyros goes on to quote as Socratic in sentiment a fragment of Euripidean dialogue (1007cN^2): 'if these things are done secretly, whom do you fear? The gods, who see further than men.' Such a view is certainly possible for Socrates, and Satyros plainly thinks that Euripides was influenced by Socrates' ethics.

The *Life* prefixed to our manuscripts cites the comic poet Telekleides (39–40K) as evidence that Socrates helped Euripides write his plays. The charge is repeated by Kallias (fr. 12K) and by Aristophanes in the *Clouds* (fr. 376K, omitted from the second edition, which is preserved).[38] Aristophanes' *Clouds* was first produced in 423 B.C.; Kallias' play has been dated about 430 and Telekleides, who started to produce about 450, is unlikely to have written much after 430. [39] According to Telekleides Socrates supplied the firewood (which cooked

[38] Diogenes Laertius, 2, 18 quotes Kallias and Aristophanes as well as Telekleides.
[39] The dates confirm A. E. Taylor's view that Socrates had abandoned science for philosophy by 430 B.C. Professor Ferguson omits this evidence in *Eranos* 62, 70f.

up the play); for Kallias Euripides was the mother and Socrates the father of the play; for Aristophanes it is Socrates who writes the talkative, clever tragedies of Euripides. He says essentially the same thing nearly twenty years later in the *Frogs*, when the chorus, after congratulating Aeschylus on going back to Athens, say of Euripides: 'it is better not to sit beside Socrates and talk, abandoning Poetry and failing in the most important part of tragic art'. According to Aristophanes it is realism and rhetoric that Euripides learnt from Socrates, and the teaching of rhetoric is Aristophanes' real charge against Socrates in the *Clouds*.

Other stories connect Euripides and Socrates.[40] Euripides lent Socrates a text of Herakleitos, which Socrates appreciated but found very difficult. Socrates walked out during a performance of the *Auge* when he heard the line: 'It is best to abandon these things as chance'.[41] He was revolted by this suggestion that there was no criterion of excellence, but he demanded an encore of the first three lines of the *Orestes*: 'There is no word nor suffering nor heaven-sent disaster so terrible that human nature could not support its burden.' According to Aelian Socrates seldom went to the theatre but always attended new productions of Euripides, and if Euripides was taking part in a contest at the Peiraieus, he even went there; for he rejoiced in his wisdom and in the excellence of his lines. Aelian's story so obviously reflects Hellenistic and later practice (the competition of new tragedies and competitions at the Peiraieus) that it throws doubt on the whole lot; and the most that we can say is that there was a tradition that Socrates admired Euripides, just as the *Lives* of Euripides show that there was a tradition that Euripides admired his younger contemporary.

The comic poets' evidence is also suspect, but it is interesting that the charge of co-operation is made just at the time when Euripides was emphasizing the conflict between passion and reason, and this may have been the starting point.[42] Aristophanes, however, ascribes the talkative, clever element in Euripidean tragedy to Socrates; he expands this later in the *Frogs* (946ff.) where Euripides describes his own drama: first of all the actor said what kind of play it was; then no character was silent, woman, slave, master, girl, old woman; I taught them all to

[40] Diogenes Laertius, 2, 22; 2, 33; Cicero, *Tusc.*, 4, 63; Aelian, *V.H.*, 2, 13.
[41] The same line occurs at *El.* 379; presumably Euripides repeated it in the *Auge*.
[42] See below, p. 76.

talk. It is realism and rhetoric which comprises the talkative and clever element; in the surviving *Clouds* Socrates is consulted primarily as a teacher of rhetoric. But, as far as we know, Socrates did not teach rhetoric. He did argue, and the object of his arguing was to make men lead better lives. This was near enough to make it possible for Aristophanes to use the familiar ugly Athenian as an envelope for everything which he most disliked in the scientific, educational, and rhetorical thought of the time. This is generally agreed, and it means that the realism and the rhetoric in Euripides are better associated, if an outside influence is felt necessary, with Protogaras and Prodikos than with Socrates.

The story that Euripides lent Socrates a text of Herakleitos points up the difference between them. Euripides, according to the *Life*, wrote his plays in a cave on Salamis to avoid the crowd, and his library is attested by Aristophanes (*Frogs* 943, 1407); Socrates borrowed Herakleitos from Euripides and heard someone reading aloud from a book of Anaxagoras (*Phaedo* 97c). Euripides read and wrote in a cave by the sea; Socrates talked to people in the agora and the gymnasia. Socrates harried those whom he met towards ethical definitions by ingenious and ruthless argument; Euripides got inside his characters by deep sympathy and this is what the realism ascribed to him by Sophocles and Aristophanes means. Euripides and Socrates were extremely different but they had some obvious points of contact. They certainly shared an interest in philosophy, in theological thought, in ethical values, and above all in personal integrity, but Euripides was perhaps more pessimistic about the possibilities of change. They both to some extent accepted traditional religion. Socrates' whole mission was the result of an oracle, and he spent his last days in prison writing poetry because a dream had commanded it; if death was not a sleep, he hoped to meet the heroes of the past in a traditional Hades. Euripides' position can only be discussed when all the plays have been surveyed, but his fondness for tying his story on to a particular cult at the end of the play surely implies that he perceived some value in traditional religion. They both abjured practical politics. We have some evidence for Socrates performing military service and sitting on the Council. For Euripides we have no evidence except Aristotle's reference to his answer to the Syracusans; the scholiast there (*Rhet.* 1384b, 15) says that Euripides was sent as an ambassador to Syracuse to ask for peace and friendship. It may be true, but the emendation of his name to Hyperides is attractive.

The ancient picture of a crowd-shy Euripides writing his plays in a cave by the sea accords ill with the attempts by modern scholars to find allusions to recent political and military events in every play.[43] Day to day political comment was the task of comedy, not of tragedy. This, of course, does not exclude a reaction to a major political or military event or to the contemporary political climate. The *Eumenides* gives the Areopagus its charter as a murder-court, just after its political powers had been removed. The resistance-plays, *Prometheus Vinctus*, *Ajax* and *Antigone*, seem, as suggested above, to be a warning against underrating the distinguished individual. In the first part of the Peloponnesian war Euripides chose Athenian subjects for the *Heraclidae*, *Supplices*, and *Erechtheus* and the Hypothesis of the *Supplices* calls the play a 'praise of Athens'; but these are only three tragedies out of the eighteen which he produced from 431 to 421 B.C. and it is arguable that the pictures of Athenian democracy and Theban tyranny in the *Supplices* owe more to Protagoras' discussions than to contemporary and personal observation. It is not nearly so clear that the *Andromache* has any contemporary political reference: Helen was a Spartan, and Peleus describes her as a modern Spartan girl (596ff.); this is the normal Euripidean formula and has nothing to do with Athens being at war with Sparta. His picture of Menelaos as the general who gets the profit while the common soldier does the work (693ff.) is not more Spartan than Athenian, as the complaints of Dikaiopolis in Aristophanes' *Acharnians* (600f.), produced in 425 B.C., show. It is true that the ancient commentator on Andromache's denunciation of the Spartans (445ff.) says that Euripides uses Andromache as a pretext for abusing the Spartans because of the present war. But this is misinterpretation: Euripides makes Andromache abuse Menelaos because he has broken faith with her, and as he is by tradition a Spartan, Euripides gives him Spartan colour.[44]

What is clear is that Euripides hated war and particularly aggressive war. In the *Heraclidae* the Athenians have to fight to protect suppliants, in the *Supplices* they fight for the Panhellenic law that the dead must be buried, in the *Erechtheus* they fight against a foreign invasion. It is only

[43] Particularly by E. Delebecque, *Euripide et la Guerre du Péloponnèse*, 1951; R. Goossens, *Euripide et Athènes*, 1962. Cf. on the other side G. Zuntz, *Political Plays of Euripides*, 1955, particularly 78ff.; A. Lesky, *Tragische Dichtung*, 1964, 173.
[44] Cf. most recently P. N. Boulter, *Phoenix*, 20, 1966, 51.

such occasions that justify war with all its horrors and degradation. In the Trojan trilogy produced in 415 B.C. he saw the Greek war against Troy as a foreign invasion in which the leaders were weak and the real power lay with the unscrupulous Odysseus; the Trojans had at least the glory of dying for their country (*Tro.* 386). The first play accepts traditional mythology, but fixes for the last play the characters of certain Trojans particularly Hekabe and Hektor. The second play, *Palamedes*, fixes the characters of the weak Agamemnon and the vengeful Odysseus. The third play shows the suffering of the defeated; but yet, as Kassandra says, invaded Troy has more blessings than the Greeks (*Tro.* 365). When Euripides had this trilogy accepted by the archon Arimnestos, who took office late in June 416 B.C., the Athenian fleet had probably already sailed on its expedition to Melos (Thuc. V, 84) and in the following winter, after their savage and brutal treatment of the Melians, they conceived the idea of conquering Sicily and sent an embassy to Segesta to reconnoitre. The embassy returned just about the time that the trilogy was produced in March 415 B.C.,[45] and the expedition sailed in the following July. The trilogy must be seen as a warning against aggression formulated when a minor aggression was being executed, and given when the minor aggression had succeeded and a major aggression was in the planning stage. But the Athenians were as deaf to Euripides' warning as the mythical Trojans of the first play and the mythical Greeks of the last play were to Kassandra's warnings. This is as near as Euripides came to direct intervention. After 415 the most that we can say is that in the debate of the *Phoenissae* and in the messenger speech of the *Orestes* he comments on the political atmosphere of Athens after the Sicilian expedition, but there, as in the *Andromache*, the political commentary is a necessary part of Euripides' conception of the story; according to his usual formula he makes the characters in the heroic situation contemporary Athenians.

In 408 he went to Macedonia to the court of Archelaos, where he died late in 407 or very early in 406.[46] Different authorities ascribe his epitaph to Timotheos and to Thucydides. Either is possible as the traditions connecting both with the court of Archelaos are credible.

---

[45] The embassy returned 'in the following summer at the time of the spring' (Thuc. VI, 8). The formula is used for a date just before the Dionysia in Thuc. II, 1 and just after the Dionysia in Thuc. IV, 117.

[46] Various stories about his death are reported in the *Lives*.

Archelaos aimed at making Macedonia a centre of Greek culture. The tragic poet Agathon, the epic poet Choirilos, and the painter Zeuxis were also at his court. How much this meant for the future we cannot tell. But here fifty years before the accession of Philip II, the father of Alexander, were the most advanced representatives of Greek poetry, art, and thought, and Timotheos at least bridged the gap since he died as a very old man when Philip was already on the throne.

II

The Early Plays

Within the first group the certain dates are 455 *Peliades*, to which *Likymnios* can very probably be added; 438 *Cretan Women, Alkmaion in Psophis, Telephos, Alcestis*; 431 *Medea, Diktys, Philoktetes, Theristai*; 428 *Hippolytus*. They are therefore discussed in the first four sections of this chapter (but it seemed obvious to include the *First Hippolytos* in the discussion of the surviving *Hippolytus*). The collocation of plays in these three years shows Euripides observing two principles: in any given year the three tragedies are drawn from different fields of legend and they are each a different kind of play: *Peliades* in 455, *Cretan Women* in 438, *Medea* in 431, *Hippolytus* in 428 are all plays about bad women, and exactly five other plays in the first group (including the *First Hippolytos*) were about bad women, so that together they account for one play in each of the nine sets of tragedies which Euripides produced from 455 to 428 B.C. Similarly one of the plays in 438 and one of the plays in 431 was about an unhappy woman: in the *Alkmaion in Psophis* Arsinoe has been deserted by Alkmaion whom she still loves; he comes back and robs her of the necklace of Harmonia, she bitterly resents her father's action in having him ambushed, and possibly is punished for her resentment; in the *Diktys* Danae has to endure the unwanted attentions of the king, Polydektes. Again the total number of plays about unhappy women can be made up to nine from the other plays of the First Group.

The undated plays about bad women and the undated plays about unhappy women are discussed in the fifth and sixth sections of this chapter. The last section is entitled 'other plays.' I was tempted to call them 'plays about men', but some of them, notably the *Theseus* and the *Heraclidae* have women's parts; it is however probably true that neither Ariadne in the *Theseus* nor Alkmene in the *Heraclidae* had such important parts as the bad women and the unhappy women in their plays. Here *Oinomaos* and *Kadmos* may also have belonged, but we have less positive evidence for placing them early than we have for those selected.)

The appended chronological table arranges the plays of the first group so that each production has three plays both of a different kind and from a different cycle of legend. The plays in italic are certainly dated and the plays without italics or question mark are probably dated: for the rest the order is uncertain, but the fact that *Stheneboia* and *Theseus* are represented on the two sides of an early South Italian vase[1] may mean that they were produced together, and various other indications for the date of individual plays are given in discussing them below.

Production	I	455	*Peliades* ? Skyrioi Likymnios
	II		Aigeus ? Alkmene ? Thyestes
	III	442/1	? Phoinix ? Kretes ? Oineus
	IV		? Stheneboia ? Protesilaos ? Theseus
	V	438	*Kressai Alkmaion Telephos Alcestis*
	VI		? Hippolytos I ? Danae ? Chrysippos
	VII	431	*Medea Diktys Philoktetes Theristai*
	VIII		? Peleus ? Alope Heraclidae
	IX	428	*Hippolytus II* ? Ino ? Bellerophon

1 *Peliades and Likymnios*

According to the *Life* Euripides' first play, produced in 455 and accorded the third prize, was the *Peliades*.[2] It would be fascinating to know something of this first play which was produced only three years after the *Oresteia*, but we only have the end of a Hypothesis on papyrus, a brief summary, sixteen short fragments, and some illustrations. The fragments are largely gnomic and in the style known from later Euripides; they have none of the grandeur of Aeschylean diction,[3] but this first Medeia, however different, must surely have owed something to Aeschylus' Klytemnestra.

[1] See list of illustrations, pp. 301, 303.
[2] Bibliographical note: L. Séchan, *Études sur la tragédie Grecque*, 467; C. Dugas, *R.E.A.*, 46, 1944, 1; W. Buchwald, *Studien zur Chronologie der attischen Tragödie 455–431*, 1939, 9. Papyrus hypothesis: M. Papathomopoulos, *Récherches de Papyrologie*, 3, 1964, 40; Illustrations, see below, p. 300.
[3] Buchwald rightly notes that fr. 604 'I do not kick against the pricks' quotes *Ag.* 1624, but this is, of course, a proverb.

The summary is in Moses Chorenensis (N^2, p. 550): 'She (Medeia) allied herself with Jason and sailed from Scythia to Thessaly. There having shown her skill in magic she decided to destroy by treachery the local king. Therefore she spoke long to his daughters about their father's great age and lack of male offspring and offered her help in restoring his youth. After this Euripides proceeds to narrate in detail how her end was accomplished, how Medeia put a slaughtered ram in a cauldron and fired it from below, how by the boiling of the cauldron she showed the appearance of a living ram and thereby deceiving the daughters managed to get Pelias butchered. And he was, says Euripides, in the cauldron and *he adds nothing else*.'[4] It is difficult to know how far we are entitled to fill this story out from other accounts, particularly Hyginus, *Fab*. 24, but the fragmentary end which is all that remains of the papyrus Hypothesis seems to agree with Hyginus' last sentence: 'he gave the kingdom to Acastus and set out to Corinth with Medeia'. Séchan argues that (1) Moses' 'allied herself with Jason' agrees with Hyginus' account that Jason went into hiding and only returned at a signal from Medeia after the murder (this would be a pleasant reminiscence of Klytemnestra's beacon-chain), (2) her demonstration of skill in magic suggests that she came in the guise of 'a priestess of Diana' (Hyginus). This arrival is shown in the Pompeian picture which illustrates the story, and Medeia similarly seems to have presented herself to Perses as a 'priestess of Diana' in the original of Pacuvius' *Medus*, a play with many Euripidean reminiscences of which this may have been one.[5] (3) her *long* discussion with the Peliades (in Moses) suggests that she met with some opposition; in Hyginus she promised to rejuvenate Pelias but his eldest daughter Alkestis denied that it could be done; after the ram experiment the five daughters, Alkestis, Pelopia, Medusa, Pisidice, Hippothoe, killed and cooked their father and then when they saw they had been tricked fled the country.

The first question here is whether Alkestis had a part in the play. In the Pompeian picture which illustrates the story she has been identified (wrongly) with the figure enthroned in the centre, who seems to be ready to receive Medeia when she has entered the palace, and (rightly) with the Peliad who dissociates herself from the ram miracle. It is

[4] These last words are corrupt in the Arabic original (Buchwald).
[5] Cf. my *Hellenistic Poetry and Art*, 283f. Euripides himself may have remembered Hera who disguised herself as a priestess in Aeschylus' *Semele*.

notable that no picture earlier than Euripides' play shows dissension among the Peliads, and the earliest of the fifth century pictures which differentiates the daughters, the Villa Giulia painter's hydria, can be dated 450/40 (the Vatican cup and the Louvre pyxis can be dated about 430; the original of the Lateran relief about 420). The earliest picture of the ram miracle is on an Attic black-figure vase of the mid-sixth century, but there is nothing on it to show that Medeia did not youthen Pelias, as she did Aison, Jason, and the ageing Maenads and Satyrs.[6] The earliest reference to Medeia's criminal intentions is Pindar (*Pythian*, IV, 250) in 474(?). It is often assumed that Sophocles treated the subject in his *Rhizotomoi* but no certain evidence either dates this play before 455 B.C. or connects it with Pelias; we may indeed ask where Medeia would find a chorus of root-pickers (who invoked Helios and Hekate) at Pelias' court. Pindar remains our earliest evidence for the murder and there is no evidence for Alkestis' resistance earlier than Euripides.

Hyginus names five Peliads; Diodorus has two new names, Amphinome, Evadne; Mikon's painting named Asteropeia and Antinoe; the rf. vase in Tarquinia has Alkandra; Arniope and Elera may be added from the British Museum hydria. The choice before Euripides was whether to make the Peliades the chorus, like the mothers of the Seven in his *Supplices* and probably the Athenian boys and girls in the *Theseus*, or to make another daughter a character (with perhaps a mute partner) as well as Alkestis. The former solution seems more likely, and Aeschylus' *Danaides* gave a precedent for Alkestis' relation to the chorus since Hypermnestra must have played a similar lone part against her sisters there. But it involves the major difficulty that the chorus would have to go into the house at least for the execution of Pelias, if not for the ram trial. It is naturally assumed that Aeschylus put the murder of the bridegrooms in the interval between the *Aigyptioi* and *Danaides*.[7] But the *Helen* gives a good parallel for the chorus entering the palace and leaving it again, and this may have been how Euripides managed the murder of Pelias; Medeia could then give her report from the roof when

[6] British Museum B 221, *A.B.V.*, 321. The two metopes of Foce da Sele (which seemed at first to attest the crime in the early sixth century) have now been reinterpreted as the murder of Minos (*A.S.M.G.*, 5, 1964, 51). The magnificent funeral games of Pelias in archaic art and the presence of his daughters at them (Kypselos chest) suggest that Corinthian and Attic artists in the early sixth century supposed him to have died a natural death.

[7] E.g. R. P. Winnington-Ingram, *J.H.S.*, 81, 1961, 142.

she signalled for Jason. If Alkestis denied the possibility of rejuvenation, Alkestis may have been the only witness of the ram trial and she could have reported this to her sisters.

Whether the daughters went into exile at the end as in Hyginus is uncertain; Medeia's picture of them living on in the house (*Med.* 504) is irrelevant, since Euripides need not there be quoting the same form of the legend which he had previously dramatized (he returns to the normal form of the Helen story in the *Orestes*, four years after the *Helen*).

Pelias himself seems to have had a part. The Vatican cup on which he receives Medeia speaks for it, and it is probable that the enthroned figure on the Pompeian picture is Pelias rather than Alkestis. Frs. 603–4N^2 sound like Pelias counselling a disobedient daughter, possibly Alkestis when she resists the experiment; 605N^2 might be Pelias' own complaints of the disadvantages of tyranny, and 608–9N^2 may belong to the same context. Pelias develops the theme of 'association', the influence of the company one keeps, into a general appeal to the young.[8] Pelias is realistically portrayed as a fussy old king who is no match for the ruthless Medeia.

The first line of the play is 601N^2: Μήδεια πρὸς μὲν δώμασιν τυραννικοῖς. It has been compared with the opening of the *Hypsipyle* 752N^2: 'Dionysos, who etc . . ., was the father of . . .'. But Hypsipyle's account of Dionysos leads gradually to herself in her present position. A flat narrative by a god is unlikely at this early date, and it is difficult to see how to continue from 'Medeia on the one hand at the palace'. But 'Medeia, on the one hand standing at the palace, let us make our plans, but afterwards I shall return to the ship and you will seek entry' is a very possible beginning if Euripides made Jason accompany her to the palace gate, and so prepares for her final signal to Jason from the roof; as Buchwald has seen, the play had a dialogue prologue.

The scheme may then have been:

Prologue: Jason and Medeia: 601N^2
Epeisodia: Medeia hears Pelias' complaints: 605, 608–9N^2
    Medeia tells of her magic to Alkestis and the chorus.
    Medeia takes Alkestis inside to see the ram-trial.
    Alkestis reports the ram-trial and the chorus are convinced.

[8] Schadewaldt, *Monolog*, 129, compares *Androm.*, 622, 950; *Suppl.*, 917; fr. 464N^2, *Kressai*.

The chorus persuade Pelias against Alkestis' protestations to take the
  cure: 603–4N².
The chorus go in to perform the cure with Medeia.
Alkestis remains outside worrying.
The chorus rush out in horror at what they have done.
Medeia on the roof reports her success and signals to Jason; Jason
  arrives and hands over the kingdom to Akastos (hypothesis).

The dating of the Likymnios depends on 473N², a description of
Herakles in anapaestic tetrameters which is quoted in Plutarch's Life of
Kimon and was probably parodied in Kratinos Archilochoi (fr. 1 Demianczuk, as reconstructed by Reitzenstein); this would date Euripides'
play at latest 449 B.C. and as his early productions were widely spaced
it may have belonged to his first production with the Peliades.

Herakles is described in 473N² as the simple man who cuts short
speech by action, and 474N² 'labour, as they say, is the father of fame'
sounds like his description of himself. 476N² 'Teuthranian forefront of
Mysian land' in conjunction with Herakles fixes the story in the earlier
Trojan war.

Schmid-Stählin[9] has suggested that the story of Argeios, the son of
Likymnios, who went to Troy with Herakles and was killed is relevant.
According to Schol. A on Iliad, I, 52, Herakles, who had promised to
bring Argeios home, had him cremated. This story could be combined
with the Hesychios note on Λικυμνίαις βολαῖς ('Likymnian bolts'):
'perhaps it recalls Euripides' Likymnios. The ship is hit by a thunderbolt
according to the story there; it was not Likymnios himself who was
hit'. This is expanded by the ancient commentators on the same phrase
in Aristophanes' Birds 1242, who refer to the messenger speech in
Euripides' play and say that Euripides introduced someone hit by a
thunderbolt. (The further note that Kallimachos says he does not refer
to this production is explained by Pfeiffer (fr. 455) as meaning that
Aristophanes was not even thinking about Euripides' play.) Buchwald[10] may be right in ascribing 982N² to this play: 'many are
destroyed by the bloodless wound of thunder'. The story of the thunderbolt on the way home does not go easily with the story of cremation.
Possibly the messenger invented the story of the thunderbolt to save

[9] Griechische Literaturgeschichte, 3, 462.
[10] Studien, 13.

Herakles' face (and so anticipated the report of Lichas to Deianeira in Sophocles' *Trachiniae*). But even if the story was false the idea may have germinated later in Euripides' mind to give the fall of Phaethon.[11]

The scene must have been Likymnios' court at Tiryns, where the king was waiting for the promised return of his son, and the chorus describe the singleminded energy of Herakles (473N²). The one hint of a development is given by the chorus' song to Apollo (477N², iambic dimeters with Theiler's Βάκχιε, quoted by Buchwald) combined with 479N² 'muzzle him and stop his mouth': this sounds as if some prophet (cf. also 478N², a strange word for 'prophesy') foretold the death of Argeios and was restrained forcibly (this anticipates Agamemnon's treatment of Polymestor at the end of the *Hecuba*). Then the messenger arrived with the story, false rather than true, that Argeios had been killed by a thunderbolt on the way home (479, 982N²), and Herakles then brought in the ashes and speaking the truth justified himself to Likymnios (474, 475N²): he had pursued his laborious path to glory and endured the burden which necessity had laid upon him.

We know too little about the economy of a play produced only three years after the *Oresteia* to say whether this is enough for the action. The only obvious parallel is Sophocles' *Teucer* where Teucer brought the news of Ajax' death to his father, but there too we know nothing either of the date or the structure.

It is at least clear that this play was entirely different from the *Peliades*, and it is interesting that the theme of the disbelieved prophet occurs so early. The third play of the production was one of the early plays about unhappy women but there is no way of deciding which: *Alkmene* can be excluded because Herakles appears in the *Likymnios*.

2 Euripides' production in 438 B.C.

The hypothesis to the *Alcestis* says that in 438 Sophocles won the first prize, and Euripides was second with the *Cretan Women*, *Alkmaion in Psophis*, *Telephos*, and *Alcestis*.

CRETAN WOMEN

Three scholia give important information. The scholiast on the reference to Aerope in *Ajax* 1297 says 'the story is in Euripides' *Cretan*

[11] Cf. below, p. 226.

Women that when Aerope had been seduced by a servant, her father (Katreus of Crete) handed her over to Nauplios with instructions to drown her, but he failed to do so and engaged her to Pleisthenes'. There is nothing to tell us here whether this was information given in the prologue or part of the action. The scholiast to *Acharnians* 433, 'the rags of Thyestes', says 'either in the *Cretan Women* or in the *Thyestes* itself'. The scholiast evidently believed that Thyestes was a character in both plays. If Thyestes was a character, then the action must have taken place in Mycenae (as frs. 467–9N^2 on the feast suggest) and the story of Katreus was prologue information. The Cretan Women were then, as we should expect, the chorus, attendants of Aerope also handed over to Nauplios with her. Thirdly, the scholiast on *Frogs* 849 gives various explanations of 'composer of Cretan monodies, dramatizer of unholy marriages'; according to Apollonios 'this could refer to Aerope in the *Cretan Women* whom Euripides introduced prostituting herself'. Whether Aerope sang a monody is perhaps not certain; but if Thyestes was a character, Aerope's seduction of Thyestes must be the subject of this reference. (Sophocles' *Atreus* probably covered the same subject matter, but nothing is known of its date.)

The prologue told of Aerope's seduction in Crete and her punishment; perhaps she would hardly have told this herself. Probably Euripides followed Hesiod in making Pleisthenes die young and leave his sons (and his wife) to Atreus. Therefore when the play opened, Aerope was married to Atreus, a young woman to an old man.[12] She seems to have offered Thyestes, the younger brother of Atreus, the golden lamb on which the kingship depended: so Phaidra in the *First Hippolytos* offered Hippolytos Theseus' throne. Two fragments of this dialogue survive: 461N^2, 'a young man should be prepared to work for his happiness' and Thyestes' answer, 462N^2 (with Snell's addition) 'I know only too well that all men are friends of the rich, but the poor have none'.

Atreus must have discovered both that Aerope was infatuated with Thyestes and that she had borne Thyestes children. This must be the shameful disaster which he is advised to conceal (fr. 460N^2), and he bursts forth into a tirade against wives and marriage (463–4N^2). His revenge was to kill Thyestes' sons and serve them up to him to eat. A difficult fragment may belong here: fr. 466N^2 can be read either as 'for

[12] Cf. *Aigeus, Phoinix, Stheneboia, Peleus*, and the two Hippolytos plays.

your sake shall I not kill the children?' or, with a slight change, 'for your sake am I to kill your daughter?' The second version has been taken as Nauplios speaking to Katreus; and even if the action takes place at Mycenae, it could conceivably belong in the prologue as a quotation of Nauplios' words; a minor difficulty is that Katreus gave *two* daughters to Nauplios. If this solution is rejected, the first version may have been spoken to Aerope by Atreus before the feast. Aerope has pleaded for the children's lives and this is Atreus' answer; his final word to her is fr. 465N² 'Death shall be the judge'. The feast itself is the subject in frs. 467-9N²; fr. 467N² belongs to Atreus' description of the rich food to Thyestes before they enter the house; 468-9N² come from an account of the feast.

The actual feast can only have been described in a messenger-speech. Presumably, Thyestes went off in distress. Here Aerope may have sung her monody if in fact she sang one. It is tempting to connect with this play Quintilian's note (XI, iii, 73) that actors borrowed the emotion from her mask to make her *tristis*, and the description in the Anthology (*A.P.*, 6, 316) 'the tears of weeping Aerope and the abominable remains of the feast and the Fury'.

All that we can recover of the scheme of the play is:

Prologue: Katreus and his daughters (Schol. S. *Aj.* 1297)
Parodos of Cretan Women.
Aerope and Thyestes: frs. 461, 462N²
Atreus discovers the plot and the existence of the children: fr. 460, 463-4N²
Atreus summons Thyestes' children, Aerope's appeal: fr. 466, 465N²
Thyestes arrives for the feast: fr. 467N²
Messenger's account of the feast: fr. 468-9N²
Aerope's lament: *A.P.*, 6, 316

ALKMAION IN PSOPHIS

Euripides' two plays about Alkmaion are separated by more than thirty years. It is nevertheless not entirely easy to disentangle the fragments. 65, 71, 73N², are expressly quoted from the *Alkmaion in Psophis*; 66N² also certainly belongs because it is quoted in Aristophanes *Knights*; 72 is spoken to Phegeus. For the *Alkmaion in Corinth*, 73a, 74, 77 are explicitly attested; 75 is fixed by Kreon, who is also the childless old man of 76; 67 and 80 are metrically late (probably also 78a since both the emendations proposed contravene Zielinski's Rule III): 84, a child's declaration of loyalty to a father in distress, belongs more naturally to the story of the later play. The interrogation on matricide, 68N², ascribed to the *Bellerophon*, should also belong to the *Alkmaion in Corinth* since Alkmaion was known in Psophis, but in Corinth he was unknown both to the chorus and to his son. 70 (Amphiaros going to Thebes), 71 (Polyneikes bringing the necklace), 81 (the unfortunate should speak humbly), and 82N² (God punishes the children of criminals) could belong to either play. 87N² is better given to *Alkmene* (q.v.). 78, 79, and 85–6N² are discussed below.

Van Looy[13] stresses the connexion between Tatian's description of the Euripidean Alkmaion and Ennius' *Alcimeo*. Tatian (*Orat. ad Graec.* 24 ap. N², p. 380) says: 'What help to me is the Euripidean madman announcing the matricide of Alkmaion? He has not even the normal bearing, he gapes wide and carries a sword; he shouts aloud and is on fire; he wears an inhuman garb'. The word 'gaping' is usual in late descriptions of the tragic mask. But Tatian is evidence for a mad-scene and for Alkmaion wearing rags as in fr. 78aN², which metrically should belong to the *Alkmaion in Corinth*. Ennius' *Alcimeo* (III–IVR) had a famous mad-scene, which dwelt on fire – *haec flamma, flammiferam hanc vim, ardentibus taedis*; and Alkmaion (IIR) complains of *exilio atque inopia* (rags). It has also been suggested that *exalbescat metu* (IIR) translates Euripides' ἀργαίνειν (fr. 73 of *Alk. Psoph.*), but there is a better clue which, as Hartung saw, leads to the *Alkmaion in Corinth*: Cicero introduces his quotation of part of the mad-scene (IIIR) with *virginis fidem implorat* 'Alkmaion begs for the loyal help of the maiden'. The only maidens in the *Alkmaion in Psophis* are the members of the chorus, but Alkmaion is surely unlikely to address them at the moment, but in the *Alkmaion in Corinth* he is accompanied by Tisiphone, his as yet unrecognized daughter. The scene must have been like the dialogue between Orestes and Elektra in the *Orestes* (particularly *Or.* 264, 268). A mad-scene is as likely in a late play as in an early play, and Euripides had not lost his liking for ragged heroes (cf. *Or.* 385, *Hel.* 420f.). But there is no reason for Alkmaion to be either ragged or mad in the *Psophis*.[14]

[13] *Zes Tragedien*, 83f., 123f.
[14] On the significance of these figures see J. de Romilly, *L'Évolution du Pathétique*, 131ff.

The story of Alkmaion in Psophis is told by Apollodoros (III, vii, 5–6) and by Pausanias (VIII, 24, 8). Alkmaion was purified by Phegeus after he had killed Eriphyle. He married Phegeus' daughter, Arsinoe (Apollodoros) or Alphesiboia (Pausanias, Sophocles, Accius) and gave her the necklace of Harmonia. A famine caused him to travel further, and he was purified again by Acheloos and married his daughter Kallirrhoe, who demanded the necklace. Alkmaion returned and told Phegeus that he could only be finally purified if he dedicated the necklace in Delphi. Phegeus believed him and gave him back the necklace, but a servant told him that Alkmaion was taking the things to Kallirrhoe. He ordered his sons to ambush Alkmaion and to kill him. According to Apollodoros, Arsinoe accused them and they put her into a chest and sold her as a slave in Tegea.

The story gives two periods in Psophis. In fr. 72 the text is too doubtful to give a decision, but fr. 71N^2: 'For, mother, he washed away your blood' refers in the past to the first period and therefore places the action of the play in the second period. Then the choral fragment, 78N^2, 'a woman brings the greatest benefit and the greatest disaster to man' may not be too general to refer to Alkmaion's two wives, and 79N^2 'a mortal should not wear divine adornment' would naturally be Arsinoe's renunciation of the necklace. Schadewaldt[15] connected the Florentine papyrus (*P.S.I.*, no. 1302), which contains fr. 86N^2, with the servant's report to Phegeus in Apollodoros: the beginnings of the lines in the papyrus show that someone is sent into the house, a woman must not be told something, and a female chorus is pledged to silence; the speaker ends with a general sentiment, 'only a fool would trust a slave', presumably to reinforce his command for silence.

The *Alkmaion in Psophis* must have started with Alkmaion's arrival at Phegeus' palace and his narrative of events up to date. For content frs. 69 and 70N^2 (Amphiaraos' departure; Polyneikes and the necklace) could belong here, but we have no evidence to which play they belonged. On the other hand, whatever the exact text, fr. 71N^2 must have come from the prologue, as Schadewaldt saw. Van Looy wonders (p. 101) whether the emotional vocative: 'Your blood, mother, he

---

[15] *Hermes*, 80, 1952, 46ff. His reconstruction is on the whole sound, but the fragments of Accius' *Alphesiboea* and *Alcimeo* cannot be used. The two plays should not be identified. *Alphesiboea* probably derives from Sophocles' *Alkmaion* (cf. 880P). *Alcimeo* IR refers to children of Alkmaion, to whom there is no reference in the Psophis story.

washed away', suits a prologue, but a prologue may surely be emotional
when the situation allows it. Here Pausanias gives the clue: Alkmaion came
back 'against his will'. His situation is like that of Bellerophon in the
prologue of the *Stheneboia* in so far as he has been asked to wrong a man
to whom he is deeply grateful: unlike Bellerophon he has consented.
This emotion he can only show now because as soon as anyone arrives,
chorus or another character, he has to play his part (like Telephos).

The chorus are identified as 'maidens' *parthenoi* by fr. 66N². One
line of the parodos survives 'I am come straight from home' (fr. 65N²).
The metre recurs in the *Medea* parodos (151). Presumably they are
friends of Arsinoe. In the next scene Alkmaion comes out with Phegeus
and persuades him of his need for the necklace (fr. 72, reading ἐκδοὺς
'You gave me your daughter, and I regard you as father-in-law, father,
and saviour'). Then Phegeus must tell the story to Arsinoe, who agrees
that a mortal should not wear divine ornaments (fr. 79N²). Perhaps
Alkmaion actually leaves with the necklace at this point, since it is not
clear why an ambush is necessary if he is still in the palace when the
servant reports his treachery.

The servant's report must belong to the next act, and his opening
words to the chorus may be parodied by Aristophanes (fr. 66N² =
Eq. 1302): 'don't you know the news from the city, girls?' Euripides
would not have written trochaic tetrameters at this date, and the words
of the original cannot be certainly recovered. The situation recalls
Sophocles' *Trachiniae*, where the messenger brings Lichas' news to
Deianeira and in due course exposes the story which Lichas has given
her; this may have been the inspiration of the Sophoclean scene. Here
too, Phegeus' slave brings the true story, which Alkmaion must have
told someone in Psophis before arriving at the palace. Rather similarly,
in the prologue to the *Medea*, the paidagogos brings news which he
has heard from the old men playing draughts (*Med.* 67). This scene
ends with the Florentine papyrus. Phegeus' attempt to conceal the
truth from Arsinoe of course means that she will learn it.

The following stasimon gives no clear lead for reconstruction.
Pausanias' comment 'many men and even more women come to
disaster with foolish desires' is exactly the sentiment which one would
expect but it cannot be traced in the ten lines of which the beginnings
are preserved. The choral fragment (78N²) about the good and bad
brought by a woman to her husband does not necessarily belong here,

but could not come in any earlier chorus: the exact wording of the last line is uncertain, but the plural verb ('you taught' or 'you showed') would make it parallel to the end of the second stasimon of the *Andromache* (486): 'the Laconian girl, daughter of the general Menelaos, showed this'.

For the rest of the play, we can only conjecture that Phegeus sent his sons to ambush Alkmaion, that they returned to report his death (perhaps bringing his body), that Arsinoe found out the truth and at least lamented Alkmaion and vilified her brothers.

The scheme of the play seems to be as follows:

Prologue: Alkmaion, 71, perhaps 69, 70N²
Parodos: maidens of Psophis, 65N²
Alkmaion and Phegeus: 72N²
Phegeus and Alkmaion: 79N²
Stasimon
Servant: 66N²
Servant and Phegeus: papyrus, 85–86N²
Stasimon: papyrus, perhaps 78N²
(plot to ambush Alkmaion, Stasimon, messenger-speech, lament of Arsinoe)

TELEPHOS

Aeschylus' *Telephos* certainly included the seizing of the infant Orestes but nothing more is known about it. Sophocles' *Telepheia* would naturally have included the wounding and healing of Telephos, and the suggestion that the third play after the *Aleadai* and *Mysoi* was the *Assembly of the Achaians* is still persuasive in spite of the discovery that the Berlin papyrus certainly and the Rylands papyrus probably belong not to that play but to Euripides' *Telephos*. The *Assembly of the Achaians* certainly had a muster of the suitors of Helen and a reference to a night voyage (frs. 143–5P), which would suit this story. As a connected trilogy, the *Telepheia* is likely to have been produced before 449 B.C.[16] and therefore when the Euripidean Achilles asks 'Where is the Assembly of friends?' (Berlin papyrus), he may be referring to the title of the third play. The story cannot have been very different; what struck Aristophanes as startling in Euripides' play was the equipment of the

[16] Cf., *Hermathena* 50, 1965, 23ff., and above p. 16.

beggar hero (whether this was only described in words, 697N², or included in his costume), his defence of the Trojans, and the search for him as an enemy spy. These elements must at least have been elaborated, if not introduced, by Euripides.

In publishing the Oxyrrhynchus papyrus (*P. Oxy.* 2460), which secures the Berlin papyrus for Euripides' *Telephos*, Mr Handley and Mr Rea[17] have discussed also the evidence of other papyri, the book fragments, Aristophanes, Ennius and Accius, so that I can limit myself to a simple statement of what seems to me the likely development of the play.

Outline of play

Prologue: Telephos, Page, *G.L.P.*, no. 17; 696N²; Accius I, XIII–XVR; 705, 705a N²; 697–8N²; Ennius I, IIIR; 701–2, 1066N²; Accius VI–VIIR, Telephos and Klytemnestra, 699, 714N².
Parodos
Epeisodion: Telephos 706, 703 (= Ennius IIR), 709, 711N²; Menelaos, 717–18, 712N²; Agamemnon and Menelaos, 722–3, 713N²; Telephos, 918N²
Stasimon
Epeisodion: Odysseus, 721N², Ennius VIR, Accius III–V, X; 704, 707, 720N², Ennius IVR. Telephos, 710N²; Ennius VIIIR, 700N². *P. Oxy.* 2460, fr. 1.
Stasimon
Epeisodion: messenger speech (727N²)
Agamemnon, Telephos, Odysseus. *P. Oxy.* 2460, fr. 9, 10, 13; Page, *G.L.P.*, no. 21.
Stasimon. Page, *G.L.P.*, no. 3.
Epeisodion: Achilles, Odysseus, Telephos. Page, *G.L.P.*, no. 3; *P. Oxy.* 2460, frs. 17–20, 11, 32; 719, 716, 724N².

The prologue is partly preserved on papyrus (Page, *G.L.P.*, no. 17) as well as in fr. 696N². There are two themes in the sixteen preserved lines: (1) Telephos' birth in Arcadia, and his establishment as king of Mysia. (2) The Achaean attack on Mysia. This description is presumably continued; perhaps Accius IR: 'the mighty mass of war stirred by the daughter of Tyndareus, the house of Menelaos, and the Trojan

[17] *B.I.C.S. (London),* Supplt. 5, 1957.

shepherd'. XIV 'ablaze with bronze and steel, alight with flags', XV 'waves of Mysian blood rolling', XIII, 'they swiftly sped in flight to the left, where the sea was calm under a mountain' belong; perhaps also fr. 705N² (spoken by Telephos): 'lord of the oar, disembarking in Mysia he was wounded by an enemy's arm' might refer to the wounding of Patroklos by Telephos. Fr. 705aN² 'chasing pirates with his spear' should describe Achilles. Finally, in this section Telephos must have referred to his own wounding by Achilles.

Telephos must go on to say how he has come to Argos. To this belong the fragments saying that he is disguised as a beggar: 697N² and 698N². Ennius IR adds that he had left home in disguise, III that his disguise was to avoid being killed, *caedem caveo*. (This fragment may be wrongly printed as trochaics, and has been rightly equated with 697N².) The story of a Greek reconciliation with Telephos before they left Mysia is therefore excluded. Telephos expects hostility; he therefore arrives disguised as an Arcadian beggar.

He must also quote the oracle of the Lycian (?) Apollo that his attacker would heal him.

The gnomic fragments about self-help, *arete*, etc. may belong here: 701, 702N²; Accius VIR = 1066N², Accius VIIR: *Nam huius demum miseret, cuius nobilitas miserias nobilitat,* 'there is pity for him whose nobility ennobles his pitifulness'.

He is admitted to the house by Klytemnestra, 699N², whom he begs to help him with his plan; he will be happy with a modest daily wage, 714N². Does he become her porter? Tzetzes on Ar. *Nub.* 922 says that Telephos with difficulty became the gate-keeper of Agamemnon's court.

Klytemnestra can tell Telephos the situation in Argos and how far preparations for the Trojan War have gone. Her emotional position and her reason for befriending Telephos are quite unclear. It is possible that at the end of the prologue she sets off with the infant Orestes to the sanctuary of the Lycian Apollo (see below on the messenger-speech).

Parodos. The chorus are either Argive soldiers or possibly chieftains of the Greek cities concerned in the expedition except for those who appear as characters – Agamemnon, Menelaos, Odysseus, Achilles.

Epeisodion. The three speaking characters are Menelaos, Telephos, and Agamemnon. Menelaos evidently demands an attack on Troy to win back Helen. Telephos, posing as an Arcadian beggar-porter, argues with them that the Trojans were justified: 'even if I had my head on the block, I would not be silent if I had a just cause to plead' (706N²); 'do not think ill of me, if a beggar dares to speak before princes' (703N², add Ennius IIR); 'if you had been attacked, would you have sat at home?' (709N²); 'are we right to be angry when we have suffered no more than we have done?' (711N²). Menelaos is horrified that Agamemnon is prepared to listen to a man who is vilifying the whole of Greece (717, 712N²). The quarrel between the brothers flares up in a dialogue in recitative anapaestic dimeters: 'Go where you like. I'll not perish for your Helen' (722N²), 'Sparta is yours, look after it' (723N²), 'City of Argos, do you hear his words?' (713N²), 'let them do their worst; I have justice on my side' (918N²). Telephos believes that he has achieved an agreement which will allow him to seek healing without jeopardizing his ties with Troy (his wife was Astyoche, daughter of Priam).

But after a stasimon, a new danger arises for Telephos. Odysseus, perhaps prompted by the discomfited Menelaos, assumes that Telephos is a spy: 'a bad man is abusing your hospitality' (721N²); 'all Argos is inflamed against him' (Ennius VIR). A series of fragments from Accius (III–V, X) mention an unknown stranger whose ragged clothes contrast with his personality; this is Agamemnon, answering Odysseus' question about Telephos. Odysseus attacks him (704, 707, 720N², Ennius IVR). Telephos defends himself (710N²). Somehow, and we cannot say how, Telephos' identity has come out. But he claims the protection of Klytemnestra: this is the implication of Ennius VIIIR 'you must make this statement to me in front of her'.

Ennius VIII shows that Agamemnon demands that Telephos shall validate his claim before Klytemnestra. But where is Klytemnestra? The obvious assumption that she is in the palace may be wrong. Telephos cries (700N²): 'Phoibos Apollo of Lycia, what will you do to me?' Metzger[18] has rightly connected this with the Attic kalyx krater on which Telephos with the child Orestes sits on an altar in a sanctuary of Apollo. The Campanian bell krater also places the altar in a sanctuary of Apollo. The Campanian hydria shows Klytemnestra restraining Agamemnon; it looks, therefore, as if Klytemnestra set out with Orestes and her women to pray to the Lycian Apollo in an earlier scene, probably the prologue. The Attic pelike shows two bearded men

[18] On the vases, see below, p. 302.

discussing together while Telephos holds the baby (probably he is sitting on a high altar, but the lower part of this vase has been broken away): they will be Agamemnon and Odysseus. (The young man who is separated from the rest on both the Attic red-figure vases is Achilles, whom the painter added because, although he had not arrived at this moment, he was essential to the story.)

It seems therefore justifiable to conclude that Odysseus, Agamemnon, and Telephos go to the sanctuary of Apollo while the chorus sings the second stasimon, then a messenger relates how Telephos seized the baby Orestes and sat on an altar threatening to kill it ($727N^2$) if he was not given protection.

The Oxyrrhynchus papyrus (2460) makes it certain that we have in the Berlin papyrus (Page, *G.L.P.*, no. 3) the end of the chorus and the beginning of the final act of Euripides' *Telephos*, in which Odysseus persuades Achilles to heal Telephos; from the Berlin papyrus we can draw the following conclusions:

1. Telephos has promised to lead the host to Troy. (Col. ii, 3.)
2. Telephos has been accepted as leader because he is an Arcadian and not a Mysian. (Col. ii, 7.)
3 Odysseus is on the stage eagerly awaiting Achilles, who comes at the right moment. Telephos has therefore been promised that Achilles shall heal him.

In front of this fits the Rylands papyrus (Page, *G.L.P.*, no. 21) as the end of the preceding act; the certain points in it seem to be:

1. That Telephos as a *Greek* is freed from some restriction.
2. That someone (presumably Odysseus) is left to make further arrangements (presumably with Achilles).

The clue to the stress on Telephos' Greek origin is to be found in Hyginus (*Fab.* 101): 'the Achaians had an oracle that without the guidance of Telephos, Troy could not be captured'. Oracles are not usually so specific – the text may have been '*with* the guidance of a foreigner' (and it is possible that a corrupt papyrus hypothesis, which may belong to this play, could be restored to refer to this oracle, *P.Oxy.* 2455, fr. 12, col. xi).

Then Telephos may have offered his guidance in return for healing, and the establishment of his Greek origin would both satisfy the Greeks and allay his own scruples. This discussion between Agamemnon, Odysseus, and Telephos presumably took place on stage after the messenger speech. The Rylands papyrus ends with recitative anapaests calling for fellow sailors for the stranger. Whoever speaks them, they probably round off the scene.

After the stasimon partly preserved in the Berlin papyrus Achilles arrives, complaining of the delay (Euripides echoed this at the end of his life in the *Iphigenia in Aulis* (801ff.) just as he also echoed and elaborated the quarrel between Agamemnon and Menelaos (331ff.)). Achilles objects to Telephos as a barbarian (719N^2) and perhaps to his ragged appearance; Odysseus answers this objection (716N^2, which is fixed here by the Oxyrrhynchus papyrus). Finally, Achilles is told how to heal Telephos' wound by filings from his spear (724N^2) and the play presumably ends when he goes in to do it.

This is a play of exciting events: Telephos has to meet a series of crises, the first dominated by Menelaos, the second by Odysseus, and the third (in which Odysseus is on the side of Telephos) dominated by Achilles. It is interesting to find such clear-cut early evidence for Euripides writing this sort of play.

ALCESTIS

The fourth play in this production was not a satyr-play, but the *Alcestis*. We have no explanation and no parallel. Phrynichos had already put the story on the stage, but whether as a tragedy or a satyr-play, we do not know; Euripides borrowed from him the figure of Death carrying a sword to cut Alkestis' hair (74ff.). The play must be briefly examined because it is the earliest surviving play, but at the same time its unique status as a pro-satyr-play must be remembered.

Apollo enters from the palace of Admetos to tell the story. He has to leave so that he may not be polluted by Alkestis' death, which is due on that day (so also Artemis abandons the dying Hippolytos). Death enters to recitative anapaests: both the ghoulish figure[19] with black chiton, wings, and sword, and the excited entry suggest the satyr-play. Apollo makes a last vain appeal, and the dialogue, perhaps intentionally, recalls Aeschylus' scene between Apollo and the Eumenides (A. *Eum.* 179ff.). Apollo then announces that Herakles will force Death to give Alkestis up. The audience should therefore have no doubt as to the

[19] Cf. A. Lesky, *Maske und Kothurn*, 10, 1964, 203.

outcome, but Euripides manages to make them forget their knowledge.

The chorus of old men arrive to ask for news; no oracle nor sacrifice can help; Asklepios might have raised her from the dead, but he is dead himself. The matter is eminently suitable; the form is curious in that the first strophe and antistrophe are followed by recitative anapaests divided between two half choruses; here again the influence of the satyr-play may perhaps be seen.[20] To answer their questions, a servant-girl heartbrokenly describes Alkestis' preparations for death. Two pointers forward deserve mention: she sums up Admetos' position – 'if he had died, he would be gone; his escape has given him a wound for which there will be no oblivion ever' (197), and she says that Alkestis wants to see the sun once more (206).

The chorus sings briefly, praying to Apollo, describing Admetos' loss as worse than suicide. They see the king and queen coming and wonder whether marriage is worth while. The staging has to be considered here. The servant said that Alkestis wanted to see the sun again. The chorus here uses the word πορεύεται which probably means 'comes' rather than 'is brought'. Alkestis sinks down on her couch at l. 266 and dies at l. 391. At l. 422, Admetos tells the chorus to wait and sing while he makes preparations for the funeral procession. At l. 476, Herakles arrives; Admetos comes *out* of the house to meet him (507) and tells him lies about Alkestis' death. Then at l. 606, Admetos comes out of the house again with the funeral procession. Clearly Alkestis' dead body on the couch, her two children, and Admetos have all been got into the house before Herakles arrives; and the couch and children must have been brought out of the house when the chorus first sees Admetos and Alkestis at l. 234. It would, of course, be possible for servants to bring on the couch and take it off again, but it would be much simpler to use the *ekkyklema*, which is attested by Aristophanes of Byzantion for the entry of Phaidra in the *Hippolytos* (170): she also wants light and air, she is brought in on a couch, and the phrasing is again ambiguous 'here is her nurse before the door, conveying her outside the house'. We have no reason to distrust Aristophanes, who may have had an annotated acting text. If we insist (like Mr Barrett in his note on *Hipp.* 811) that the *ekkyklema* is used only to bring the

[20] Satyr-play choruses seem to divide into semi-choruses easily and also have *ephymnia* after strophe and antistrophe.

interior of a house into view, we can say that Alkestis and Phaidra move from an inner room into the courtyard of the palace and the *ekkyklema* brings the courtyard into view. Euripides made several daring uses of the *ekkyklema* and this is one of them, in his earliest surviving play. Its entry is marked by the lines of the chorus, 233–243, and it rolls in again as they start their stasimon, l. 434.

The iambic dialogue between Alkestis and Admetos is framed between two lyric dialogues. Both are strophic and in both Admetos speaks iambic trimeters. In the first, Alkestis sees Charon in his boat and the dark, winged Hades coming to fetch her. In the second, the elder child sings of her death and of their loneliness. (Miss Dale has shown that the singer was in fact the actor who took Alkestis, while the children mimed.[21]) Between the two lyric dialogues, Alkestis reminds Admetos of her own nobility in dying for him and of the ignoble behaviour of his mother and father (Pheres is to appear later), and begs him not to marry again: 'A stepmother is no kinder than a viper' (310); of the stepmother plays, the *Aigeus* at least was earlier than this. Admetos promises that he will remain single for his life. He will give up the music and feasting that he has always loved. He will have a statue of her in his bedchamber (a clear reminiscence of the earlier *Protesilaos*[22]), and he begs her to prepare a house for him in Hades.

Alkestis dies. Her children lament her. Admetos gives his instructions and the *ekkyklema* rolls in. The chorus in their stasimon repeat themes from the preceding scene, her nobility, his parents' ignobility, his treachery if he marries again. When they sing of her future fame, they say that poets will celebrate her not only in Athens but also at Sparta 'when the cycle of the season of the Karneian month comes round'. The Karneia was a festival of Apollo, and Euripides must have known that Alkestis was celebrated then; the ancient story is anchored in a modern cult, as so often in his plays.

In sharpest contrast to their lament, Herakles arrives on his way to capture the mares of Diomedes. Admetos, whose shorn hair shows his mourning,[23] tells him that he is mourning a woman whose father had left her in his house, and sends Herakles indoors to the guest chambers. The chorus criticize his conduct and then sing of the hospi-

[21] *Euripides: Alcestis*, xx.
[22] See below, p. 97.
[23] 512, the long locks of the mask have been removed, cf. *Hel.* 1087, 1187.

tality of the house, the benefits which Apollo as a guest brought, the different standards of behaviour that the good can permit themselves. The audience heard Apollo promise that Herakles would face death to give Alkestis life. The arrival of Herakles, followed by the chorus' song of Apollo's favours, must remind the audience of this, but Herakles has seemingly been diverted by a lie and the funeral must go on.

The procession comes out of the house, but at the same moment Admetos' father, Pheres, arrives with attendants bringing offerings for Alkestis' funeral. Admetos renounces both him and his mother; he takes the line that Alkestis had already taken: they were ignoble not to die for him. Pheres answers that life is sweet; Admetos is the murderer of his wife, and will no doubt marry other women and make them die for him as well. Formally, as a debate, this ugly scene is parallel to and balances the earlier scene between Alkestis and Admetos. The earlier scene showed Admetos' desolation; this scene shows the damage that his selfishness has done him.

The procession moves off and with it the chorus. Euripides allowed himself both an unusual procedure and an improbability, because Herakles' decision must be taken in their absence. Thus his return will be a surprise. Aeschylus and Sophocles use the exit and re-entrance of the chorus to mask a change of place, and Euripides may have used this device in the *Andromeda*.[24] Here and in the *Helen* (385), the only purpose is to leave characters unwitnessed so as to achieve a later surprise (the use suggested above for the *Peliades* is different again). A servant (a man this time, contrasting with the girl of the first act) complains that he has to entertain a drunken Herakles when he wanted to go to Alkestis' funeral. Herakles pursues him on to the stage: 'all men have to die, therefore drink and womanize as much as you can.' This is the glutton Herakles of satyr-play and comedy. The servant is goaded into telling him the truth, and he immediately decides to go to Alkestis' tomb and wrestle with Death.

The improbability mentioned above is that Herakles can go to Alkestis' tomb without meeting Admetos and the chorus, who are on their way back. In the theatre a producer could avoid this by sending Herakles out one side as they come on from the other, and hope that the audience would not notice the difficulty. A long lament follows in

[24] See below, p. 196.

which recited anapaests from Admetos alternate with choral stanzas, largely iambic and dochmiac.[25] Then shatteringly Admetos realizes the truth (934): his dead wife is happier than he is. She has no pain and her reputation is assured. He has emptiness at home, weeping children, and lamenting slaves. Outside he will be taunted with still being alive. This speech is the fulfilment of the maid-servant's prophecy in the first act that his escape has given him an unforgettable wound (197). The chorus sing that he is caught in the webs of necessity and Alkestis will now be honoured as a god. Herakles returns with Alkestis and after mocking Admetos a little, leaves him with his wife.

Within this essentially light-hearted play, the devotion of Alkestis and the self-discovery of Admetos are beautifully realized. The fully preserved play shows how accomplished Euripides was in constructing a swiftly moving whole of contrasting incidents and intervening songs.

3 Euripides' production in 431 B.C.

The hypothesis to the *Medea* says that in 431 B.C. Euphorion was first, Sophocles was second, and Euripides was third with the *Medea*, *Philoktetes*, *Diktys*, and *Theristai*. The formula for the three tragedies was the same as in 438 B.C.: three plays from different cycles of legend, one about a bad woman, one about an unhappy woman, and one about men.

MEDEA

This was Euripides' third play about Medeia. He showed her ruthless and triumphant in the *Peliades* in 455 B.C., ruthless but defeated in the *Aigeus* soon after 450 B.C.,[26] and here ruthless, much more seriously provoked, and heartbrokenly victorious. Each time, an old man – Pelias, Aigeus, Kreon – is shown to be no match for her. In the chronology of the story, this play comes second because the Corinthian episode preceded the Athenian episode; how much of the Corinthian episode Euripides told as past history in the *Aigeus* we do not know. For Medeia in Corinth knowledge of a possible asylum in Athens is essential, but the connexion between Aigeus and Medeia was long established and

[25] In 903ff. a reference has been seen to Anaxagoras' bearing on hearing the death of his son (Diels-Kranz, *Fragmente der Vorsokratiker*, II, 14).
[26] See below, p. 79.

the audience did not need to have seen the *Aigeus* to understand the
Aigeus scene in the *Medea*.

The play opens with Medeia's old nurse, who has come outside to
vent her misery (48). Medeia was in love with Jason but he has betrayed
her and married the daughter of Kreon, king of Corinth. Medeia is
wasting away in misery. 'She hates her children and takes no pleasure in
seeing them. I am afraid she may plan something new.' The nurse is as
loyal as Alkestis' servant and describes her very different mistress in the
same detail. The old paidagogos comes back with the children; he has
heard gossip among the old men playing draughts that Kreon is going
to banish Medeia and the children (he brings news which was being
concealed, like the servant in the *Alkmaion in Psophis*).[27]

The parodos is an extremely effective tripartite structure. The nurse
recites anapaests on the stage, Medeia sings anapaests inside the house,
the chorus enter the orchestra and sing with them, partly in anapaests,
partly in other lyric metres (largely aeolo-choriambic).[28] Medeia prays
for death and curses her children, Jason, and his new wife. The nurse
philosophizes on her character and fears for her children (whom she
sends into the house, presumably with the paidagogos, telling them to
keep away from their mother in her fury). The chorus have heard
Medeia's cries and have come to comfort her.

Medeia comes out because she knows that it is difficult for a foreigner
to be accepted. All women are in a worse position than men, and she is
in addition an exile, misused by her husband. She begs them to keep
silent if she finds any means of vengeance. Kreon arrives to banish her.
She pleads with him not to let her reputation for cleverness damage her,
and persuades the foolish old man to give her a day's respite. Left alone,
Medeia thinks how to kill Kreon, his daughter, and Jason. If she had an
asylum, she could use poison. Otherwise she will use the sword even if
it means her own death. A granddaughter of the Sun cannot be mocked
by the descendants of Sisyphos.

The chorus sing in dactylo – epitrites that men have become more
faithless than women and in aeolo-choriambics of the complete desolation of Medeia. Jason arrives to offer her money for the journey. She
answers that his shameless visit at least allows her to say what she thinks:
she saved him, she betrayed her home for him, she gave him children,

[27] Cf. above, p. 42.
[28] On 131ff. cf. A. M. Dale, *Wiener Studien*, 77, 1964, 26f.

and where does he think she can go now. He retorts that she was only driven by Eros to save him, and he has made her a Greek instead of an unknown barbarian; his marriage is a device to provide them with money and legitimate brothers for her children (the situation which Alkestis feared if Admetos married again). Medeia refuses his money and sends him home to his new wife.

The chorus sing of the troubles caused by excessive passion and the miseries of exile (again dactylo-epitrites are followed by aeolo-choriambic). Then Aigeus, the hoped for asylum, appears. It is reasonable that he should pass through Corinth on his way from Delphi to Troizene in pursuing a cure for childlessness. She tells him her story and promises drugs to cure him if he will grant her asylum. He agrees provided that she herself can reach Athens. Alone, she elaborates the plan; she will pretend a reconciliation with Jason and so send her children with a poisoned robe and crown to kill Kreousa. Then she will kill them so that Jason will have no chance of children. The idea[29] that Aigeus' childlessness suggested to Medeia that she should make Jason childless is attractive, but Euripides would have told the audience if he had wanted them to think this. What he has told the audience is that Medeia hates her children, and this hatred now finds its possible fulfilment; he makes this clear because the servant sent to fetch Jason is the nurse, who told us of this hatred (820, with Page *ad loc.*). The chorus naturally view her deed with horror, and she herself 'cries in horror' at what she has to do and describes it as a deed of unholy daring (791, 796).

The chorus sing of Athens, its wisdom, its music, the breezes sent by Kypris. Athens can never accept her if she kills her children. How can she ever have the heart to do it? The description of Athens in the first strophe and antistrophe (dactylo-epitrites) is the only place in this play where Euripides uses the rich, decorated style, which has its analogy in the art of the Eretria painter and Meidias painter. The chorus escape for a moment from their horror to an idealized Athens. Then they return. The direct address to Medeia in the second strophe (aeolo-choriambic) makes her return to the stage after preparing the robe and crown. Jason comes in and Medeia asks his pardon. She calls out the children with the paidagogos (again we remember the first scene of the play) and tells them to embrace Jason. She persuades him to ask Kreousa to obtain pardon for the children from her father and reinforces this request by

[29] See D. L. Page, *Euripides Medea*, p. xxix.

her gifts. In this scene she nearly breaks down (899ff., 922ff.) but can pass it off as sorrow at parting.

The chorus sing that there is no hope for the children. The short song (the last in dactylo-epitrites and aeolo-choriambics) masks the interval until the old paidagogos comes back with the children to announce that they will be allowed to stay in Corinth. He too thinks that her distress is merely due to her impending departure. Left alone she goes through it all again in a speech which recalls Admetos' self-discovery.[30] They have a home, she will go into exile, deprived of all her hopes for their future and her own. They will never see her again, when they move into another kind of life (this deliberately ambiguous). Then they look at her and her resolve fails and she proposes to take them with her into exile. But she cannot bear the thought of her enemies' laughter. She pleads with her passion not to drive her on, then she reflects that she has already taken the fatal step and Kreousa is dying. Once more she embraces the children and is overcome by sight, touch, and scent. 'I know what evils I am going to do, but passion is stronger than my reason, passion which causes the greatest evil to men' (1079).

The chorus in a long passage of recitative anapaests argue that the hazards awaiting children are so great that it is better not to have children (this is parallel to the thoughts on the inadvisability of marriage voiced by the chorus of the *Alcestis* when they see Alkestis at the point of death, 238). Medeia receives one of Jason's servants who recounts the death of Kreon and Kreousa. Medeia steels herself to kill her children and leave. The chorus in shocked dochmiacs invoke the Sun, her grandfather, to stop her but their song is interrupted by the cries of the children. The chorus can only think of Ino as a parallel: she was driven mad by Hera and killed her two sons.[31]

Jason arrives to save his children from the revenge which Kreon's family may be expected to take. But as he bangs on the door, Medeia appears above the roof in a chariot drawn by winged snakes.[32] He attacks her furiously as a barbarian traitress who murdered her brother and now has murdered her children. She puts the responsibility on him.

[30] Cf. above, p. 52.
[31] This version probably occurred in Sophocles, *Athamas A* (cf. my *Hellenistic Poetry and Art*, 149); in the *Ino* (see below) Euripides followed quite a different story.
[32] Euripides probably remembered the unassailable Bellerophon at the end of the *Stheneboia* (see below, p. 84).

She will not let him bury the children or even touch them. She will bury them at Perachora and they will be celebrated with ritual for ever (this is the familiar connexion of the story with an existing cult); she will go to Athens; Jason will die in dishonour.

The construction is brilliantly simple, as in the *Alcestis*. Here too there is a tendency to balance the central scenes: Medeia–Kreon, Medeia–Jason, Medeia–Aigeus, Medeia–Jason, Medeia–Messenger, which is the completion of the Kreon story. But the continuous thread after the description of Medeia by the nurse really consists of the five monologues of Medeia to the chorus – before Kreon's arrival (214), after Kreon's departure (364), after Aigeus' departure (764), when the children have come back (1021), and after the messenger speech (1236). In no other surviving play, except perhaps the *Agamemnon*, is the motive power so completely given to a single character, whose attitude is already defined by a retainer in the prologue. If we had the *Peliades*, we should have another link between Aeschylus' Klytemnestra and the surviving Medeia, but Medeia in the *Peliades* had no reason for the misgivings which haunt our Medeia from the moment that she conceives the murder of the children.

Sophocles' *Tereus* according to some suggested to Euripides the idea of making Medeia murder her children. This cannot be proved because, although the argument for dating the *Tereus* shortly before 431 B.C. seems to me sound,[33] Euripides, if indeed he invented Medeia's murder of her children, did not need Sophocles to remind him of the Tereus story. It is more interesting to see Sophocles and Euripides, as we shall see also in the Phaidra story, working on a similar story at the same time. The *Tereus* is linked to the *Trachiniae* by its picture of the lonely heroine (583, cf. also *Med.* 230f.), by the sequence of false report (585P, Tereus) and true report (586P, 588P Philomela's messenger), and by its doxology (590P).[34] The metamorphosis of the chief characters into birds by Zeus (581P) is announced by someone (surely himself a god rather than a messenger) who follows it with the assessment (589P) 'Tereus was mad, but the women were madder still . . .' and the chorus end with the moral (590P): 'mortals should have mortal thoughts in the

[33] Cf. my *Sophocles*, 3, 176.
[34] The *Trachiniae* itself has recently been shown to be near the *Oedipus Rex* by an analysis of its lyric metres, H. A. Pohlsander, *A.J.P.*, 84, 1963, 280; D. S. Raven, *A.J.P.*, 86, 1965, 225.

knowledge that Zeus is the steward of all that will happen'. Prokne and Philomela suffered worse provocation than Medeia, but Sophocles comments that 'to apply in anger a remedy that is worse than the disease is the sign of a bad doctor' (589P). For Sophocles the women were cruelly provoked; they gave way to the provocation and killed Tereus' child, who was also Prokne's child; this was to have more than mortal thoughts in their anger, because somehow they were taking on themselves the function of Zeus in arranging the future. It is not certain whether the doxology of the *Medeia* belongs, since it comes at the end of other plays too; in this doxology Zeus' stewardship only guarantees the unpredictability of events; Medeia is not judged by the same standards as Prokne, and the events are not accepted with the same resignation as the will of Zeus.

Deianeira also was probably a Klytemnestra-like figure in the original story as her name implies, but Sophocles, as has often been pointed out,[35] carefully distinguished her from Klytemnestra by reminding his audiences here and there of the *Agamemnon*. The timid, pathetic, middle aged Deianeira cannot face rivalry with the youthful Iole. Eros is a god whom Herakles has been unable to resist and whom she recognizes as ruling her. But she never thinks of killing Herakles, and though in her heart of hearts she knows that magic is dangerous, she believes that she is using a love-philtre and not a fatal poison. She also is cruelly provoked; the provocation is of the same kind as Medeia's, but she has no anger against Herakles. Sophocles has cast the story so that the will of Zeus is achieved by the stupidity of a loving woman, who never suspected a dying Centaur of hating and accurately assessing his killer. Euripides is only interested in the human predicament of Medeia: 'passion is stronger than my reason, passion which causes the greatest evil to men.'

PHILOKTETES[36]

Outline of play

Prologue: Odysseus, frs. 787–9N²; Dion Chrysost. *Or.* 59. Philoktetes, fr. 790, 790aN² (exeunt into cave).

[35] E.g. my article in *Greek Poetry and Life*, 164; H. S. G. Kapsomenos, *Sophokles Trachinierinnen und ihr Vorbild*, 39ff.

[36] The vase by the Dirke painter (Séchan, 490, fig. 144); A. D. Trendall, *Paestan pottery supplement*, no. 7 (6), *LCS*, 204; Bieber, *History*, fig. 119; S. Setti, *Dioniso*. 38, 1964,

Parodos of Lemnians: fr. 791N²(?).
Philoktetes and Aktor (supplies, and news of Trojan ship?).
Debate with Trojan envoy: Paris, fr. 794N² Odysseus, fr. 796–9N².
Philoktetes, fr. 795N² (Etruscan urns).
Arrival of Diomede: Philoktetes' sickness, fr. 792, 801N². Diomede
    steals the bow (Etruscan urns).
Exodos (hypothesis).

Bibliographical note: L. Séchan, *Études*, 485; W. H. Friedrich,
Philologus, 94, 1941, 157. Hypothesis: *P. Oxy.* 2455, fr. 17.

Dion Chrysostom in his comparison of the plays by Aeschylus,
Sophocles and Euripides (*Or.* 52) says that in Aeschylus Odysseus was
accepted by Philoktetes because he told of the complete ruin of the
Greek army and that he stole the bow while Philoktetes was in a
paroxysm of sickness. (All three poets had the sick scene, and Euripides
used one of Aeschylus' lines with a slight alteration (792N²).) For
Euripides Dion gives us the following points: the chorus were Lemnians,
and they apologized for not having visited Philoktetes before; Aktor
was introduced as a Lemnian friend of Philoktetes (in Hyginus, *fab.* 102,
Philoktetes is given food by a shepherd who belongs to the king, Aktor,
and the papyrus summary (*P. Oxy.* 2455, fr. 17) speaks of 'the pity of
those who met him being his livelihood'); Odysseus spoke the prologue,
which included the announcement of a Trojan embassy; Odysseus was
not there alone but with Diomede; the songs were full of exhortations
to virtue.

In *Oration* 59 Dion paraphrases the prologue. Odysseus characterizes
his own restless energy (frs. 787–9N²); he has not told the kings of
Helenos' prophecy; Athena persuaded him in a dream to come and
changed his appearance so that Philoktetes should not recognize him;
he knows that the Trojans also are sending an embassy to capture
Philoktetes. Then he sees Philoktetes arriving and wonders at his

---

214, shows Philoktetes sitting in his cave, while outside it Athena talks to a young man and
an older man holds up his sword as he talks to a young woman – probably a nymph of the
island. This has no valid connexion with Euripides' play unless we make the daring sup-
position that the young man is Odysseus youthened by Athena. The vases, which Mrs
Hooker (*J.H.S.*, 70, 1950, 35f.) thinks draw their subject, a sacrifice to Chryse in the first
Trojan War by Herakles and Philoktetes, from a speech in this play are better referred to a
dithyramb, as one of the vases shows a tripod prize; even if Mrs Hooker were right, they
would only illustrate a single reminiscent speech of Philoktetes.

dishevelled appearance (cf. Aristophanes, *Ach.* 423). Odysseus announces himself as returning from the Trojan campaign and Philoktetes nearly shoots him (a theme which Sophocles transferred to the end of his play (1299)). He pretends to be a friend of Palamedes, and Philoktetes invites him into his cave (frs. 790, 790aN²). If Dion's statement that Odysseus spoke the prologue is right, it is difficult to refuse to accept this whole sequence as belonging to the prologue. Friedrich has suggested that Dion overran at least one chorus, but the only obvious break is before the arrival of Philoktetes and if the chorus came to visit Philoktetes it is very unlikely that he was not at home when they arrived. Probably then we should accept the sequence as given by Dion. There is no mention of Diomede; he may have been a mute character, but it seems hardly possible that neither Odysseus nor Philoktetes should have mentioned him, and we must suppose that Diomede did not take the stage till later.

The prologue ends with Odysseus and Philoktetes going into the cave. The chorus of Lemnians arrive and defend themselves for not having visited Philoktetes before. They presumably imagine his life, and the choral fragment fr. 791N² 'May I die before disaster (i.e. such disaster) falls on my chattels or my person' may belong here. Séchan has made the interesting suggestion that Aktor may be the ancestor of the *autourgos* in the *Electra* (but perhaps he is more like the old man who brings Elektra supplies to entertain Orestes and Pylades). There are two possible functions for Aktor here. He may bring Philoktetes supplies and he may bring Philoktetes news; he may indeed do both. The reason for suggesting the former is that Hyginus speaks of the shepherd nourishing Philoktetes and the papyrus summary calls the pity of those who met him 'his livelihood'. The news which is needed and which Odysseus cannot give is the arrival of a Trojan ship.

Then after a chorus the Trojan envoys arrived. Six fragments may belong to the following scene. Odysseus comes out with Philoktetes; he has a part to play which is not unlike the part played by the disguised Telephos when he defends the Trojans from the attack made on them by Menelaos.[37] The Trojan (fr. 794N²) says that Philoktetes should follow the principle of the gods and accept the riches (including the crown) which the Trojans offer. He has presumably also told Philoktetes the prophecy that success belongs to the side which possesses Philoktetes

[37] Cf. above, p. 46.

and his arms. Philoktetes, now or perhaps later after Odysseus has made his speech, answers that prophecy is impossible for men and is only used as a means of persuasion (fr. 795N²); he presumably goes on to say that his own miserable plight is due to a prophet and that he does not propose to listen to a prophet again (the theme which we have already noticed in the *Likymnios*). Odysseus breaks in with the line parodied by Aristotle: 'But when the whole Greek expedition is at stake, it is base to be silent and to allow the barbarians to speak' (fr. 796N²). He goes on 'I will speak even if he seems to have destroyed my argument by admitting the wrong that he has done' (fr. 797N²). This description identifies the Trojan speaker as Paris, and in any case after the death of Hektor and the capture of Helenos he is the most likely to lead the embassy. Like Telephos, Odysseus cannot give himself away, but he can claim that the injustice done to Palamedes and the injustice done to Philoktetes does not justify sacrificing their country to the Trojans (fr. 799N² 'anger should not be eternal' and probably fr. 798N² 'individual success depends on the success of one's country' may belong here). Odysseus may also quote Helenos' prophecy that Philoktetes' arms will take Troy, and it may be here rather than earlier that Philoktetes answers with his attack on prophecy.

An interesting possibility is offered by the Hellenistic Etruscan urns published by Brunn and Körte (*Urne Etruschi*, I, 80, pl. 69–72). Two types are relevant. On nos. 1–3, Odysseus and a younger man look in astonishment towards the centre where Philoktetes with his arrows moves towards two young men one of whom wears a Phrygian cap. Surprisingly this is interpreted as deriving from Sophocles, although the Phrygian cap is exactly like that worn by Paris on the urns illustrating the *Alexandros*. The young man must therefore be the leader of the Trojan embassy in the Euripidean play: the action is not entirely clear; but it looks as if Philoktetes threatened to shoot Paris, as he had earlier threatened Odysseus.

Philoktetes is still in possession of his bow and has shown himself as unwilling to help the Greeks as he is to help the Trojans. Something new has to happen, and in Euripides this probably means a new arrival. Perhaps Diomede now comes, whether he has been waiting on Odysseus' ship or has been sent later by the Greek army on his own ship. The second type of Etruscan urns (nos. 4 to 7) suggest that he steals the bow and arrows while Odysseus expresses sympathy with Philoktetes' sickness. A fragment 'he breathed out (or he has just breathed out) his soul' (fr. 801N²) has naturally been interpreted as Philoktetes fainting after a new attack of his disease. This would give Odysseus the opportunity to pretend kindness and Diomede the opportunity to steal the bow and arrows. At that stage Odysseus would reveal his identity. The play must have ended with Philoktetes going off with the Greeks. The words at the end of the papyrus hypothesis 'compels him to go with them to the ship' suggest one of the Greeks rather than a god as a subject: 'the assurance' that he offers is perhaps the assurance that Philoktetes will be healed. 'Compels' is hardly compatible with the idea that Philoktetes goes willingly or that he has yielded either to divine or human persuasion. Philoktetes in this play seems to be the victim of Greek intrigue, and Odysseus to be the ruthless self-seeking schemer whom we know later from the *Hecuba* and *Palamedes*.

DIKTYS

Outline of play

Prologue: fr. 330b. 331, ? 341, 344N² (Perseus). ? Polydektes. Exit Perseus.

Parodos: women of Seriphos?

Danae and Diktys, scene of consolation: frs. 332, 343, 346N².

Diktys, Polydektes, Danae: frs. 333–340; ? 347N².

Recital of Gorgon exploit?

Polydektes and Perseus?

Messenger speech of petrification of Polydektes.

Return of Perseus. Diktys made king. Departure of Perseus with Danae.

We do not know anything about Aeschylus' *Polydektes*. For this play the story of Danae's arrival in Seriphos is excluded by fr. 332N² in which Diktys supposes that Perseus is dead; Hyginus' story (*fab.* 63) in which Akrisios is accidentally killed by Perseus at the funeral games of Polydektes is excluded because it has no part for Diktys. The fragments fit, however, into the story which is known from various sources.[38] Polydektes, King of Seriphos and brother of Diktys, fell in love with Danae and was prevented from seducing her by Perseus who had

[38] The Cyzicene epigrams (*Anth. Pal.* 3, 11), Strabo (487C), Pherekydes (ap. *Schol. Ap. Rhod.*, 4, 1515a) and more fully from Apollodoros (II, iv, 2–3).

grown up. Polydektes sent Perseus to fetch the Gorgon's head as his part in an *eranos* or as a wedding present for Hippodameia. When Perseus returned to Seriphos, 'he found that the violence of Polydektes had caused Danae and Diktys to take refuge on an altar; he entered the palace and when Polydektes had summoned his friends, he showed them the Gorgon's head and they were changed into stone'. He then made Diktys king.

The likeness of the altar scene and its sequel to the *H.F.* is obvious, and Euripides may well have modelled the earlier part of that play on his own earlier *Diktys*. This gives an outline for the later part of the *Diktys*: Danae and Diktys seated on an altar; Perseus arrives (perhaps on the *mechane*?); Perseus learns their plight and recounts his story of the Gorgon; then he punishes Polydektes.

Polydektes is the king, and it looks as if Euripides followed the tradition which made Diktys, his brother, a fisherman; Wilamowitz[39] suggested that in Euripides, as in Pherekydes, they were half-brothers with a common mother. We have to ask whether the action takes place before Polydektes' palace or Diktys' hut. When Danae laments Perseus' absence (fr. 332N²), she is surely outside her own house rather than outside the palace, and there is no reason why the altar should not be here rather than outside the palace. (If this is right, Euripides remembered the setting when he wrote his *Electra*.) Then Perseus returned, as he naturally would, to Diktys' hut, and the scene ends with Danae and Diktys persuaded to go into the hut. Perseus went off to the palace, unless Polydektes came back to attack Danae again (like Lykos in the *H.F.*) and Perseus persuaded him to summon his friends to the palace to see the Gorgon's head. Two analogies in later Euripides are Agave's request to Kadmos to summon his friends to celebrate her hunting (*Bacch.* 1241) and Merope's feigned reconciliation with Polyphontes.[40] Euripides may here too have made Perseus promise Polydektes a reconciliation with Danae after celebrating the Gorgon's death. After a stasimon the messenger from the palace will recount that Polydektes and his friends were all turned to stone. Perseus returns and makes Diktys king and leaves for Argos with Danae.

The point at which the story begins is not clear. 'Seriphos washed by the sea-surge' (fr. 330bN²) is the first line of the prologue and presumably

[39] *Kl. Schr.* V, 2, 135.
[40] See below, p. 142.

continued 'is here, where once' but gives no clue as to who told the past history. The two possible moments to begin are, (1) before Perseus goes to fetch the Gorgon's head, (2) when Perseus has already departed and Polydektes is trying to get hold of Danae. The second is paralleled in the *H.F.* and involves no unreality of time and Perseus' long absence accounts well for the desolation of Danae (332N²): it is perhaps questionable whether it leaves enough action for the play. The first involves a major unreality of time, but in the *Stheneboia* also the prologue is much more easily understood if Bellerophon has not yet been sent to meet the Chimaira. One fragment (331N²) is closely linked in sentiment to the *Stheneboia* (prologue l. 30 = fr. 672N²) and to the *Theseus* (fr. 388N²).[41] The sense must be 'it is my hope that an Eros may capture me which does not lead me to folly or Kypris' and Nauck's emendation is as likely as any. Perseus, like Theseus and Bellerophon, is set on a career of glory; both of them were themselves entangled with undesirable women, Perseus must here be referring to Polydektes' passion for Danae (but his sentiments also exclude Andromeda, who has no part in this version of the story). Perhaps 'may I never surrender to bribes or associate with bad men' (fr. 341N²) also belongs here. 'Young and not unexercised in courage by adventure' (fr. 344N²) must describe Perseus but need not come from the prologue. It is then possible that Perseus spoke the prologue and that either in the prologue or in a scene immediately after the *parodos* he accepts Polydektes' challenge to bring him back the Gorgon's head.

We have no evidence for the composition of the chorus. If Perseus has already departed they may be women who comfort Danae. Danae laments Perseus' probable death and Diktys comforts her with the general misery of mankind (fr. 332N²) and perhaps with the thought that Justice is strong (fr. 343N²). She answers with the common love of children shown by gods, men, and animals (fr. 346N², cf. *H.F.* 280, 633). The next clear scene is Polydektes' attempt to seize Danae: at some stage Danae, like Megara to the chorus at *H.F.* 277, tries to dissuade the aged Diktys from quarrelling with the King (fr. 337N²). The beginning of Diktys' speech is preserved (fr. 334N²) he feels himself forced to speak because he has been abused by a villain. The root idea is the same as Odysseus' opening against the Trojans in the *Philoktetes* (769N²). Here also perhaps fr. 333N² 'a bad father could not have a

[41] Stobaeus in fact joins the two quotations from the *Diktys* and *Theseus* together.

good son'; fr. 335N² 'tyrants make long speeches'; fr. 336N² 'nobility depends on virtue rather than birth'. Certainly fr. 338N² 'when you have children, do you propose to beget new children and so cause hatred', is a direct argument against marriage with Danae. The abuse of which Diktys complains may be contained in frs. 339, 340N²: 'fathers often help their sons and sons their fathers in their love affairs'. 'Kypris only makes more havoc if you try to repress her.' These arguments are familiar in the mouth of the nurse in *Hippolytos II* (460ff.). Polydektes may have had a similar *confidant*, of whom all trace is lost, but these could equally well have been arguments used by Polydektes himself against Diktys to show the way in which he should behave to help his brother to possess Danae, arguments which Diktys could only hear as 'abuse by a villain'. (A difficult fragment, 347N², may belong here if it belongs to this play at all: 'if you were not an utter villain, you would not dishonour your country and praise this city'. Danae, though not a Seriphian, is excluded because the 'you' is masculine. Perseus is also a foreigner, but there does not seem any reason to accuse him of playing the Seriphian. The pedigree of the brothers is obscure but they both seem to have been foreigners. It is perhaps easiest to suppose that Diktys is attacking Polydektes for living in the immoral manner of his Seriphian friends.)

This scene ended with Diktys and Danae taking refuge on the altar and Polydektes retiring with a threat that he will return with soldiers (this seems a reasonable interpretation of violence). Perseus arrives, Diktys rouses Danae (fr. 342N²). Perseus promises them his aid (fr. 345N²).[42] The rest we have discussed.

4 *The Phaidra plays*[43]

The preserved *Hippolytus*, which was produced in 428 B.C., was the second play that Euripides wrote on the theme. The Hypothesis says:

[42] Note that this is an admirable example of the general sentiment which fits only loosely to the particular situation: 'a father loves his children, and sons love their parents', although here a mother and a foster-father are the parents involved.

[43] The Phaidra plays are fully discussed by W. S. Barrett in *Euripides Hippolytos*, 10ff., and by Bruno Snell in *Scenes from Greek Drama*. C. Zintzen, *Analytisches Hypomnema zu Senecas Phaedra* (Meisenheim, 1960), extracts the maximum of evidence from Seneca for the First Hippolytos, but does not discuss how Seneca uses his sources. Cf. also F. Scheidweiler, *Würzburger Jb. für die Altertumswiss.*, 3, 1948, 232; R. Merkelbach, *Rh. Mus.*, 100, 1957, 99; W. H. Friedrich, *Euripides und Diphilos*, 110ff.

'It was clearly written later. All that was unseemly and worthy of condemnation has been corrected in this play.' Aristophanes must therefore have been referring to the earlier play when he made Aeschylus say (*Frogs* 1043): 'But *I* never made Phaidras or Stheneboias into whores': the other Euripidean woman labelled 'whore' in ancient sources is Aerope in the *Cretan Women* produced in 438. The essential meaning seems to be a woman who offers herself to a younger man, and the earlier play is twice called *Hippolytos Kalyptomenos*: Hippolytos covered his head to avoid being polluted by Phaidra's approach, as Herakles covers his head after killing his children in the *H.F.* (1159).

The play shares the essential idea of the wife who throws herself at a young man with the *Cretan Women* of 438, and with the *Stheneboia*, *Phoenix*, and probably *Peleus*, all of which belong to Euripides' first period, which closes with the preserved *Hippolytus*.

The scene was laid in Athens (the corrupt 'in Thebes' in the Hypothesis may conceal 'in Troizen and not as for the first play in Athens'). If the scene was Athens, then the Attic cult of Hippolytos, which comes awkwardly into the prologue of the surviving play (29), was presumably introduced as an aetiological allusion at the end of the first play (and the cult may in fact have been a recent one):[44] this is the honour which, according to the choral anapaests, Hippolytos wins for his *sophrosyne* and *eusebia* (446N²). It must previously have been announced by a *deus ex machina*. The occasion for Phaidra's attempt was presumably Hippolytos' visit to Athens for the mysteries, which is also related in the prologue of the surviving play (24).

In the second play Phaidra's visit to Troizen and Theseus' absence were manufactured for the needs of the plot. Theseus was probably also absent at the beginning of the earlier play. In Sophocles' *Phaidra* (686P) he returned from Hades in the course of the play, and his supposed death may have been used as a justification for Phaidra's conduct, but this would not prevent Euripides from using it too. Euripides' Phaidra justified her love for Hippolytos by the 'transgressions of Theseus' – an accusation which Plutarch, to whom we owe this (*Mor.* 28A), compares to Helen's statement in the *Trojan Women* (919) that Hekabe caused the Trojan War by giving birth to Paris.[45] Plutarch regards her words as

[44] Cf. Barrett, *op. cit.*, 4.
[45] Zintzen, *op. cit.*, 13, compares rightly Pasiphae's attack on Minos in the *Cretans* (cf. p. 90).

shameless and hopes that the young reader will see through them. Phaidra's attitude to her husband is in fact the opposite of Andromache's who helped Hektor in his love-affairs (*Andr.* 222ff.). Plutarch's 'accusing' does not necessarily mean that Phaidra accused Theseus to his face, and it is difficult to see when she could have spoken of her love of Hippolytos to him in these terms; the accusation must have been a self-justification. Such a speech would be more likely if Theseus was absent, whether his 'transgressions' at the moment consisted of chasing Persephone or some other joint enterprise with Peirithoos, which Plutarch would regard as a natural duty. Plutarch's account has naturally been connected with Phaidra's monologue at the beginning of Seneca's play (*Phaedr.* 91f.) where the same sequence, Theseus' infidelity and her love for Hippolytos, occurs: however much he has remodelled, Seneca was using the *First Hippolytos* here.

The beginning of the *First Hippolytos* is probably preserved in the address to the light of day ($443N^2$).[46] The speaker, like the nurse in the *Medea* (57), has come out of the house to tell her misery. Here the speaker must be Phaidra as no one else in the play is 'born unfortunate', and her misfortune is first her desertion by Theseus and secondly her love for Hippolytos.

Two other fragments have been attributed to the prologue. Friedrich suggested that $444N^2$ (inborn and heaven-sent evils cannot be avoided) belonged to the context of Seneca 114, where Phaidra compares her love to Pasiphae's fatal love, a theme picked up also in the surviving play (337). Barrett's suggestion that Phaidra herself is described by another is less likely.

The Scholiast to Theokritos 2, 10 says: 'It is natural for women possessed by Love to summon the moon, as Euripides makes Phaidra do in the *First Hippolytos*.' Barrett suggests that the Nurse described Phaidra's behaviour in the prologue. But the scholiast says that Euripides made *Phaidra* call on the moon, so that both this and the common equation with the Nurse's prayer to Hekate and the Moon in Seneca (406) are impossible. But Phaidra may have prayed to Hekate and have identified her with the Moon, which disposes of Barrett's difficulty about a prayer to the Moon in daylight (Sophocles had already made the identification, fr. 535P); her prayer, like the prayer in Seneca and like Simaitha's prayer in Theokritos, may have been for the attraction

[46] Snell equates with Seneca 85-90.

of Hippolytos, but there is no reason to ascribe it to the prologue.

The next scene of which we can be certain is Phaidra's approach to Hippolytos, when he covered his head in shame (and perhaps rushed from the stage, cf. S. *Aj.* 245). To this or to the prelude to this must belong Phaidra's statement that Eros is her teacher in confident daring (430N²). She swears Hippolytos to silence (435N²); Barrett has shown how this would work in stichomythia. Hippolytos answers with the penalty to be incurred if he breaks the oath (in the surviving play the nurse has sworn Hippolytos off stage (611)).

Three fragments: 'Act first and then call on the gods' (432N²),' in danger revere necessity rather than law' (433N²), 'success is won by daring and unrestrained hands, not by piety' (434N²) fit very well with a suggestion to Hippolytos that he should seize the royal power (and the charge of having attempted this is answered, although Theseus never made it, by Hippolytos in the surviving play, 1013). In Seneca also Phaidra offers him the throne (617). Hippolytos' answer may begin with the wish that facts had voices so that they could not be misrepresented by eloquence (439N²) (and 445N² 'but now the gods order things wrong' may also belong here). It is true that a parallel idea – 'would that the house could speak and bear witness to me' – occurs at the end of Hippolytos' defence to Theseus in the surviving play (1074), but in the earlier play the obvious instance of misrepresentation is Phaidra's speech to Hippolytos.[47]

The strongest evidence for an intervening scene in which someone advises Hippolytos to unbend is 428N²: 'Those who exceed in shunning Kypris are as sick as those who exceed in hunting her.' An echo of this in the surviving play is the short scene between the Therapon and Hippolytos after his prayer to Artemis (88f.). With this the difficult fragments about *hybris* being the child of wealth rather than of poverty (437, 438N²) should probably be associated. The attractive identification with the Nurse's speech to Phaidra in Seneca (204ff.) – *libido* is the comrade

---

[47] The other components in this scene and the links forward and backwards are unclear. Merkelbach suggested that, as both Seneca (646) and Heliodorus make Phaidra see in Hippolytos a younger Theseus, this derives from Euripides. The surviving play gives no hint of this idea; Phaidra thinks of Hippolytos as the son of the Amazon. In two cases it is an older outsider who sees the son as a reminder of the father, Helen seeing Telemachos in the Odyssey (4, 142) and Hekale seeing Theseus (Callimachus, fr. 367 Pf.). Is either possibly the source both for Seneca and Heliodorus? One would not willingly debit Euripides with such a false piece of psychology. Sophocles' Phaidra is more likely, cf. *Phil.* 356ff.

of great fortune; it seldom enters poor homes – must be rejected; *hybris* could be *either* Phaidra's refusal to yield to her passion *or* Hippolytos' refusal of love *or* Hippolytos' supposed seduction of Phaidra, but *not* Phaidra's passion for Hippolytos. I find attractive Scheidweiler's suggestion that 438 (reading τί for τε and keeping ἤ) should precede 437 and both be spoken by Hippolytos: 'What produces *hybris*? Wealth or thrift? I see that in most men their existing prosperity produces *hybris*. (But I am a thrifty and chaste hunter.)' Barrett refers the fragments to a late debate between Theseus and Hippolytos (as in the surviving play), but we have no evidence for such a debate, and the emphasis on excess in 428N² leads naturally to a charge of *hybris*, the same *hybris* of repression in Hippolytos with which the nurse charges Phaidra in the surviving play (474). Hippolytos defends himself by an account of his *sophrosyne*, which is more effective and sympathetic here than in the Theseus debate of the surviving play (995ff.).

But who is the speaker of 428N²? The Therapon or the Nurse? The scene in the surviving play when the Therapon criticizes Hippolytos for not revering Aphrodite, is effective because the audience has just seen Aphrodite. In the first play this justification was absent; but the sequence in Seneca – Phaedra persuades the Nurse to approach Hippolytos, and the Nurse tries to make Hippolytos relax – is entirely natural, and this may have been Euripides' structure. If it was, it is justifiable to note the close connexion between Seneca 469 and fr. 898N² pointed out by Friedrich: the Nurse tells Hippolytos that Aphrodite is the cause of all increase (an argument which is transferred in the surviving play to her scene with Phaidra, 447ff.). The appeal to *Aidos* may start Hippolytos' answer (436N²), and the theme may have been repeated in recitative anapaests by the chorus (897N²).[48]

The first approach to Hippolytos cannot advance beyond the general position – 'make some concessions to Aphrodite' – to the particular proposition: 'Phaidra is in love with you'. If Hippolytos heard that he would run away. If then the Nurse is the speaker (and this has the double advantage of more natural motivation than the Therapon and of providing someone other than the chorus who knows the truth), she

[48] Formally these anapaests are parallel to the choral anapaests on the undesirability of having children in *Med.* 1081ff. They imply that the audience have already seen Hippolytos and might follow either his scene with the nurse or his scene with Phaidra (if they are rightly ascribed to this play).

never gets to the particular proposition. Hippolytos reacts violently against the general proposition. Possibly, as in Seneca, Phaidra breaks in on the scene before the Nurse can tell her what has happened.

After the great scene between Phaidra and Hippolytos, a choral ode (or perhaps recitative anapaests including 897N²) intervenes before Theseus appears. For the rest of the play we have three certainties: (1) 429N², choriambic dimeters A, the chorus sing 'We women are a fire worse than fire, much more invincible'; (2) 442N², 'going straightway to the stables', messenger speech, cf. *Hipp.* 1178; (3) 446N², the epilogue, already discussed. If a female chorus speaks of women as an invincible fire, some woman has just done or is about to do something extremely damaging to men. Here the reference must be to Phaidra's accusation of Hippolytos to Theseus. In the second play she commits suicide out of shame when she is betrayed by the Nurse, and her suicide note is an improbable device to allow the play to proceed on its traditional lines. In the first play she evidently accused Hippolytos to save herself. In Apollodoros, *epit.* 1, 18–19, she provides broken doors and torn clothes as evidence of rape (and she may have described them in Euripides). In Seneca (863ff.) Theseus finds her pretending to commit suicide with Hippolytos' sword, which he had thrown away as polluted when she grasped it in supplication; Theseus recognizes the sword and so accepts her story. This demands an *ekkyklema* scene, but that is no difficulty.[49]

In the surviving play Theseus debates with Hippolytos before cursing him: Hippolytos' return is skilfully but artificially contrived (661, 902). The debate is necessary to fill out the picture of Hippolytos with details which in the first play were given in the scenes with the Nurse and Phaidra. Barrett's argument that a debate is also necessary in the first play because Hippolytos cannot vanish so early from the action is worthless as a glance at the *Alcestis, Andromache* and *Phaethon* shows. He claims 439N² for the debate, but it is better accommodated as we have seen in Hippolytos' answer to Phaidra. He also interprets 440N², 'Theseus, I give you the best advice, if you are wise. Don't believe a woman even if she speaks the truth', as said by a servant after Phaidra's accusation but before Theseus has acted upon it, but in the preserved play the messenger

---

[49] Friedrich suggests that the chorus enters the house while the *ekkyklema* comes out. If one could think of a suitable reason this would be attractive, cf. above on *Peliades* and *Alcestis.*

says that he refuses to believe that Hippolytos is base even if the whole female sex hangs itself and fills every pine-tree in Ida with accusations (1250), and 440N² with 441N² ('time is apt to prove the truth') may very well come from the messenger speech.

Why and how does Phaidra commit suicide? Presumably not on the stage after a confession as in Seneca. According to Apollodoros she hanged herself when her love was made public. The Nurse is the only person outside Phaidra and Hippolytos who could have told the whole story; we have a clear parallel for a servant betraying his mistress in the *Second Phrixos* (see below): Ino's servant saves Phrixos by informing Athamas that Ino has both caused the famine and forged the oracle commanding the sacrifice of Phrixos. It is also probable that Aerope was betrayed to Atreus by a servant in the *Cretan Women* (see above). The Nurse may have given similar information to Theseus too late and Phaidra overhearing rushed in to commit suicide, pursued by the Nurse, who then reports her suicide however briefly. Alternatively, and perhaps more economically, Phaidra with Theseus hears the messenger speech and rushes into the house to commit suicide, and the Nurse reports both the suicide and the cause: then Phaidra died as Servius says *impatientia amoris* – her accusation of Hippolytos was an effort to save herself and she now sees that its consequence is his death.

In either case Theseus knows the truth, and probably her body is brought out on the *ekkyklema* as Hippolytos is carried in (did Euripides remember the end of the *Antigone* here?). In the surviving play Artemis has to enlighten Theseus, and this shapes the whole moving scene of Theseus' reconciliation and Artemis' farewell to the dying Hippolytos. Artemis there cannot stay to see Hippolytos die (1437); in the earlier play, therefore, Hippolytos must be dead before the *deus* arrives, probably before his body is brought on (if it is brought on). This is also implied by the use of ἥρως in the final anapaests (446N²). The end was like the end of the *Andromache* and the only function of the *deus* is to announce the cult. Poseidon for his connexion with Theseus, Artemis for her connexion with Hippolytos, or Aphrodite for her connexion with the Attic cult are the obvious possibilities.

The probable scheme seems therefore to be:

Prologue: Phaidra 443N²; Plut. *Mor.* 28 A; ? 444N²; ? Schol. Theocr. 2, 10.

Epeisodia   Phaidra and Nurse.
  and Stasima: Nurse[50] and Hippolytos: 428, 898, 436–8N².
                 Phaidra *porneuousa* and Hippolytos *kalyptomenos*:
                 430, 435, 432–4, 439, 445N².
Stasimon: (or ? choral anapaests, 897N²).
                 Return of Theseus: *ekkyklema* scene with Phaidra.
Stasimon: 429N².
                 Messenger: 440–2N².
                 Suicide of Phaidra: report by Nurse; body on
                 ekkyklema.
                 Arrival of Hippolytos' body.
                 Deus ex machina.
                 Exodos: 446N².

In the surviving play the scene is moved to Troizen, which also had a Hippolytos cult. Perhaps Euripides felt now that Athens should not be burdened with this cruel story; the chorus of the *Medea* (846f.) in 431 B.C. disliked the thought of Athens as a refuge for a murderess. Aphrodite speaks the prologue, partly because the new Phaidra cannot tell her love and the exposition must therefore be given to a god, partly because the hypostatization of a psychological force in the form of a vengeful goddess also seems to take the responsibility away from Phaidra.[51]

Hippolytos enters with a chorus of huntsmen who sing with him to Artemis and he places a wreath on Artemis' statue. No obvious reason accounts for the subsidiary choruses[52] in Euripides; here their intervention is charming but unnecessary; perhaps they were always due to the generosity of a particular *choregos*. Hippolytos claims that his inborn and pervading modesty (*sophrosyne*) gives him the right to pick the flowers for this garland. Most simply, Hippolytos' devotion is the devotion of a hunter to the patroness of hunting, but hunting must at least be widened to include all forms of sport; and if we consider the

[50] Leo, *De Senecae Tragoediis*, 178, suggested that the Nurse took a letter from Phaidra to Hippolytos. The evidence is representations on paintings, mosaics, reliefs, sarcophagi of the 1st to 2nd century A.D. (see Roscher, III, 2223ff.; Reinach, *R.P.*, 209/2; *Acta Antiqua*, 14, 1966, 211). This must have come from some well-known source, *not* Lykophron, suggested by Rohde. Either this play or Sophocles' *Phaidra* seems the most likely.
[51] Cf. A. Lesky, *Entretiens Hardt*, VI, 137.
[52] Cf. below on *Alexandros, Antiope, Phaethon, Supplices*.

parallel between Hippolytos' 'a long good-bye to your Kypris' (113) and Theseus' 'good-bye to Kypris, the daughter of Zeus' (388N²),[53] it is tempting to suppose that Euripides conceived of devotion to career, as opposed to the pleasures of wine and women, as a psychological force like the sexual urge, which he might hypostatize as a goddess, here as Artemis and perhaps in the case of Theseus as Athene. The old servant opens the door[54] to Hippolytos and begs his master to do honour to Aphrodite whose statue also stands beside the door; this little dialogue is a substitute for Hippolytos' dialogue with the nurse in the earlier play (cf. above, p. 68). It is contrived here, but prepares the audience for future developments.

The parodos introduces Phaidra. The elements are the same as in the *Medea*: lyrics from the chorus, recitative anapaests from the nurse, sung anapaests from Phaidra; but here the sequence is chorus, then nurse and Phaidra. The opening song is a lovely decorated beginning in the style reserved for the praise of Athens in the *Medea*. They heard at the washing-trough that the queen was ill. Has she sinned against some god or goddess? Has Theseus been unfaithful? Or bad news from Crete? or pregnancy? The *ekkyklema* rolls out with the nurse standing beside Phaidra who reclines on a couch.[55] The dochmiacs of the chorus (362ff.) mark its rolling back and Phaidra makes her great speech to the chorus (372ff.) standing on the stage. The anapaestic dialogue shows Phaidra's distress, her physical weakness, her desire for the mountains and the chariot-track, and her shame at her madness. Urged by the chorus, the nurse extracts the truth: if Phaidra dies, her children will not inherit their father's house; their master will be the bastard who behaves as a legitimate son, Hippolytos. The name extracts a cry from Phaidra, and then she gradually confesses: like her mother Pasiphae, and like her sister Ariadne, she is fatally in love – with Hippolytos.

After the horrified exclamations of the nurse and the chorus, Phaidra states her position in a considered speech: 'We recognize ideals and know them, but we fail to carry them out from lack of energy or because we prefer pleasure.' This being her view, when she fell in love she first tried silence, then repression, and when that failed she decided on suicide. She utterly hates adulterers. She must not shame her husband

[53] Cf. below, p. 107.
[54] Cf. Hourmouziades, *Production and Imagination*, 18.
[55] Cf. above, p. 49, on its use here and in the *Alcestis*.

or her children: they must live free with reputation unharmed. Thus she picks up the nurse's point about her children, and we know that she is deeply concerned about them. The nurse answers that love is the common lot of men and gods, and it is *hybris* to resist (these are arguments that the nurse in the first play used to Hippolytos): she pretends that she has a philtre which will cure Phaidra's disease. She takes over the responsibility.

She goes in and Phaidra remains outside while the chorus sing of the power of Eros which destroyed Iole and destroyed Semele. Phaidra stops them. She can hear through the door Hippolytos abusing the nurse and she decides on suicide. She stands back as Hippolytos comes out into the sunlight cursing the whole race of women. He decides to go away until Theseus returns. Phaidra's dochmiac monody of agony (669ff.) corresponds metrically to the chorus' earlier song of horror at her revelation (362ff.) so that the two clamp the whole disastrous sequence together. In a final scene of bitter reproach with the nurse, Phaidra asks the chorus not to betray her if she can preserve her children's reputation and punish Hippolytos for his pride.

The chorus escape into the decorated world of Phaethon and the Hesperids in a song which stylistically recalls the parodos. The nurse cries from within that Phaidra has hanged herself. Theseus arrives with wreathed head and hears the cries. The *ekkyklema* rolls out with Phaidra's body and Theseus laments her in bitter misery. Then he sees the tablet hanging from Phaidra's hand which announces that Hippolytos had raped her. He immediately calls on Poseidon to grant him one of the three wishes which the god had promised: to kill Hippolytos that day, and he adds that he will exile him. Hippolytos arrives and Theseus accuses him as a hypocritical puritan. Hippolytos defends himself as a virgin whose only desire is to be a successful athlete. Theseus drives him away, and he goes off with a farewell to Artemis, Athens and Troizen. The chorus sing of their doubts about divine justice when they witness the cruel fate of Hippolytos.

One of Hippolytos' servants reports that a bull rose from the sea and terrified Hippolytos' team so that he was thrown and hopelessly injured. The messenger swears to Hippolytos' innocence; Theseus regards the disaster as proof of his guilt. The chorus sing of the power of Aphrodite and Eros; then Artemis appears (presumably on the roof of the palace). This sequence recalls the prologue appearance of Aphrodite followed by

Hippolytos' hymn to Artemis. Aphrodite has in fact used Phaidra to ruin Hippolytos so that the chorus' song is in place here. Artemis bitterly and unsparingly tells Theseus the truth. Hippolytos is carried on dying, and after a lament (in anapaests and lyrics) bids farewell to Artemis, who announces the vengeance that she will take on Aphrodite and the worship that will be paid to Hippolytos, and at her bidding he is reconciled to Theseus before he dies.

Given its assumptions, the play is beautifully constructed. The same kind of balance can be seen as in the *Medea* and *Alcestis*. The whole is framed by the balancing sequences: Aphrodite–hymn to Artemis; hymn to Aphrodite–Artemis. After the *parodos*, the first *ekkyklema* scene starts the Phaidra story, which is punctuated by the metrically corresponding expression of horror by the chorus (362) and monody of Phaidra (669) and by the Eros chorus, which makes a centre-piece (525); the Phaidra story ends with the second *ekkyklema* scene which itself starts the Theseus story.

The assumption is that Phaidra tries to conquer her love, that she is essentially different from the Phaidra of the first play. But Hippolytos must nevertheless be accused of trying to seduce her or Theseus will have no reason for cursing him. Euripides saw that this Phaidra could only accuse Hippolytos to preserve her own good name for the sake of her children and that she has no need to do this unless she has lost her good name. He emphasizes the importance of Phaidra's good name early both when the nurse says that her death will make Hippolytos the children's master and when Phaidra herself says that her honourable death will allow them to live free and unharmed. Thus Phaidra can only lose her good name if she is betrayed, and therefore Euripides makes the nurse betray her. On this ground, the suicide note with accusation of Hippolytos is intelligible.

But sympathy for Phaidra is bought at the expense of sympathy for Hippolytos. In the first play Hippolytos defended his clean athleticism first to the nurse and then to his passionate stepmother. In the second play when he denounces all women to the nurse (in terms which remind us of Jason in *Medea* 574ff.), our sympathy for Phaidra is already won and all we think of is that he completely misunderstands her. And when he defends his own way of life, the utter desolation of Theseus has again won our sympathy and makes him seem priggish and odious. Hippolytos is no more reprehensible than any of the other young men who resist passionate women, but he is only allowed to speak in situations which make him appear reprehensible.

As far as we know, this is the only time that Euripides rehandled a story which he had himself used before.[56] The author of the Hypothesis says: 'all that was unseemly and worthy of condemnation has been corrected in this play.' This statement develops out of the criticism of ancient comic poets, who labelled the first Phaidra, like Stheneboia and Aerope, a 'whore'. The statement is true, but it does not provide any explanation of Euripides' behaviour. Two explanations have been given in modern times and they may very well both be true.

The first is that Sophocles answered the first play with his *Phaidra* and then Euripides answered Sophocles' play with the second *Hippolytus*. This would give a sequence as in the later sequence Euripides' *Electra*–Sophocles' *Electra*–Euripides' *Orestes*. Sophocles found that Euripides' chief character is not the sort of person one ought to portray, and Euripides found that Sophocles' chief character is not the sort of person that exists.

The certainties about Sophocles' *Phaidra* are that Theseus returned from Hades and therefore that Phaidra had believed him dead (686P), that Phaidra pleaded to the chorus that her love was a sickness sent from heaven, a shameful thing sent by Zeus (680P), and begged them to conceal what measures she proposed to take (679P). The measures were probably to send her nurse to approach Hippolytos, since someone reported Hippolytos' indignant rejection of her overtures (678P), and from the scene between the nurse and Hippolytos may come the sentiment: 'a noble man ought not to allow himself a pleasure which is unjust' (677P). It is possible that 685P ('children anchor a mother to life') is part of Phaidra's decision to bring a false charge against Hippolytos. Fr. 683P (on the analogy of 191–2P) seems to be Theseus' attack on Hippolytos as a glib demagogue. It is very tempting to place this play between the first and second versions of Euripides.[57] Its likeness to *Trachiniae* and *Tereus* suggests that it is close to them in date. Then the sequence would be: Euripides portrays an entirely shameless Phaidra who throws herself at Hippolytos' head (perhaps urging as an excuse that Theseus is chasing Persephone); Sophocles answers with a Phaidra who has the excuse that Theseus is believed dead, who really believes

[56] The two Melanippe plays are different stories. On the two Phrixos plays see below, p. 131.
[57] Cf. H. Friis-Johansen, *Lustrum* 7, 1962, 284; Barrett, *Hippolytus*, 12.

that Aphrodite's power is invincible, who, more decently to Athenian eyes, uses a go-between to approach Hippolytos, and who, when rejected, accuses him to save her children's name; as Pearson notes, it is Phaidra's play, and Hippolytos may have been as secondary as Hyllos or Lichas in the *Trachiniae*; Euripides then takes over the indirect approach to Hippolytos and Phaidra's honour as the basis of the false accusation. But he puts Aphrodite on the stage (as earlier in the *Cretans*)[58] not as a venerable goddess, but as a spiteful personification of passion, and his Phaidra describes in purely human terms the feelings of a woman who has fallen in love with her stepson and is completely honest about it. She cannot excuse herself either by the death of her husband or by appealing to traditional religion.

The other explanation is that Euripides' interest had changed and that he had become more interested in portraying the conflict of passion and reason than simply in portraying passion. Medea in 431 B.C. is more passionate than Phaidra, but in her too Euripides showed this conflict which she finally formulated as 'passion is stronger than my reason'. Professor Snell[59] has supposed a sort of dialogue between Euripides and Socrates. Socrates answered Medeia that, if you know what is right, then you do it. Phaidra comes back in 428 B.C.: 'we know what is right and recognize it, but we do not work it out.' Euripides himself gives something very like Socrates' answer in the *Iphigenia in Aulis*, where the chorus sing (558ff.): 'Modesty is wisdom and has the exceeding grace of perceiving the right by force of intellect', and they seem to refer back to Phaidra: 'it is a great thing to pursue virtue – for women in secret love'. In the *Medea* and *Hippolytos* he makes his characters state the Socratic problem, but they give their own un-Socratic solutions of it. It may partly have been Euripides' preoccupation with this problem that caused the comic poets to speak of Socrates as part-author of his tragedies at just this time.[60]

Medeia and Phaidra are not the only examples of this conflict. We shall meet other instances in the fragments, and in the surviving plays Alkmene in the *Heraclidae* and Hekabe in her name play show it in another form: both are essentially good women driven to an act of cruel vengeance by brutality.

[58] See below, p. 89.
[59] *Scenes from Greek Drama*, 59ff.
[60] Cf. above, p. 26.

5 *Other plays about bad women*

Four other plays about bad women remain to be discussed: *Aigeus, Stheneboia, Phoinix, Peleus*. All belong to the first period on metrical grounds. *Phoinix* is quoted in Aristophanes' *Acharnians* (425 B.C.),[61] *Stheneboia* in his *Wasps* (422 B.C.), *Peleus* in the second edition of his *Clouds* (421–417 B.C.), *Aigeus* on the evidence of the vases which seem to illustrate it was produced soon after 450 B.C. and may refer to a temple which was built about 450 B.C.[62]

AIGEUS

Outline of play

Prologue: Theseus arrives and describes his journey: 11a, 12N^2 (Sydney vase).

Parodos: Chorus question him and show him Athens: 2, 1N^2; Ennius 243–4R.

Epeisodia: Theseus makes his claim perhaps to Medeia: 10, 905N^2 = Ennius, *Medea* XVR.
Medeia discusses Theseus with Aigeus: 389, 7N^2.
Theseus undertakes to fetch the bull of Marathon: (here perhaps commentary on Medeia: 3, 4, 858N^2; Ennius, *Medea* XVIR and Aigeus' answer: 5N^2).

Stasimon: 11N^2.
Messenger speech (Attic vases).

Stasimon: 9N^2.
Medeia plots with Aigeus to poison Theseus.
Theseus arrives and is invited into the house.
Messenger speech of poisoning and recognition (Attic vases; Apulian vase; Bactrian plate).
Banishment of Medeia.

Bibliographical note: U. von Wilamowitz-Moellendorff, *Analecta Euripidea* 172; *Kl. Schr.*, I, 18, 205; V, 2, 114 n. 1; *Euripides Hippolytos*, 42ff., 423; W. Buchwald, *Studien*, 42; B. B. Shefton, *A.J.A.*,

---

[61] Aristophanes probably, as Schmid-Stählin (4, 198) suggests, parodied this play between 419 and 412 B.C. in the *Anagyros* (cf. Demianczuk, fr. 6). This is more plausible than to suppose that Euripides borrowed an Attic legend about Anagyros to fill out the Homeric story.

[62] See below.

60, 1956, 159; T. B. L. Webster, *Ant. Class.*, 34, 1965, 519. Illustrations, see below, p. 297.

Three fragments give Theseus' arrival in Athens. The lyric fragment (2N²) 'What did your mother name you?' is compared by Buchwald with *Hcld.* 86, where the chorus discover Iolaos seated on an altar. This, too, is an excited chorus questioning a stranger. Three iambic lines (1N²) ask where he has come from, his country and his father; the plural φῶμεν is probably a true plural and the speaker the leader of the chorus. A fragment ascribed by Nonius to Ennius' *Medea* (243–4R) may also belong to this opening: 'Stand and consider Athens, ancient rich town, and see the temple of Ceres on the left.' According to Plutarch (*Theseus*, XII) Aigeus lived on the site of the Delphinion, and the temple of Demeter may have been the Ilissos temple, which was built about the middle of the fifth century B.C.[63] Theseus, now or later, told of his journey – Panaktos (12N²), as Buchwald saw, is where he killed Kerkyon, and 'the flower-strewn bed before a spring' (11a) may be where he begot Melanippos (Plutarch, VIII).

Theseus arrives into a dangerous situation like Telephos and the young Kresphontes. And he is prepared to undertake a dangerous task: 'death is the appointed end also for the man who sits at home and eschews enterprise' (10N²). The dactylo-epitrites (11N²), 'It is possible even in disaster to show manhood by death', should come from a chorus sung while he is absent performing the enterprise, and the anapaests (9N²) 'Success is sometimes better than high birth' from a comment after the enterprise and before Theseus has been recognized.

Someone evidently scorns Theseus' idealism (905N² = Ennius, *Medea*, XV) 'I hate a sage who cannot help himself'. Perhaps these are the words of Medeia (and a fragment attributed both to this play and to the *Theseus* (389N²); 'a poor and energetic young man is likely to rob the rich', could very well be her misrepresentation of Theseus to Aigeus).[64] On the other side, 'Better than money or rich harvests is the company of just and good men' (7N²) is so like the doctrine of the aged Pelias (609N²) that it is tempting to attribute it to the aged Aigeus as a defence of Theseus.

[63] R. E. Wycherley, *Phoenix*, 17, 1963, 96; Travlos, *Exelixis*, 66.
[64] Unfortunately 271N² 'child, you are pursuing a winged hope', is attributed both to *Auge* and *Aigeus*; if it were to be *Aigeus*, it would suggest an early dialogue between Aigeus and Theseus.

Medeia herself is the brazen wife of a cowardly king ($3N^2$), the second wife who hates his earlier children ($4N^2$): both are phrased as maxims and we cannot tell who applied them to Medeia, or who called her mind 'hot-planning' ($858N^2$), or who wished she had never left Kolchis (Ennius, *Medea*, XVI). At least these fragments prove that there was considerable opposition to Medeia and perhaps they suggest that her schemes failed. If, as is very possible, Theseus criticized Medeia, Aigeus may have answered ($5N^2$) 'if you will not restrain your tongue, it will go ill with you'.

The elements that we can detect in the fragments – arrival of Theseus, Theseus undertaking an enterprise, hostility and perhaps defeat of Medeia – fit admirably into the framework of what has been called the 'variant legend', best known from the epitome of Apollodoros (I, 4–6): Theseus arrived, Medeia persuaded Aigeus to beware of him as a threat to his throne, Aigeus sent him against the bull of Marathon. When he returned successful, Aigeus gave him a cup of poison which he had just received from Medeia. As the cup was being brought, he gave his father his sword. Aigeus recognized the sword and dashed the cup from his hand. Theseus was thus established as Aigeus' son and expelled Medeia. The unsuccessful poisoning and the recognition were presumably reported, but Euripides put an equally dangerous recognition scene on the stage later in *Kresphontes*; and repeated the foiled attempt at poisoning with variations, in the *Ion*.

Mr Shefton in his review of the vase evidence for the variant legend concluded that from about 430 there is substantial evidence for the currency of the variant version and that it is quite likely that Euripides' *Aigeus* gave it this currency.[65] The only question which needs further discussion is his date. In his list of vases[66] Mr Shefton refuses to recognize Medeia until she appears about 430 in Oriental costume. It seems, however, more likely that there were two stages in the pictorial tradition: first the fleeing figure was changed from a dismayed nymph to Medeia by the addition of jug and phiale which alluded to her attempt to poison Theseus. Then Medeia was made more recognizable

[65] We know nothing about the date of Sophocles' *Aigeus* nor at what stage Medeia tried to poison Theseus. It certainly told of Theseus' journey, of the bull of Marathon, and included his mission against Pallas and his sons (cf. H. A. Thompson, *A.J.A.*, 66, 1962, 339f.).

[66] See list of illustrations.

by Oriental costume. It is this second stage which started about 430.[67]
The earliest vases with Aigeus, Theseus and the bull, and Medeia are
earlier than 430 but it is doubtful whether any of them could be dated
before 450. It is therefore likely that the *Aigeus* was produced in the
early 40's and possible that it was produced in the late 50's; but if the
allusion to the Ilissos temple is valid and the date for that is right,
the early 40's are indicated.

STHENEBOIA

Outline of play

Prologue: Bellerophon, Page, *G.L.P.* no. 16; 672N² Bellerophon
and Proitos, *adesp.* 292N². Proitos, on Stheneboia's accusation and
the letter to Iobates.

Parodos of women.

Epeisodion. Nurse and Chorus fr. 664–5N². Nurse and Stheneboia
(? fr. 663N²).

Chorus.

Return of Bellerophon with Pegasos. Chimaira story, fr. 665a, 668N².
Accusation of Proitos, fr. 667N².

Chorus.

Bellerophon and Nurse: fr. 666N².

Bellerophon and Stheneboia: 669N². Exeunt on Pegasos.

Chorus.

Fisherman of Melos (fr. 670N²). Messenger speech.

Return of Bellerophon on *mechane*. Bellerophon and Proitos (fr.
671N²).

Bibliographical note: G. G. A. Murray, *Athenian Drama* III, 1906, 343;
U. von Wilamowitz-Moellendorff, *Kl. Schr.* I, 275; L. Séchan,
Etudes, 494; M. Pohlenz, *Gr. Trag.*, II, 114; H. Friis-Johansen, *General
Reflection*, 134; B. Zühlke, *Philologus*, 105, 1961, 1; Korzeniewski,
Philologus, 108, 1964, 45; N. Hourmouziades, *Production and Imagina-
tion*, 152.

Illustrations, see below, p. 301.

---

[67] Similarly in the sequence of representations of the *Peliades* (q.v.) Medeia does not
appear in Oriental costume until the Lateran relief and the Meidias painter's hydria.
Professor Page (*Medea*, lxii, n. 1) may very well be right that Euripides' *Medea* started this
fashion in 431.

Sophocles dramatized the Bellerophon story in the *Iobates*. The title shows that the scene was set in Lycia and we have no reason to suppose that Stheneboia was a character nor do we know the date. The argument of Euripides' play is preserved by a scholion to Gregory of Corinth and in a slightly shortened form by Johannes Logothetes, who also gives the prologue (Page, *G.L.P.*, no. 16). The outline of the story is as follows: Bellerophon was purified after a murder by Proitos of Tiryns; his wife Stheneboia (daughter of Iobates) fell in love with him; Bellerophon refused her; she accused him to Proitos, who sent him to Iobates with a letter; Iobates sent him against the Chimaira, which he killed and returned to Tiryns. Learning of another plot, he persuaded Stheneboia to mount Pegasos and threw her into the sea near Melos. Fishermen brought her body back to Tiryns. Bellerophon also returned and claimed that he had taken a fitting vengeance.

Wilamowitz reconstructed the play on the assumption that after the prologue speech Proitos sent Bellerophon to Iobates. More recently Zühlke, later followed by Korzeniewski, argued that the double un-reality of time (Bellerophon's mission to kill the Chimaira and the drowning of Stheneboia) was too great and proposed to exclude the first by making the play start with Bellerophon's return to Tiryns after killing the Chimaira. At first sight this is attractive and had already been proposed by Gilbert Murray in 1906. Then we reflect that the general shape, two unsuccessful attempts against a young man, is paralleled in the *Aigeus* (although there no major unreality of time is involved), that in the *Diktys* it is possible that Perseus' adventure with the Gorgon took place during the course of the play, that the dispatch of Bellerophon to Proitos is represented on three South Italian vases, which are likely to have been inspired by this play, and that these pictures are more likely to have been based on a stage scene than on a brief report in Bellerophon's prologue speech, and finally that nothing in the prologue suggests the return of a victor to punish those who have plotted against him: it presents rather a worried young man.

The prologue, as Holger Friis-Johansen points out, is shaped like the prologue of the *Heraclidae*. Bellerophon starts with a general reflection on the partiality of happiness. Proitos is rich and noble but has a foolish wife. (Here a line may have fallen out giving Stheneboia's name, because she is the subject of the next line. Bellerophon's name is not necessary, if, as Dr N. Hourmouziades suggests, he is leading Pegasos.

Tiryns also need not be named if, when Proitos enters, Bellerophon addresses him, fr. 292 *adespota*, 'lord of this land of Tiryns'). Stheneboia's nurse is always approaching him with offers of bed and throne (like Aerope in the *Cretan Women* and Phaidra in the earlier *Hippolytus*). He is not prepared to yield; he reverences the laws of hospitality and Proitos who purified him; and, like Theseus in the *Theseus* and Perseus in the *Diktys*, he wants only the clean love which leads to glory. After two corrupt lines he ends: 'It is no use to sit here and be abused because I will not sin, nor indeed to tell the truth and besmirch Proitos' wife and disrupt his home.' The two corrupt lines can easily be emended to mean: 'I propose to live and die in modesty. Now I am minded to go away.' Then the whole makes sense as the utterance of a man who (rather like Alkmaion at the beginning of the *Alkmaion in Psophis*) is being asked to wrong a host and benefactor. It seems to me impossible therefore to follow either Zühlke, who expands the corrupt lines to contain a reference to Bellerophon's plot to kill Stheneboia as a revenge for his sufferings with the Chimaira, or Korzeniewski, who makes Bellerophon say here that he has fought with the Chimaira and has now come back to find that Stheneboia is as bad as ever.

Bellerophon intends to keep out of the way, like Hippolytos when he has heard the proposals of the nurse (*Hipp.* 659f.). Presumably he is prevented by the arrival of Proitos, who sends him off to Iobates with the letter. The presence of Stheneboia in this scene on the vases does not necessarily imply that she is present, only that she is responsible. For the audience, who have heard from Bellerophon of Stheneboia's attempts on his virtue, Proitos will tell that Stheneboia accused Bellerophon of seducing her; this must have been a soliloquy after Bellerophon's departure, and Proitos presumably also told the audience the contents of his letter to Iobates. The time difficulty is slightly less if Bellerophon is dispatched in the prologue.

As the play is called after Stheneboia, the chorus are presumably her friends, and it is probable that fr. 664N² 'whenever she drops anything, she says "in memory of the Corinthian stranger" ' and fr. 665N² 'So distraught. Eros presses harder when chidden' are spoken to them by Stheneboia's nurse. Fr. 663N² 'Eros teaches even the illiterate to write poetry' has naturally been compared to Phaidra's remark in *Hippolytos I* (fr. 430N²) that Eros teaches her daring. Here the illiterate man is an example, and the nurse will continue 'in the same way you can win

Bellerophon'. This may, however, come in a later scene. The main point of this first act must have been to show Stheneboia desolate for love of Bellerophon.

Bellerophon returns in triumph and fury leading Pegasos. He told of his battle with the Chimaira (the reference to 'this (horse)' in fr. 665aN² proves that Pegasos was on the stage) and accused Proitos of deceiving his guest (fr. 667N²). The three accounts of his treatment of Stheneboia differ slightly: the scholiast to Aristophanes *Peace* 140 '*he deceived her as though he were going to make her his wife* and mounted her on Pegasos etc.'; the scholiast to Gregory of Corinth '*he threatened to strangle her.* But learning (that the wife of) Proitos was again plotting against him he retired having mounted Stheneboia on Pegasos' etc.; Johannes Logothetes 'he cheated Stheneboia *as though he were going to take her to Caria.* But learning from him a second plot from Proitos, he anticipated it by retiring. And he put Stheneboia on Pegasos.' The fragments give an attack on a woman, fr. 666: 'Utter villain and woman, what could one call you worse than this?' (quoted as Euripides' Bellerophon, i.e. the character, *not* the play; Wecklein suggested that Bellerophon so addressed the nurse; if so, this preceded the scene with Stheneboia; cf. however *Med.* 1323, Jason attacking Medeia), and a description of the coming journey on Pegasos (fr. 669), which must belong to the scene in which Stheneboia is persuaded. The second 'plot' is obscure because the accounts seem to be contradictory;[68] Johannes Logothetes' 'from him' must be wrong: Wilamowitz emended 'from her', but Pohlenz objected that Bellerophon could not then have killed her, and therefore accepted – 'from someone' (Rabe). But possibly the second plot of Proitos against Bellerophon was an invention of Stheneboia's to make Bellerophon take her away, which he understands and uses for his own purposes. Then the sequence of this scene is Bellerophon's attack on Stheneboia (perhaps after a preliminary scene with the nurse), Stheneboia pleads her love and claims that she is protecting him from the hostility of Proitos, Bellerophon promises to take her away.

After a chorus which covers a considerable lapse of time the fishermen of Melos arrive and describe their miserable life (fr. 670N²). This anticipates the descriptions in later comedy and Hellenistic poetry.

[68] Note that the words of the scholiast to Gregory bracketed above could be restored equally well to read 'from her that Proitos' which would bring him into line with Johannes as emended by Wilamowitz.

Diktys may have been described as a poor fisherman but no fragment survives to show it; it is unlikely that this theme had already occurred in the Aeschylean *Diktyoulkoi*; the unhappy sailors of Sophocles *Skyrians* (fr. 555P), quoted by Goossens, are not a parallel because the dangers of sea-faring was a well-established literary tradition. Presumably the fishermen bring the body with them and describe to Proitos how they saw it fall from the winged horseman.

The body is still on the stage when Bellerophon returns on Pegasos and admits his deed to Proitos and claims that he has taken a fitting vengeance for the double plot by killing her and causing him to grieve. It looks as if Proitos only now learns the truth; and therefore now tells the servant to carry the body in: 'a sensible man would never trust a woman' (fr. 671N²). If Bellerophon for this scene comes in on the *mechane* (like Medeia at the end of her play), he is safe from any assault by Proitos and has something of the quality of a *deus ex machina*. It is tempting to see an illustration of this on the Tarentine fragment in Würzburg (*Greek Theatre Production,* pl. 10): the central akroterion of the palace shows Bellerophon on Pegasos, on the left an attendant flee-ing, on the right Proitos attacking. The main scene on the fragment will then be Bellerophon's earlier despondent return to Proitos, observed by Stheneboia and the nurse.

PHOINIX

In Homer the mother Alkimede played a part. This seems unlikely in Euripides. The corrupt fragment 804N² seems to say: 'Children are a trouble to an old man. He pays (the penalty) who marries late. For a wife lords it over an elderly bridegroom.' The natural interpretation is that the aged Amyntor says this early in the play before Phoinix has been accused and that he is excusing himself for having a young con-cubine (818N²) rather than a young wife; this would imply that Alkimede is already dead. This passage may indeed come from the prologue, which starts (813N²) 'Wealth is an easy burden, but involves much difficulty and corruption'.

Phoinix is expressly said by the Iliad scholiast to be 'blameless in Euripides'; therefore the temptation of Phoinix by the young concubine probably came early in the play: 'an old man is unpleasing for a young woman' (807N²). He refused her, and she accused him to his father. Amyntor believed her: 'secrets are discovered by evidence' (811N²), which should be printed as iambics, *not* as a trochaic tetrameter. 'After this present disaster I would never advise anyone to give a son authority' (806N²). His attack on Phoinix contained a near quotation of Homer (*Il.* IX, 455): 'May you never put a child on your knees' (Ennius 363R). Phoinix defended himself by his character and by the company he kept (810, 812N², cf. Ennius IIR). Amyntor told someone, perhaps the concubine, that he has ordered his slaves to blind Phoinix (815N²). The great debate between father and son must have been famous as it is echoed by Demeas in Menander's *Samia* (128f.). It is probably earlier and certainly more effective than the debate between Theseus and Hippolytos in the preserved play.

We do not know what then happened to the concubine or to Amyntor, but at this late stage Peleus arrived to take Phoinix to Cheiron for healing; presumably his reason for coming was that he wanted to make Phoinix king of the Dolopes. The Latin fragment (*inc. inc.* 214R) 'my father, strangers, my father blinded me' has reasonably been ascribed to Ennius' *Phoenix*; the strangers, *hospites*, are then Peleus and his attendants. This scene had two anticipations of later plays. The arrival of Peleus to help a friend in disaster and take him home anticipates the arrival of Theseus when Herakles has murdered his wife and children (*H.F.* 1163). The entry of Phoinix blinded is earlier than the entry of Polymestor in the *Hecuba* (1056). Whether either or both of these is earlier than Oidipous' entry in the *Oedipus Tyrannus* is impossible to say. The much earlier case of Thamyras in Sophocles' play was entirely different: Thamyras, as the note about the double-sided mask implies, was struck blind by the Muses on the stage; he did not have his eyes put out.

Phoinix is led out wondering that human love of life is so great that he is prepared to bear such misfortunes (816N²) and he bids farewell to his native country.

PELEUS

The fragments give very little. Peleus presumably is the man who maintains that no action is successful without the gods (617a = 1025N²) and he is offered advice by some older man (619N²). The only likely story for a tragedy about Peleus in his youth is the story to which Aristophanes alludes in the *Clouds* (1063): Peleus was purified by Akastos; Akastos' wife, Astydameia, attempted to seduce him. When

86   THE TRAGEDIES OF EURIPIDES

he refused her she accused him falsely; Akastos believed her and threw
him out into the forest unarmed, but the gods saved him by giving him
a sword.

6 Other plays about unhappy women

The remaining plays about unhappy women fall into two groups: the
women with irregular babies (*Cretans, Alkmene, Alope, Danae, Skyrioi*)
and the others (*Protesilaos, Ino*). Strictness of metre places them all in
Group I. The *Protesilaos* was probably earlier than the *Alcestis*, as
Wilamowitz[69] saw: the story of the substitute statue for the dead
partner is essential to the *Protesilaos* and Admetos remembers it in the
Alcestis (348); Admetos wishes he had leapt into Alkestis' tomb (898),
which recalls Laodameia's suicide in the blaze which consumed the
statue; thirdly, Alkestis, like Protesilaos, is brought back from the dead.
Otherwise, Phaidra's allusion to Pasiphae in *Hipp.* 337 may place the
Cretans before that play and possibly before *Hippolytos I* (see above,
p. 66). The argument for placing the *Skyrioi* very early is not con-
vincing: Körte thought that the story of Achilles on Skyros must have
been dramatized before the Neoptolemos story and that Sophocles'
treatment of the Neoptolemos story could be dated about 450 by vase-
paintings. There is no reason to suppose that Sophocles needed a
Euripidean precedent; he could take the story from epic; and one of
the vase-paintings[70] which certainly shows the departure of Neoptolemos from Skyros must be dated nearer 460 than 450 (in any case there
is no reason to connect the vase-paintings with Sophocles). It is equally
arguable that Euripides' play was later than Polygnotos' picture and the
Boston krater by the Niobid painter (about 450 B.C.)[71] because they
show Achilles among a plurality of daughters of Lykomedes, whereas
Euripides makes Deidameia an only daughter; but the painters may
have followed the normal version unperturbed by Euripides. Nor is
there any justification for seeing an allusion to the desertion of the
Thessalians at Tanagra in 457 B.C. in a fragment of the *Ino*:[72] their
perjury was no doubt demanded by the plot. We cannot even argue
safely that the *Ino* must be later than the *Medea* because in the *Medea*

[69] *Kl. Schr.* V, 1, 524.
[70] *ARV*[2] 536/4. The story is implied even earlier by the Douris cup, *ARV*[2]429 26.
[71] *ARV*[2] 600/12; E. Simon, *A.J.A.*, 67, 1963, 57.
[72] Goossens, *Euripide et Athènes*, 14, on 422N[2].

(1282) Euripides makes Ino kill *both* her children. But on grounds of character drawing Ino does seem to belong with Medeia, the second Phaidra, and Alkmene in the *Heraclidae*.

CRETANS

Outline of play

Prologue, Aphrodite? Minos' account of the Minotaur: summoning of Mystics.

Parodos, chorus of Mystics. Fr. 472N²; *P. Oxy.* 2461, fr. 2; Schol. to *Frogs* 1359. Invocation of gods to avert evil.

Epeisodion: Minos and chorus. *P. Oxy.* 2461, fr. 1.

Epeisodion: Minos interrogates the Nurse and finds out the whole story.

Pasiphae brought out. Minos attacks Pasiphae. Pasiphae's defence (Page, *G.L.P.*, no. 11).

Pasiphae and Nurse imprisoned.

Epeisodion: Minos attacks Daidalos, fr. 988N². Imprisonment of Daidalos and Ikaros.

Epeisodion: Messenger speech of escape. Daidalos and Ikaros: Schol. *Peace* 140.

Ikaros' monody: Schol. *Frogs* 849. Minos searching. Final speech by Helios or Poseidon?

Bibliographical note: U. von Wilamowitz-Moellendorff, *Analecta Euripidea*, 155; *Kl. Schr.* I, 191; M. Croiset, *R.E.G.*, 28, 1915, 217; C. Zintzen, *Analytisches Hypomnema zu Seneca's Phaidra*, 13; H. J. Mette, *Hermes*, 91, 1963, 256; H. Lloyd-Jones, *Gnomon*, 35, 1963, 447f.; R. Cantarella, *I Cretesi*, 1963.

Illustrations, see below, p. 299.

The fragments have been recently augmented by *P.Oxy.* 2461, frs. 1–4, which are fixed as belonging to this play by Mette's identification of fr. 4 with fr. 472N². Fr. 1 is a description of the Minotaur in stichomythia (taking with it frs. 996–7N²) and presumably precedes Pasiphae's self-defence preserved in the Berlin papyrus (Page, *G.L.P.*, no. 11). Fr. 2 certainly contains chorus in the first column and the last two lines of the second column may belong to the succeeding iambic scene. Fr. 3 also has the end of a chorus and the beginning of an iambic scene but it is quite uncertain where it belongs.

In addition to this complex of fragments dealing with Minos and Pasiphae, Wilamowitz added fr. 988N² : 'you are a craftsman but the work that you did is no carpenter's'. If the attribution is right (it is just possible that such a taunt could also be thrown at Palamedes), a dialogue between Minos and Daidalos is certain. On Etruscan urns (nos. 4 and 5), which almost certainly illustrate this play, he is shown in custody with his hands tied behind his back, and once (no. 5) with Ikaros beside him. A fourth century Apulian vase fragment in Amsterdam shows Daidalos (probably with Ikaros) kneeling in supplication to Minos in the presence of Pasiphae; Sir John Beazley referred this to Daidalos' arrival in Crete; this is the natural interpretation, but the costume is tragic and we know no tragedy on this theme; either, therefore, the vase is based on a lost play, or it illustrates his supplication to Minos in this play (we do not know that Euripides followed the version in which Pasiphae died in prison).

The scholiast on *Frogs* 849 explains 'Cretan monodies' as a reference to Ikaros' monody in this play 'for he played a somewhat daring part'. The scholiast on *Peace* 140, 'What if he falls into the watery depths of the sea, how will he be able to escape with his wings?', says first that Aristophanes is mocking at the tragedians because of what happened to Ikaros; then gives an alternative reference to the *Stheneboia*. Aristophanes' chief source is *Bellerophon* there but he also alludes to *Aiolos* and *Stheneboia*. He may, therefore, also have borrowed a line from *Cretans*. Pasiphae's intercourse with the bull and Ikaros' fall from heaven were subjects of pyrrhic dances performed for Nero according to Suetonius (*Nero*, 12); their source may have been this play. Two South Italian vases show Daidalos fastening the wings on Ikaros.

It is difficult to reconstruct this play or to see for certain what line Euripides took. The chorus (fr. 472N²) are white-robed vegetarian mystics, initiated in the rites of Zeus, Zagreus, and the Mountain Mother, who have left their wooden temple to visit Minos. The address to Minos which opens this anapaestic beginning of the parodos implies that Minos is on stage; the chorus are priests who have come to the palace for a special purpose and will take some part in the action. It is natural to assume that Minos has summoned them to deal with a portent, and as they must be told what the portent is, it is tempting to place next the description of the Minotaur in fr. 1 of *P. Oxy.* 2461 (particularly as the questioner there has clearly heard a report that something strange has happened).

One of the Etruscan urns (no. 3) shows Minos starting back in horror at the sight of a woman holding the baby Minotaur. It may not be fanciful to remember Menander's *Samia* (50) where Demeas' whole agony of suspicion was aroused by seeing Chrysis suckling the baby; this might be a remodelling of the Euripidean theme. Then the last part of the prologue will have been a speech of Minos describing the horrible sight that he has seen and stating that he has sent for the Mystics to help him deal with the portent. The audience must have been told of the arrival of Daidalos and Ikaros, that Pasiphae fell in love with the bull, that Daidalos helped her by constructing the model cow, that she became pregnant and gave birth to the Minotaur. Presumably Minos knew nothing until the Minotaur was born. Whether he found the whole story out from Pasiphae (or from her nurse) before he sent for the Mystics is unclear. He cannot know the reason for Pasiphae falling in love with the bull, and the audience must have been told this by a god at the beginning. Pasiphae herself puts the responsibility on Poseidon, who was angry because Minos failed to sacrifice the bull to him. Hyginus (*fab.* 40) says that Pasiphae herself had failed to sacrifice to Aphrodite; the Scholiast to *Hippolytus* 47 says that Aphrodite was angry with all the daughters of Helios because Helios had reported her adultery. My feeling is that Euripides made Aphrodite responsible and gave her the prologue speech so that Pasiphae is more like Phaidra than she herself maintains. Croiset thinks of her, like Phaidra and Medeia, as denying the Socratic equation of knowledge and virtue; but the speech shows no sign of a split personality.

The description of the Minotaur in *P.Oxy.* 2461, fr. 1, on this theory comes after the parodos; the questioner is the leader of the chorus and Minos himself gives the information. The relation of fr. 2 to fr. 1 is uncertain. The placing of fr. 2, Col. ii immediately above fr. 1 (Lloyd-Jones and Cantarella) is, as Turner states, only a possibility. One reason for supposing that fr. 2 belongs before fr. 1 is the nature of the lyric preserved in Col. i, where an invocation to Apollo and Artemis is recognizable. They might very well be invoked in the parodos to avert any disaster which is portended by the birth of the monster. An invocation to Diktynna Artemis occurs in Aeschylus' parody of a Euripidean monody in Aristophanes' *Frogs* (1359) and scholiasts refer both this and the preceding (1356) 'But Cretans, children of Ida', to the *Cretans*. There is no reason to suppose that the invocation to Diktynna comes from a monody rather than a chorus, and it may belong here. (The earlier line may, as has been suggested, come from Ikaros' monody.) If fr. 2 contains the end of the parodos, Professor Lloyd-Jones's suggestion that the letters before the first two lines of the iambic scene stand for Chorus and Minos is very attractive.

The chorus learn from Minos the nature of the portent, a bull-headed child. What comes between this and Pasiphae's self-defence on the Berlin papyrus is unknown. Her defence is a beautiful piece of rhetoric; Croiset notes a connexion with Teisias the Sicilian rhetorician, and Zintzen rightly compares Phaidra's accusation of Theseus in the *First Hippolytos* (cf. above, p. 65). Pasiphae says that her passion must have been sent by the gods since she could not have either fallen in love with a bull or have wanted him to sire her children; Minos caused the anger of Poseidon to fall on her because he did not sacrifice the bull. She 'the guiltless mother, concealed the blow of heaven, he publishes it to everybody'. He may kill her but she will die innocent. Minos must, therefore, before this have told the story and have threatened to kill her.

There are several difficulties here: why is her speech preceded by a lyric line of the chorus? How does Pasiphae come on the stage? Why is nothing said about the Minotaur? It is strange to have a lyric between two speeches of an Agon; presumably it is justified by the horror that the chorus felt at Minos' revelation: 'for I say that no other woman has ever committed such a crime, but you, O King, should consider how to conceal it'. Perhaps the choral strophe that intervenes in the *Hippolytus* (362) between the revelation that Phaidra loves Hippolytos and her self-defence provides some sort of parallel. Pasiphae's words 'concealed the blow of heaven' perhaps cover the fact that the Minotaur is now safely hidden in the labyrinth. What happened we can only guess. The Mystics consulted about the portent may have counselled that the monster should be destroyed, like Hellen in the *Wise Melanippe*. Minos failing to find it may have interrogated the Nurse: the woman carrying the Minotaur on some of the Etruscan urns is probably the Nurse; she is also a known character in the story of Ariadne from the sixth century.[73]

[73] J. D. Beazley, *Development of Attic Black-Figure*, 33f.

The interrogation may have told him both of Pasiphae's passion for the bull and of Daidalos' part in the story. Minos then summoned Pasiphae out and accused her. Some such development would lead up to the Berlin papyrus.

After Pasiphae's speech Minos gives orders that she and her accomplice shall be imprisoned. They have then both been on the stage up till now. Cantarella tries to avoid this conclusion by reading τῆσδε instead of τήνδε in l. 47; but 'take *them* within the house' is certain. If the accomplice is the Nurse, which seems the natural explanation (Ariadne has been suggested but we have no trace of her otherwise), she may be a mute character in this scene.

The papyrus ends with the chorus trying to restrain Minos and Minos saying that punishment must not be delayed. Two scenes on the Etruscan urns must be quoted here. In one (no. 3) a woman is seated on an altar clinging to a statue; this may be Pasiphae and she may have taken refuge on an altar at this moment or earlier inside the palace. On the others (nos. 4-6) a woman, half-naked, kneels at the feet of Minos, who has raised his sword. Körte interprets this as Ariadne praying for the life of Pasiphae, but it would be more natural to suppose that the artists thought of Pasiphae herself and the scene may have been described in a messenger speech. Croiset supposes that the chorus saved Pasiphae; undoubtedly they tried to restrain Minos, but success is perhaps beyond the power of a tragic chorus.

Equally unclear is the detail of the scenes with Daidalos and Ikaros. The evidence quoted above suggests that Minos accused Daidalos (fr. 988N^2) and had him imprisoned (Urns nos. 4-5), that Ikaros was fitted with wings and discussed them with Daidalos (South Italian vases, and Scholiast to Ar. *Peace* 140), that Ikaros sang a monody (Scholiast to Aristophanes *Frogs* 849), and that Ikaros' fall was reported (Suetonius). Hyginus says that Pasiphae liberated Daidalos from prison; in Zenobius Daidalos made wings in the labyrinth and flew away.

The two escapes which survive in Euripides are the escape of the Phrygian in the *Orestes* (1366) and the escape of Dionysos in the *Bacchae* (604). The latter is a possible analogy. If a supernatural happening, thunderclap or divine appearance, both prevented Minos from murdering Pasiphae and released Daidalos, this could have been told in a messenger speech and then the scene between Daidalos and Ikaros could have followed, Ikaros sang his monody and they escaped (perhaps on the *mechane*),[74] Minos entered to find them gone, and a god, Helios or Poseidon, told of Ikaros' fall and prevented further violence to Pasiphae; he may also, as Croiset thinks, have ordered Minos to sacrifice bloodless offerings to him, which would account for the scene on the short side of the Louvre sarcophagus. In the Platonic *Minos* (318d) Minos is said to have been represented as savage and angry and unjust by the tragedians; the writer may have been thinking of this play as well as of the *Theseus* and *Polyidos*.

ALKMENE[75]

The scene is Thebes. The choice of moment lay between the morning after Alkmene had been seduced by Zeus and the day on which she gave birth to the twins. I have argued that in the *Amphitruo* Plautus (or rather the author of the Greek comedy which he adapted) combined a play of Sophocles, which chose the earlier moment, with the play of Euripides, which chose the later moment.[76] Two doubtful fragments could be combined with this: Wilamowitz[77] attributed fr. 87N² to this play on the ground that it must refer to midwifery, and Erotian may easily have miswritten *Alkmaion* for *Alkmene*. Arrighetti[78] has shown that fr. 913N² was wrongly ascribed to the *Auge* by Wilamowitz; Satyros quotes it as referring to Herakles. 'Who despises the gods so much that when he sees these things he does not believe in god and throw away the crooked lies of the meteorologists?' The anapaests sound like a choral comment and would better suit the birth of Herakles in this play

[74] In Aristophanes, *Daidalos*, fr. 188K, someone tells the crane-man, as he pulls the machinery upwards, to say 'Hail, light of the sun'. Is this reminiscence and quotation of the flight in the *Cretans*?

[75] Two fragments, which have been attributed to this play would on metre give a date after 415 B.C. Fr. 67 is ascribed in an early edition, but suits the situation of the *Alkmaion in Corinth* and need not be considered. P. Hamburg 119, Col. III, speaks of the Taphians and then of Alkmene's refusal to marry anyone except the avenger of her brothers. As it is now clear (as Siegmann suggested) that the papyrus contained prologues (cf. H. Lloyd-Jones ap. G. W. Bond, *Euripides Hypsipyle*, 157, 160), this must be a prologue. The lines seem to be quoting an oracle given in the past; the story must have been told in the prologue of the *Alkmene* but may have been told again in the prologue of a late play e.g. *Auge, Temenos, Temenidai*. There seems therefore no valid reason to reject the early date of the *Alkmene* given by the absence of resolved syllables in the book fragments. Nothing is known about Aeschylus' *Alkmene*.

[76] *Later Greek Comedy*, 86ff.

[77] *Kl. Schr.* I, 186.

[78] *Stud. Class. et. Or.*, 13, 1964, 110.

than anything in the *Likymnios*. Nauck ascribed *adesp*. 400: 'Herakles was the son of the one and Iphiklos of the other'. This must have been a statement after the birth by someone other than Zeus who knew the truth: perhaps Teiresias, who was already in the Pindaric account (*N*., i, 32) or perhaps Eos, who is shown on the Paestan vase. The difficulty here is that fr. 89N^2: 'I did not allow Sthenelos to deprive you of your rights' has very reasonably been ascribed to an epilogue speech by Zeus to Amphitryon, and it must be admitted that *adesp*. 400 may have come from any play by any tragic poet about Herakles. Finally the report of the birth by Bromia in Plautus' play (1053f.) made to Amphitruo, who is prostrate with fear of Zeus' thunderbolt, and followed by the intervention of Zeus, who stops Amphitruo consulting Teiresias, has obvious analogies with Euripidean scenes.[79]

To the messenger speech also belongs the description of the transformation of Alkmene's room into a bower (fr. 88N^2)' (perhaps this was effected by the golden rain which is portrayed on the Paestan vase and reported by Pindar I, vii, 5 (cf. *O*. vii, 34)) and presumably the description of the dismissal of Alkmene's servants by the midwife (fr. 87N^2). But it must in fact have started the story further back. 'How did you come to think of using a torch' (fr. 90N^2) has been connected with the two South Italian vases[80] showing Amphitryon burning Alkmene off an altar and the Clouds quenching the fire. This cannot have been acted, and the famous storm (referred to in Plautus' *Rudens* 86) must have been reported; fr. 90N^2 is a reprimand spoken perhaps by Zeus to Amphitryon during the storm and also reported. The narrative reported, therefore, Amphitryon's attempt to burn Alkmene off the altar, the storm, and the birth of the twins. The audience saw Alkmene flying from Amphitryon into the house to take refuge on the altar; this was followed by a choral ode, punctuated by a thunderclap, while Amphitryon staggered out of the house, then the messenger (who may well have been the nurse of Alkmene) made her report to him, and this was followed by the appearance of Zeus to speak the epilogue, and the choral comment on the power of the gods (913N^2). The only fragments of any significance from an earlier scene are those which indicate Amphitryon's suspicions that Alkmene has been seduced by a rich lover (frs. 95–6N^2). The prologue must almost have been spoken by a god,

[79] E.g. *Med*. 1317, *H.F*. 905, *Ion* 1546.
[80] See list of illustrations p. 298.

perhaps Hermes, as the audience must have been informed of the intricacies of the situation.[81]

ALOPE

The fragments fit into the story of Hyginus *Fab.* 187. The scene is Eleusis. The description of Poseidon making Alope pregnant and deserting her (fr. 106–7N²) may come from the prologue, as Wilamowitz[82] suggested, and the speaker may be the Nurse, who was given the infant Hippothoon to expose: she certainly expresses her loyalty in fr. 108N². Alope's situation is very like that of the wise Melanippe. The chorus are specially characterized as athletes, because her father Kerkyon was a great wrestler (fr. 105N²). The arbitration scene, adapted by Menander, presumably came soon after the parodos: the new fragment[83] 'do not be bad-tempered', could very well be said by Kerkyon to the herdsman who did not wish to give up the decorated garment in which the baby was wrapped. Recognizing the garment, Kerkyon interrogated the Nurse, and she betrayed her mistress while professing her loyalty (108N²). Kerkyon then stormed at Alope (fr. 109–11, *adesp.* 510N²).[84] This sequence must have been closely parallel to the sequence in the *Cretans* (q.v.). Kerkyon certainly punished Alope, but how far Hyginus can be trusted for the rest is unclear. It is a possibility that he exposed Hippothoon again and that Poseidon prophesied that Theseus would kill Kerkyon and give the kingdom to Hippothoon: in that case Poseidon presumably also announced that Alope would be transformed into a spring.[85]

DANAE[86]

Johannes Malalas tells us that Euripides' Danae was put into a chest and cast in the sea because she was raped by Zeus in the form of gold.

[81] Cf. O. Skutsch, *H.S.C.P.* (forthcoming). The new vase in Taranto (see below, p. 298) shows Hermes as well as Zeus.

[82] *Menander: das Schiedsgericht*, 127.

[83] H. J. Mette, *Lustrum*, 9, 1964, 32, no. 233a.

[84] See Nauck's note on 112N² (which is a quotation from comedy).

[85] A very good discussion and comparison with other plays about women with irregular babies by B. Borecky, *Studia Antiqua* (*A. Salac*), Prague, 1955, 82f.

[86] Sophocles' play may have been earlier if it was produced as part of a connected trilogy (cf. above, p. 16) with *Larisaioi* and *Andromeda*; it is only clear that Akrisios was terrified at the oracle which foretold death at the hands of his grandson, and Danae prefaced her defence by saying that a short speech to parents becomes an Argive girl.

According to Pollux (4, 111) the chorus were women. The fragments are difficult to interpret. Schmid-Stählin[87] wished to date the play late because he saw a three-actor scene between Akrisios, his wife, and Danae, but it is more probable that pieces of at least two different dialogue scenes survive (and in any case the criterion is worthless). One is a scene between Akrisios and his wife: Akrisios is an old man who wants a son (316N[2]); his wife (like Amyntor in the *Phoenix*) maintains that old parents should not have children (317N[2], without l. 4 deleted by Nauck) answered perhaps, as Goossens[88] suggested, by 1007e, fN[2]: 'children who have grown up may be dangerous . . . young sons are sweeter to a father'; he wants a son (318N[2]); she agrees that women are no use without men (319N[2]). Whether Akrisios had sent to Delphi and received the oracle that his grandson should kill him we do not know, but the word 'oracle' suggests this (330a); he certainly punished Danae for allowing herself to be seduced. When she is discovered to have a child, he (like Amphitryon in the *Alkmene*) supposes that a rich man has seduced her (322, 324–8N[2]),[89] and his wife apparently believes him (320–1N[2]). Danae pleads with him for her child (323N[2]). Perhaps he is persuaded by her not to kill the child, and adopts the alternative of putting her and the child to sea in a chest (as apparently Aleos in the late *Auge*). This interpretation is suggested by fr. 329N[2]: 'Ah, how shining in courage is the stamp of the noble.' No one else but Danae in this play can deserve this comment, presumably from the chorus; and it is deserved if she chooses a remote hope of safety for herself and her child in preference to certain death for the child and safety for herself: Andromache would have done the same. A god must have announced the future, and the long comparison of human fortunes to the weather (330N[2]) may have been Akrisios' comment.

SKYRIOI

The papyrus Hypothesis (*P.S.I.* XII, no. 1286) says that Thetis knew the future and dressed Achilles as a girl and placed him on Skyros with Lykomedes, who did not know his identity and brought him up with his orphan daughter (in Statius Thetis passed Achilles off as her

[87] *Op. cit.*, 595.
[88] *Chronique d'Egypte*, 16, 1941, 109.
[89] On 325N[2], cf. above, p. 25.

daughter). When Achilles grew up, he raped Deidameia. The Greeks as a result of an oracle sent Diomedes and . . . (here the papyrus breaks off).

Apollodoros (III, xiii, 8) is nearer to this hypothesis than Hyginus (*Fab.* 96) because he makes no mention of the other daughters. Apollodoros implies that Neoptolemos was born before Odysseus discovered Achilles by the ruse of a trumpet-blast, and Statius puts the two events on the same day; Körte[90] is therefore likely to be right in attributing this sequence to Euripides.

The play started with an invocation to Helen (681aN²). Gallavotti[91] gave this to Thetis, but Körte gives it to Deidameia's nurse. It is true that Thetis' plans are shattered but this surely does not prevent her, as Körte thinks, from speaking the prologue; and although the nurse may now know that Achilles is not a girl, how could she know the whole story which Achilles himself is unlikely to know? The speaker who invokes Helen at this point evidently has complete knowledge.

The dialogue in which the nurse tells Lykomedes that his daughter is suffering from a more dangerous disease than pleurisy and they decide to conceal the trouble (682–4N²) probably comes early and may form the second part of the prologue. This must lead to a confrontation of Lykomedes and Achilles, and Körte plausibly supposes that the birth of Neoptolemos took place in the play.

Bickel[92] suggested that the one fragment of Livius Andronicus' *Achilles* was spoken by Deidameia threatening Achilles: *si malas imitabo, tum tu pretium pro noxa dabis.*[93] Unfortunately we have no other evidence for the play and *malas* has usually been emended to *malos*. But it must be admitted that the other fragment (*inc.* V) which has been attributed to the *Achilles* would fit the subsequent debate with Odysseus: *haut ut quem Chiro in Pelio docuit ocri.*[94] But this is too slender evidence to use.

Presumably then Neoptolemos has been born and Achilles has consented to marry Deidameia when Diomede and Odysseus arrive, perhaps announced as *parasangai* by the chorus of Skyrians (686N²).

[90] *Hermes* 69, 1934, 1.
[91] *R.I.F.C.*, 61, 1933, 177.
[92] *Rh. Mus.* 86, 1937, 1.
[93] 'If I imitate bad women, then you will pay for your guilt.'
[94] 'Unlike Cheiron's pupil on rugged Pelion.'

Lykomedes has now every reason not to betray Achilles so that Odysseus may have needed the trumpet ruse to arouse him from his female disguise. The remaining fragments (683a, 880, 885N²) are direct addresses of Odysseus to Achilles, reproaching him for spending his time among women instead of fighting: this scene must have been a debate in which Achilles was persuaded to abandon Deidameia and go to Troy. The earlier part of the play, the strange pregnancy of Deidameia, connects it with the *Danae*, *Alkmene*, and *Cretans*; the later part, Achilles' conflict of duties, with the *Telephos* and *Philoctetes*.

The sequence of scenes which we can detect is then:

Prologue: Thetis, 681aN².
             Nurse and Lykomedes, 682–4N².
Epeisodia: Achilles and Lykomedes
             (Birth of Neoptolemos).
             Arrival of Odysseus and Diomede: 686N².
             Odysseus and Lykomedes, discovery of Achilles.
             Odysseus and Achilles 683a, 880, 885N².

PROTESILAOS

The return of Protesilaos to the upper world, Laodameia fainting when he comes, Hermes taking Protesilaos back to the underworld are figured on Roman sarcophagi[95] (which often take scenes from tragedy). According to Hyginus (*Fab.* 103–4) Hermes brought Protesilaos back for three hours. 'Only follow me when I lead you' (646aN²) is perhaps more likely to be said by Hermes when he takes Protesilaos back again to Hades. There was certainly a meeting between Protesilaos and Akastos, Laodameia's father (647N²), and perhaps Protesilaos talked about marriage in praising Laodameia (657N²), while Akastos said that she should marry again (652–3N²). Laodameia could not endure her grief when Protesilaos went back. Frs. 649, 650, 651N² are conventional consolation, whether spoken by her father or the chorus. She made a statue of Protesilaos and put it in her room, pretending that it was a god whom she was worshipping. A slave looked through a chink and saw her kissing it. He reported to Akastos that she had a lover. Akastos burst into her room and found out the truth and ordered the statue to be

[95] Cf. Robert, *Sarkophagreliefs*, III, 3, 496; M. Lawrence, *A.J.A.*, 69, 1965, 210.

burnt. Presumably what the audience saw was (i) Laodameia's decision to have the statue made and a plea to the chorus to keep her secret (perhaps 648N^2 belongs here: 'no unlawful person may penetrate this room'), (ii) the slave betraying her to Akastos, (iii) Akastos giving orders for the burning of the statue in spite of her protests (655N^2: 'I would not betray even a lifeless friend' was spoken by Laodameia; 654N^2 the comment of the chorus on the debate). Left to herself she considers different methods of suicide (656N^2) and finally decides to throw herself into the blaze. This was probably reported, but it is the ancestor of the scene in the *Supplices* where Evadne throws herself into Kapaneus' pyre.

INO

Hyginus *Fab.* 4 is headed *Ino Euripidis*: Athamas in Thessaly had two sons, Learchos and Melikertes, by Ino. She went as a Bacchant to Parnassos (like Dirke in the later *Antiope* and the women in the *Bacchae*). Athamas, thinking she was dead, married Themisto and had two sons by her. When he found that Ino was alive, he had her brought back. Themisto thought she was a captive (and according to Hyginus *Fab.* 1 she was employed as a nurse to all four children, an anticipation of Hypsipyle) and confided to her her scheme for killing Ino's children, telling her to dress them in black and the other pair in white. Ino switched the clothing so that Themisto killed her own children and then when she discovered her error committed suicide. Athamas went mad and killed his son Learchos;[96] Ino threw herself into the sea with Melikertes and became a goddess (thus the play ends like the Hippolytus with a reference to an established cult).[97]

There is just enough other evidence to show that this was the outline of Euripides' play. Horace's *flebilis Ino*, contrasted with *Medea ferox*, suits the oppressed Ino of this story. Aristophanes speaks of her rags in the *Acharnians* (434), and in the *Wasps* (1413) the yellow-faced bakeress is compared to 'Ino hanging on to the feet of Euripides'; possibly Ino wore a specially-coloured mask to show her ill-treatment,[98] and this

[96] The evidence that this incident had already been described by Aeschylus in the *Athamas* is tenuous in the extreme, cf. however Mette, *Lustrum*, 9, 1964, 50.
[97] On the cults see Pindar, *Threnos* IV, 2; *Isthm.* VI, 5; O. ii, 30; P. xi, 2.
[98] T. B. L. Webster, *Festschrift für A. Rumpf*, 147.

suggests that she made an appeal to Athamas.[99] The preface to Athamas' hunt may be given by the hymn to Artemis equipped as a huntress, which, according to Terentianus Maurus (1931), Livius Andronicus made the chorus sing in his *Ino* (the actual verses are not by Livius but do not destroy the value of the testimony).

It is therefore worth considering how many of the fragments can be fitted into Hyginus' outline. $398N^2$ can be excluded because Plutarch, *Ant*. 36, shows that the true reading is δεινὴ and not δ᾽ Ἰνοῦς. A number of fragments seem to refer to Ino's view of Themisto and some of them at any rate belong to a 'debate' between Ino and Themisto. Their relative positions have on one side a parallel in the relation of Andromache and Hermione, on the other side in the relation between the nurse and Hermione in the *Andromache* and the nurse and Phaidra in the *First Hippolytos*.

Plutarch speaks of the *parrhesia* (freedom of speech) of Euripides' Ino when she says about herself that she knows how to be silent where she should and to speak where it is safe, an accomplishment defined in the first line of the quotation as 'all that the well-born need to know' ($413N^2$), Orion adds a line 'to see what I should and not see what I do not'; two further lines about controlling the appetite added by Stobaeus cannot belong here, both because they are unsuitable for a woman in Ino's position and because the speaker is a man. Probably Ino's statement has some connexion with $410N^2$, which sounds like Athamas commending Ino to Themisto as a frank servant who will speak the truth; this may be closely followed by $412N^2$: 'may I have a beggar or worse if his goodwill to me overcomes his fear and he speaks truth from the heart', and $401N^2$ 'Do not be too scornful of the unfortunate, when you are a mortal yourself.'

Ino's *parrhesia* displays itself in a speech which begins $415N^2$: 'Queen, many human beings have sufferings; for others they have just ceased, for others there is a risk they will come . . .'. This continues in $420N^2$: 'You see mighty tyrants are overturned . . .' and ends with $417N^2$: 'Be wise and possess what you have without doing anything blameworthy . . . do not behave like a bad shipowner who through his greed loses everything' (cf. 416, $419N^2$). $418N^2$ 'Do not grieve too much; you are not the only sufferer' (cf. $409N^2$), may be Ino's answer

[99] Whether 'Euripides' is a simple *paraprosdokian* or, as M. Taillardat, *Images d'Aristophane*, 1962, 213 suggests, a pun on Euripos commonly used as a synonym for instability.

to a speech in which Themisto has said that Athamas favours Ino's children rather than hers. Alone Ino may speak of the horrors of jealousy (403N²),[100] the difficulties of marriage (402N²), and the frailties of women (400–1N²).

After this scene Themisto plots with Ino the killing of the children: here presumably the demand for secrecy is made (411N²). Somehow Themisto must have been able to make the sacrifice appear necessary (in the *Phrixos B* an oracle was forged commanding the sacrifice of Phrixos and Helle). Then the children had to be dressed for death as in the *Hercules Furens* (329, 442, 526) and in the *Melanippe Sophe* (see below, p. 148). This gave Ino the chance to dress up Themisto's children instead of her own. We have, I think, no reason to suspect that the clothing of sacrificial victims was *black*, and probably the black and white colouring of the clothes are inventions of Hyginus or his source.

How the stage action proceeded here is unknown. We must presumably trust Hyginus that Themisto killed her own children, then discovered the truth, and committed suicide. Perhaps the whole sequence from when Ino was sent indoors to dress the children was told in a messenger speech, presumably to Athamas. The next trace of the story is 399N², the beginning of Ino's speech of repentance to the chorus: 'Dear ladies, how could I have my life with Athamas over again, having done nothing of what has been done.' This must be near Ino's appeal to Athamas, which is attested by Aristophanes. After that we are in the dark. Does Athamas take Learchos to the hunt? The chorus sang to the huntress Artemis, and this may have masked the interval before the messenger returns with the news that Athamas has gone mad (like Herakles later in the *H.F.*) and killed Learchos: 421N² 'in a hollow cave without a light, like a beast, alone' has been attributed to this speech and 422N² (the untrustworthy Thessalians) may well belong. When she heard the news, Ino presumably announced her intention of throwing herself into the sea with Melikertes. Wilamowitz[101] has suggested that two unattributed tragic fragments belong to a *deus ex machina*: adespota 100N² 'wanderers on the sea (shall worship you) as Leukothea' and 101N² 'he shall be called holy Palaimon by sailors'.

[100] There is no justification for Kuiper's transference of this fragment to the *Ixion* (*Mnem.* 41, 1913, 241).
[101] *Kl. Schr.* I, 201.

This suggests the following outline:

Prologue: Perhaps Athamas?
Epeisodia: Athamas commends Ino as a nurse to Themisto, 410,
                412N².
            Debate of Themisto and Ino, 413; 415–420, 409N².
            Commentary of Ino: 400–403N²;
            Themisto's plot: 411N².
            Report of sacrifice of Themisto's children, followed by
                Themisto's suicide.
            Ino's repentance and appeal to Athamas, 399N², Ar.,
                Wasps 1413.
            Athamas goes off to hunt.
Stasimon: To Artemis the huntress (Livius Andronicus).
            Messenger speech of Athamas' madness and murder of
                Learchos, 421, 422N².
            Ino proposes suicide with Melikertes.
            Deus ex Machina: Adespota, 100, 101N².

7 Other plays

Seven plays remain which on metrical grounds belong to the first
period. We cannot tell which one of them was in fact produced after
428 B.C. A mention in Aristophanes' Acharnians gives a bottom date of
426 B.C. for the Bellerophon, Oineus, and Thyestes; but the Telephos is
quoted in the same context and the Telephos was produced in 438 B.C.,
so that any of these plays may have been produced long before 426 B.C.
Political allusions have been said to fix the Heraclidae in 430, in 429–7,
and in 426 B.C.;[102] the contradiction shows that none of them is valid
but Eurystheus' prophecy (1035) would hardly have been emphasized
long before the beginning of the Peloponnesian war. The figure for
resolved feet (5.9%) associates it with the Medea (6.5%) and Hippolytos
(5.4%) and implies a certain distance before the Hecuba (14.7%), which
was itself produced before 423 B.C. The Theseus is quoted in the Hippolytus of 428 B.C.,[103] and the herdsman, describing the letters which
make up Theseus' name, clearly distinguishes the eta in the second place

[102] Zuntz, Political Plays of Euripides, 81; Goossens, Euripide et Athènes, 175; Wilamowitz,
Analecta Euripidea 152.
[103] Frs. 385–6N² with Hipp. 1144–5, as well as the reference to Ariadne (339), which may
derive from the First Hippolytos.

from the *epsilon* in the fourth place. *Eta* first appears in Attic inscriptions about 450 B.C.,[104] and one would suppose a lapse of ten years or so before it would be the obvious letter to use. *Oinomaos* and *Chrysippos* are quoted together in the corrupt hypothesis of the *Phoenissae*, but this merely means that the writer was using a set of Hypotheses which put the stories together in their chronological sequence.[105] For the *Oinomaos* we have no clue except metre. The two fragments (840–1N²) of the *Chrysippos* in which Laios admits that passion has overcome his reason have rightly been compared to the similar assessment of their actions by Medeia and Phaidra, and the long anapaestic fragment (839N²) about Earth and Aither, which ends with the statement that earth returns to Earth and air to air, was referred by Kranz to consolation by the chorus after the death of Chrysippos: he noted as similar the long anapaestic passage in the *Medea* (1081) in which the chorus comment on the hazards of having children after Medeia has agonizedly decided to kill hers.[106]

It is likely, therefore, that the *Theseus* was produced soon after 440 B.C., and the *Chrysippos* near the *Medea*, and the *Heraclidae* is among the latest productions of the group. They are here arranged in the order *Heraclidae, Theseus, Bellerophon, Chrysippos, Oineus, Thyestes, Oinomaos*, as it is more convenient to study the preserved play first.

HERACLIDAE

Euripides wrote this play in the general tradition of Suppliant plays, and in particular he had Aeschylus' *Heraclidae* before him. The general tradition appears in many forms as different from each other as Aeschylus' *Hiketides, Heraclidae, Eleusinioi*, and *Eumenides*, Sophocles' *Oedipus Coloneus*, and Euripides' *Heraclidae* and *Supplices*. Common elements are the taking of asylum, an attempt to remove the suppliant, an appeal to the people before the suppliant is accepted, and a battle, which the party who accepts the suppliant wins. It is certainly possible,

---

[104] Schwyzer, *Gr. Gramm.* I, 147; H. Immerwahr, *Ullman Studies*, 40.

[105] Cf. above, p. 10, on *Peliades, Medea*.

[106] W. Kranz, *Stasimon*, 202. Fr. 839N² has also been compared or identified with Pacuvius, *Chryses* VI, VIIR and Ennius ap. Varro, *L.L.*, VII, 88 (cf. O. Skutsch, *C.Q.*, 14, 1964, 89), but neither poet, as far as we know, wrote a *Chrysippus*. The theory is not unique, cf. e.g. E. *Suppl.* 532ff.; fr. 971N² and the Poteidaia epitaph of 432 B.C. (Tod, *G.H.I.*, no. 59), and may therefore have been quoted in many tragedies. We have no reason to doubt Clement's ascription of fr. 839N².

as suggested by Mette (on fr. 111M) that Aeschylus' play included the youthening of Iolaos.

Euripides' play is set in Marathon. Iolaos, Alkmene, and the younger children of Herakles have taken refuge there from the pursuit of Eurystheus, Iolaos with the boys at an altar, Alkmene with the girls inside the temple. Hyllos and the older sons are looking for another refuge in case Demophon and Akamas will not receive them in Athens. The Argive herald enters and tries to drag them from the altar. Iolaos shouts for help, and the chorus of Marathonians enters and in excited dochmiacs question him and reprimand the herald. Demophon arrives accompanied by the silent Akamas, and both sides plead their case before him (two contestants before a judge as earlier in the *Telephos* and *Philoktetes*): the herald offers an Argive alliance in return for the fugitives; Iolaos argues that exile from Argos does not entail exile from Greece and stresses the kinship of Herakles and Theseus, saying also that Herakles saved Theseus from Hades. Demophon accepts Iolaos, and the herald departs threatening war. Iolaos expresses his gratitude and Demophon goes to make his arrangements; Iolaos refuses to leave the altar. The chorus sing defiance of Eurystheus in an aeolo-choriambic stasimon.

Demophon returns with the news that the Argive army is approaching; that he has made his preparations but that the prophets demand the sacrifice of a virgin of noble birth to Persephone, and he is not prepared to sacrifice an Athenian. Iolaos is in despair; he cannot think of another refuge, and he offers himself – they may surrender him to Eurystheus. Demophon tells him that Eurystheus wants to kill the young not the old. Makaria has heard Iolaos' lamentations and comes out. The Athenians are helping them; they must share the toil with the Athenians. Her death is a noble solution. Iolaos proposes that the daughters shall draw lots but she refuses. She asks to die in Iolaos' arms but he refuses. She asks Demophon to let her die among women. Then she bids farewell. If they get home, they may give her a fitting burial. She hopes that death means nothingness. Iolaos collapses.[107] The chorus sing conventional consolation in dactylic metre: the changes of fortune and Makaria's glory.

Euripides has here written a type of scene which he was to use again in the *Hecuba* (Polyxene), *Erechtheus* (the daughter), *Phrixos B* (Phrixos),

[107] On falling figures in Euripides see J. de Romilly, *L'Évolution du pathétique*, 80.

Phoenissae (Menoikeus), and *Iphigenia in Aulis* (Iphigeneia). Clearly the heroism of a girl or boy was good theatre, but it is fair to suppose that youthful idealism was a value which Euripides respected and wanted to emphasize. We have no evidence that either of the other tragedians made the sacrifice voluntary. We know nothing useful about Sophocles' *Iphigeneia*. Whether Aeschylus introduced the Sacrifice of Makaria in his *Heraclidae* is quite uncertain. If the first chorus of the *Agamemnon* is any evidence, his Iphigeneia is unlikely to have gone willingly to the knife when her father decided to sacrifice her. It is tempting to suppose that Euripides saw the *Agamemnon*, if not the Aeschylean *Iphigeneia*, in his youth, and felt that the story cannot have gone like this. In every Euripidean scene parental resistance plays a part.

Nothing more is heard of Makaria, and many have felt that her death must have been reported. But it is arguable that Euripides has prepared for this omission by arranging that Iolaos shall not be present at her death, that she shall die among Athenian women (who have no part in the play), and that her burial shall not take place until the Herakleidai are restored to Argos. He is hurrying on to the second part of the play, the effect of the battle on Iolaos and Alkmene.

A retainer of Hyllos arrives with good news. Alkmene thinks that he is another herald from the Argives and has to be reassured. Hyllos is marshalling his forces with the Athenian army. Iolaos proposes to join them and totters off with the retainer carrying his armour. The chorus mark the time while the battle takes place by asking Sun and Moon to tell the gods that Athens is involved in a dangerous war because of her refusal to surrender suppliants: they claim the help of Athena. (The metre is aeolo-choriambic as in the first stasimon.)

The messenger returns with the news that the battle has been successful, that Iolaos prayed to Hebe and to Herakles and was rejuvenated and that he captured Eurystheus, who is being sent back to Alkmene. The youthening of Iolaos is evidently an essential part of the story, and Euripides has treated it as realistically as he can: he emphasized Iolaos' age and weakness while he was on stage, the youthening was not seen by the messenger himself but is only a report from another (847f.), and Iolaos is not allowed to appear on stage again.

The chorus sing (again in aeolo-choriambics) that victory means dancing and music and women, and this victory has proved that the gods punish injustice and that Herakles is in heaven. Eurystheus is brought in by a retainer of Hyllos, and the second big debate of the play is staged: instead of Iolaos and the Argive herald here Alkmene and Eurystheus. Alkmene bursts out in passionate hatred. The retainer[108] says that a captive may not be killed. Eurystheus attributes to Hera his whole quarrel with Herakles; from that beginning his whole life has been dictated by fear. The chorus say again that he must not be killed. Alkmene answers that he can be killed but his body will be given to the Athenians. With some dignity, he accepts death and says that his grave will give benefits to the Athenians and a bad return to the Herakleidai when they forget their gratitude and invade Attica. The chorus apparently accept Alkmene's proposal and he is marched off to die.

The end is clearly determined by the known position of Eurystheus' grave. Euripides could not give this act of vengeance either to the Athenians or to the essentially noble Iolaos. It was a master stroke to give it to the aged Alkmene who is crazed by triumph after such long suffering. Her act of vengeance is a balance to Makaria's self-sacrifice, a cruelty which sinks as far below Iolaos' steady decency as Makaria's heroism rises above it. This is not a great play, but it is well constructed with careful preparation for the part of Alkmene in Iolaos' opening speech, with the balance of the two great debates, with the Athenian chorus commenting on the moral issues for Athens all through the action, and with Makaria's great scene to end the first part.

THESEUS

This play was discussed several times by Wilamowitz.[109] He usefully removed 383–4N² and gave them to the *Peirithoos*; they must surely be the threats of an underworld official to an intruder, Theseus, and the scholiast was misled by the name Theseus into making them threats against Minos.

Less convincingly he supposed that the play contained Theseus' visit to Poseidon to get the wreath of Amphitrite, and that the play was produced in a connected trilogy between the *Aigeus* and *Hippolytos I*. The trilogy was assumed because Wilamowitz felt that Euripides must have made it clear that the wish used to kill Hippolytos was the third and last (and therefore irrevocable). Theseus used his second wish to escape from Hades and according to this theory this was mentioned in *Hippolytos I*;

[108] The distribution of speakers is doubtful: I follow G. Zuntz, *Political Plays*, 125f.
[109] *Kl. Schr.* I, 19; V, 2, 114; *Analecta Euripidea*, 172; *Hippolytos* 43.

but we have in fact no evidence that in *Hippolytos I* he was in Hades when Phaidra made love to Hippolytos or that a wish of this kind could ever be revoked. The *Theseus* according to Wilamowitz showed the audience what he did with the first wish. He may well have used it here,[110] but the wish cannot have been of exclusive importance if he got out of the labyrinth by using Ariadne's thread, and it is difficult to see to what other tragedy fr. 1001N² could belong: 'he took a ball of thread and carried it with him'. Wilamowitz' connexion between *Theseus* and *Hippolytos I* remains entirely hypothetical and it is in any case doubtful whether Euripides would have juxtaposed the hero of the *Aigeus* and *Theseus* with the cuckold of *Hippolytos I*.

P. Oxy. 2452 has been claimed by Professor Turner for Sophocles' *Theseus*. Professor Lloyd-Jones[111] says that the language suggests Sophocles rather than Euripides, but that the evidence does not justify more than a very tentative conclusion: either Sophocles' *Minos* or *Theseus* might be thought of. It must be pointed out that Sophocles' *Theseus* depends on a single quotation, so that we know nothing about its content, even if it existed; and Pearson conjectures that the single fragment of the *Minos* belonged to the *Kamikoi*, Minos' adventures in Sicily. As therefore at least one usage, the repeated κατελεήσατε of P. Oxy. 2452, fr. 5, 11 is certainly Euripidean, the papyrus should be tentatively considered with the fragments of Euripides' play.

Euripides' *Theseus* certainly dealt with the tribute to the Minotaur (385–6N²). The scene must be Crete, and the youths and girls are probably the chorus; as Theseus is officially one of them they must arrive together. They were not necessarily brought by Minos himself as in Bacchylides. The passage in which the illiterate herdsman describes the letters of the name of Theseus (382N²) became famous, but we are not told where in the play it occurs or to what it refers. What is likely to be inscribed with a name so that a herdsman could take it in at leisure and describe it to an interested party? A sword of course (cf. Theseus' sword in the *Aigeus* and Hippolytos' sword in *Hipp. I*), but here inevitably one thinks of the herdsman in the *I.T.* 260, who saw Orestes and Pylades by the sea, and of the shepherds in Apollonios Rhodios (IV, 313) and in Accius' *Medea* who observed the Argo arriving. Probably then Theseus' name was on the sail or stern (?) of his ship and

[110] Cf. below on P. Oxy. 2452, fr. 6.
[111] *Gnomon*, 35, 1963, 436.

the herdsman who saw it 'by the very skirts of Europe's land' ($381N^2$) reported it to Minos in the prologue.[112] Then Theseus and the chorus arrive for the parodos, to which the ionic lament lines $385-6N^2$ may belong.

After that we have little help. Theseus must either have been commanded or have volunteered to be first offering to the Minotaur; this was presumably a scene with Minos. Ariadne must have instructed him in the use of the thread. There are three pointers to Ariadne: $1001N^2$, the fragment about the thread; $387N^2$ 'Yet I will tell the tale though it be blameworthy', which could very well introduce her disloyal planning to save Theseus; $388N^2$ (quoted from this play by Plutarch) 'But there is another love among men, the love of a just, temperate, and brave soul. This ought to be the rule for men, that the temperate should love the pious and say good-bye to Kypris, the daughter of Zeus.' Professor Erika Simon has made the attractive suggestion that this fragment comes from a final speech by Athena, sending Theseus from the bed of Ariadne to his duty in Athens and prophesying Dionysos' union with Ariadne in Naxos; she finds this illustrated on a kalyx-krater by the Kadmos painter.[113] Other explanations of the fragment are conceivable: someone warning Minos to keep his hands off Eriboia or someone warning Ariadne to leave Theseus to his fate. But a warning to Theseus seems much the most probable (Stobaeus in fact combines the lines with a similar wish of Perseus in the *Diktys*, $331N^2$, and Bellerophon in the *Stheneboia* prays also for a sober love which leads to excellence, $672N^2$); on the analogy of these passages Theseus himself should be the speaker and the phraseology suits a mortal rather than a god. At the least then the fragment suggests that Theseus is warned or warns himself not to abandon Athens for the love of Ariadne. Athena may, however, very well have prophesied in an epilogue (when Theseus, or at least, Ariadne, had already left for the ship and the chorus were still on stage), that Theseus would leave Ariadne to Dionysos in Naxos, and the play then ended with the chorus making for Theseus' ship: in the *Iphigenia in Tauris* Athena in the epilogue speaks both to Thoas on the stage (1435) and to Orestes on his ship (1446).

[112] Gilbert Murray suggested the sail of the ship, *Aeschylus*, 67. Euripides may have remembered the Aeschylean report of the passage of Glaukos, on which see R. P. Winnington-Ingram, *B.I.C.S.*, 6, 1959, 58.

[113] *Antike Kunst* 6, 1963, 14: see also list of illustrations, below, p. 303.

Ariadne betrayed her country for love of Theseus. She appears then as a true sister of the Phaidra of the *First Hippolytos*, who encouraged Hippolytos to take Theseus' kingdom, and we understand why in the surviving play Phaidra (339)[114] thinks of Ariadne's love as a parallel to her own and Pasiphae's. (So also Tzetzes on *Frogs* 849 'Cretan monodies and unholy marriages' quotes Ariadne with Phaidra and Pasiphae.)

The longer and partly intelligible fragments of *P. Oxy.* 2452 fit into this outline. In fr. 2 someone describes to another some strange phenomenon in the stars; the celestial phenomenon connected with this story is Ariadne's wreath. It is possible that its appearance in the heavens is reported to Minos at the beginning of the play and that it is ominous whether it implies that Dionysos has temporarily abandoned Ariadne or that he is going to join her in Naxos.

In fr. 4 Ariadne speaks trimeters and Eriboia sings dochmiacs, and this alternation seems to be continued in fr. 5. Ariadne speaks in pity; Eriboia asks for pity. In Bacchylides Eriboia is one of the fourteen and in Pindar, *N* 5, 45, the wife of Telamon and mother of Ajax. In the play to which the papyrus belongs (whether Sophocles or Euripides wrote it) two of the fourteen, Theseus and Eriboia, were distinguished from the rest; it is perhaps easiest to suppose that Eriboia was the leader of the chorus (possibly also we should suppose that in the *Peliades* Alkestis was a character and another named Peliad was leader of the chorus of her sisters). In fr. 3 Theseus describes his labours to someone who seems to have denied his capability of killing the Minotaur. This must be after he has been chosen or has volunteered as the first victim. The hearer is a sympathizer, who tries to dissuade him, probably Ariadne. In fr. 1 someone tells Theseus he must either give up or act; he answers that he will go in the confidence that heaven favours the pious. The chorus sing that they wish that they could go with him (?). Fr. 6 is a description of a *xenos*, presumably then of Theseus by a Cretan: the stranger calls on someone and probably makes a vow (it is tempting to think that Theseus calls on Poseidon).

If all these hints are accepted, a possible outline is:

[114] I am not convinced by Mr Barrett that in the *Hippolytos* Euripides thought of the *Odyssey* story to the exclusion of the subsequent union with Dionysos in Naxos: if the Syracuse vase is evidence for the *Theseus* he certainly envisaged there that Dionysos would find or rejoin Ariadne in Naxos, but that is, of course, not necessarily evidence for the *Hippolytos*.

Prologue: Herdsman and Minos, 381–2N², *P. Oxy.* 2452, fr. 2.
Parodos: Theseus, Eriboia, and the chorus (? 385–6N²).
            Minos proposes that Theseus enter the labyrinth.
Kommos: Ariadne and Eriboia: *P. Oxy.* 2452, fr. 4 and 5.
            Ariadne and Theseus: 387, 386aN², *P. Oxy.* 2452, fr. 3
            and 1.
Stasimon:
Messenger
speech: *P. Oxy.* 2452, fr. 6; 1001N².
Return of
Theseus: Theseus and Ariadne leave for ship (? here 388N²).
Epilogue: Athena prophesies Naxian episode.
Exodos of chorus to Theseus' ship.

BELLEROPHON

The parody in Aristophanes' *Peace* 135ff. (cf. also 148, *Ach.*, 426) shows
that Bellerophon flew to heaven on Pegasos, was thrown off, and
appeared broken and dying at the end (like Hippolytos). The actual
flight was shown (fr. 306–8N²), whether Bellerophon took off on the
stage or inside the house like Trygaios in the *Peace*:[115] 306 is said to
Pegasos as he starts (it is the end of an iambic speech primarily addressed
to the chorus or another character), and 307–8 come from a monody in
anapaests. Bellerophon fell in Lycia, therefore we should naturally
assume that he took off from Lycia.

In the prologue (285N²) he speaks of his former prosperity in
contrast to his present misfortune. An obscure fragment (305N²) quoted
on the trial of Orestes in Argos (*Or.* 872), about a speech made 'on the
polished bank of Danaid seats' may be his announcement that the
Argives condemned him for the murder of Stheneboia.[116] This condemnation may have been the reason for his return to Lycia and for his
misfortunes. The male chorus have entered before he declares that the
corruption of the world convinces him that the gods do not exist
(286N²). A number of fragments fit into the general context, but someone evidently counters with the advice not to be angry with events but

[115] Technically and dramatically it would be easiest if Bellerophon went *in* to fetch
Pegasus after his debate with Iobates. Cf. N. Hourmouziades, *op. cit.*, 151ff.
[116] If Bellerophon did describe his trial, this may account for the ascription of the
interrogation fr. 68N² to the *Bellerophon* instead of to one of the Alkmaion plays.

to use them skilfully (287N²), and presumably the same character says: 'My son, young men are energetic but old men are wiser' (291N², cf. 619N², an older man advising Peleus). Probably Iobates tried to restrain Bellerophon and failed. The disastrous flight to heaven followed. Presumably a messenger told of Bellerophon's fall before he was brought in, but the account of Pegasos, that he yielded too willingly to Bellerophon (309N²) and that he is now carrying Zeus' thunderbolts (312N²) can only have been given by a god in an epilogue speech, perhaps Hermes. When Bellerophon was brought in, he spoke of his own past life: 'you were pious to the gods, you helped your hosts, and you were unwearied in aiding friends' (311N²). This must have been one of the great speeches of self-revelation, like that of Admetos when he discovers that life is worthless or the repentant speech of Ino in the *Ino*. After this Bellerophon is taken into the house to die (310N² cf. 673N² from the *Stheneboia*).

What remains of this strange play suggests that Bellerophon belongs to the tradition of heroic resisters: he may owe something to the Aeschylean Prometheus and to the Sophoclean Ajax, and he may have bequeathed something to Phaethon and even to Pentheus. But we are left unsatisfied. The fragments do not come clear. In the great debate Bellerophon's contention is that divinity must mean divine justice to reward the pious and punish the sinner, so he lists instances of the wicked flourishing and the pious failing or only succeeding by efforts which have nothing to do with piety (286N²). Guile succeeds in private life and in war (288-90N²). Jealousy (294-5N²), evil associations (296N²), evil protected by money (297N²), evil inherited (298N²), this is what he sees and the sight makes life not worth living (293N²). The difficult fr. 292N² seems to be a sort of summing up: 'doctors choose the particular drug needed for the particular disease, some diseases are sent by the gods but we cure them by *nomos* (the doctor's rules derived from practice?). If the gods do anything base, they are not gods.' If Iobates' experience only produced the philosophy that the world is unpredictable (301N²), the simile of the doctors may be Bellerophon's answer: the gods should behave like skilful doctors.

To go and ask them about this is to court disaster: on a much smaller scale Ion is prevented from consulting Apollo (*Ion* 1547). But what is the end? 'Alas. But why alas? I have suffered what comes to a mortal' (300N²), must have been said by Bellerophon and implies some sort of acceptance of the death which according to Aelian (to whom we owe 311N^2) he faced heroically. If these fragments are taken together, Bellerophon's statement of his own virtuous behaviour is not necessarily bitter. He accepts a world which has room for human courage and kindness even if there is no divine punishment of human failings or reward for human virtue.

CHRYSIPPOS[117]

The play certainly dealt with Laios' passion for Chrysippos, the son of Pelops. Aelian (*N.A.* 6, 15) describes a dolphin which loved a boy: 'they lay there, one dead and the other dying. Laios did not do this for Chrysippos, my dear Euripides.' This implies that in Euripides Laios survived Chrysippos and fits much better the story in the Scholiast to E. *Phoen.* 1760, that Chrysippos committed suicide out of shame, than the story in pseudo-Plutarch, *Parall.* 313e, that Hippodameia murdered him. The papyrus hypothesis (*P. Oxy.* 2455, fr. 17, xxi) gives a few letters of the first line and Professor Turner offers either fr. 1027N^2 or fr. 972N^2 to complete it. Fr. 1027 can be dated metrically in Group III and at that date a long generalizing piece of advice to a young man would be a most unlikely beginning to a prologue; but fr. 972 'By many forms of wisdom the gods' is a blameless beginning for a play of Group I. It may even be that Chrysippos' prayer for wisdom and courage combined with ugliness rather than beauty combined with cowardice also belongs in the prologue (842N^2).

The fragments of Accius give a little. 'If he wins here, I give him Sparta and Amyclae' (IIIR), is a promise of a prize by Pelops, not necessarily, as Mette thinks, a prize in war, but possibly a prize in the games; this would suit the tradition that Laios carried off Chrysippos at the games (games at Olympia rather than Nemea, which Hyginus names), and the indication of a race-course in two of the illustrations. Fr. 844N^2 describes Laios urging on his horses (cf. *I.T.* 1423). The fragment (Accius IR) about everyone finding some missile to throw recalls several Euripidean messenger speeches in which slaves try to restrain free men from doing what they want to do (e.g. *Melanippe Desmotis*,

[117] Bibliographical note. U. von Wilamowitz-Moellendorff, *Kl. Schr.* I, 176; L. Séchan, *Etudes*, 311ff.; W. Schadewaldt, *Monolog*, 251 n. 3; B. Snell, *Scenes from Greek Drama*, 63; F. Wehrli, *M.H.* 14, 1957, 108ff.; H. J. Mette, *Lustrum*, 9, 1964, 136. For illustrations, see below, p. 298.

Page, *G.L.P.*, no. 13, 49; *I.T.* 318ff.) and may therefore come from the account of the games, when they tried to stop Laios driving off with Chrysippos: a pedagogue and a young man appear in this role on three of the illustrations. ' "What am I to do? It is his voice." We all hear it too' (VR). This again must come from a messenger speech, and the likeness to S. *Ant.* 1206–20, where Kreon is reported as hearing Haimon's voice in Antigone's tomb, suggests that someone, perhaps the pedagogue, is reporting the suicide of Chrysippos and perhaps an attempt by Laios to prevent it. Finally the messenger consoles Pelops with a general reflection on the mutability of human fortune (843N²). It may be at this point that the chorus in anapaests (839N²)[118] reflect on the nature of immortality – earth to earth and air to air – and the anapaests recovered by Wilamowitz from Plutarch *Mor.* 750B 'Laios, forgetful of reason, forgetful of his country' may belong to the same context.

Laios survived Chrysippos and had to face his heartbroken father. Presumably he came back or was brought back with the body of the boy. As in the scene between Theseus and Hippolytos (but here the charge was true), Pelops may have cursed him. It is to this scene probably that the two fragments about the conflict of desire and reason belong (840–1N²) 'None of what you chide escapes me. But Nature overcomes my intellect.' 'Alas, this is an ill sent by the gods to men, when they know the good and do not do it' are phrased in the present but must be Laios' confession. (The only person to whom he could have said this earlier is Chrysippos, and there must have been an earlier scene in which he persuaded Chrysippos to be a passenger in his chariot, but if he had admitted his passion so openly Chrysippos would have refused to go with him.) A curious fragment of Accius (IIR) speaks of 'sharing alternate riches'; this sounds like the sharing between Eteokles and Polyneikes, and it seems possible that this unreal possibility was envisaged either in Pelops' curse or in a prophecy by a god at the end of the play. If the writer of the Hypothesis included it, this would account for the play being quoted as from the same cycle as the *Phoenissae*.

Outline of play

Prologue: Fr. 972, 842N²: Chrysippos.

Parados: Competitors in Olympic games?

[118] Cf. above, p. 21.

Epeisodia: Pelops announces the prizes (Accius IIIR).
         Laios and Chrysippos.
Messenger speech of the games, the rape, and the death of Chrysippos (?): illustrations; Accius IR, VR; 843–4N^2.
Choral anapaests: 839N^2, Plutarch, *Mor.* 750B.
Laios returns with Chrysippos' body; Pelops and Laios, 840–1N^2.
Accius IIR (Pelops or *deus*).

OINEUS

Pacuvius' *Periboea* and Accius' *Diomedes* both seem to be adaptations from this play. Diomedes returns from Troy with Sthenelos, son of Kapaneus, and salutes his native country (558N^2) telling the story of the capture of Thebes (559N^2, Accius IVR) and presumably of Troy. The description of how Agrios and his sons used the aged Oineus as a kottabos mark at dinner (as Gilbert Murray saw) is not given by himself (562N^2, cf. Pacuvius XIIR): 'they pelted the old man's head'.[119] So Diomedes and Sthenelos (like Kresphontes) were met by a sympathizer (who also spoke fr. 564N^2 'O Strangers'); he told them that Agrios and his sons had robbed Oineus of his kingdom and were maltreating him. At the end of the prologue Diomedes goes to find Oineus in the fields (Accius XIIR, reading *agros*). After the parodos Oineus himself describes his misery (561, 563, 565, 569, 570N^2; Pacuvius I–VII, XIII, XIV, XX; Accius VI–VIIR). This must have led to a plan for vengeance (Accius VIII; Pacuvius VIIIR). The rest is unclear: Agrios appears and apparently is going to kill Oineus' wife Periboia (Pacuvius XR). Perhaps Diomedes tells her to take refuge in the temple of Dionysos (Pacuvius XVIIIR). Agrios summons his son Melanippos to help him (Pacuvius XIR). Oineus hopes that he is still strong enough to prevent his taking refuge on an altar (Pacuvius XXIIIR). He presumably failed,[120] but whether with the help of a *deus ex machina* or not, in the end the kingdom was given back to Oineus.

THYESTES

The fragments give very little hint of the contents of the play – a suggestion by Thyestes to Atreus that many unlikely things happen

[119] *Athenian Drama*, III, 1906, 335. The situation had already occurred in Aeschylus' *Ostologoi* (179–80N^2). The relation of Sophocles' *Peleus* to Euripides' *Oineus* is unknown.
[120] See below, p. 299.

(396N²), with which perhaps goes 'the light in your eyes is misty' (397aN²) and someone's choice of energetic action rather than words (394, cf. 393N²). Lesky[121] found echoes of two fragments of Aristophanes' *Proagon* (361–2K), which parody Thyestes' horror at having eaten his children, and of the Thyestean rags (Ar. *Ach.*) in Seneca's *Thyestes* and claimed that for Euripides, but Seneca may have combined several sources and we do not know that Aristophanes in the *Proagon* was parodying this play; if his source was Euripides, it may rather have been the *Cretan Women*. But the suggestion remains a possibility if we assume that Euripides dramatized the same story differently in the *Thyestes*, putting Aerope's seduction of Thyestes before the beginning of the play and delaying the feast until Thyestes had returned from exile.

The claim that Ennius translated Euripides' play, which has been revived by Mette,[122] depends on the identification of Ennius' *Thyestes* VIIR 'Look at this shining height which all call Jupiter' with Euripides fr. 941N² and the consequent attribution of that fragment to Euripides' *Thyestes*. This identification is supported by the fact that Cicero after quoting Ennius goes on to give his own closer translation of Euripides fr. 941N². The Ennius fragments include the arrival of an unknown old man (IVR), presumably Thyestes, who also begs strangers (presumably the chorus in a lyric dialogue) not to come near him because of his pollution (VIIIR, Cicero, quoting this, says 'Will you condemn yourself, Thyestes, for another's crime', which must mean that Atreus has already given him his children to eat); he laments an evil which has fallen on him this day (IX, XR) and calls down curses on Atreus (XIR). This is compatible with the other outline provided we assume that Thyestes' fear of contagion (VIIIR) comes *after* the feast and is not part of Thyestes' arrival (IVR). It is, of course, tempting to combine them and make Thyestes' arrival parallel to Oidipous' arrival in Sophocles' *O.C.*, but that would mean that the feast had already happened and some other disaster ensued in the course of the play. But if we assume that the feast is the crime and is central in the play, then the Euripidean fragments about energetic action will refer to Atreus before the crime; and someone in Ennius (IIIR) describes Atreus making his intrigue.

Mette also suggests that the fragment *P. Hamburg* 119, col. ii, may be part of the prologue. The papyrus with 118 seems to be a collection of Euripidean prologues, and a father in misery, complaining that someone will not let him meet his children, may well be Thyestes. The beginning of the prologue was genealogical, the proud lines (*inc. inc.* LVIIR) which Cicero quotes first to contrast them with Thyestes' self abasement in fr. VIIIR, which, on our assumption, came late in the play.

It is therefore possible that for this play Euripides placed a long period between the seduction of Aerope and the feast, a period in which Thyestes is in exile and Atreus has control of his children. Thyestes arrives back. There is some sort of a seeming reconciliation with Atreus (Ennius, fr. VI ?), which gives Atreus the chance to plan the feast. After the feast Thyestes comes out shattered and goes again into exile cursing Atreus.

OINOMAOS

This play shows no resolved syllable in twenty-four lines; its relation to Sophocles' play, which was produced before 414 B.C., is unclear. The Sophoclean play dealt with the well-known story reflected on vases of the late fifth and fourth century, and the fragments show Hippodameia's love for Pelops, the disaster to earlier suitors, their heads affixed above Oinomaos' doors, the compact with Myrtilos. (Accius probably followed Sophocles.) The few fragments of Euripides show nothing of this, but the difficulties of parenthood (571N²), the impossibility of enduring disaster (572N², the phraseology of ll. 4–5 recall Medeia and Phaidra), the relief given by lamentation (573N²), the miseries of old age (575N²), and the mistakes of excessive zeal (576N²). If Euripides did treat the same part of the story, it looks as if he completely changed the emphases and made Oinomaos an unhappy father who was outwitted by the unscrupulous Pelops.

III

The Second Group

In Euripides' early productions a pattern seems to appear. Each year he produced one play about a bad woman, one play about an unhappy woman, and one play of a different kind. From 415 B.C., by when perhaps the conditions of production had changed, a new pattern of interrelated plays can sometimes be seen. For the second group the principles are not so clear, partly because Euripides is no longer so interested in bad women (only *Phrixos B* belongs to this class), and the unhappy women are now so various in kind that there is no reason why two such plays should not be produced together. *Aiolos* and *Melanippe Sophe* continue the line of plays about women with irregular babies. In the first group Ino in her name-play was a woman of high birth in a servile position: she is followed now by Andromache, Elektra, and Melanippe in the *Melanippe Desmotis*. Merope in the *Kresphontes* is faced with a horrible marriage like Danae in the *Diktys*. Hekabe in her name-play is in a similar position to Alkmene in the *Heraclidae*. Apart from echoes of the earlier unhappy women, we shall also notice other themes from the first group echoed in this group.

The only absolute date is 422 B.C. for the *Erechtheus*; Plutarch dates it to the one-year truce which started after the Dionysia of 423 and ended after the Dionysia of 422 (*Nic.* 9). Quotation in comedy dates *Kresphontes* before 424 B.C. and the *Aiolos* and *Hecuba* before 423 B.C. *Electra* must be later than the second edition of Aristophanes' *Clouds* (which cannot have been produced before 422) and earlier than the plays of the next group, which probably starts in 416 B.C. The *Ixion* was written after the death of Protagoras, which probably occurred about 420 B.C. The figures for resolved syllables in iambics in the preserved plays are *Andromache* 12%, *Supplices* 14.2%, *Hecuba* 14.7%, *Electra* 17%.

The figures for fragmentary plays are obviously not so reliable but *Melanippe Sophe* with 16% clearly precedes *Melanippe Desmotis* with 19.2%: this relation is confirmed by the difference in the stories – *Sophe* follows the tradition of the *Alope*; *Desmotis* precedes the later plays in which a mother is discovered by grown-up sons. Other suggestions for dating the two Melanippe plays have been made: Gilbert Murray[1] attractively found the origin of the gibes about Euripides' greengrocer mother (made already in the *Acharnians* of 425 B.C.) in Melanippe's ascription of wisdom to her mother (fr. 484N, particularly), but a date for the *Sophe* before 425 seems excluded by the metrical statistics. Goossens[2] dated the *Sophe* between the *Erechtheus* and the *Ion* on the ground that Xouthos and Ion are not mentioned in the *Erechtheus* but are mentioned in the *Sophe* and the *Ion*. This argument is worthless: Euripides is not consistent – he uses the *eidolon* story of Helen in the *Electra* and *Helen* but not in the intervening *Troades* and subsequent *Orestes*. Nor have we any evidence to exclude Xouthos and Ion from the *Erechtheus*, and in the *Sophe* no mention is made of Ion's two fathers (the essential theme of the *Ion*). Goossens also wanted to date the *Desmotis* to the time of the Sicilian expedition because of its Western setting, but Athenian interest in the West long preceded that date.

These datings make the placing of eleven plays in the five productions of Group II highly probable. But we do not know which the other four plays were. Of the plays listed below *Phrixos A* may rather belong to Group I and *Polyidos* to Group III.

Group II

X	Before 424	Kresphontes	Andromache	? Phrixos A
XI	Before 423	Aiolos	Hecuba	Supplices
XII	422	? Melanippe Sophe	*Erechtheus*	? Oinomaos
XIII		? Phrixos B	? Ixion	? Kadmos
XIV		Electra	? Melanippe Desmotis	? Polyidos

For the purposes of discussion the most suitable grouping is (a) *Andromache, Hecuba, Supplices, Erechtheus*; (b) *Phrixos A, Phrixos B*; (c) *Kresphontes, Electra*; (d) *Melanippe Sophe, Melanippe Desmotis*; (e) *Aiolos, Ixion, Polyidos, Kadmos*.

[1] *Euripides and his age*, 27: perhaps Medeia's magic in the *Peliades* and the *Aegeus* was derived from her mother?

[2] Budé Euripides: *Ion*, 158.

1 *Andromache, Hecuba, Supplices, Erechtheus*

ANDROMACHE

The *Andromache*[3] (which on metrical statistics comes early in the group) probably belongs to the same production as the *Kresphontes*, after 428 and before 424 B.C. Andromache speaks the prologue: she tells the past history – her capture by Neoptolemos, his marriage with Hermione, and Hermione's hatred, which has made her take refuge in the Thetideion (for stage purposes this is a statue of Thetis behind the usual stage altar) and send her child away to safety, while Neoptolemos is asking Apollo's pardon in Delphi. Andromache, Hermione, and Neoptolemos are the three points of a triangle, and as the play proceeds Euripides examines them successively. A servant reports that Menelaos has discovered the hiding place of the child; Andromache sends her again to summon Peleus' aid.

The parodos of Phthian women who come to console Andromache is preceded by her lament in sung elegiacs: Andromache sings of Paris, Helen, Hektor and her present misery as Hermione's slave. They pity her, but warn her that she had better put up with her position. The dactylic metre of the chorus picks up the elegiacs of her monody. If the preserved text is correct Hermione enters saying that Menelaos gave her royal robes on her marriage so that she might be able to speak as a free woman. This is clearly the prelude to her tirade against Andromache, but it is a curious beginning if addressed to the chorus, who have just expressed their fear of Hermione; perhaps Euripides wanted from the start to emphasize her feeling of insecurity. She accuses Andromache of poisoning her so that she is childless, while Andromache, like a typical incestuous barbarian, gives children to her husband's murderer. Andromache answers that she has no wish for children: Hermione is always taunting Neoptolemos with the greatness of Sparta; a wife ought to help a husband even in his love-affairs. Hermione then threatens to burn Andromache off the altar of Thetis. This is the only surviving debate between a bad woman and a good woman (the debate between Klytemnestra and Elektra is a very special case), and enables us to imagine what the clash between Themisto and Ino in the *Ino*[4] was like.

[3] Nothing is known of the relation of this play to Sophocles' *Hermione*.
[4] Cf. above, p. 98.

The chorus sing of the Judgement of Paris and wish that Hekabe had killed him when Kassandra prophesied: Andromache would still be a queen, and Greek wives and parents would not be desolate. Metre and theme links this with the parodos; the style is perhaps less decorated than in the parodos of the *Hippolytus* but can be classed with it. Menelaos arrives with the child and offers Andromache the alternatives of dying herself or seeing the child die. Andromache attacks. Should the conqueror of Troy fight with a slave? Her death will be murder. The child's death will mean the expulsion of Hermione, and who will marry her? Menelaos again offers her the alternatives, and Andromache. saying that life has no pleasure for her, gives herself up. (We have suggested above that Danae in her name-play[5] was faced with a rather similar choice.) Having lured Andromache off the altar, Menelaos says that he will give the child to Hermione to kill.

The chorus sing of the evils of double marriages – like double tyrannies, quarrelling poets, discordant steersmen; the proof lies in Hermione. Then they see Andromache and the boy being led out by Menelaos to die. Andromache and the boy sing glyconics; Menelaos recites anapaests. (Again as in the *Alcestis* the actor who takes the mother must also sing the child's part.) At this lowest moment the aged Peleus arrives. A furious altercation with Menelaos follows: all Spartan women are unchaste; you had not the sense to see you were well rid of Helen nor to kill her when you got her back; you got all the glory as general while others did the work; get out and take your barren cow with you. Menelaos can only answer that the Trojan War taught Greece military skill and that Peleus is setting up the Trojans to rule the Greeks; he then retires saying that he will return. Peleus takes Andromache and the boy off to his palace.[6]

The chorus sing (again in dactylo-epitrites) of the value of Arete and the worthlessness of unjust victory: they believe in the great exploits of Peleus. The nurse reports that Hermione is trying to commit suicide, and she comes out to sing a lyric dialogue – she sings dochmiacs and prosodiacs; the nurse speaks trimeters. The nurse regards her present fears that her father has abandoned her and that Neoptolemos will throw her out as no less excessive than her savage treatment of Andromache.

[5] See above, p. 94.
[6] Note the reminiscences of *Telephos* fr. 723N² in 581; of the rejuvenation of Iolaos in *Heracl.* in 551f., 761ff.

(Here again this scene gives us some idea of how Euripides may have treated Phaidra at the end of the *First Hippolytos* and Themisto after the death of the children in the *Ino*.) Orestes arrives, like Aigeus in the *Medea*, unprepared but well motivated. Hermione begs him to save her: she has listened to the Siren words of gossips (again as with Peleus' description of Spartan women and generals the colouring is completely modern). Orestes has been waiting for this and takes her home: he has planned death for Neoptolemos in Delphi.

The chorus sing, again in dactylo-epitrites, of the sack of Troy, the death of Agamemnon and Klytemnestra (with Apollo's part hushed in an aposiopesis); Hellas and Troy both suffered. Peleus returns having heard of Hermione's flight. He is met by the messenger who recounts Neoptolemos' death in Delphi, the result of Orestes' plot and Apollo's complicity – Apollo, whom the chorus could not believe to have commanded matricide. Euripides has been very careful to indicate time here:[7] Neoptolemos at the beginning of the play is said to be in Delphi. The messenger reports that Neoptolemos devoted three days to sightseeing during which Orestes sowed his rumours; so that we should think of Orestes leaving Delphi for Phthia before the day on which Neoptolemos decided to sacrifice and was murdered. The messenger-speech is followed immediately by the arrival of the body, and Peleus and the chorus burst into a lyric dialogue, the last of the three lyric dialogues in this play. Thetis appears on the *mechane* and instructs Peleus to bury Neoptolemos in Delphi, to establish Andromache in Molossia, and to join her for eternity.

Once it is seen that Euripides is dealing in turn with each of the three persons whose lives have become intertwined, the structure of the play becomes admirably clear. Each of the chief parties has a low point marked by a lyric dialogue before relief comes: Andromache when she is led out to die, Hermione when she tries to commit suicide, Peleus when he receives Neoptolemos' body. The characters are conceived realistically, and the vulgarity and self-interest of Hermione and Menelaos contrast uglily with the nobility of Andromache, Peleus, and Neoptolemos. As a foil to the rather sordid happenings in Greece the story of the Trojan war is told in dactylo-epitrites (or kindred metres) in the first, third, and fourth stasimon; and it is with these that the elegiac

[7] Cf. A. Lesky, *A.A.W.*, 84, 1947 = *Ges. Schr.*, 144f.

lament of Andromache at the beginning and the first strophe and anti-strophe of the lyric lament of Peleus at the end are associated, emotionally and thematically as well as metrically.

HECUBA

Euripides also composed choruses in decorated style about the Trojan war as a foil to the realism of the iambic scenes for the *Hecuba*, which probably belongs with the *Aiolos* and the *Supplices* to his next production. It is a reasonable conjecture that Sophocles' *Polyxene* was earlier, because Euripides echoes at the beginning lines spoken in that play by the ghost of Achilles (523P). Sophocles' play seems to have followed the order of the *Nostoi*, and the ghost of Achilles appeared in the course of the play after the quarrel between Menelaos and Agamemnon. Euripides started with the ghost of Polydoros, just as later he started his *Andromeda* with the spectacle of Andromeda already chained to the rock, whereas Sophocles had echoed the binding scene of the *Prometheus Vinctus*.[8] How Sophocles developed the play we do not know. The voluntary death of Polyxene in Euripides is more likely to have come from his own *Heraclidae* than from Sophocles.

Polydoros is able to tell the audience both the story of his own murder and the proposal to sacrifice Polyxene, which make the two themes of the play. The parodos starts with Hekabe coming out on her stick, helped by her attendants (who will be needed for more gruesome work later): she sings an anapaestic monody in terror at her dreams about Polydoros and Polyxene. The chorus of captive Trojan women enter with a long passage of recitative anapaests: they can report the Greek debate about the sacrifice to Achilles; Odysseus will come to fetch Polyxene. This is followed by an anapaestic lyric dialogue in which Hekabe expresses her misery and summons Polyxene; Polyxene is told her fate, and in the antistrophe she grieves more for her mother than for herself.

Odysseus (who belongs to the same breed as Menelaos in the *Andromache*) enters to fetch Polyxene. Hekabe argues that she saved him; he is merely an ungrateful demagogue; Achilles ought to demand the sacrifice of Helen rather than Polyxene; he should persuade the Greeks not to kill a slave girl whom they have already spared. Odysseus answers

[8] See below, p. 193.

that there is a patriotic necessity to honour the heroic dead. Hekabe calls on Polyxene to plead for herself, but Polyxene refuses: she would rather die than live as a slave when she was born to be a queen. As in the *Heraclidae*, Euripides has made a situation in which youthful heroism is entirely natural; here too Hekabe begs to be allowed to die instead. Polyxene tells Odysseus to lead her away, and Hekabe falls to the ground cursing Helen.

In a wonderful decorated aeolo-choriambic ode the chorus wonder where they will be taken – Doris or Phthia or Delos or Athens – now that Troy is in flames and they are slaves. Talthybios, Agamemnon's herald, enters full of pity for Hekabe. She hopes he has come to kill her (a variant on Alkmene's mistake in the *Heraclidae*, 545f.). But he tells the story of Polyxene's death. Hekabe muses on the immutability of noble character when assisted by education.[9] (This is one answer to Phaidra's dilemma in the *Hippolytus*.) She sends her old slave to fetch water to wash Polyxene's body. A brief beautiful ode traces the misery of Troy and Greece back to Paris' voyage and the Judgement on Ida. The old slave comes back with others carrying a dead body which she has found on the shore. Thus the two stories are linked, and Hekabe in a lyric lament recognizes the truth of her dream: Polydoros has been killed by his host, Polymestor.

Agamemnon comes in, to fetch Hekabe for the burial of Polyxene. Hekabe hesitates for a long time and then begs him to punish Poly-mestor. It is his duty to uphold the law on which all civil and religious order is based. (Agamemnon draws away.) She turns to persuasion: he loves Kassandra. Agamemnon fears he may be slandered by the army. Hekabe then asks him to give her freedom to act alone with her women (the women who supported her on to the stage at the beginning of the play) and to get her maid through with a message to Polymestor. Agamemnon agrees also that Polydoros shall be buried with Polyxene (894–8, this is the signal for removing his body).

The chorus sing another decorated song about the last night in Troy and the Greek capture, ending with a curse on Helen. Polymestor arrives with his children, excuses himself for not visiting Hekabe before, tells her that Polydoros is well (perhaps one may recall the Sophoclean Tereus' return to Prokne here, 585P) and Hekabe lures him into her hut with his children by promising him gold and secrets. This is the first

[9] On the idea cf. above, p. 23.

preserved of several 'luring' scenes: later Klytemnestra in the *Electra*, Lykos in the *H.F.* and Lykos in the *Antiope* are obvious examples.

The chorus excitedly sing in dochmiacs of his punishment. Then he is heard crying out that he is blind and that he cannot get out. Hekabe comes out and says 'You shall see him soon, coming in front of the house, blind, with blind, mad gait, and the bodies of his two children. . . . As you see, he is coming out of the house' (1053); then later (1117) Agamemnon says, 'Who blinded you and killed these children?' As earlier in the *Alcestis*,[10] the terminology suggests entrance, but the bodies of the children must have been brought out on the *ekkyklema*. Probably the *ekkyklema* rolls out, as Hekabe speaks (1053) with the bodies of the children and Polymestor on all fours. Polymestor sings mostly in dochmiacs of his misery, of his incapability of taking vengeance, of the impossibility of escape.

Agamemnon arrives in answer to his shouts, and is prepared to listen to both sides. Polymestor claims that he killed Polydoros to prevent a reoccupation of Troy and the need for another Trojan war, which would also have threatened him. Then he tells what the women did to him (which is, in effect, a messenger speech spoken by a character). Hekabe tears his defence to pieces: he killed for gold, otherwise he would have killed earlier and given Agamemnon the gold. Agamemnon gives judgment for Hekabe. Polymestor prophesies her transformation into a bitch and the murder of Kassandra and Agamemnon. Agamemnon gives orders for him to be cast away on a desert island, tells Hekabe to bury her children, and the chorus to go to the tents of their masters.

The likeness of the end of this play to the end of the *Heraclidae* is clear. Euripides has developed further the portrait of a mother driven mad by suffering to take a cruel vengeance on her torturer. Here the vengeance is fully portrayed instead of only being threatened. But here too, like Eurystheus, Polymestor after his terrible blinded entry (prepared by the *Phoinix*, if not also by the *O.T.*) attains a certain dignity, and Euripides has made him, like the prophet of the *Likymnios*, the seer whose dreadful truth is not believed.

There are points of comparison also with the *Andromache*, particularly in the pattern made by the choral odes and the lyric dialogues, but unlike the *Heraclidae* and *Andromache* this play is dominated by a single

[10] Cf. above, p. 49.

figure, Hekabe, whose suffering turns to mad fury beneath the strain, as she reacts in turn to the odious Odysseus, the heroic Polyxene, the sympathetic Talthybios, the weak Agamemnon, and the villainous Polymestor.

SUPPLICES

The *Supplices* is so close to the *Hecuba* on metrical statistics that it was probably produced in the same year. It also is connected with the *Heraclidae* because it is a traditional suppliant play. More particularly Aeschylus[11] had dealt with the same subject in the *Eleusinioi*, but there Theseus persuaded the Thebans to allow the Seven to be buried, and made a truce instead of fighting a battle: perhaps Euripides introduced the battle to show for what ideals a democracy should be prepared to fight.

As in the *Heraclidae*, the suppliants are at a temple, here the temple of Demeter and Kore at Eleusis, to which Aithra has come to sacrifice for the harvest. The suppliants are the mothers of the Seven, the sons of the Seven (106), and Adrastos, the father-in-law of Tydeus and Polyneikes, who looks after the women and boys, as Iolaos looks after the sons and daughters of Herakles. But here the mothers form the chorus and the boys a subsidiary chorus at the end of the play. Euripides had probably used such a special chorus in the *Peliades* and *Theseus*,[12] but here the compelling analogy was the Aeschylean *Hiketides*. Aeschylus had felt no qualms about representing fifty daughters of Danaos by a chorus of twelve. Euripides makes his chorus of fifteen say that they are *seven* mothers, although he can hardly have included Iokaste among them and is careful to exclude Amphiaraos, as well as Polyneikes, from the funeral orations (925).

In the parodos the Mothers sing two ionic strophes and antistrophes begging Aithra to ransom the bodies of their sons, followed by an iambic strophe and antistrophe of lamentation. Theseus arrives in answer to Aithra's summons. Adrastos pleads with him to secure the burial of the dead. Theseus answers with a general account of civilization

---

[11] This is implied by Plutarch, *Theseus*, 29. Mette suggests that Aeschylus' *Argeiai* had a chorus composed of the wives of the Seven. This may have suggested to Euripides his chorus of the mothers of the Seven and the lament of Evadne; but Mette's conjecture cannot be confirmed.

[12] See above, p. 34.

as the gift of god; Adrastos' difficulties arise from his disregard of divine warnings against the expedition, led astray by young men who did not belong to the safe middle class. Theseus' beginning would be much more intelligible if Adrastos had said that the gods have no control over human affairs and Murray's transference of 549ff. after 179f. would provide for this. Theseus' account of civilization and of the three classes in the state perhaps comes from Protagoras, and in any case puts the story into modern Athenian terms, like Hekabe's description of Odysseus as a demagogue and Peleus' description of Menelaos as a *strategos*.[13]

Theseus rejects Adrastos. Adrastos tells the Mothers to call the gods to witness that their prayers have no effect. Someone appeals to kinship: Pittheus, the father of Aithra, was the son of Pelops. The beginning is lost, so that it is not clear whether the lines are spoken by Adrastos or the chorus, but Adrastos seems to have finished. The Mothers then make their appeal in hexameters. Aithra weeping, enters the argument: do not dishonour the gods; the Thebans are confounding the common customs of all Greece by refusing burial to the dead. Theseus yields; he will get the bodies of the Seven back by persuasion or force; but first he must secure the goodwill of the people and take Aithra home. The chorus sing an excited little ode, wondering what the city will decide.

Theseus returns to report the city's decision and to send his herald to Thebes, but a Theban herald arrives at the same moment. He asks who is the tyrant here. Theseus answers that Athens is a democracy. The herald enlarges on the vices of democracy and Theseus on the evils of tyranny (again a purely fifth-century political debate). Then the Theban tells Theseus to expel Adrastos and have nothing to do with the corpses of the Seven, or else meet war with Thebes: it is foolish to choose war instead of peace in unsure hope; the gods punished Kapaneus and the rest justly. Theseus, preventing Adrastos from breaking in, replies that he will preserve Panhellenic law and bury the Seven; what have the Thebans to fear from the burial? The herald is sent off. Theseus makes his preparations, leaving Adrastos behind.

The Mothers call on the gods, wondering what is happening in the battle and how they will get home. The messenger, a servant of

[13] *Hec.* 244; *Andr.* 694. Cf. above, p. 23.

Kapaneus who had been captured in the earlier battle of the Seven, reports Theseus' victory. Adrastos is told that the bodies of the Seven are being brought, and he goes out to meet them. The Mothers welcome the news, but wish they had never been married and had children (like Iphis later). Adrastos enters with the corpses and laments them in a lyric dialogue with the Mothers. Theseus asks who these incredibly brave warriors were. Adrastos praises the five, and Theseus says that he knows about Amphiaraos and Polyneikes. Adrastos' portraits are in conscious contrast to the purely military portraits of the same heroes in their splendour, which Aeschylus had given in the *Septem*. Each is a great warrior: Kapaneus eschewed banquets, Eteoklos rejected gifts of money, Hippomedon was a rustic who had no use for the Muses, Parthenopaios (like Hippolytos) was uninterested in male or female lovers, Tydeus was greedy of honour. In later plays Euripides continually returns to these contrasting elements in men's lives. Here he stresses the military virtues of the Seven by denying them other forms of enjoyment.

Theseus arranges that Kapaneus shall be buried 'beside this building' (and his body is carried by attendants through the central door). The sons will go with Theseus and Adrastos to cremate the others and will return with their bones. This sets the scheme for the end of the play, which might be termed war as it affects individuals. First, the Mothers sing of the utter misery of childless old age. Then startlingly the *ekkyklema* rolls out with the tomb of Kapaneus and his wife Evadne perched on a rock above it. She sings of her marriage day and her intention to leap into the flaming tomb (her song is linked by its aeolic metre to the preceding song of the mothers).[14] Thirdly the aged Iphis, father of Eteoklos as well as father of Evadne, comes to find her and tries vainly to stop her leaping into the tomb. (Euripides has converted the reported suicide of Laodameia in the *Protesilaos* into a stage scene for this play.)[15] The old man speaks (like the Mothers) of the utter misery of old age and is then led off. The sons are seen carrying the bones of their fathers. They share the lamentation with their grandmothers. (For this their parts are probably taken by a subsidiary chorus, unless we can suppose that Euripides adapted the technique which he had used in the *Alcestis* and *Andromache*: there an actor sang the child's part and the

[14] Wilamowitz, *Griechische Verskunst*, 550ff.
[15] See above, p. 98. On Euripides' purpose here see J. de Romilly, *L'Évolution du pathétique*, 37.

child mimed it. Here it is conceivable that the chorus sang the sons' part while the sons mimed it and the chorus then sang their own part and mimed it themselves. The subsidiary choruses of which we know in Euripides – in *Hippolytus*, *Alexandros*, *Antiope*, *Phaethon* – are different; they are firmly associated with a single character.[16] The subsidiary chorus at the end of Aeschylus' *Eumenides* is more like this, but they do not sing a lyric dialogue with the main chorus.) It only remains for Athena to remind Theseus that he must take an oath from Adrastos and consecrate the place where the bodies had been cremated, thus tying the play on to a well-known Athenian monument.[17]

Finally she prophesies that the sons will capture Thebes so that this play, in which Theseus was outspoken against a war conducted against the omens, and only fought himself to secure a Panhellenic ideal, this play in which the effects of war on mothers, wives, fathers, and children had been so devastatingly demonstrated, ends with the prophecy of another war, but the prophecy tells us nothing of Euripides' views: the epilogue takes the story back to mythology again. Euripides' own view is rather given by his casting the traditional story into a fifth century mould so that Theseus' sanity has its full impact, and by the devastating parade of sufferers at the end of the play.

ERECHTHEUS

The *Erechtheus*[18] was produced in 422, probably with the *Melanippe Sophe* but the third play cannot be named with certainty. The outline is given in Lycurgus (in *Leocr.* 98) and Plutarch (*Moralia* 310D). Athens was facing an invasion from Eleusis by Eumolpos, son of Poseidon, and his Thracians. Erechtheus inquired of Delphi and was told to sacrifice his daughter. With the agreement of his wife Praxithea, he did so and the invasion was repelled.

The prologue told of the birth of Eumolpos (349N²) and presumably gave the past history in the form that Euripides wanted it. Fr. 366 'Beyond I think the hostile' (so Goossens) 'barbarians dwell' should describe the Thracian-occupied territory beyond Eleusis, and 'I think'

---

[16] See pp. 71, 171, 209, 227.

[17] Cf. G. E. Mylonas, *PAE* 1953 (1956), 81ff.; L. H. Jeffery, *BSA* 60, 1965, 50.

[18] Bibliographical note: U. von Wilamowitz-Moellendorff, *Analecta Euripidea*, 174; *Kl. Schr.*, I, 72; *Ion* 6; R. Goossens, *Euripide et Athènes*, 477; H. J. Mette, *Lustrum* 9, 1964, 179.

fixes the speaker as a man rather than a god, perhaps Erechtheus. But the people who sleep on the ground with unwashen feet (367N²) cannot be the Thracians as Meineke thought; both the sources who quote this refer to the Selloi and fr. 368N² is also referred to Dodona. Erechtheus therefore consulted the oracle at Dodona as well as Delphi.

The great discussion with Praxithea, his wife, must come after the parodos.[19] Erechtheus' feeling that he must overcome his *aidos* (365N²) may belong to the beginning; perhaps Praxithea suggests that an adopted child might be sacrificed instead of his own child (359N²) and is told that they are not valid. She then agrees to the sacrifice of her daughter (360N²): Athens has the peculiar virtue of being autochthonous; the purpose of having children is to protect the city; one family should suffer for the many Athenian families; 'If there was in the house a male crop instead of women, should I not have sent them out to fight?' Mothers should gladly give their children for the city. This is a unique glory for my daughter. 'She will save her mother and you and her two sisters.' Never shall Eumolpos and his Thracians worship Poseidon in this city.

A fragment asking why so many cakes are being sent out of the house (350N²) may belong to the daughter who perceives the preparations for the sacrifice. The only hint that the daughter does not accept self-sacrifice as cheerfully as her mother offers it is a fragment of Ennius (IIR): 'Many are stony-hearted and pity nobody.' In the end she undoubtedly agrees: 'honourable death is a truer life than ignoble life' (361N²): 'I win them liberty by my trouble, I save them from slavery by my misery' (Ennius IR) – whether this is part of her final speech or part of the report of her death. It is perhaps when she is led off to die that Erechtheus tells the other daughters to love their mother (358N²).

After the report of her death Erechtheus makes a long speech of advice to 'his son' in case he shall die (362N²) telling him to behave fairly to rich and poor, to get his wealth justly, to choose worthy friends, not to seduce the children of the worthy poor, nor to give authority to bad favourites. Eteokles' last speech to Kreon in the *Phoenissae* (748) is similar in intent, though very different in content. But who is this 'son'? The words of Praxithea (360, 22) quoted above

[19] Possibly 370N², 'notes of the Asian lyre' (parodied in Ar. *Thesm.* 120) comes from an appeal to Apollo in the parodos.

rule out his being a son of Erechtheus, and Mette must therefore be wrong in invoking the tradition that a younger Kekrops was Erechtheus' son. Wilamowitz suggested the grandson Ion. But if he is a grandson old enough to succeed, would Praxithea have omitted to mention him? Adopted children are mentioned (359N²), and the easiest solution may be to suppose that in this play Xouthos appeared as a young adopted son of Erechtheus.

A few more fragments belong to Erechtheus' preparations (352–4N²); he insists on the justice of his position and on the folly of going to war without the goodwill of the gods. This, as we have seen, was the position of Theseus in the *Supplices*, and we know that Erechtheus has consulted Delphi and Dodona. Curiously in the *Phoenissae* (852f.) Teiresias says that he is tired by the journey from Athens, where he had made the Erechtheidai victorious over Eumolpos. Perhaps then Erechtheus had also summoned Teiresias to help him, and this scene may have been accommodated here. Before his departure for battle Erechtheus calls on the women to sing cheerfully that Athena may come and help the city (351N²). Wilamowitz supposed that these women formed the chorus, and that the lyric prayer for peace (369N²) was sung by a subsidiary chorus of victorious soldiers. There are two difficulties here: the lesser is that such a subsidiary chorus would not conform to the pattern as known.[20] The greater is that 'may I crown my *hoary* head' and 'read books' is a curious sentiment for victorious soldiers. It is more likely that this is the main chorus, elderly defenders of the city, and that the women told to sing are Praxithea and her household. It is of course very possible that the period of the battle was covered by a monody or lyric dialogue of Praxithea praying for victory followed by the chorus's prayer for peace; and the prayer for peace may be followed as in the *Heraclidae* (371ff.) by a statement of belief in just war.

A messenger reported the battle (Ennius, fr. IIIR), the death of Eumolpos, and presumably the death of Erechtheus. Perhaps his body was brought back, and Athena announced that he would be paid divine honours (but fr. 930N², 'Oh dear! half of me is already a snake', ascribed to this play by Wilamowitz must surely come from comedy and is referred by the Scholiast to Kekrops). Certainly the transformation of the daughters into Hyades was mentioned (357N²) and

[20] See p. 127 above, on *Supplices*.

this can only have been in an epilogue speech. Three girls are mentioned, and Praxithea speaks of the girl who is to be sacrificed and her two sisters whom she will save. One of the sisters may have been Kreousa and her marriage to Xouthos may have been forecast by Erechtheus (unless it had already taken place). This would bring the mythology into line with the prologue of the *Melanippe Sophe*, where Euripides must have had some reason for introducing Xouthos, Kreousa, and Ion into the pedigree of Hellen; his reason may have been that he was going to use this version in the *Erechtheus*. The catasterism of the daughters is therefore a distant, not a near future.

It is difficult to assess this play. The political philosophy clearly comes from the same spirit as the *Supplices*, and the sacrifice of the daughter is in the tradition of the *Heraclidae* and the *Hecuba*. Klytemnestra in the *Electra* (1024f.), condemning Agamemnon's sacrifice of Iphigeneia, says that 'it would be excusable if he had killed one girl to save many, to save the city from capture or to benefit his house and save his other children'. The reference back to this play is clear, and Erechtheus was prepared to face death himself and was probably killed. Praxithea's speech to the modern ear is unforgivable, but we do not really know how it was counterpoised in the economy of the play.

Additional note. I owe to Dr Colin Austin knowledge of a new papyrus which he is to publish in *Récherches de Papyrologie IV*. This gives the end of the play. What can be made out with some certainty is as follows: the male chorus sing of their hopes of victory (this may perhaps be the end of the same chorus as 369N^2). A messenger announces to Praxithea that both Eumolpos and Erechtheus are dead. Praxithea laments her husband and her daughters. Then some excited lyric lines seem to accompany an earthquake. Athena appears and instructs Praxithea about the burial and cult of the daughters (they are to be called Hyakinthides *not* Hyades; and all three had died at the same time – if therefore, as I think, Kreousa was mentioned earlier, she was already married to Xouthos), about the burial and cult of Erechtheus–Poseidon 'in the middle of the city', and about the priesthood to be given to Praxithea herself. Finally she tells what arrangements Zeus is making for the succession of Eumolpos in Eleusis. It is tempting to connect Athena's speech with the building of the Erechtheion, which housed the cult of Erechtheus–Poseidon. (It looks as if the new fragment may raise the percentage of resolutions to about 20%.)

2 *Phrixos A and B*

The Oxyrrhynchos hypotheses must now be the starting point in reconstructing the two plays about Phrixos. The hypothesis of *Phrixos A* (*P. Oxy.* 2455, fr. 14, col. xvi) shows that 821N² was the prologue: a man states that he is already broken in to misery and today's misery is not the beginning (his identity is unknown). Such a beginning recalls the *Heraclidae, Andromache, Stheneboia,* and would suggest a date before 420 B.C. Athamas in this play was king of Thessaly. Ino was apparently his second wife and behaved like a stepmother. Van Looy[21] finds in συνκαλε – a reference to Ino gathering the women to roast the seed corn, but this is hazardous. Then after a considerable gap the papyrus ends with the enigmatic statement 'but thinking him nearer kin than one who used his father's thunderbolt because of a woman'. Professor Turner suggests that the subject is a son of Zeus but 'his father's' may only refer to the subject of 'used'; this was perhaps Dionysos, if in this version he saved or had saved Ino by a use of Zeus' thunderbolt.[22] We cannot therefore say whether the statement means that Phrixos sacrificed the ram to some other god whom he thought 'more akin' than Dionysos or that Hermes gave Phrixos the ram because he thought him 'more akin' than Dionysos. If the second is right, the play ended with the salvation of Phrixos, and must have covered the same span of action as Phrixos B.

But the end of the hypothesis is so obscure and so difficult to read that the subject of the play may have been quite different. Tzetzes (N², p. 627) expressly calls the second play the first play: if he was using a collection of hypotheses which numbered the plays by the chronological sequence of their actions,[23] this confusion would be natural, if the action of what we call *Phrixos A* took place after the action of what we call *Phrixos B* and ended with Phrixos' sacrifice of the ram. The only case of a second play being a straight revision of a first play is the *Hippolytus*, which is a very special case. A clue may be given here by the two Melanippe plays: there Euripides completely altered the story and changed the setting from Greece to Italy but preserved the names of Melanippe and her sons. In *Phrixos B*, according to the hypothesis

[21] *Zes Tragedien*, 132ff.
[22] For Dionysos using lightning cf. *Bacch.* 594–5 with Dodds' note.
[23] Cf. the hypotheses published in *Récherches de Papyrologie*, III, 37f.

(*P. Oxy.* 2455, fr. 17, col. xix) Athamas was king of Orchomenos instead of king of Thessaly. I suggest that Euripides changed the setting not so much with reference to *Phrixos A* as to contrast his new play with the *Ino*,[24] which also had Athamas and Ino as characters but quite a different story. In *Phrixos A*, if the main story was Phrixos' adventures in Kolchis, Euripides may have left Athamas and Ino in Thessaly because this was only prologue information. The sacrifice of the ram is painted by a Lucanian vase painter[25] who often draws scenes from the theatre, but we cannot even guess at the course of the play.

The hypothesis of *Phrixos B* fixes 819N² as the prologue, which gives the genealogy of Kadmos.[26] The genealogy may have been given by a god but perhaps Ino is a more likely speaker, as Iphigeneia in *I. T.* and Melanippe in the *Melanippe Sophe*. *Telephos* already had a genealogical prologue, but it is alive because Telephos has returned to the land of his ancestors; the earliest example of this kind of flat genealogical narration is the *Melanippe Sophe*, which was probably produced in 422 B.C.

The hypothesis puts Athamas in Orchomenos instead of Thessaly. He is living with Ino. Nephele's children Helle and Phrixos are then mentioned, but it is not clear whether their birth postdates (Turner: προσεγέννησεν) or antedates (Parsons: προγεγεννηκώς) the marriage with Ino. Then after an obscure passage the hypothesis ends: 'to him who was being plotted against (Phrixos). She (Ino) having summoned Dionysos escaped certain death. For Dionysos drove Phrixos and his sister Helle mad and led them into a deserted place to cause their destruction by the maenads. Nephele flew down and rescued her children and gave them a ram for a good journey.'

Here we know both the artistic and the literary tradition. The Attic neck amphora[27] which shows a woman with an axe (a maenad rather than Ino?) attacking Phrixos as he takes to the ram is too early for Euripides' play, and attests the story before him. The Paestan kalyx krater by Assteas is inspired by Euripides: Nephele and Dionysos appear in the background as the ram carries Phrixos and Helle over the

[24] See above, p. 98.

[25] See list of illustrations, p. 304.

[26] 820N² perhaps also belongs here: Europa was probably the sister rather than the niece of Kadmos according to this version; R. Cantarella, *I Cretesi*, 46 gives the fragment to the *Cretans*.

[27] See list of illustrations, p. 303.

sea. Hyginus, *Fab.* 2, 3–5; 3, 1, gives the same story (I give only the portions given by the hypothesis because Euripides may not be the source for the rest): *rex facinore cognito uxorem suam Ino et filium eius Melicerten Phrixo dedidit necandos. quos, cum ad supplicium duceret, Liber pater ei caliginem iniecit et Ino suam nutricem eripuit . . . Phrixus et Helle, insania a Libero injecta cum in silva errarent, Nebula mater eo dicitur venisse et arietem inauratum adduxisse, Neptuni et Theophanes filium, eumque natos suos ascendere iussit et Colchos ad regem Aeolum* (sic) *Solis filium transire ibique arietem Marti immolare.*

The other fragment expressly ascribed to *Phrixos B* shows that the earlier part of Hyginus, *Fab.* 2 also comes from Euripides: 827N² 'and yet you did not think of opening the corn-bins'. According to Hyginus *Fab.* 2, 1–3, Ino, wanting to kill Phrixos and Helle, made a plot; she persuaded the women to roast the corn which she was to issue for sow- ing. The result was famine and pestilence. 2. Athamas sent a *satelles* to Delphi; Ino ordered this *satelles* to report that the sacrifice of Phrixos would relieve the famine. Athamas refused to sacrifice his son; Phrixos volunteered. 3. *itaque cum ad aram cum infulis esset adductus, satelles misericordia adulescentis Inus Athamanti consilium patefecit; rex facinore cognito* etc. 'Therefore when he had been brought to the altar arrayed for sacrifice, the *satelles* out of pity for the young man betrayed Ino's plot to Athamas.'

Long ago Schadewaldt[28] discussed a Florence papyrus (Page, *G.L.P.*, no. 32) in connexion with the *Phrixos* fragments and Hyginus. The papyrus gives the confrontation of Ino, Athamas, and the *satelles*. The old man says that he received the seed to sow the fields from Ino. Ino denies it. The old man reiterates his charge and accuses Ino of slaying Athamas' son. Now that the new hypothesis shows that Hyginus was drawing on Euripides, the double agreement with Hyginus and with 827N² makes it fairly certain that this papyrus also comes from *Phrixos B*. Whatever is the correct reading of 827N² it clearly came near the papyrus passage.

Schadewaldt naturally worked other fragments into the Hyginus structure: 819N² prologue; 828N², description of the famine, which is very close to the priest's appeal to Oedipus in *O.T.* 56f.; 830N², description of the old man (Schadewaldt noted that *penestes* is used here in a non-technical sense as in *Hcld.* 639, and it is arguable that Euripides

[28] *Hermes*, 63, 1928, 1.

would *not* have used this Thessalian term in a play with a Thessalian setting like *Phrixos A*); 833N^2, Phrixos' proposal of self-sacrifice[29] – here the obvious parallel is the death of Menoikeus in the *Phoenissae*, and Kreon's attempt to prevent it (852ff.).

A new papyrus in Oxford[30] gives us an earlier moment. The details are obscure, but the general line seems to be (1) Athamas laments in despair; the nine lines are either a monody or the end of the antistrophe or epode of a kommos: the metre is mixed anapaestic, dochmiac, dactylic with closest parallels in *Or.* 1363–4, *Hel.* 383–5. (2) The chorus see a procession of slaves bearing offerings coming out of the house followed by Ino.[31] Pheres similarly appears with slaves bringing funeral offerings in the *Alcestis* 611f. The sex of the chorus of Orchomenians is not clear. (3) Iambic dialogue between Ino and Athamas. Ino seems to say that she is using her dowry to give offerings for the funeral of Phrixos (fr. 1, 19f.). Athamas tells her to go in (fr. 2, 7). She answers at length on the virtues of a wife in helping her husband (10–13 = 822N^2) and the chorus apparently support her (823N^2).

It is at least possible that the old man is part of the funeral procession, particularly if he came from Ino's home, which seems to me the natural interpretation of 830N^2 λάτρις πενέστης ἀμὸς ἀρχαίων δόμων.[32] If this is so, presumably he breaks into Ino's protestations of loyalty to Athamas with the truth about the forged oracle, and the story of the corn is then extracted from him (Florence papyrus). The extraction of truth has obvious analogies with the scenes with the Corinthian and the Theban in Sophocles' *O.T.* Iokaste like Ino tries to prevent the revelation. Here the treachery of Ino's servant is remarkable. The nurse in the *First Hippolytus* may have similarly betrayed her mistress to Theseus. We have no reason to doubt Hyginus' statement that he acted out of pity for Phrixos.

The rest of the play is outlined by the hypothesis and Hyginus but they do not distinguish between action, messenger-speech, and *deus ex*

[29] For the sentiment 'the dead have no suffering' in this situation cf. *Alc.* 937; *Hcld.* 591ff.; *Hec.* 378 (variant); *Erechtheus*, fr. 361N^2.

[30] I am grateful to Dr John Rea for showing me this.

[31] Such sequences in anapaestic dimeters are common, cf. particularly *Or.* 1012, *Hyps.* I, iv, 10; *I.T.* 456–66.

[32] Cf. the description of Klytemnestra's dower-slave, at the moment when he betrays his master (*I.A.* 868, where the MSS. reading should be kept).

machina. Athamas must condemn Ino to death on the stage. Presumably he sent the old man into the house to be incarcerated, and thus Euripides gained an actor to play Phrixos. The hypothesis apparently says nothing of Ino's son Melikertes and he may have been introduced by Hyginus from the Ino story, but Helle, who is mentioned in the hypothesis, must have been a mute character who came out with Phrixos. Perhaps we may suppose here a lyric dialogue between Athamas and Phrixos, Athamas overjoyed at his son's escape from sacrifice. 835N², justice at length overtakes the evil-doer, may well belong to the context when Athamas hands Ino over to Phrixos.

The simplest solution for the rest is to suppose that the scene closes with Ino's prayer to Dionysos to save her in return for her nursing him in the past, and that she is then led off by Phrixos and Helle. Then after a chorus one of Phrixos' attendants returns and tells the story. Euripides could, of course, have dramatized the madness of Phrixos, but this would have left Ino on the stage, and the curious word of the hypothesis διώλισθεν implies rather that she faded out of the story.

The messenger can relate that Phrixos and Helle suddenly went mad when Phrixos was on the point of killing Ino. Ino escaped and the messenger followed Phrixos and Helle into a deserted place (Hyginus says a forest) where they were attacked by maenads, but Nephele flew down and gave them the ram. The play may have ended with Athamas' acceptance of the messenger's news but it is perhaps more likely that either Nephele herself or Dionysos appeared *ex machina* and told the story of the flight to Kolchis. If we knew that *Phrixos B* contained Euripides' description of the Stymphalian birds (838N²) we could be certain that the play had such an epilogue, but the fragment may belong to *Phrixos A*.

Neither the hypothesis nor Hyginus tell us where the play started but the difficulties of timing and the analogy of the O.T. suggest that the play began when the old man had nearly arrived back in Orchomenos from Delphi.

This suggests the following outline:

Prologue: Ino fr. 819, 820N² tells of her hatred of Phrixos and Helle, her roasting the seed-corn which the old man distributed; the famine; the mission of the old man to Delphi.

Parodos: Orchomenian women (?) pray for release from the plague (in this context fr. 828N²).

Epeisodia: The old man arrives. Ino commands him to tell Athamas that the oracle demands the sacrifice of Phrixos (fr. 824N² may belong here).

The old man tells Athamas and Athamas refuses to sacrifice his son (like Kreon with Menoikeus in the *Phoenissae*).

Phrixos learns the situation, whether from Ino or from Athamas himself, and heroically confronts Athamas with his decision (fr. 829; 832–3; 834N² may belong here). Phrixos goes into the house to be dressed for sacrifice.

Athamas abandons himself to grief. Ino comes out of the house with attendants bearing rich offerings for the sacrifice, among them the old man. She affirms her ability to comfort Athamas (*P. Oxy. ined.*; fr. 822–3N²).

The old man bursts out with the truth and the whole story is extracted from him in the presence of Ino (Page, no. 32; fr. 827, 830N²).

The old man is sent in to punishment. Phrixos and Helle are summoned out. Lyric dialogue between father and son. Ino is handed over to Phrixos for punishment (fr. 835N²). Ino's prayer to Dionysos. Exeunt Phrixos, Helle, Ino, Attendants.

Stasimon.

Messenger-speech: Ino's escape. Madness of Phrixos and Helle. Attack of the maenads. Nephele and the ram.

Deus ex machina: the voyage to Kolchis.

For the last time Euripides seems to have given here an uncomplicated portrait of a bad woman, but the play belongs to Athamas and Phrixos rather than to Ino, and Ino's plot leads to the devastating scene where a father knowingly and against his will sends his son to death and then is reprieved by an almost equally shattering revelation of the truth about his wife. Ino's plot and her use of Athamas to execute it recalls Medeia's plot against Theseus in the *Aigeus*, but Aigeus did not know the identity of his son and the foiled execution was told in a messenger speech, whereas here the whole sequence was acted on the stage.

3 *Kresphontes and Electra*

The reason for treating these two plays together is that in the *Kresphontes* Euripides can be seen trying out ideas which he uses again in his very original *Electra*. The bottom date of the *Kresphontes*[33] is 425 because fr. 453N² is quoted in Aristophanes' *Georgoi*. The top date is unlikely to be much higher because the number of resolutions 16.6% put it in Group II rather than Group I, i.e. after the *Hippolytus* in 428. It was probably produced with the *Andromache* but the third tragedy of this production cannot be identified.

Plutarch (fr. 456N²) quotes the scene in which Merope is stopped by the old man when she has already raised the axe to kill her son. This agrees closely with Hyginus (*fab.* 137) 'Merope came into the *chalcidicum* with an axe to kill her son, not knowing him; the old man recognized him and stopped the mother committing the crime.' This dramatic scene was also mentioned by Aristotle in the *Ethics* (1111a11) and the *Poetics* (1454a5). Hyginus may therefore be used as a guide in reconstructing Euripides' play.

Hyginus' outline is as follows: the elder Kresphontes was killed by his brother Polyphontes, who took possession of his kingdom and his wife Merope. Merope managed to get the baby, young Kresphontes, to a friend in Aetolia (Andromache was unsuccessful in a similar attempt in the *Andromache*, but the old man was successful in saving the child Orestes (E. *El.* 16)). Polyphontes put a price on the boy's head, like Aigisthos (E. *El.* 32). The boy grew up and came back to take vengeance (also like Orestes). He obtained entry by demanding a reward for having killed the young Kresphontes, and Polyphontes told him to wait while he made inquiries. The old man who had acted as a messenger between Merope and her son arrived and reported to her that the young Kresphontes had vanished from his place of exile. Merope assumed that the young man, who had in the meantime gone to sleep, was her son's murderer and was only just prevented from killing him (as described above). She then saw an opportunity of vengeance and pretended to be reconciled to Polyphontes. He made a sacrifice to celebrate this and was killed by Kresphontes, 'who pretended that he had killed the victim and killed him': this sentence only makes sense if it is read with the messenger speech in *Electra* 810ff., where Orestes was invited to cut up the sacrificial calf and then while Aigisthos was looking at the entrails

[33] Bibliographical note: U. von Wilamowitz-Moellendorf, *Analecta Euripidea*, 154 n. 5; N. Hourmouziades, *Production and Imagination*, 105; J. Jory, *B.I.C.S.*, 10, 1963, 67; H. J. Mette, *Hermes*, 92, 1964, 391; *Lustrum*, 9, 1944, 66; E. G. Turner, *Hermes*, 93, 1965, 256.

Orestes killed him. The *Electra* murder is a later variation of the *Kresphontes* murder.

The fragments of Euripides' play and of Ennius' adaptation[34] can be fitted into this story. New evidence is provided by *P. Oxy.* 2458. Fr. 1 consists of parts of three columns. The second column is stichomyth: the first character is told by the second the past history of the house: Polyphontes is ill-disposed to strangers, he killed the old Kresphontes and two of his sons; the baby was smuggled away and may be still alive. The character who is given this information must be the young Kresphontes; he is extracting information without revealing his identity and discovers that he has at least one sympathizer. The audience must know the identity of Kresphontes and he must have revealed it himself in the prologue (not later because the chorus must be kept in ignorance); the preceding column with the words 'father' and 'children' could come from such a monologue. Ennius fr. IR about the partition of the Peloponnese by the Herakleidai must come from this (but the ascription of fr. 1083 N² describing the geography of Messenia is impossible because its iambics are typical of Group IV and Zielinski's ascription to *Temenos* is likely). The first preserved line of the papyrus dialogue 'Is the master of the house inhospitable?' implies that Kresphontes has asked for hospitality and is rebuffed like Menelaos in the *Helen* (437). This fits with Polyphontes' fear of the young Kresphontes. The identity of the second speaker is unclear. Professor Turner's suggestion of Merope is attractive because Euripides liked scenes between mothers and sons who failed to recognize each other. It is a more economical suggestion than Professor Mette's old man, who cannot be the go-between and yet is a sympathizer. But if the speaker is Merope, there are four difficulties, none of which is perhaps fatal: (1) Why does Kresphontes not disclose himself to Merope? He knows who she is and he has come to help her. (2) Why does Merope, if she has seen this sympathetic young man, assume later that he is her son's murderer rather than her son? (3) Why does Merope open her own front door to a stranger? (4) Why is Merope labelled $\overline{\Gamma}$ in the papyrus? The labelling of the speakers $\overline{A}$ and $\overline{\Gamma}$ is unique in a tragic text. The signs (which are ordinal numbers) have been convincingly interpreted as First Actor and Third Actor. It is tiresome that Merope was once played by Theodoros before Jason of Pherai (Aelian, *V.H.* 14, 40) and Theodoros would not have taken a

[34] Ennius fr. III was rightly claimed for comedy by Wilamowitz.

third actor's part; and Kresphontes was played by the third actor Aischines according to Demosthenes (18, 180), but Demosthenes is generally supposed to have confused Kresphontes with Polyphontes, since the third actor often played tyrants. However that $\bar{A}$ is Kresphontes here is inescapable. The interpretation of the third column of fr. 1 is also a factor to be considered before deciding on the identity of the other speaker.

The difficult question is the relation of fr. 1, col. iii, to this dialogue and the relation of fr. 2 to both of them. Professor Turner finds no certain physical association between fr. 2 and fr. 1, and takes fr. 1 col. iii, l. 36, as the beginning of the scene where Merope raises her axe against Kresphontes; this involves (besides other difficulties) the assumption that the papyrus contained extracts, since the great scene cannot have come so soon after the prologue. Professor Mette [35] places fr. 2 columns i and ii below fr. 1 columns ii and iii, and makes continuous sense of a kind. The major difficulty is the choral lament: (1) there is no conceivable reason for a lament parodos in this play, (2) if it is not the parodos but a later utterance of the chorus, then (a) how was Kresphontes' identity made known to the audience before the stichomythia without also being revealed to the chorus, (b) what has the chorus got to lament about in the arrival of the young Kresphontes and his acceptance by a friendly old man? The first step then must be to disassociate fr. 2 from fr. 1, and then their interpretation can be considered.

Fr. 1 col. iii starts with four lines which seem to describe Merope, ending with 'and weeping she hopes'. This may be the conclusion of the dialogue in col. ii; if it is, the speaker must be $\bar{\Gamma}$ because Kresphontes does not know this, and on this evidence $\bar{\Gamma}$ cannot be Merope but must,

---

[35] He completes fr. 2 col. i, 1.2 with fr. 1060N² 'may enemies have a hostile wife', which is quite uncertain, as the only two words 'to have a wife' preserved in the papyrus occur also at the end of the line in *I.T.* 696. He supposes that the stichomythia ends at l .7 and that $\bar{\Gamma}$ then speaks from there until $\bar{A}$ comes in again in fr. 1 col. iii with 'Alas, what shall I do?' $\bar{\Gamma}$ takes up again with 'Now, if ever' down to 'my dearest' (Mette supposes that the sympathetic old man has now recognized the young Kresphontes) and they both go into the palace before the chorus start their lament in fr. 2, col. ii. This has two advantages: first, we need not assume that the text was composed of extracts (which is made unlikely by the inclusion of a chorus in fr. 2 col. ii) and secondly $\bar{A}$ stands for the same character in fr. 1 col. ii and iii. A minor disadvantage is that the bottom of fr. 2 col. i appears to contain an instruction to go in, but the characters remain on stage for another thirty lines.

as Mette suggests, be a friendly servant, male or female. Then $\overline{A}$ speaks. For Professor Turner this is Merope about to slay her son. This involves the unlikely assumption that the text gave extracts, as well as other considerable difficulties. Why does she speak of a 'whetted sword' when Plutarch and Hyginus give her an axe? Secondly the identification with fr. 456N[2] assumes deep-seated corruption since in the second line Plutarch has the necessary πληγὴν and the papyrus has Ἅιδη δ[. Thirdly, there is no sign of the old man stopping Merope or of Kresphontes awaking and intervening. The only possible place for a change of speaker is in or after the lost line (l. 43 of P. Oxy.). Fourthly, Merope is now taken by the actor who had taken Kresphontes in the earlier scene. The alternative is to suppose with Mette that Kresphontes speaks. The passage is in fact continuous. Kresphontes has obtained all the information he needs in the dialogue, and now he nerves himself for action by summoning various assistants. The first line is corrupt and Mette's τί δράσω; 'What shall I do?' is possible. The 'whetted sword' now belongs to Kresphontes. The general shape of l. 40–50 is 'O father in the underworld . . . and I pray to Hades . . . and you gods of the country remembering my father . . . Dearest Hermes.' This then is an invocation like the invocation in the later *Electra* (671ff.), where Orestes and Elektra pray to Zeus, Gaia, and the dead Agamemnon before Orestes goes off to kill Aigisthos.

The clue to interpreting fragment 2 must be the beginning of the chorus in col. ii. This is a lament and is clearly marked as such by the beginnings of the lines. It is tempting, but quite uncertain, to restore the beginning of the last iambic line ἔθανες but in any case the chorus must be lamenting someone whom they believe to be dead. As they would not lament the death of Polyphontes, they must be lamenting the supposed death of the young Kresphontes. If this is right, the remains of fr. 2 col. i should belong to the scene in which he claims the reward from Polyphontes. All we have is something about a wife, something about a husband, something about 'a neck before' (i.e. someone has died or will die before?), something about enemies, something about 'will exact a penalty', and then 'go (and sit by the) hearth'.In this context 'will exact a penalty' could be 'Kresphontes will never exact the penalty from those who killed his father and brothers.' If Polyphontes sends Kresphontes in with 'go (and sit by the) hearth', the lost twenty lines at the top of fr. 2 col. ii will be Polyphontes summing up of the situation, including his need for further information. (This phrase is left unexplained by Hyginus; it is difficult to see whom he can ask but Merope.)

With these two fragments placed we can consider the book fragments. The three columns of fragment 1 must cover most, if not all, of the prologue. It is not clear whether Kresphontes goes in at the end of his prayer or remains outside the palace. If he remains outside, then the chorus discover him: the *Heraclidae* parodos is a special case of this kind of discovery (cf. also the *Aigeus*). The lyric appeal for peace, which Aristophanes took over, may belong here (453N²); the whole city is upset by the strife between Polyphontes and those like Merope who are loyal to the memory of the old Kresphontes.

Then the scene between Polyphontes and the young Kresphontes follows: Ennius fr. IIR, 'listen and pay for what you hear' may be Kresphontes' opening, and the end of the scene is partially preserved by the papyrus fr. 2. Kresphontes goes into the house and falls asleep, as Hyginus says and Plutarch implies. The next scene after the choral lament, I think, introduces Merope. The audience needs to see the enmity between Merope and Polyphontes, fr. 451N² 'For if my husband had the intention to kill you, as you say, you ought also to have had only the intention until the time had passed.' Polyphontes answers that he is not ashamed of the common human experience of self-love (fr. 452N²), and Ennius fr. VR, 'When I spare my own life, am I to remove death from an enemy?', should belong here. This debate on the death of the older Kresphontes belongs more easily here, where probably Polyphontes confronts Merope with the report of her son's death in the hope of obtaining confirmation, than later in her feigned reconciliation.

Merope is left alone, and the old man who has taken messages between her and the young Kresphontes arrives to say that he is no longer with his Aetolian host but has vanished. Merope assumes that Polyphontes' story is true and that the young man asleep in the palace has murdered her son (she must, therefore, have heard the story from Polyphontes). She plots with the old man to murder him (this is the ancestor of the scene between the old man and Kreousa in the *Ion*).

Plutarch's description of the audience's excitement and their fear that the old man will not stop her in time proves that the murder scene was acted and not related by a messenger. In Sophocles' *Mysians*, which, if it was included in the *Telepheia* was probably produced before 450

B.C., Auge was according to Robert about to kill her son in the marriage-chamber, when a snake appeared to separate them; but this must have been told in a messenger-speech. The attempted murder of Paris in the *Alexandros* in 415 followed by his recognition was probably a stage-scene but it only demanded an altar, which was already on the stage. Hyginus says that Merope came into the *chalcidicum*. The word means 'porch' in Vitruvius and 'bedroom' in Ausonius, so that its meaning here cannot be fixed. As Dr Hourmouziades has seen, the only possible way of staging this is to use the *ekkyklema*. Luckily we have a close parallel in the attempted murder of Lykos in the *Antiope*,[36] which also shows how little need be said while the platform is rolled out. Here, however, the chorus must cover the interval while Merope and the old man go in and the platform rolls out.[37]

The murder scene changed into a recognition scene, and the recognition scene gave place (as in the later *Electra*, *I.T.*, and *Helen*) to an intrigue to kill Polyphontes. Here Merope tells Kresphontes her own misfortunes: she was not allowed to bury her husband or her sons (Ennius VIIIR); Polyphontes married her in the hope of children (Ennius IVR). The new full form of fr. 457N[2]: 'Reverence is in the eyes, my son; it has not reached my heart' is Merope's description of how she will behave to Polyphontes. Kresphontes' argument that even the all powerful gods are reconciled to each other (Ennius VIR) suggests the way the intrigue should go. When he says that Herakles if dead has no strength (fr. 450N[2]), he implies the conclusion 'if he is in heaven, he will see justice done', and Polyphontes the Heraklid can expect no help from him either way.

The intrigue is that Merope shall pretend to be reconciled to Polyphontes and persuade him to celebrate this by a sacrifice, to which the young Kresphontes still posing as his own murderer shall be invited. Presumably the old man is sent to fetch Polyphontes. A stasimon gives time for the *ekkyklema* to roll in again. Fragments are left of Merope's persuasive speech: 458N[2] 'my losses have made me wise'; 454N[2] 'I am not the only mortal who has lost children'; 455N[2] 'Niobe lost fourteen children'; 449N[2] 'we ought to mourn the new born and congratulate the dead'; 459N[2] 'we should have our treasure where there won't be tears hereafter'. Polyphontes is persuaded. An earlier pretended recon-

[36] See below, p. 210.
[37] Cf. above, p. 49, on *Alc.* 233f.

ciliation of this kind is the scene between Medeia and Jason (*Med.* 869ff.) and later Euripides uses the type again for the plot against Klytemnestra in the *Electra* (651ff., 1123ff.) and the plot against Theoklymenos in the *Helen* (1049ff., 1230ff.). Here, as in the *Medea*, the feigned reconciliation balances an earlier scene of complete estrangement (*Med.* 446f.).

Whether the sacrifice is performed inside the palace or whether Polyphontes, Merope, and Kresphontes go to some holy place off stage, we do not know. In any case a stasimon must intervene before the messenger makes his report. If the relief in Kyzikos is based on Euripides (*Anth. Pal.* 3, 5), Merope took her part in the slaughter and beat Polyphontes on the head with a stick. This is brutal, but Euripides showed how suffering could brutalize women in the *Heraclidae* and *Hecuba* too. Presumably at the end Merope and Kresphontes appeared in triumph.

Outline of play

Prologue: *P. Oxy.* 2458 fr. 1. Kresphontes' monologue: Ennius fr. IR.

Kresphontes and servant. Kresphontes' monologue.

Parodos: fr. 453N².

Polyphontes and Kresphontes: Ennius fr. IIR; *P. Oxy.* 2458 fr. 2.

Stasimon: *P. Oxy.* 2458, fr. 2.

Polyphontes and Merope: fr. 451–2N²; Ennius fr. VR.

Merope and the old man.

Stasimon or strophe.

Attempted murder, recognition, and plot: ekkyklema scene, fr. 456N²; Ennius fr. VIII, IVR; fr. 457N²; Ennius fr. VIR; fr. 450N².

Stasimon or antistrophe.

Reconciliation of Merope and Polyphontes: fr. 458, 455, 449, 459N².

Stasimon.

Messenger-speech.

Exodos.

The *Electra* which, although it uses ideas from the *Kresphontes* is completely different in tone, probably belongs to the last production of this second group. It was inspired by the revival of Aeschylus' *Choephoroi* which shortly preceded Aristophanes' *Clouds*. Euripides' approach to the story is shown by his criticism of the recognition scene in Aeschylus' play. The Aeschylean Elektra recognizes Orestes by family hair and family foot (*Cho.* 168f.); the Euripidean Elektra (520ff.) says 'Nonsense, a young man's hair is toughened by the *palaistra* and a woman's hair is soft and long; a man's foot is much bigger than a woman's.' He transfers the story from heroic legend to contemporary town-life. Similarly the great lyric dialogue which is the centre of the *Choephoroi* and nerves Orestes for his crime is reduced to twelve iambic lines invoking the gods and the spirit of the murdered man, as Kresphontes also invoked them before putting his plan into action. Euripides asked what nowadays would Klytemnestra and Aigisthos do with these uncomfortable children: put a price on Orestes' head (again as in the *Kresphontes*) and marry off Elektra to someone safe. This involved changing the scene from Agamemnon's palace to the farmer's hut, as in the earlier *Diktys* the scene seems to have been Diktys' hut.[38] This change carried with it a complete remodelling of the two murders.

The play starts with the moving monologue of Elektra's farmer husband, who has been loyal to the family and has not touched Elektra. Elektra leaves the hut with her hydria to fetch water for the household: a startling contrast with the Aeschylean Elektra, who enters with libations sent by Klytemnestra to Agamemnon's tomb. Euripides' Elektra is doing the housework to spite Aigisthos. As she and the farmer go off to their tasks, Orestes enters with Pylades, who is mute all through this play but expresses a friendship as valuable to Orestes as the farmer's is to Elektra (compare 67f. with 82f.). He has arrived secretly (this is the modern conspirator) to find Elektra, and they stand aside as she comes back with her water-pot. She sings a strophic aeolic monody on her misery, the absence of Orestes, and the murder of Agamemnon. The chorus of Mycenaean women enter to invite her to a festival and offer to lend her clothes, but she is only concerned with misery. The lyric dialogue continues with variation the aeolic metre of the monody, and is in the decorated style of the parodos of the *Hippolytus*.[39]

Orestes and Pylades emerge. Elektra describes to the unrecognized Orestes her misery, the luxurious life of Klytemnestra, and Aigisthos

[38] See above, p. 62. On the *Choephoroi* in contrast to E. *Electra* see J. de Romilly, *L'Évolution du Pathétique*, 16, 117.
[39] See above, p. 72.

dancing drunk on Agamemnon's tomb. The farmer returns and invites them in. Orestes is deeply disturbed at the difference between honest poverty and corrupt wealth. His discussion of criteria (367ff.) points the values which Euripides has emphasized by introducing the farmer into the story. Elektra sends the farmer to ask for supplies from the old man (who had saved Orestes and who alone, as she has said (285), could recognize him). The chorus sing a lovely decorated aeolic song about Achilles going to Troy and the arms which the Nereids brought him; the lord of such a man was slain by Klytemnestra, and she shall die for it. The world of epic glory stands in contrast to the reality in which Agamemnon's children live.[40]

The old man arrives with the farmer (who is mute in this scene – unless he has gone off to his fields never to be seen again). Séchan[41] suggested that Aktor in the *Philoktetes* was the original of the farmer, but if he brought Philoktetes supplies, he was more like the old man who brings a lamb, wreaths, cheeses, and wine. The recognition scene follows. Their joy is expressed in three iambic lines shared between the two characters (579ff.) and eleven lines of dochmiac from the chorus in contrast to the long lyric dialogues after the recognition in Euripides' later plays. Then the plan is made; both sections are entirely new – the killing of Aigisthos at a sacrifice (which is very like the killing of Polyphontes in the *Kresphontes*) and the luring of Klytemnestra by the story that Elektra has given birth to a child. Another decorated aeolic ode tells of the golden lamb and the Sun's change of course; the chorus comment that they do not believe this legend but it is a useful moral story, which the murderess Klytemnestra forgot – again mythological fantasy but here with a modern 'sophistic' explanation, and again ending with Klytemnestra.

A servant of Orestes reports Aigisthos' death. The chorus sing for joy. Orestes and Pylades return with Aigisthos' head (a foretaste of the much crueller return of Agave in the *Bacchae*). After crowning the pair, Elektra vents her hatred: you killed my father; you found you had married a tyrant; wealth is no good compared with character; you used your youth and beauty to seduce girls. This combination is in conscious contrast to Orestes' earlier description of the standards which the farmer embodies. The picture of Aigisthos corresponds to the

[40] On the relation of this chorus to the whole play, cf. O'Brien, *A.J.P.*, 85, 1964, 13.
[41] See above, p. 59.

146

THE TRAGEDIES OF EURIPIDES

pictures of the tyrant in the *Supplices* (452f.) and the *Erechtheus* (fr. 362, 22f. N²). Then Klytemnestra is seen in the distance. Orestes has doubts, and unlike the Aeschylean Orestes he doubts Apollo: the oracle was a great folly; could it have been an avenging spirit taking on the likeness of the god? Elektra tells him not to be a coward, and sends him in to wait.

Klytemnestra arrives in a carriage, attended by Trojan captives. Euripides means us to see her first as a vulgar, snobbish, insecure, domineering woman, a suitable mate for Aigisthos; he, therefore, makes mother and daughter quarrel at once. Klytemnestra brings up the sacrifice of Iphigeneia and the arrival of Kassandra; Elektra answers that she was unfaithful to Agamemnon from the day he went to Troy. Then he shows her as the helpless victim of her ruthless children: Klytemnestra asks why Elektra summoned her; Elektra asks her in to make sacrifices for her child. 'Take care my sooty room does not dirty your frock. You shall make the sacrifice you ought.' The chorus sing excited dochmiacs while the murder is being committed.

Orestes and Elektra come out and sing a lyric dialogue with the chorus. Both are bitterly repentant, and this is entirely new. Elektra accepts the responsibility from the beginning; the chorus says that she forced her brother against his will; and she agrees that in the actual deed she drove him on and put her hand on his sword. The Dioskouroi appear on the *mechane* to finish the play: Klytemnestra has been justly punished but Orestes' deed was unjust; Apollo is wise but his oracle contained no wisdom for Orestes (later in 1302 they speak of 'the unwise words of Apollo's tongue'). But Orestes will be acquitted in Athens (the Dioskouroi see the Furies coming in 1342), and Pylades will marry Elektra and establish the farmer in Phokis.

The motive force in this human story is Elektra's hatred of her beautiful but unprincipled mother and of the vicious young opportunist Aigisthos. Most significantly it is she who nerves Orestes for the murder, whereas in Aeschylus Pylades intervenes for that sole purpose with the voice of Apollo. As in the *Andromache* the choral odes provide a foil of decorative mythology and it is into the world of traditional mythology (not, I think, into a divinely-ordained world-order, as A. Spira[42] suggests) that the Dioskouroi reinsert these characters at the

[42] *Deus ex machina*, 112.

end. But Euripides stresses also another contrast: opposed to the misuse of wealth by Klytemnestra and Aigisthos, which breeds the hatred of Elektra and Orestes, is the chivalrous poverty of the farmer and the loyal friendship of Pylades.

4 *Melanippe Sophe and Desmotis*

The main lines of the two Melanippe plays are fairly clear, particularly since the careful work of Van Looy,[43] but the details are difficult. The prologue of the *Sophe* is preserved by Johannes Logothetes (Page, G.L.P., no. 14; fr. 480N² is probably best taken as a parody of the first line): frs. 481–8N² are either expressly quoted from the *Sophe* or obviously belong to it. Fr. 489N², the naming of Boiotos (one of Melanippe's two sons; the other is called Aiolos after his grandfather) could belong either in the epilogue of the *Sophe* or in the prologue of the *Desmotis* (in the messenger speech of the *Desmotis* Boiotos is known by this name). Fr. 497N², an appeal to punish a woman is ascribed to the *Sophe* by Wilamowitz and to the *Desmotis* by Van Looy; the *Sophe* is more likely as Hellen could speak of his granddaughter in such terms, but the King in the *Desmotis* could hardly speak so of his wife. Fr. 500N² should be Hellen to his son, the elder Aiolos, in the *Sophe*. Fr. 505N² could belong in either play. Fr. 506N² probably belongs to Melanippe's great speech in the *Sophe*. Fr. 508–10N², an old man and young man, suits Hellen and Aiolos here better than the putative shepherd and the young man in the *Desmotis*. The context of 512–3N² is completely unclear. Fr. 514N², 'the gardens of Adonis', probably describes Melanippe's children when she is afraid that they will be killed. Ennius' *Melanippa* was clearly based on the *Sophe*.

An abbreviated hypothesis and the first twenty-two lines of Melanippe's prologue are preserved by Johannes Logothetes (Page, G.L.P., no. 14). She gives the genealogy Zeus–Hellen–Aiolos, who was her father, and her mother who was Cheiron's daughter Hippo. She must have gone on to tell that Aiolos had been in exile for a year after committing a murder (like Theseus in the *Hippolytus*); she herself has been raped by Poseidon and has borne twins, whom she has given to her nurse to put in a cowshed at Poseidon's bidding.

[43] *Zes Tragedien*, 185ff. Cf. also Vysoky, *Listy Filologicky*, 12, 1964, 17.

We do not know whether Aiolos returned before or after the parodos or who formed the chorus. On Aiolos' return herdsmen, who had found the twins being suckled by a cow, brought them to him as monstrous births of the cows. Aiolos' father Hellen persuades him to give orders that the children shall be burnt. Two fragments of Ennius (I, IIR) give the text for this. Four fragments of Euripides come from a dialogue between Hellen and Aiolos, 500, 508–10N²: 500, 'A young man who has a gloomy and unsocial father in his house, suffers greatly', this must be Hellen's self-depreciatory approach to Aiolos; 508 'young men are strong in action but old men in wisdom'; 509 'What is an old man but a voice and a shadow?' might be either self-depreciatory or Aiolos' strong reaction; 510 'Alas, that a young man can be so stupid' is Hellen's reaction to Aiolos. We cannot say for certain that these all belong to this dialogue rather than to a later dialogue. The words of the hypothesis 'persuaded by' show that Aiolos put up some resistance to this sacrifice of the children. Finally he ordered Melanippe to dress them for death (ἐνταφίοις κοσμῆσαι).

Melanippe, like Ino in the *Ino*, has to prepare her own children for death; unlike Ino she has no easy way out. She defends her children without giving away that they are her children. We can see three parts of her defence: (i) the account of creation given to her by her mother does not leave any room for monstrous births: 483N² has probably been rewritten by Aristophanes, and perhaps ἐγὼ γυνὴ μέν εἰμι, μοῦσα δ'ἔστι μοι, 'though I am a woman, I have some wisdom' was the original first line; 482N² 'who first prophesied', she must have introduced her mother Hippo already and the thought continues 'but then she gave an account of the creation'; this was followed immediately by 484, 'the creation of the physical world', which presumably ended in asserting the impossibility of monstrous births;[44] (ii) the monstrous births are not punishment for Aiolos' sin (this must have been the reason that Hellen gave for them), the theory of Zeus' recording individual sins is nonsense, 506N²; (iii) 'if the children were exposed by a girl who had been seduced and was frightened of her father, you will be a murderer' (485N²). This was one of the great dangerous speeches like Pasiphae's speech in the *Cretans* (and the whole conception of the monstrous birth and the King's desire to destroy it recalls the *Cretans*).

[44] Ennius' hexameter fragment (IVR) placed by some here, was probably wrongly attributed to this play by Macrobius (see Jocelyn, *C.Q.*, 15, 1965, 134).

The next stages are unclear. Presumably Aiolos rejected his daughter's appeal.[45] Presumably also the truth that they were Melanippe's children then came out. Van Looy's suggestion that fr. 487N[2] 'I swear by holy aether, the dwelling of Zeus' is an oath that Melanippe's seducer was the god Poseidon is attractive, whether this revelation was brought about by the nurse or by Melanippe's own desperate confession. This revelation did not remove the threat; if it had, Hippo's appearance *ex machina* would have been unnecessary. Here, I think, another intervention of Hellen is likely. The fragment of Ennius (VIR)[46] that women who are not too beautiful preserve their chastity need not necessarily belong to Hellen rather than to Aiolos, but fr. 497N[2] only suits Hellen: 'You (plural) must punish this woman. For this is why women go wrong. Men who have taken a bad wife do not destroy her, either in hope of children or because of her family. . . .' The plural means 'you, my son, and your henchmen'. The sentiment is quite general: Aiolos has not taken a bad wife, but if Melanippe is not put to death, he will presumably marry her off and so the evil will spread, which is what Hellen fears. This must be immediately before the appearance of Hippo *ex machina*; if this is right, the three actors are needed for Hellen, Aiolos, and Hippo; Melanippe cannot therefore be on stage, but the deictic pronoun τήνδε can so be used of her if she has just been sent into the palace.[47] Hippo had a special mask in this play (fr. 488N[2]) and therefore she certainly appeared. She could instruct her husband Aiolos (like Thetis at the end of *Andromache*) and she could prophesy the future of the twins, Aiolos and Boiotos: this was accepted by Aiolos and Hellen as ensuring the future of the royal house (Ennius, fr. IIIR).

Outline of play

Prologue: Melanippe, Page, no. 14; fr. 481N[2].
Return of Aiolos. Herdsman with babies (hypothesis).
Hellen and Aiolos: frs. 500, 508–10N[2]; Ennius I, IIR.
Aiolos and Melanippe: frs. 483, 482, 484, 506, 485N[2]. ?514N[2].
Revelation that the babies are Melanippe's: fr. 487N[2].

[45] The comparison of the children to 'gardens of Adonis' (514N[2]) may belong here.
[46] Cf. H. J. Mette, *Lustrum*, 9, 1964, 73.
[47] Cf. A. M. Dale, *J.H.S.*, 84, 1964, 166.

Hellen and Aiolos: fr. 497N²; Ennius VIR. Condemnation of
Melanippe.
Hippo *ex machina*: fr. 488N²; Ennius IIIR; 489N²(?).

For the *Melanippe Desmotis* part of a messenger speech on papyrus
(Page, *G.L.P.*, no. 13b; fr. 495N²), part of a rhesis on papyrus (Page,
no. 13a; frs. 499; 492, 6–7; 494N²) and frs. 490–1, 493, 498N² may be
regarded as certain; fr. 492 1–5 cannot be excluded, although ll. 6–7
are now found in the papyrus rhesis with different lines in front of
them. Fr. 498N² may well be the attack on women which inspires the
papyrus rhesis in their defence. Fr. 501–3N² are comments on marriage,
which suit this play better than the *Sophe*. Fr. 504N², a reflection to a
young person on the advantages of poverty, would more easily be said
to one of the sons of Melanippe than to Aiolos in the *Sophe*. In fr.
507N², 'Why not allow the dead to be dead?', the reference must be to
Melanippe's children whom she thinks are dead. Fr. 511N², 'Many
slaves are better than freemen', may be a remark about the sons of
Melanippe after they have been unmasked and before the final
recognition.

The general theme, recognition and rescue of oppressed mother by
grown-up twins, has been thought to connect this play with Sophocles'
Second Tyro, which was produced before 414 B.C. and (since Sophocles
did not produce in 415) at latest in 416 B.C. But we have no evidence
which play was the earlier, or even that one was influenced by the
other. The obvious Sophoclean parallel for the *Tyro* is the Sophoclean
Electra: Tyro persecuted by Sidero as Electra by Klytemnestra, possibly
even a dream (649, 661P) and a false report of death (653P), and the
recognition late.[48] If this is right, the whole action will have been
focused on Tyro's emotions and the subsidiary characters will have
been made to display the heroine, whereas in Euripides' *Melanippe*
each had his or her independent part to play.

The story is told with much variation of detail and names by
Diodoros (IV, 67) and Hyginus (*Fab.* 186). Hyginus calls Melanippe's
father Desmontes which shows that he had some knowledge, direct or
indirect, of Euripides' play. For the setting Strabo and Athenaeus
provide firm ground. Strabo (VI, 265) not only places Metapontos,
Melanippe Desmotis, and her son Boiotos in Metapontion but also

[48] Schol. E. *Or.* 1691.

implies that Melanippe was brought there from elsewhere. Athenaeus (532d = 496N²) says that according to Euripides in the *Melanippe Desmotis* the town Siris was named after a woman Siris, but Archilochos says it was named after a river. The analogy with the epilogue of the *Antiope*, where the spring Dirke is to be named after the persecutor of Antiope, has been pointed out. We can accept then as facts for the *Melanippe Desmotis* that the setting was Metapontion, that Melanippe had been brought there, that the King was Metapontos, and that in an epilogue the town Siris was said to derive its name from his wife Siris: the god may have given instructions for her ashes to be thrown into a river on which the town would stand.

The messenger speech (495N²; Page, *G.L.P.*, no. 13b) also allows certain conclusions: the messenger tells his story to a woman; two boys out hunting have been attacked by the woman's two brothers, whom they believed to be their uncles; these men said that the boys were sons of a slave and ought not to have the succession to the throne; one of the boys, Boiotos, killed both the men (perhaps Boiotos has the speaking part throughout the play). The messenger winds up that courage and justice can make even the children of slaves nobler than those with an empty reputation.

The nearest parallel to this ending among those quoted by Professor H. Friis-Johansen[49] is the end of the messenger speech in the *Medea*, spoken by a servant of Jason and drawing a moral hostile to Medeia; it is followed by five lines of chorus before Medeia's speech. Here the speaker certainly took part in the ambush, and the speech seems to have been followed by three lines of chorus and a speech by the woman, whom we may name Siris. (The ambush story itself may have been borrowed from the *Alkmaion in Psophis*.)

The messenger speech fits with Hyginus' account of the hunt, except that in Hyginus the plot is made with the Queen's sons instead of her brothers, and Poseidon takes a decisive part in the battle (this may, perhaps, have come in the gap in the papyrus after the uncles' announcement that the boys cannot have the kingship). The boys must have gone out to hunt before this, and Siris must also have plotted with her brothers to kill them. The boys think that they are the sons of Siris and the plot is to prevent them inheriting the kingdom. Hyginus' account

[49] *General Reflection*, 152.

that the queen was childless and had got the twins as babies from the shepherds and pretended that they were her own fits with this. But why did Siris turn against them? Hyginus says that she later bore children of her own, which would be a sufficient reason (but he may have imported this from the Ino-Themisto story). Wilamowitz[50] suggested as the reason for the plot that Melanippe's arrival threatened Siris with exposure. Van Looy thinks that Hyginus' story is excluded by fr. 491N² 'It is folly for the childless to get children from outside. If the gods do not grant children, one should not fight against the divine decree but let things be.' But this does not exclude the possibility that the woman who imported children bore children later herself and bitterly repented her earlier action (so Kreousa in *Ion* 1291–1305 denies that the foreigner Xouthos or Ion, as Xouthos' son, has any rights in Athens except to bear arms). It is difficult to see on Wilamowitz's theory why the uncles should taunt the boys with the truth if the object of the plot was to prevent the truth coming out (the obvious way to achieve this was to kill Melanippe). (Fr. 491N² will then be Siris introducing the plot to her brothers; fr. 490N² may also belong here, 'with the help of god the wise twist their plans to achieve the expedient'.)

Wilamowitz was also concerned to give Melanippe a part in the play before the late moment when she was rescued by her sons, and this is surely necessary. As he showed, fr. 507N² 'Why don't you let the dead be dead? Why do you collect forgotten woes?', must be said to Melanippe at a time when she believes her sons to be dead, and said either by someone unsympathetic, like Siris, or by some would-be comforter like the chorus. This even suggests that the parodos was a lyric dialogue between Melanippe and a chorus of women. A chorus of women is likely, and the masculine participial ending in the lines spoken by the chorus after the messenger speech, from which Blass deduced a male chorus, may rather refer to the sons who are expected to take vengeance on Siris (only the ends of the lines are preserved). Melanippe must then have lived on in the palace after her children were exposed. Diodoros' version, that her father Aiolos handed her over to Metapontos when he found she was pregnant, may be the Euripidean story. It looks as if, in order to get her to Italy, Euripides

[50] *Kl. Schr.* I, 440ff.

borrowed this theme from the Aerope story in the prologue of the *Cretan Women*.[51] Wilamowitz and others think Melanippe arrived during the course of the play (from where?) and was imprisoned by the queen, who feared exposure. One difficulty in this theory has already been discussed: the fact that the uncles taunted the sons with their birth suggests that the queen did *not* fear exposure. Another is the title, the adjectival form *Desmotis* (as distinct from a participial form) should mean that she was a captive from the beginning of the play. For stage purposes *Desmotis* may only mean that her hands were tied, like Andromache's when she is led out to die (*Andr.* 501, 555) or like Hypsipyle's for the trial scene where she calls herself *desmia* (fr. 60, 29); and she may have appeared like this for the *parodos* and, one would expect, in the scene when her sons set out to the hunt.

The story of the past sixteen or so years back to Melanippe's pregnancy must have been told in the prologue. Poseidon was presumably reserved for the epilogue. Another god could have spoken the prologue; or, as Van Looy suggests, the herdsman who discovered the children knows their history back to the time when he discovered them (and in that case their names were given them either by the herdsman or by Siris) and Melanippe can tell her own story. But we must admit our ignorance here. After the parodos the twins must have set out to hunt. Hartung's suggestion,[52] that the attack on jesters (fr. 492, 1–5N²) was delivered by one of the twins, who preferred hunting to the symposion, is very attractive and it is difficult to see a more suitable context for the fragment which is expressly attributed to this play by Athenaeus.

The question of where the long defence of women (Page, no. 13a) belongs is difficult. It is generally agreed that the attack was made by a man and that fr. 498N² 'except for my mother, I hate the whole race of women', belongs to it. The defence is certainly made by a woman: women are better than men; they are honest and thrifty; '*we*' perform essential religious services; but women differ in nature. Van Looy seems to me right in placing fr. 493N² here as a transition to women in marriage. I am inclined to think that the two other fragments about good and bad marriage may belong too (fr. 501–2N²). The general line is that there are bad women and good women, but men also make marriage go wrong by marrying for the wrong reasons.

[51] See above, p. 38.
[52] Ap. Van Looy, 297.

The speakers of fr. 498N² and of the papyrus defence of women have been variously identified. Wilamowitz says that there is no room for the debate *after* the messenger-speech: the defence should belong to Melanippe; the king was the attacker. Schmid[53] also made the king the attacker but the queen the defender. Van Looy argues that the defence cannot have been given to a murderess, that Melanippe must therefore be the speaker, that the defence can only be made after a woman has committed a crime and therefore must come after the messenger-speech, and that the other speaker is the king (this is a development of Wilamowitz' argument). If fr. 498N² is part of the debate (and the links both with the papyrus fragment and with fr. 493N² 'hated race of women' make this practically certain, as everyone has seen), the king seems to me to be excluded as the attacker. Why should a middle-aged or elderly king mention his mother? No one has any suggestion for her name, and there is not the smallest reason to suppose her present: Admetos and Oidipous have special reasons for remembering their mothers. Surely the only possible speaker is one of the twins, and 'except for my mother, I hate the whole race of women' sounds remarkably like Hippolytos (*Hipp.* 616f.; particularly 664, which Barrett wrongly regards as interpolation. Cf. Seneca, *Phaedra* 578).

If this is right, it is tempting to go several steps further. The tone is like that of fr. 492N² 'I hate laughter-makers'. This, we have seen, may have been an attack on the symposion as inferior to the athletic life; the energetic youth may well have gone on to attack the other great hindrance to the active life, women. If this is right, the addition by Athenaeus of a line and a half from the defence of women to the attack on jesters has a very simple explanation: Athenaeus' eye skipped an intervening column which contained the attack on women and the beginning of the defence. Fr. 498N² also gives the safest clue for identifying the defender of women. If the speaker says 'except for my mother', the woman whom he regards as his mother cannot be present. If the debate preceded the messenger speech the twins still think that Siris is their mother, and Melanippe can then be the defender. This seems the simplest solution, and fr. 504N² (statement to somebody young that the simple life is sometimes better than wealth) may belong, spoken by Melanippe to her unrecognized son.[54] The obvious place for the debate is after the parodos before the twins go out to hunt and before Siris plots with her brothers.

The length available after the messenger-speech was reckoned by Blass and Wilamowitz as 350 lines on the assumption that the messenger speech was the first leaf and the fragment identified as the end of the play came from the last leaf of a quaternion. (It should be noted, however, that we do not know the exact size of the pages nor whether in fact the surviving pieces are rightly identified as lying at the end of a quaternion nor indeed whether the book was made up in quaternions.) On their assumption a possible parallel is given by the 400 lines after the end of the messenger speech in the *Ion*; they are made up as follows: 20 lines of lyric; Kreousa's arrival, Ion's arrival and dialogue with Kreousa, 70 lines; priestess and Ion, 70 lines; recognition scene and aftermath (which is here very long), 165 lines; epilogue 70 lines. Here we can only guess: Siris was either put to death or more likely, as in Hyginus, committed suicide. The recognition may have been brought about by a confrontation of Melanippe and the herdsman. Poseidon presumably foretold the wanderings of the twins and perhaps the marriage of Melanippe and Metapontos. We have no trace of Metapontos in the play; he may have arrived at the very end of the play like Lykos in the *Antiope* or have been absent for the whole play like Lykourgos in the *Hypsipyle*. Brunn and Körte[55] connected the scene represented on some Hellenistic Etruscan urns with this play: a woman identified as Melanippe on the left seated by an altar with a statue above it; the sons with a winged Victory between them; a bearded man attacking restrained by an old man; a woman on a bier. If this identification is right, Siris did commit suicide and Metapontos arrived (rather like Theseus in the *Hippolytus*) after her death but was restrained by the herdsman when trying to take vengeance. His presence at the end is almost necessary since someone must receive the gods' instruction to throw Siris' ashes into the river.

Outline of play

Prologue: ? 1. Herdsman (? fr. 489N^2). 2. Melanippe.

[54] Melanippe could, of course, also be the speaker later, provided that the twins do not yet know who their mother is; but after they have recognized Melanippe, Siris would have to be the speaker.

[55] *Urne Etrusche*, II, 232.

Parodos: lyric dialogue between Melanippe and chorus of women:
fr. 507N².

Debate between the twins and Melanippe: fr. 492, 1–5; 498N²;
Page, no. 13a; fr. 493; 501–2N²; ? 504N².

Siris plots with her brothers to ambush the boys while hunting: fr.
491; 490.

Messenger-speech fr. 495N²; Page, no. 13b: death of the uncles;
triumph of the twins; told to Siris.

Suicide of Siris.

Arrival of the twins with shepherd: fr. 511N²(?)

Recognition scene: shepherd, Melanippe, Boiotos (and Aiolos silent).

Arrival of Metapontos?

Poseidon *ex machina*: fr. 496N².

The *Melanippe Sophe* is in the tradition of plays like the *Cretans*,
Danae, and *Alope*, but in the *Desmotis* Euripides cut himself free from
the story, and preserved little but the name of the heroine and her sons
and the fact that the babies were exposed and discovered by a herdsman. As on other occasions, when he is inventing, he invents on the
lines of earlier scenes from other plays. Whether the idea of grown-up
twins discovering their mother came to him from Sophocles or not,
he certainly remembered, besides the earlier *Melanippe Sophe*, the *Ino*,
but he here gave the plot a new twist because Siris had previously
passed the children off as her own; the *Cretan Women* provided a
model for the banishment of Melanippe, the *Alkmaion in Psophis* for the
ambush (but here it was unsuccessful), and perhaps the *Hippolytus* for
the return of the King to find his wife dead.

If the interpretation given above of the debate is right, it introduced
two themes which Euripides used repeatedly later. One is the sympathy felt between parents and adult children who have not yet recognized each other. 'I hate the whole race of women except for my
mother' (498N²) is a peculiarly poignant remark if addressed by
Boiotos to his mother whom he has not yet recognized. Mother and
son meet each other unrecognized in the *Ion*, mother and twin sons
again in the *Antiope* and *Hypsipyle*, father and daughter and son in the
Alkmaion in Corinth. Many different nuances can be given to this relationship: we do not know, for instance, whether Melanippe felt
sympathy for Boiotos and Aiolos here as obviously as Kreousa does for

Ion, and we have lost the scene in which Antiope met her sons in the *Antiope*.

The other fruitful theme is the comparison of lives. Euripides had always been concerned with choice of lives: Achilles had to choose between Deidameia and Troy in the *Skyrioi*, Hippolytos had to choose between women and athleticism. What is perhaps new here is that the compulsion to choose a life or even to defend an ideal is not so strong here as in the *Skyrioi* or *Hippolytus* or in any of the plays where a virtuous young man resists a seductive woman. The ancestor of this debate seems to be rather the set of funeral orations in the *Suppliants*.[56] Boiotos combines the virtues of Kapaneus and Parthenopaios. We do not know whether the other twin took the other side, but the great speech of Melanippe in defence of women perhaps excludes a third statement of ideals. The obvious successor to this debate is the debate in the *Antiope* which arises similarly without compulsion, but we shall find that with different degrees of compulsion and with variations in the details of the lives the essential contrast between the energetic life and the quiet life is stressed in the *Polyidos*, *Phaethon*, *Palamedes*, *Ion*, *Oidipous*, and *Archelaos*.

5 Other plays

AIOLOS

The play was produced before 423 B.C. and may have belonged to the same year as *Hecuba* and *Supplices*. The papyrus hypothesis (*P. Oxy.* 2457) agrees with the account given by Stobaeus and Plutarch (N², p. 366) in placing Aiolos' kingdom in the Tyrrhenian sea, but differs in making Makareus the youngest instead of the oldest of his sons. Makareus raped his sister Kanake; she tried to conceal the birth of the child by pretending to be ill (this picks up a theme from the *Skyrioi*).[57] The young man persuaded his father to let his sons marry his daughters. Aiolos drew lots, and the lot gave Kanake to another of the sons. Then after an obscure sentence the hypothesis breaks off; the other accounts go on immediately after the rape to Aiolos' discovery of it, his sending Kanake a sword with which she committed suicide; Makareus won Aiolos over but only arrived to discover Kanake dying and himself

[56] Cf. above, p. 126.
[57] Cf. above, p. 96.

committed suicide. The suicide of Kanake has been recognized on a Lucanian hydria[58] of about 415 B.C.; Aiolos threatens her, and Makareus is standing with his hands bound at the foot of her couch.

The prologue started 'Strange and unintelligible are the plans of god' (fr. 13aN²). The speaker (who cannot be Aiolos) goes on with a genealogy: Aiolos was the son of Hellen and the father of Sisyphos, Athamas, Kretheus, and Salmoneus (fr. 14N²). Euripides was very free with the Aiolos pedigree as the two Melanippe plays show. Here presumably the strange plan of god was to get Aiolos the father of Sisyphos to the Aeolian islands where he had six sons and daughters. The lyric dialogue 'Is it true, Aiolos, that you are going to marry off your children?' 'It is a matter of opinion, maidens, I cannot say for certain' (fr. 17–18N²) has reasonably been regarded as the parodos. If this is right, Aiolos must be on stage before the parodos. But the audience must be told that Makareus had raped Kanake and that she is trying to conceal the birth of the child, so that the suggestion that the first speech of the play belonged to the nurse is likely. After that Aiolos appeared, and his desire for male grandchildren who will be good fighters and wise counsellors may have come here (fr. 15–16N²).

After the parodos came the debate on marriage between Aiolos and Makareus. Aiolos proposes various criteria, wealth, birth, age, which Makareus rejects (fr. 20–24N²). Makareus then in a magnificently dangerous speech (like the wise Melanippe's defence of her babies) proposes that Aiolos shall marry off his daughters to his sons: 'nothing is base if it does not seem so to those who practise it' (19N²). This inspires the chorus to sing, recalling the first stasimon of Sophocles' *Antigone* (332), of the ingenuity of man (27N²). Aiolos then announces to his sons that he will draw lots to decide who shall marry whom (28, 39N²): presumably the sons, except Makareus, are mute.

So far all is clear. For the rest we know that Kanake's lot did not fall to Makareus. Probably the drawing of lots took place off stage, and Makareus came out to announce the disastrous result, and he may have considered exile (30N²). It used to be assumed that at this point Kanake gave birth to her child, and Nero was quoted as evidence. Suetonius says that Nero sang tragedy (*Nero* 21): *inter cetera cantavit Canacen parturientem, Oresten matricidam, Oedipodem excaecatum, Herculem insanum.*

[58] See list of illustrations, p. 303.

In the last two what Nero 'sang' (whatever that means) about 'Oidipous blinded and Herakles mad' must have been a messenger-speech, and we have therefore no right to suppose that Kanake sang a monody when she was on the point of giving birth. What Nero 'sang' may have been the prologue speech.[59] Now that we have the hypothesis, this is the only interpretation compatible with its statement: 'she tried to conceal the birth by pretending to be ill'. The last preserved sentence of the hypothesis is corrupt. After saying that 'the lot married off Kanake to live with another' (cf. W. Morel quoted by H. Lloyd-Jones[60],) it seems to say 'when they ran together to the same part of the house, the nurse (did something with) the baby, and' (I owe this shaping of the sentence and the connexion back from συνδραμόντες to συμβίωσιν to Mr E. W. Handley). Presumably 'they' are Aiolos and the son allotted to Kanake; they go to find her in her room; perhaps the nurse is caught with the baby, Aiolos guesses or extracts the truth, and sends Kanake a sword. For economy it seems likely that this all happens during a chorus, and that Aiolos comes out and tells the whole story to Makareus, who confesses. A comment of the chorus is probably preserved in fr. 33N[2]: 'Alas, who cannot grieve at this disaster? Who could hear this without weeping?' The end given in Stobaeus and Plutarch is so reminiscent of the Sophoclean *Antigone* that it is probably right (the only obstacle is the Lucanian vase which shows Makareus with his hands bound before the couch of Kanake): Makareus persuaded his father to pardon Kanake, but when he entered her room she was dying and he committed suicide with the same sword. This was told in a messenger speech, to which Gilbert Murray[61] finds the conclusion in the fragment about Aphrodite (26N[2]): 'She brings the greatest joy and the greatest pain. When I meet her, may she be kind.' Lloyd-Jones suggests that the child survived because Kanake was the mother of Triopas, the founder of Knidos. Euripides may well have adapted the tradition to make Makareus the father of Triopas, and a god could announce that Triopas' descendants would in due course colonize the Aeolian islands.

The movement in this play is given by the story of Kanake and

[59] Strepsiades in the *Clouds* (1371) objects to his son 'singing' the earlier part of this speech.

[60] *Gnomon* 28, 1963, 443.

[61] *Athenian Drama*, III, 1906, 313f.

Makareus, and the debate on marriage is entirely relevant to this story. But this is the first of a number of such debates and it rather looks as if one reason for the decrease in the number of bad women is the switch in interest from the problems that arise after marriage to the problems of marriage itself. This last group of plays only has two bad women of the old type: Ino in *Phrixos B* is the classic case of the stepmother who plots against her stepchildren, and Klytemnestra in the *Electra* recognizably belongs to the class of wives who have chosen a young lover instead of an elderly husband; the career of Aigisthos as portrayed by Euripides should be remembered by those who think that Hippolytos should have treated Phaidra more kindly. The new problem which the debate in the *Aiolos* poses in the next production after the staging of the marriage triangle in the *Andromache* is the problem of how to choose a wife, a problem in which as in later Comedy parents have a large say. This problem recurs in the *Phaethon*, *Meleager*, *Andromeda* and *Antigone*.

IXION[62]

Philochoros found in this play a reference to the death of Protagoras which took place about 420 B.C.,[63] the play must, therefore, have been produced shortly after his death. Someone evidently advised Ixion against ambition ($425N^2$); someone else (or Ixion himself) advised a just reputation to cover crime and the audacity which wins tyrannies ($426a$, $426N^2$). A reference to pollution ($427N^2$) shows that Ixion had already murdered Deioneus. Plutarch (*Mor.* 19e) tells the story that when people criticized Euripides' Ixion as a sacrilegious villain he answered 'I did not take him off the stage until I had nailed him to the wheel.' It is tempting to follow Séchan in finding an illustration of Euripides in the Campanian vases[64] which show Hermes and Hephaistos looking at Ixion after he has been tied to the wheel. This may have been told in a messenger speech but could have been done in front of the audience if the *ekkyklema* was used to carry the wheel, a reminiscence of the binding of Prometheus in Aeschylus' *P.V.* and of Andromeda in

---

[62] Nothing useful is known about Aeschylus' or Sophocles' treatment of the Ixion story.

[63] *R.E.*, 23, 911; J. A. Davison, *C.Q.*, 3, 1953, 33. Does Zeus' readiness to overlook Ixion's pollution point to Protagoras (cf. above, p. 25)? Or did some comic poet equate Ixion and Protagoras as two atheists who came to a bad end?

[64] See list of illustrations, p. 303.

Sophocles' play. The fragments suggest that Ixion had something of the Odysseus of Euripides' *Philoktetes* and Plutarch quotes him with the Eteokles of the *Phoenissae* (426aN²).

KADMOS

There is no reason to doubt the existence of the play, although the only fragment is certainly a forgery.

POLYIDOS

The high percentage of resolutions (26.5%) and particularly the occurrence of three in one line (641, 3N²) may place this play in Group III rather than Group II. The main lines of the story are given by Hyginus (*Fab.* 136). The portent of the three-coloured cow and the guiding owl are attested for Euripides by the Scholiast to Aristides and Aelian respectively (N², p. 558). The timing of the action is indicated by fr. 636N². Polyidos deduces from the flight of a sea-eagle that the child is on land and not on the sea. This is an early stage when Polyidos has already solved the riddle of the three-coloured cow. The owl then leads him to the jar of honey, one of the palace storage jars in which the boy is found. The audience see the body of the boy brought out and Polyidos led out with him for burial in the tomb. A messenger will later relate that sounds were heard coming from the tomb[65] and finally Polyidos will enter with the boy restored to life.

At some time there was a debate between Minos and Polyidos in which Minos stood for wealth and power and Polyidos for wisdom and virtue (634–5, 640–645N²): a contrast of lives, here the rich tyrant and the poor artist, like the debate in the *Antiope*. Gilbert Murray[66] suggests that the offerings placed in the tomb of Glaukos were a superstitious extravagance which Polyidos condemned (640N²), as Hekabe, having given what she can for the burial of Astyanax, says that rich funerals merely show the useless arrogance of the living (*Tro.* 1347). This would suggest that the debate came when the boy had been found and ended, after Polyidos had criticized the extravagance of the funeral, with Minos condemning Polyidos to burial with the boy. The prophet who tells unpleasant truth appears as early as the *Likymnios*;

[65] Cf. above on *Aiolos* and *Chrysippos*.
[66] *Op. cit.*, 341.

Polymestor in the *Hecuba* is a very special case, so is Kassandra in the *Alexandros* and *Trojan Women*. Here it looks as if Polyidos was not only right but was sympathetically portrayed. The new anapaestic fragment (654a) 'unhappy mothers who bear children for Hades' perhaps suggests that the chorus were women.

IV

The Third Group

The beginning of the third group may have coincided with a change in the arrangements of the Competition.[1] From now on each poet had the service of all three protagonists (and their assistants) so that he could again produce his three tragedies and satyr-plays on a single day. Connected trilogies again became possible, and Euripides produced a Trojan trilogy in 415 B.C. If we follow the grouping most easily given by the metrical statistics, the *Ion* was produced with the *Andromeda* and *Helen* in 412 B.C. and here we can see a kind of strophe, antistrophe, epode pattern: two plays about the rescue of a woman from an exotic country followed by a third play which is much less light-hearted. The Scholiast to *Frogs* 53[2] seems to have preserved a didaskalic notice recording the production of *Antiope, Hypsipyle, Phoenissae*, probably in 410 B.C.; here again Euripides uses a similar pattern: two plays about grown up mothers rescued by their twin sons are followed by a play with an unhappy ending. But here the stories are also linked: the *Antiope* belongs to early Theban history; the *Hypsipyle* and *Phoenissae* are two later chapters. Metrical considerations place the *Iphigenia in Tauris* and the *Hercules* between the Trojan trilogy and the *Helen*. Again an exciting play with a happy ending is linked with a tragedy: the strange Euripidean *Antigone* would make a possible complement to the *Iphigenia in Tauris*. This leaves *Phaethon, Meleager, Pleisthenes* for the first production: the fragments of *Meleager* and *Pleisthenes* show a very high resolution figure but the plays are both quoted in Aristophanes' *Birds* of 414 B.C.; this means that they must have been produced at latest in 416 B.C. since 415 B.C. is occupied by the Trojan trilogy. (It must also be remembered that *Polyidos* may belong to this group rather

[1] Cf. *Hermathena*, 100, 1965, 21f.
[2] Cf. *The Classical Tradition: Essays presented to Harry Caplan*, 83f. B. Snell, *Scenes from Greek Drama*, 70ff., has suggested that *Antiope* was the first play. *Antiope* was parodied in *Thesm. B* (fr. 327K), *not* in *Thesm. A* (411 B.C.).

than to the second group, in which case one of these plays belonged to the second group.)

Apart from the new patterns of grouping the plays together in a trilogy, the single plays themselves seem to show a different emphasis on family relationships. It is not easy to define this difference. Perhaps one might say that earlier Euripides was more interested in family crimes and in strange events, like the irregular babies or the sickness of Telephos, than in family relationships, but that later Euripides is more interested in the family relationships than in family crimes and strange events. In the plays about bad women in Group I generally three people at most seem to have borne the brunt of the action – Medeia and Jason only in the *Medeia*; Phaidra, Hippolytos, Theseus in the *Hippolytos*. In the *Andromache* at the beginning of Group II more people are brought in beside the essential triangle of Andromache, Hermione, and the absent Neoptolemos: Peleus, Menelaos, and Orestes. The *Electra* (late in Group II) has Elektra's husband and the old man, who had originally saved Orestes, as well as Pylades (who was mute) and Klytemnestra; and Aigisthos, though only his severed head appears, has much more personality than in Aeschylus or Sophocles. Sophocles' only purpose in introducing Chrysothemis was to illuminate sides of Elektra's character. But Euripides wants us to see Elektra in her family setting, and the members have each their independent value. I would not, of course, deny that here still the main interest is the matricide and its effect on its perpetrators rather than the family relationships themselves, but the chivalry of the farmer and the loyalty of Pylades are very real values asserted against the corrupt relationship of Klytemnestra and Aigisthos.

In the *Phoenissae* at the end of Group III the emphasis has been completely switched from the fratricide to the relationship between the characters. Aeschylus' *Seven against Thebes* has as characters only Eteokles, a messenger, and perhaps the two sisters to lead the laments at the end. Euripides, telling the same stretch of story, introduces Antigone with her old slave very early to prepare us for her part at the end and adds to Eteokles Iokaste, Polyneikes, Teiresias, Creon, Menoikeus, and finally Oidipous (all members of the family except Teiresias who is the family seer). The duel of the brothers is told in a magnificent messenger-speech, but the point of the play is not the horror of fratricide, nor even Eteokles' decision to meet his brother, but the effect of his lust for power on the whole royal family, who are somehow so very human in their diversity. It is sad that we cannot say more of Euripides' *Antigone*, which was earlier, and of his *Oidipous* which was later, but at least we know that Antigone was not the lonely figure contrived by Sophocles: that Haimon helped her in the burial of Polyneikes and she bore him a child. And the one point that is clear in the very strange *Oidipous* is that Iokaste stuck to him loyally when Kreon had him blinded and when the secret of his birth had been revealed. Something of the same change separates the *Hecuba*, early in Group II (dominated by the cruel things which happen to Polyxena and Polydoros) from the Trojan trilogy of 415 B.C., where we see mother, father, three sons, and a daughter in the first play, *Alexandros*, and mother, daughter, two daughters-in-law and a grandson in the last play, *Trojan Women*.

How Euripides displays the relationship between family and friends in all its diversity of love, hostility, loyalty, overbearingness, and ignorant sympathy can only be seen by examining the plays in detail and noting in particular the kinds of scene that are most used. The productions will be taken in their probable chronological order, except for *Phaethon*, *Meleager*, *Pleisthenes*, which, as being the most uncertain trio, are left till last.

1 *The Trojan trilogy, 415 B.C.*

In this year according to Aelian (*V.H.* ii, 8) Xenokles was first with *Oidipous*, *Lykaon*, *Bakchai*, and a satyr-play *Athamas*, Euripides was second with the *Alexandros*, *Palamedes*, *Troades*, and a satyr-play *Sisyphos*. Xenokles produced four unconnected plays; Euripides followed his story through from the recognition of Paris to the capture of Troy, and even the satyr-play was relevant since Sisyphos was a reputed father of Odysseus, who had a major part in the *Palamedes* and contrived the death of Astyanax in the *Trojan Women*.

ALEXANDROS

Sophocles' *Alexandros* certainly told of Paris' victory in the games (93P) and of his being suckled by an animal (95, 98, 99P). The likeness of the description of the victory to fragments of the *Aleadai* (84, 86–7P), which was probably produced about 450 B.C. may suggest that Sophocles' play was earlier than Euripides' play.

Outline of play

Prologue: Aphrodite: *Inc. Inc.* VR; 867N².

Kassandra and Priam (Kassandra to temple of Apollo, Priam to Games).

Parodos: Chorus of Trojan Women and Hekabe: 44–6N²; 6 Snell (= Page, *G.L.P.*, no. 9a).

Kassandra and Hekabe, Kassandra's prophecy: 7 Snell, Ennius V–IXR; *Inc. Inc.* VIIR; 42a–c, 64N².

Priam returns, Priam and Kassandra(?): 16 Snell.

Stasimon: Chorus and messenger: 18 Snell (= Page, no. 9b).

Priam and messenger: Ennius II–IVR, *Inc. Inc.* VIR, 47N².

Priam, Hektor and Deiphobos: 23 Snell (= Page, no. 9c).

Paris and subsidiary chorus: Schol. E. *Hipp.* 58.

Priam, Paris, and Deiphobos: Deiphobos 48–51, 59N²; Paris 54–7, 61N²; Priam 60N².

Stasimon: 52–3N².

Hekabe and Deiphobos, Hektor: Ennius *Inc. nom.* XIIR; 43 Snell (= Page, no. 9d).

Stasimon.

Deiphobos, Paris, Hekabe (altar scene): 58, *adesp.* 286N².

Recognition scene: Paris, Hekabe, Nurse or old man.

Paris, Hekabe (recognition duet).

Apollo *ex machina*: 1082N².

Bibliographical note: B. Snell, *Hermes*, Einzelschriften 5, 1ff.; G. G. A. Murray, *Greek Studies*, 127ff.; F. Scheidweiler, *Phil.*, 97, 1948, 321; L. Strzelecki, *Soc. Sc. de Lettres de Wroclaw*, 1949; L. Lanza, *S.I.F.C.*, 34, 1963, 230; J. Hanson, *Hermes* 92, 1964, 171; T. C. W. Stinton, *Hell. Soc.*, Supplt. Paper no. 11; M. F. Jouan, *R.E.G.*, 70, 1957, XV; P. G. Mason, *J.H.S.* 79, 1959, 80.

The reconstruction of Euripides' *Alexandros* from the Strasbourg papyrus,[3] the book fragments, and Ennius' Latin adaptation is insecure in detail but the outlines can be seen. The prologue must have told of Hekabe's dream, which led to Priam first consulting Apollo, then exposing the infant Paris and so to the institution of annual games in his memory; Snell gives this to Kassandra and ascribes to Ennius the eleven Latin lines which describe the dream and the oracle (*Inc. Inc.* VR).

[3] Snell, *op. cit.*, gives the whole text; Page, *G.L.P.*, no. 9, gives the readable portions.

'Mother' used of Hecuba and 'father' of Priam do not necessarily make the speaker Kassandra; they refer to the baby which must have already been mentioned. The audience must be told that the boy has been saved by the shepherds and has grown up and the story of his bull may have been included. Kassandra might see this in prophetic frenzy but only a god could tell it in a flat prologue. The long Latin fragment shows that Apollo cannot be the speaker as he is mentioned in the third person. Aphrodite is the most likely speaker, and if the speaker is neither Apollo nor Kassandra, a possible final line for the prologue speech is fr. 867N²; 'but – for here is the prophetic woman (I will go)'. If this is right, Kassandra appears as the prologue speaker retires. There are two problems here. The first is insoluble: with whom does Kassandra speak? Either Priam or Hekabe (Snell) are possible, but perhaps it is more likely that Hekabe makes her first iambic-speech after the parodos. The second question is the scene. This depends on the line announcing Kassandra's second entry: if the restoration ἤκουσα]ν ἀδύτων ὧ[δε Φοιβείων πάρος, which Page (*G.L.P.*, no. 9a = 6 Snell) translates 'coming hither before the shrine of Phoebus', is accepted, the scene must be the temple of Apollo. But even if we cannot be certain that Paris took refuge on the altar of Zeus Herkeios in this play (as in Hyginus, *Fab.* 91), Priam's palace would be a more natural centre for the comings and going of Priam, Hekabe, Kassandra, Hektor, Deiphobos than the temple of Apollo; μολοῦσα]ν ἀδύτων ὧ[δε Φοιβείων ἄπο is an equally plausible restoration. This involves the assumption that the speaker (probably the chorus) guesses that Kassandra is coming from the temple, because she is Apollo's priestess and where else would she come from? But this is, of course, not certain.

Snell makes the chorus Trojans; Hanson prefers Trojan women. There is no evidence either way in the text. But Hekabe's comforters are more likely to be women than men, and it is possible that the parodos itself was a lyric dialogue between Hekabe and her comforters.

The papyrus starts with Hekabe inconsolable for the loss of her baby, our first picture of her. The chorus try to comfort her, and then they see Kassandra entering like a Bacchant from Apollo's shrine; this is the wild maenad Kassandra and here, according to Snell, she has her vision of the judgment of Paris, of the fleet approaching Troy, the torn body of Hektor, and the Wooden Horse. Hekabe chides her for talking nonsense.

This sequence consists of frs. 3–15 Snell. The links between Snell's fragments 6, 7, and 8 are good. At the end of 6 the chorus see Kassandra coming; in 7 Hekabe (presumably) says βακχεύει φρένα; in 8 Ennius (VIR) translates this or a neighbouring phrase *oculis rabere . . . ardentibus*. The Ennian passage is in trochaic septenarii, but he may always use these for Greek iambic trimeters. The Ennian passage is known from Cicero (*de Div.* 1, 31, 66) and is followed after a comment by 10 (VIR) *adest . . . restinguite* (also in trochaic septenarii) and then after another brief comment by *iamque mari . . . litora* (dactylic). This again is followed shortly, according to *de Div.* 2, 112, by *eheu videte: iudicavit* (trochaic octonarii, VIIR). If we accept, as I think we must, that Cicero is quoting three stages in a single scene, then in Euripides also Kassandra may have advanced from sober speech to excited lyrics and have then returned to speech in that scene. Formally, the lyrics may have been a monody inserted between passages in iambic trimeters like Kreousa's monody in the *Ion* (859). The other two passages in Snell's fr. 10 (VIII–IXR) are quoted from different sources, but must belong in this context, since another great polymetric scene of prophecy in the same play is unlikely. Strzelecki has ingeniously conjectured from Seneca's *Agamemnon* (748f.) that Kassandra also foresaw the death of Deiphobos. Thus the entry of both brothers in this play, as well as that of Paris, is prepared by the vision.

Kassandra begins with apology: she must prophesy but she is no use (VIR, 44–7). Her comparison of herself and her useful brothers is quite general; Strzelecki argues from it that Kassandra's prophecy comes late in the play, but there is no specific reference in *prodesse . . . obsequi*. I should put here fr. 11 Snell (42bN²): 'For god has made me prophesy what none believe.' Then she appeals to Apollo (*Inc. Inc.* VIIR) presumably to make the Trojans believe her. Then she sees Paris as the dangerous firebrand near at hand (VIR, 48–9), for which 42aN² may well be the Greek version. So far the metre is still trochaic in Ennius, and VR 'wherefore the shepherds now call Paris Alexander' could conceivably belong here. Then she bursts into lyrics. There is no reason why she should not go chronologically: judgment of Paris from which Helen will come as a Fury to Troy (VIIR), as later Kassandra will return as a Fury to Argos (*Tro.* 457), fleet (VIR, 50–3), Hektor's body VIIIR, the Wooden Horse IXR. Fr. 62N² is perhaps the chorus' comment on Kassandra's prophecy (unless the Budé editor is right in placing it at the end of the play after the recognition of Paris). Hekabe, of course, cannot believe, and it may be that her disbelief stings Kassandra to prophesy that she shall be a dog to serve Hekate (fr. 14 Snell, 42cN^2): this recalls the dialogue at the end of the Polymestor scene in the *Hecuba* (1273).

Presumably Hekabe and Kassandra go into the house, and the chorus sing a stasimon. (On the other assumption that the scene is before the temple Kassandra goes into the temple; Hekabe goes to inform Priam.) What happens between the Hekabe/Kassandra scene and the arrival of the messenger announcing Paris' victory in the games is unclear. After a stasimon Snell gives first entrance of Priam (with the bird on his sceptre),[4] then the arrival of the old man to announce that Paris has come to town to take part in the games. In this fr. 16 Snell 'horse-car' is a pointer to Priam. We should naturally like to know whether Priam is coming or going, and to whom he is talking. We must note that after the games we have separate entries of the messenger, Hektor and Deiphobos, and Paris with the chorus of shepherds. It would therefore be convenient if Priam returned now and only had to be summoned out of the palace for the debate between the brothers and Paris. If this is right, he may well have gone out at the same time as Kassandra in the prologue. He must then have appointed someone else to be Agonothetes for the games. Hektor could perhaps have acted for him.

Scheidweiler supposes Kassandra, and Hanson supposes Hekabe to be Priam's interlocutor. Hektor and Deiphobos are also possibilities. But there is another factor to be considered. A stasimon between this scene and the messenger speech reporting the games is certainly needed; a stasimon after the arbitration scene is probably attested by fr. 52–53N^2; a third stasimon must intervene while Deiphobos fetches Paris to be butchered. It is unlikely that there were more than three stasima; therefore Priam's return may immediately follow on the Hekabe/Kassandra scene. If the Etruscan urns (see below) which show Priam holding back Kassandra when she storms towards Paris with an axe derive from the *Alexandros*, Kassandra is the other speaker in this scene and she threatens to seek out the so far unknown and unheard of Paris with an axe. Priam persuades or orders her into the house.

[4] Aristophanes, *Birds* 512.

Snell's second assumption, that an old servant arrives and tells of Paris' upbringing and his arrival to take part in the games, has the double point that we should hear of Paris' arrival before the messenger speech and that the old man is the means by which according to him the final recognition of Paris is brought about. Stinton (p. 67) has pointed out that the arguments for the Old Man as a character are not conclusive: the supposed reference back to him in Helen's speech in the *Trojan Women* (921) is more easily taken of Priam. The great difficulty, however, is that, if he is a known servant of Priam who exposed the baby (and only this would make him useful in the recognition), he cannot tell the story of Paris' youth without giving away that Paris has survived. It is essential that nobody connected with Priam's household should know this before the last moment. For the audience the prologue and Kassandra's prophecy is sufficient warning.

The next certain point is that a messenger brings the news that an unknown young herdsman has won the prize over the sons of Priam (presumably he described Nike or Aphrodite, 'flying from heaven with wreath and fillets', Ennius IR).[5] Hekabe is furious. Her sons, Hektor and Deiphobos, enter discussing their defeat; Hektor takes it lightly, Deiphobos wants vengeance. Thus Hektor is fixed for us as a noble and generous character. The young herdsman appears with a subsidiary chorus of shepherds. Deiphobos and the herdsman plead before Priam, and Priam confirms the award of the prize to the herdsman. Hekabe incites Deiphobos to murder.

This sequence starts with fr. 18 Snell (= Page, no. 9b). Snell assumes that Hekabe rather than Priam hears the messenger-speech. The fragment of Ennius (IIR), 'my mind and ears have long been awaiting news' could apply to either or to the chorus. Snell gives 47N² to the chorus when Priam appears to decide between Deiphobos and Paris, but Murray suggests that it is the close of the messenger speech itself: 'Whence you should win, you fail, Sire. Whence you should not, you succeed. For you conquer by your slaves, not by your free men.' If this very attractive suggestion is right, the messenger speech is spoken to Priam rather than to Hekabe, and presumably Priam is still on the stage (having soliloquized to cover the messenger's change of role to one of the brothers) when Hektor and Deiphobos appear (Page, no. 9c). But a later arrival of Priam in that scene is possible.

[5] Cf. however O. Skutsch in *H.S.C.P.* (forthcoming).

Probably no stasimon intervenes before the arrival of Paris with his subsidiary chorus: the subsidiary chorus may sing as briefly as the chorus of huntsmen in the *Hippolytos*. He claims his prize and Priam awards it to him after Deiphobos has disputed the slave's claim. Deiphobos argues that slaves who are better than their masters are dangerous (48–51, 59N²); Paris argues that poverty produces energy (54–7; 61N²): Priam concludes that Time will show (60N²). It seems to me probable that the chorus of shepherds goes off with Paris and that frs. 52–3N² belong to the ensuing stasimon.

The next scene develops between Hekabe and Deiphobos, who has told the story to his mother: Ennius, *Inc. nom.* XIIR, 'he has the crown, basking in his victory', belongs to him rather than to her. She cannot bear defeat by a slave and urges Deiphobos to kill him.[6] Hektor apparently intervenes in l. 79 and tells Deiphobos that he should have got himself into better training for the games. His moderation towards Paris is rejected by Hekabe and Deiphobos. During a stasimon Deiphobos goes to lure Paris 'who is filling the town with his glory', back to the palace.

The next certain point is fr. 58N²: 'I shall be killed for my nobility, which for the rest is a salvation.' (The second of these lines is repeated by Andromache in the *Trojan Women* (743), where it refers to Hektor's nobility which will destroy Astyanax.) We know from this that Paris is threatened with death, and it is a reasonable guess that he has jumped on an altar for asylum. But we do not *know* that he is on stage: his words may have been quoted by a messenger. The *Telephos* provides an analogy for a messenger speech recounting an asylum scene which took place off stage, just as the *Ion* provides an analogy for this kind of asylum scene on stage.

The interpreters have all assumed that the scene took place on the stage. According to Snell Deiphobos and Hekabe attack Paris. Hekabe discovers that he might be her son.[7] Deiphobos fetches the old man, who completes the recognition. The old man goes off and Aphrodite tells Paris that he will marry Helen. This can be worked with three

---

[6] In fr. 43, 32–3, 37 Page's supplements are good. Murray pointed out that in l. 39 τῆιδε is not necessary and suggested σῆι δὲ or πιστῆι δε. Perhaps ἄτρωτος in l. 40 picks up πρωτὸς in the line before. οὐ τρωτός ἐστι; σῆι δὲ χερὶ δεῖ θανεῖν.

[7] Jouan suggests that Paris said that he was a foundling and this made Hekabe suspect the truth.

actors, and it is possible that the likeness of Paris to the sons of Priam
(*adesp.* 286N²) strikes Hekabe when she sees him for the first time so
forcibly that she calls off the attack. The attack on Paris by his mother
and another repeated the very successful scene of the *Kresphontes*, but
here it was probably the mother who recognized her son in the nick of
time.

An alternative for the old man is suggested by a very interesting set
of tragic masks in terracotta of the mid-fourth century discovered in
two tombs at Lipari.[8] They are an elderly man with a wreath round
his head, a wide-eyed young man in a Phrygian cap, a young man with
gold in his hair also in a Phrygian cap, a very beautiful boy in a Phrygian cap, an elderly woman showing great distress, a young woman
who looks like a maenad, an old Aethiopian woman. The three youths
in Phrygian caps surely must be Trojans; it is difficult to date the story
late in the Trojan War because the youngest of the three Trojans is too
old for Astyanax, on the other hand he fits beautifully with Paris in
the *Alexandros*. Then the vain youth is Deiphobos and the oldest youth
is Hektor. The elderly man is Priam wreathed for the funeral games.
The sorrowing elderly woman is Hekabe and the maenad is Kassandra.
It is possible that the old Aethiopian woman is Paris' nurse and that she
brought about the recognition.

Murray (followed with variations by Scheidweiler, Hanson, and
Stinton) makes Kassandra responsible for the recognition. Stinton
solves the problem of number of actors by dropping Hekabe so that
Kassandra stops Deiphobos' attack by her announcement. Why, when
Kassandra's prophecy is disbelieved, her identification of her brother
should be believed he does not say, nor does he say how Hekabe,
Priam, or Aphrodite appear. Hanson solves the problem of disbelief by
making Aphrodite appear to reinforce Kassandra's identification but
this would need more than three actors. In any case Aphrodite is unlikely to have spoken the epilogue as well as the prologue and Apollo
is a better guarantor of Paris' identity and of the future course of events.
'Zeus, wishing evil for the Trojans and woe for Greece, planned these
things, my father' (1082N²) sounds like the end of the play and is much
more appropriate for Apollo than for Aphrodite.

These accounts of the recognition scene arise from Hyginus and the
thirty-four Etruscan urns of Hellenistic date identified by Brunn (*Urne*

[8] L. Bernabo-Brea, *Meligunis – Lipari, II,* 321, pl. 141–3.

Etrusche I, 1–34).[9] In Hyginus (*Fab.*, 91) 'Paris wins in the games.
Deiphobos in fury draws his sword against him but he jumps on the
altar of Zeus Herkeios. When Kassandra prophesies that he is her
brother, Priam recognizes him and receives him in the palace.' Clearly
this is an abbreviated account: the altar of Zeus Herkeios was not where
the games were held. But there are two serious discrepancies with
Ennius' Euripides. At the beginning of Hyginus' account Hekabe
dreams that she gives birth to a burning torch from which many
snakes issued. The torch is in Ennius (*Inc. Fab.* VR) but not the snakes.
Secondly, in Hyginus the baby is called Alexander; but in Ennius
and Euripides (Ennius VR = 64N²) the shepherds give Paris the name
Alexander because he defends them (as in Apollodorus 3, 150). Hyginus
may be using Euripides but he is certainly not only using Euripides.
There is therefore no compulsion from Hyginus to introduce Kassandra in the Euripidean ending.

The Etruscan urns are not easy to interpret as they have a large
number of variations on a central theme. Three figures occur on nearly
all: a young warrior attacking from the left, a figure of Aphrodite
intervening, a young man in Phrygian cap with sword and victory palm
in his hand who has taken refuge on an altar. They may reasonably be
identified as Deiphobos, Aphrodite, Paris. Another warrior usually
appears on the right of Paris; he is not attacking as actively as Deiphobos; sometimes he raises his hand as if surprised at an apparition;
twice at least he is forcibly held back (nos. 20, 21). Priam often appears
further on the right, usually pointing at Paris, twice himself restrained
by a woman (nos. 10, 11), several times holding back a young woman
who rushes on Paris with an axe (nos. 18, 26–28). The young woman
sometimes attacks from the other side and on that side too is in some
versions restrained. She is presumably Kassandra. Twice (nos. 29, 30) an
older woman, presumably Hekabe, appears on the left restraining a
warrior. Aphrodite herself sometimes has wings like Nike and is sometimes duplicated by a Nike figure on the other side of Paris. Twice a
winged Fury appears on the extreme right (nos. 14, 15).

It is extremely difficult to interpret the literary and artistic ancestry
of these urns. Euripides' *Alexandros*, as a famous play known in later
antiquity, is certainly attractive as a source. The Furies on nos. 14, 15

[9] Nos. 3, 6, 17, and 26 are reproduced in J. U. Powell, *New Chapters in Greek Literature*,
Third Series, pp. 140ff.

could well illustrate Kassandra's prophecy that Helen will act as a Fury. We should then have to suppose that the more crowded scenes were combinations from a series of cyclic illustrations into a seemingly significant new composition, which is not really significant because different moments are put together. We know such series in Greek art in the Telephos frieze in Pergamon and in the Homeric bowls. The Homeric bowls are particularly relevant because some of them illustrate situations from tragedy, and the situations may be either actual stage-scenes or situations narrated in messenger speech or prologue. It is therefore possible that the attack of Kassandra is an illustration of her early appeal to extinguish the firebrand (Ennius, VIR, 48–9), that Priam is derived from the arbitration scene, that Hektor's anger is directed against Deiphobos rather than Paris, that Hekabe is restraining Deiphobos when she has guessed the truth, and that Aphrodite spoke the prologue.

The urns do not therefore impose attack and recognition by Kassandra, and they are compatible with an attack by Deiphobos which is first supported and then restrained by Hekabe. If the attack on Paris was played on the stage (and it is difficult to suppose that Euripides lost such a chance), an actor must be freed to play Apollo, but Deiphobos may have gone off before the jubilations of Hekabe and Paris (the end of the *Hypsipyle* is parallel here). It is possible that Deiphobos went off to fetch the Old Man (Snell) or the nurse (Lipari terracottas) and returned mute with him or her; then both went off before a lyric duet between Hekabe and Paris, which led up to the appearance of Apollo. Of course this ending is conjectural, but for the economy of the trilogy it seems probable that the play ended with Hekabe's joy and Apollo's forecast of the Judgment, the Rape of Helen and the Trojan War.

However the details worked, the impression is clear of Hekabe in her sorrow, her attempted murder, and her exultation, of Kassandra's Bacchic frenzy and the disbelief which greeted it, of the generosity of Hektor, and of Paris' youthful beauty, an impression strong enough to survive the next play.

PALAMEDES

Outline of play

Prologue: Odysseus. ? Arrival of soldier with forged letter.

Parodos: Greek patrols: 589N².
Agamemnon and Odysseus: investigation.
Trial scene. Odysseus: 580, 583N². Palamedes: 578, 581N². Condemnation and death of Palamedes.
Oiax' lament, 588N² and plan (Aristophanes, *Thesm.* 770f.).
Deus ex machina 584, 585N².

The second play, *Palamedes*, took the action into the Greek camp. Already in the *Philoktetes* of 431 B.C. Euripides had made the disguised Odysseus ingratiate himself with Philoktetes by claiming to be a friend of Palamedes, who had been destroyed by Odysseus on a false charge of treachery. In the *Orestes* of 408 B.C. Palamedes' brother Oiax is working against Orestes, because he holds Agamemnon responsible for 'the hateful thing which happened in Troy' (432). The fragments of the *Palamedes* include (1) Odysseus' speech to Agamemnon, 580N²: 'all men, whether interested in the arts or not, labour to get money and whoever has most is wisest', and perhaps 583N², 'I do not commend a clever speaker whose actual practices are dishonourable', (2) Palamedes' defence, 578N², 'I invented writing and so made possible overseas letters, wills, and contracts.' He is a modern Prometheus who quotes civilized uses of writing. Presumably he also invented number, though the lines describing this are perhaps better given to Aeschylus (*adesp.* 470), but Aeschylus' Palamedes was primarily interested in military affairs (303–4M = 182N²). Aeschylus also brought Nauplios to the camp to accuse the Greeks of murdering Palamedes (fr. 181N² = 305 Mette). This version is given by the Scholiast to E. *Orestes* 432: Nauplios heard (that Palamedes had been stoned) and came to Troy to go to law with the Greeks for the murder of his son. It looks as if this was the major trial scene in Aeschylus and Euripides transferred the emphasis to the debate between Odysseus and Palamedes; we do not know anything useful about how Sophocles treated the story. Palamedes must have appeared contumacious if he also said: 'Countless of us could become generals but only one or two in a long time could become wise men' (581N²). (3) Oiax made Palamedes' death known to Nauplios by inscribing the news on oars, which drifted across the sea. This comes from the parody in the *Thesmophoriazusae* (770f.) and its scholia. This slow method of sending the news answers the realistic question, how did Nauplios hear, but excludes Nauplios' arrival in

Troy. Oiax can only have announced his intention of inscribing the oars; Aristophanes for his own purpose converted it into action on the stage.[10] A *deus ex machina* may have foretold the arrival of the oars and Nauplios' arrangements to wreck the Greek fleet, which are foreshadowed again in the *Trojan Women* (54). The fragment (588N[2]) which was wrongly connected with the death of Socrates, 'you Danaans killed the harmless wise nightingale of the Muses, persuaded by a shameless man', is probably part of Oiax' lament for Palamedes rather than of a choral ode: Oiax can well call Agamemnon and his friends *Danaoi*. On the other hand, two fragments, though possible for Oiax, seem more likely to belong to a *deus ex machina*: 584, 'a single just man is superior to countless unjust men', 585, 'only the just man's reputation abides for ever'.

The only hint we have of the beginning of the play is fr. 589. Euripides evidently made some reference to the bell-men who went round to see that the sentries were awake. Goossens has noted the parallel with the opening of the *Rhesus* and with Ion's *Phrouroi* (45N[2]). It seems likely that the parodos was a dawn chorus of Greek soldiers and that they were somehow concerned with the capture of the forged letter in which Priam purported to have sent gold to secure Palamedes' treachery. Variants of this story are found in Hyginus (*fab.* 105), Apollodorus (*Epitome* III, 8), and the Scholiast to E. *Or.* 432. It does not much matter which particular variant Euripides used. Presumably Odysseus related his plot in the prologue, when he was perhaps waiting for the return of his soldier with the forged letter. Then after the parodos the letter was read to Agamemnon, who decided to search Palamedes' hut.

Even on our scanty knowledge it is clear that the *Palamedes* fixes Odysseus as vengeful and unscrupulous and Agamemnon as a general who either cannot see through or fails to withstand the machinations of his subordinate. Odysseus as a careerist had interested Euripides at least as early as the *Philoktetes* in 431 B.C., and contemporary political issues appeared obviously in the plays of the Second Group. Here the trial provides a contrast of lives, the careerist succeeds in getting the pure scientist condemned. Palamedes has no chance of proving himself like Polyidos in his play, but his brother prepares a vengeance to which allusion is made again in the *Trojan Women*.

[10] Cf. E. W. Handley, *B.I.C.S.*, Supplement no. 5, 1957, 24, 37.

TROJAN WOMEN

With all this experience (and much more that we have lost) the audience saw the *Trojan Women*. In the prologue Poseidon (37) points to Hekabe 'lying before the doors' (of the huts which contain the Trojan captives including Helen) 'weeping many tears for many. Her daughter, Polyxene, has been killed ruthlessly at the tomb of Achilles. Priam is dead and her children. Kassandra, the girl whom Apollo let run wild, Agamemnon, disregarding god and piety, will force to be his mistress'. We have seen Hekabe in the *Alexandros* weeping for her lost child; now she has more to weep for – all her children and Priam, whom she recalls almost at the end of the play (1312): 'Priam, Priam, you perished without a tomb, without a friend and now you see not my disaster.'

When Athene joins Poseidon, she tells of yet another insult to Kassandra, Ajax' attempted rape, unpunished and uncensored by the Greeks (70f.). She and Poseidon agree to wreck the Greek fleet: 'Fill the hollow recesses of Euboea with dead' (84), 'The capes of Kaphereus shall have the bodies of many dead' (91). The audience know (and have probably been told already in the *Palamedes*) that Nauplios will light beacons on the cape to guide the fleet on to the rocks and so avenge the murder of Palamedes. 'The man who sacks cities is a fool: he makes temples and tombs, the shrines of the dead, a desert, and then perishes himself.'

Hekabe rises slowly, describing her misery physical and mental in recitative anapaests. She changes to decorated melic anapaests to describe the ships which brought Helen to Troy. She calls on the chorus to lament Troy. They enter in two semi-choruses (probably, as normally, up the parodoi, each of which is thought of as leading from a different hut) and first sing a lyric dialogue with Hekabe (who begs that Kassandra may not be sent away) and then sing to each other of the parts of Greece to which they may be sent, all in lyric anapaests.

The arrival of Talthybios, Agamemnon's herald, is announced in recitative anapaests. Then in a long dialogue in which he speaks iambics and Hekabe comments, chiefly in dochmiacs, the Trojan women learn that Kassandra has been chosen to be Agamemnon's mistress, Polyxene has been sacrificed at Achilles' tomb (but Talthybios with the tact of the humble in Euripides fails to make Hekabe understand), Andromache has been chosen by Neoptolemos, and Hekabe has been allotted to Odysseus.

Talthybios gives orders for Kassandra to be fetched and is startled to see torches burning inside. Kassandra enters brandishing torches like a maenad and singing her own wedding song (in dochmiacs mingled with glyconics and iambics) for her marriage with Agamemnon. We have seen her enter like this before, in the *Alexandros* when she prophesied the fall of Troy and no one believed her. Again Hekabe tries to restrain her and takes the torches from her. She then changes to spoken iambics: she will ruin the house of Agamemnon. She can prove that Troy is happier than Greece: war in self-defence is better than a war of aggression; Hektor has his glory, and Paris married the daughter of Zeus. Talthybios is as uncomprehending as the Trojans in the *Alexandros*, the Argives in the *Agamemnon*, and Euripides' own audience on the eve of the Sicilian expedition.

She goes on to tell of the death of Hekabe and the wanderings of Odysseus, and finally changes again to recitative trochaics – to prophesy again Agamemnon's death and her own, to throw away the wreaths which she wears as priestess, and to say farewell to Hekabe. 'Hurry to catch the breeze in your sails, lead me away from here: I am one of the three Furies (456f.).' Her coming to Greece will be as disastrous as Helen's arrival in Troy, which she had prophesied in the *Alexandros*: 'By his Judgment the Spartan woman will come as a Fury' (Ennius, *Alexander*, VIIR). This last speech is a travesty of the speeches of heroic self-sacrifice, just as the wedding-song is a travesty of wedding-songs.

Hekabe falls on the ground in utter misery (as in the earlier *Hecuba*, when Polyxene left her to be sacrificed, 438), and the scene ends with her describing her past glory, her sons killed, Priam killed at the altar, her daughters deprived of marriage, her future slavery, and now the loss of Kassandra and Polyxene; she only wishes for death. As in the earlier *Hecuba*, Hekabe's despair is followed by a wonderful decorated choral description of the last night of Troy when the wooden horse was dragged to the temple of Athena and the Trojans sang and danced until the Greek soldiers got out of the horse and captured the city.

Again an elaborate entrance: Andromache with Astyanax on a chariot (should we remember here Priam's entry in the *Alexandros*?), announced in recitative anapaests which are followed by a lyric lament between Hekabe and Andromache. Andromache tells Hekabe clearly at last that Polyxene has been sacrificed (thus Euripides goes round the theme of his earlier play; Polydoros, however, is omitted altogether). Her death is better than Andromache's life, which statement Hekabe denies. But Andromache goes on: her fame as Hektor's faithful wife has brought her to the bed of Neoptolemos. Hekabe counsels her that loyalty to Neoptolemos gives her the chance of bringing up Astyanax to re-establish Troy. That hope is immediately dashed by the arrival of Talthybios to say that the Greeks have been persuaded by Odysseus to kill Astyanax. Andromache knows there is no hope: Hektor cannot save his son, Helen has destroyed Troy. Themes of the first two plays recur in this scene: at the beginning Andromache speaks of the ill will of the gods who spared Paris; Hektor, the generous prince of the *Alexandros*, is in our minds all through the scene; Odysseus is as vengeful as in the *Palamedes*. Hekabe is left alone and the chorus sing another decorated ode, going back to the first Trojan War and the gods' love for Ganymede and Tithonos, which has been no help to Troy.

A third startling entrance: Menelaos arrives to fetch Helen. We have known from the beginning of the play that she is in the same huts as the other captives, and we have been reminded of her by Andromache's curse in the last scene (766f.). Having seen the *Alexandros* with the reference to her in Kassandra's prophecy (Ennius, *Alexander* VIIR) and surely also in the epilogue speech, the audience probably expected to see Helen in the third play as they have seen Paris in the first play; or if they did not expect, at least they were not so surprised as we are, reading the *Trojan Women* by itself. Menelaos seems to be going to kill her, and Hekabe in amazement believes that there is some justice in the world, whatever may be the divine, physical, or human force which makes it operate (884f.). Helen defends herself to Menelaos: Hekabe and Priam were responsible because *she* bore and *he* failed to destroy Paris (this is the presupposition of the *Alexandros*); the judgment of Paris resulted in the end in a Greek victory; Menelaos should have been more careful of his wife; no one can fight with Aphrodite; after Paris died, Helen claims, she tried to get back to the Greeks. This is magnificent rhetoric and within the mythical framework of the story. Hekabe answers: the goddesses were not so foolish as to have a beauty contest; what you call Aphrodite, was simply the disastrous impact of a beautiful young Oriental on your small-town wits; when you got to Troy, so far from wanting to get back to the Greeks, you refused when

I begged you to go; and now when you ought to be in sackcloth and ashes, you have put on your best clothes to meet Menelaos. Menelaos says that Helen shall die at once, but a last appeal from her changes his mind and all that Hekabe achieves is that Helen will sail on another ship to Greece (the audience knew the sequel from the *Odyssey* or indeed from the *Andromache*, and could see Menelaos, the only Greek hero who appears in the play, as only moved by his own pleasures).

The chorus sing another decorated ode: Zeus has betrayed Troy; they are being taken to Greece; may Menelaos and Helen never reach home. Talthybios brings the body of Astyanax and the shield of Hektor in which he is to be buried. Heartbreakingly Hekabe pronounces his funeral oration (and we first saw Hekabe weeping for her own lost baby in the *Alexandros*). This goes over into a lament with the chorus singing in answer to her spoken iambics: Helen destroyed him; Hektor's shield is more worthy of honour than Odysseus's arms; our sacrifices had no answer, but our misery will be a theme for poets. The body is carried off in the shield.

The chorus see flames in the huts. Troy is being burnt and the captives are to go to the ships. Hekabe tries to run into the flames (like Evadne in the *Supplices*), and Talthybios stops her because she is reserved for Odysseus. The play ends with the lyric lament of Hekabe and the chorus for Troy.

In this play (as to a lesser extent in the *Hecuba*, *Andromache*, and *Electra*) the beautiful mythological world of the choral odes contrasts sharply with the present misery of women in war and in particular of these women, Hekabe, Kassandra, and Andromache, the victims of un-scrupulous, dishonest, and inefficient conquerors. But in this play Euripides seems at one point to deny the mythological world.

Helen's speech starts from the mythical framework, which the audience have seen realized through the trilogy. Hekabe's speech, pre-pared by her strange outcry to Zeus (884) smashes it. Euripides seems to have given her a moment of extreme clarity in her suffering, when she sees that the story is a lie, a just Zeus may be only a concept in the human mind, and Aphrodite is another name for lust. If there are gods, they are not like the gods of mythology. Similarly Herakles in the moment of revelation when he decides for life instead of suicide rejects the mythological comfort proffered by Theseus: 'these are the unhappy figments of singers' (*H.F.* 1340ff.), and thereby destroys also, like

Hekabe, the mythological framework within which the play has hitherto moved.

But this is not the only and perhaps not the final word. In addition to the beauty of the choral odes, when Kassandra claims that Troy is happier than its victors, she says that if the Greeks had stayed at home, Hektor's valour would have passed unnoticed, and 'Paris married the daughter of Zeus. If he had not, no one would have spoken of his homely wedding' (394ff.). It is this view that Hekabe echoes at the end of the play (1242): 'if god had not utterly destroyed and buried our city, we should have been unseen and unpraised; we should have given no song to the Muses of posterity.' Gilbert Murray[11] has interpreted the trilogy in these terms: the first stage is an exhibition of the injustice of a world in which the innocent suffer and the irony of a world in which the unworthy victors are unhappy. 'But beyond that first stage there is a glimpse of another scale of values, in which there is something – call it a glory, or splendour, or for lack of a better name, beauty – something at any rate which is material for eternal song, in playing one's part to the last word and enduring what fate sends.' I do not feel certain that Euripides would have approved of the last phrase any more than I feel certain that the epilogue of the *Electra* represents in any real sense a restoration or order of harmony in the world.[12] But that Euripides in some plays asserted both scales of values and that for him as a poet both had validity is clear.

2 *Antigone, Iphigenia in Tauris, Hercules Furens*

ANTIGONE

The chronological position of the *Iphigenia* and *Hercules*, as has been pointed out, is secure on metrical grounds. The *Antigone* is not the only possibility as a first play, but the strange exciting story in which a young woman plays a heroic part would make it suitable to be placed in parallel with the *Iphigenia in Tauris*, and the percentage of resolutions (22.2%) in forty-three lines suggests that it belongs to the third group.

Any reconstruction is incompatible with the Antigone of the *Phoenissae* (1675) who is prepared to murder Haimon rather than marry

[11] *Greek Studies*, 148.
[12] Cf. above, p. 146.

him, but this is no more strange than the incompatibility of the *Helen* in 412 B.C. with the *Orestes* in 408 B.C. Two main suggestions have been made, (1) that the action was a variation on the action of Sophocles' *Antigone* (the natural interpretation of 'the story is also in Euripides' *Antigone*'),[13] (2) that the action took place when Antigone's son Maion had grown up in seclusion and came to Thebes for the games as in Hyginus (*Fab.* 72), and was recognized by the birthmark of the Spartoi, 'the spear which the earthborn carry' (fr. 164aN^2 = Ar. *Poet.* 1454b, 22). The writer of this line is not named and there is no reason to give it to Euripides; Astydamas' *Antigone*, which won the prize in 341 B.C., is early enough for quotation in this part of the *Poetics* and for the vases which illustrate Hyginus.[14] On the other hand, even if the notice in the argument of Sophocles' *Antigone* (and the scholiast to S. *Ant.* 1350) could refer to information given in the prologue of Euripides' *Antigone* rather than to the whole play, fr. 176N^2 must refer to the death and burial of Polyneikes: 'Death is the end of quarrels *(νεικέων)* . . . who will hurt a corpse by dishonour, if they can perceive none of their sufferings?' What was common to the two plays must have been that Antigone was discovered burying Polyneikes, but in Euripides (as our authorities say) she had the assistance of Haimon and was given in marriage to him and bore him the child Maion. The birth of Maion was presumably foretold at the end of the play and the speaker was evidently Dionysos: 'Son of Dione, how great a god you are, Dionysos, and mortals cannot withstand you' (177N^2). This is the unwilling acquiescence of a mortal in a future which has been described for him by a god; if fr. 176N^2 belongs here too, the future includes the burial of Polyneikes as well as the marriage of Haimon and the birth of Maion, and all this Kreon has to accept. It is at least possible that in the latter part of the play a messenger speech announced that Haimon and Antigone had been caught, Haimon and Antigone arrived bound (one of them a mute character), Kreon threatened them with death (or ordered Haimon to kill Antigone), and then Dionysos intervened.

The prologue started with a description of Oidipous (157, 158N^2, which should be run together). The lyric fragment describing the shield of Kapaneus (159N^2) may come from a parodos narrating the defeat of the Seven, as in Sophocles. If the above interpretation of fr. 176N^2 is

[13] Hypothesis of Sophocles, *Antigone*; Scholiast to S. *Ant.* 1350.
[14] Séchan, *Études*, 274ff.

right, Euripides altered the Sophoclean order of events so as to make the arrest of Antigone and Haimon the climax, and thereby gained the point that both acted in express disobedience of Kreon's orders. We can only guess what happened, and the echoes of Sophocles' play[15] may be misleading. Kreon certainly announced his decree and met with opposition: 'the King should please the majority' (171N^2); 'it is folly to have sole rule over one's peers' (172N^2); 'a divided city ends in civil war' (173N^2). In this play Antigone herself rather than Haimon used these arguments, and the likeness of fr. 170N^2 to Theonoe's words in *Hel.* 1002 suggests that she started with this praise of Persuasion.

There was also a debate on marriage. Kreon says a beautiful woman is no good unless she has sense (212N^2); beauty is as surfeiting as rich food (213N^2); marriage partners should be equal (214N^2); good women have good children (215N^2).[16] Antigone is as mad as her father (166N^2, with αὐτῇ for αὐτῷ). Haimon objects that children need not be like their parents (167N^2, with Nauck's suggested text); Antigone's parentage may be irregular but this does not affect her character (168N^2); a man can have no better possession than a sympathetic wife (164N^2). 'I was in love, and it is true that love is madness' (161N^2): the natural interpretation of this last fragment is that Haimon admitted that he had seduced Antigone and used this as an argument for marriage. It is not certain whether the marriage debate also belongs to the earlier part of the play (like the debate between Aiolos and Makareus in the *Aiolos*) before Haimon joins Antigone in burying Polyneikes, or whether this was his final attempt to win Kreon after they have both been arrested. The late position is perhaps more likely, and then 'listen. For the unfortunate do not lose their speech as well as their success' (165N^2) and 'we have come to the very edge of disaster' (169N^2) will also belong here, and Kreon answers on the difficulty of guarding a lover (162N^2); the scene ended with the intervention of Dionysos. If the marriage debate is late, we should perhaps suppose that after telling Kreon that she intended to disobey him Antigone persuaded Haimon to help her.

Euripides must have felt, like many modern readers, that Sophocles was too harsh in his treatment of Antigone's love for Haimon; he saw

[15] Notably fr. 165 with *Ant.* 563; 166 with *Ant.* 471; 172 with *Ant.* 739; 215 (which should be given to *Antigone* rather than *Antiope*) with *Ant.* 570.

[16] Frs. 212–5N^2 were rightly ascribed by Von Arnim (*Supplementum Euripideum*, 17) to *Antigone* rather than *Antiope*.

their love as central to the story, not as a secondary motive which merely created a foil to display Kreon's isolation. The pair of lovers are nevertheless a rather special pair in that Antigone defies Kreon's decree. Makareus and Kanake are a special pair because they are brother and sister; Meleager is in love with a virgin huntress; Phaethon is loved by a goddess. Only in the *Andromeda* are the pair more equally matched and, in spite of the romantic setting, the *Andromeda* is more obviously a reflection of contemporary life and a prototype for later comedy.

IPHIGENIA IN TAURIS

In the *Iphigenia in Tauris* Euripides has added a new chapter to the Orestes story. In the *Cypria* Artemis took Iphigeneia from Aulis to the Taurians and made her immortal. Herodotus (IV, 103) had already identified the goddess of the Taurians in South Russia with Iphigeneia. The temple of Artemis at Brauron in Attica and the Heroon of Iphigeneia had been fairly recently rebuilt.[17] Euripides could therefore tie his play on to a cult at the end (1448f.). His innovation was to introduce Orestes into the story.

The play opens with Iphigeneia recounting the story of the sacrifice at Aulis and her dream that the palace was shattered by an earthquake but for one pillar, which turned into a human being and she prepared to sacrifice him. She conjectures that Orestes must be dead, and she goes in to wait for her Greek handmaidens, the chorus. Orestes and Pylades enter to spy out the ground, and see the signs of human sacrifice. Orestes suggests flight. Pylades says they should remain concealed for the day and return to steal the statue by night. The nervy Orestes and the bold Pylades are contrasted, and this arrangement of the prologue gives the audience the necessary exposition from both sides.

The parodos is a long dialogue in melic anapaests between the chorus and Iphigeneia. They have come to ask for news. Her brother is dead and she wants to pour libations for him. They answer her lamentation and recall Pelopid themes – the changing of the sun's course, the golden lamb. She sings of Aulis and Achilles, her life here far away from the songs and weaving of Greek girlhood, sacrificing strangers and now lamenting her brother. This is Elektra's sister, and the sacrifice at Aulis was for her what the murder of Agamemnon was for Elektra. The tone

[17] *Archaeological Reports*, 1958, 3; 1959, 7.

of the parodos is darker than in the *Electra* and more like the *Trojan Women*, because here Euripides wants the maximum of gloom at the beginning of the play.

A herdsman reports that he and his comrades saw two young men by the shore; one went mad and started to kill the flocks; the shepherds then fell on them and with difficulty overcame them; and the King Thoas is sending them to Iphigeneia to sacrifice. The speech recalls the messenger speech of the *Melanippe Desmotis*, which has the same emphasis on the courage of the heroic young pair. Here Euripides emphasizes also (310) Pylades' care for Orestes (foreshadowing the sick-bed scene of the *Orestes* as well as the central scene of this play), and anticipates the messenger speeches of the *Orestes* and the *Bacchae* in dividing the spectators into a pious man (who thinks the pair are gods) and an impious man, who says they are shipwrecked sailors. Iphigeneia's misery wells up: she has no pity now that Orestes is dead; she wishes she could have Helen and Menelaos to sacrifice. Then with a sudden twist she sees that human sacrifice cannot be the pleasure of the goddess; the local killers have attributed to her their own evil desires. There is something of Medeia in this speech of indecision, but the insight at the end recalls rather Hekabe in the *Trojan Women*.

In a decorated aeolo-choriambic song the chorus ask who are the strangers? Are they traders? How did they get past the clashing rocks and the White Shore of Achilles? Good if Helen came to be sacrificed. Better still if a Greek would take us home. The captives are led in by attendants, whom Iphigeneia orders to untie their hands and go into the temple. Iphigeneia's sympathy with her unrecognized brother and his friend is immediately clear. Orestes refuses her sympathy. But she gradually extracts information about home, and finally learns that Orestes is alive. So her dream is untrue, and Orestes answers that even the gods are no truer prophets than dreams. Iphigeneia says she can send one of the two home with a letter. Orestes insists that it shall be Pylades. She will see that Orestes is richly buried. She goes in to get the letter, and a little lyric dialogue with the chorus punctuates the long scene. Both men wonder who Iphigeneia can be: Pylades cannot bear to desert Orestes, but Orestes persuades him that he cannot abandon his wife Elektra and attributes his own destruction to Apollo, who is ashamed of having commanded him to kill his mother. Iphigeneia comes out with the letter and Pylades insists on having the message read to him in case the tablet gets lost at sea. Iphigeneia's letter is addressed to Orestes and tells her story. Pylades gives it to Orestes and the recognition follows.

Euripides had a single good precedent for the use of writing in the heroic age: Proitos' letter to Iobates about Bellerophon, to which he had at least referred in the *Stheneboia*.[18] In the *Palamedes* Palamedes names letters to friends overseas as one of the benefits which came from his invention of writing. Presumably Euripides felt the real difficulty of establishing for Orestes certain proof of Iphigeneia's identity: for this purpose he stresses (584) that the letter was written beforehand in the hope that a messenger might arrive, and for this purpose he has concealed Orestes' identity from her up to this moment; this brought him also the advantage of the long sympathetic scene between brother and sister, with also the growing possibility that the sister might put the brother to death.

Orestes establishes his identity by memories of his childhood, and brother and sister share a long lyric dialogue in which Iphigeneia sings and Orestes speaks iambic trimeters (832 must be given to Iphigeneia); this, like the earlier lyric dialogue while Iphigeneia fetches the letter, punctuates the long scene. Iphigeneia sings of her near-death at Aulis and his near-death here; how are they to escape? Pylades, who is now made known to Iphigeneia as her cousin and brother-in-law, stirs them to action. Orestes tells his story and his mission. Together they plan escape: Iphigeneia is to tell Thoas that the statue and the two men need purification in the sea. Iphigeneia begs the chorus to conceal her plans, and finally prays to Artemis to save them and come with them to Athens: otherwise she will prove Apollo a liar (a slightly quizzical prayer for which there are later parallels).[19] The whole sequence of scenes here: near-murder of kinsman, recognition, making of plan, persuasion of tyrant, messenger-speech on execution of plan, is like that in the earlier *Kresphontes*, and between the two plays the *Electra* is a special variation on the same general scheme. The lyric dialogue underlining the recognition[20] is a new element here which becomes standard later, and the plan is a plan to escape, not a plan to kill.

[18] Cf. above, p. 82.
[19] See below, pp. 195, 201, 209, 214.
[20] Cf. above, p. 17, for possible influence of Timotheos. The form may have been invented for the *Alexandros* of 415 B.C.

Before the tyrant is persuaded the chorus sing another decorated aeolo-choriambic song, comparing themselves to the halcyon lamenting its husband, in their desire for Delos and Greece, in their misery at their captivity. Iphigeneia will go home in glory, and they pray that they may go home too. Thoas arrives (and his arrival was prepared not only by Iphigeneia's references to him but also by the herdsman's statement that he had taken the captives first to Thoas, 333). Iphigeneia appears carrying the statue of Artemis, and explains that the statue and the victims must be purified in a lonely place by the sea. The metre changes to recitative trochaic tetrameters when she gives her instructions, then she describes the two Greeks, the animals for sacrifice, and the torches coming out of the temple, and ends with a prayer to Artemis. This is a second procession echoing the earlier arrival of Orestes and Pylades with the herdsmen. The recitative trochaics have an urgent solemnity here like Kassandra's farewell in the *Trojan Women* (444).

The chorus sing, in decorated style again, of Apollo's birth in Delos and his slaying of Python, of the contest between dreams and prophecy and the triumph of Apollo's oracle. The messenger enters to tell of the escape, the chorus vainly try to send him elsewhere to look for Thoas; Thoas comes out of the temple and hears the story, summons his forces for pursuit and promises to put the chorus to death. Athena stops him and arranges for the cult at Brauron and tells Thoas to send the Greek women (of the chorus) back to Greece.

This beautifully constructed play is light-hearted. Euripides has darkened it all he can in the earlier part by Iphigeneia's dream, her harping on the sacrifice at Aulis, and by the account of Orestes' madness. But we cannot quite believe in Orestes' danger as we believe in Kresphontes' danger, and Thoas is so completely the victim of Iphigeneia that we cannot really believe in his power to stop the fugitives; his fury is real enough but he is only made dangerous because Euripides wants to introduce Athena and ground the story in the Brauron cult. Apollo is justified whatever the humans may say about prophecy. The young trio are striving to do their best, two of them sorely handicapped in quite different ways by their past, all three touching in their sympathy for each other, and their efforts are rewarded. The *Antigone* also ends happily, but the danger is greater and on the way serious problems of marriage and statecraft are discussed. The third play, the *Hercules Furens*, is a tragedy in the modern sense of the word.

HERCULES FURENS

Amphitryon speaks the prologue and tells the past history in the form into which Euripides has cast it. Herakles has married Megara, the daughter of Kreon, king of Thebes. Herakles' labours are a price paid to Eurystheus for return to Argos, from which Amphitryon is exiled. Herakles has now gone to Hades to fetch the three-bodied dog. Meanwhile Lykos, the son of the Lykos who was husband of Dirke (Euripides perhaps foresaw already his own *Antiope*), has killed Kreon and his wife and wants to kill Megara, Amphitryon, and the sons of Herakles. They are now seated on the altar of Zeus, shut out from their house. This opening situation recalls the *Heraclidae*, partly because Herakles' children are again involved, but that is a more normal asylum play, and Euripides has come nearer here to the situation of the *Diktys* where Diktys and Danae took refuge on an altar to avoid the unwelcome attentions of Polydektes.[21] Megara asks for consolation for herself and her children, but all that Amphitryon can offer is the thought that prosperity does not endure for ever.

The chorus of old men arrive on their sticks, lamenting their old age: at the end they admire the children and lament what heroes Hellas will lose. Lykos comes in and asks why they are so slow to die: Herakles only killed animals[22] and that with a bow; he is not prepared to leave Kreon's grandchildren alive. Amphitryon indignantly defends Herakles' courage by quoting his labours and enunciates the strategy of the bow; Thebes and Hellas fail to defend the children of Herakles, and he is too old. Lykos makes preparations to burn them off the altar. The chorus leader calls on his fellows to resist Lykos and defend the children of Herakles. Megara (and here again something of Makaria in the *Heraclidae* comes through) refuses their offer; let us at least die decently, and she persuades Lykos to open the house so that she may get adornments for the children (here we remember the *Ino*). Amphitryon ends with a reproach for Zeus as divine father of Herakles: either Zeus has no knowledge or he is unjust.

The chorus sing a decorated aeolo-choriambic account of the labours of Herakles in three pairs of strophes and antistrophes each with an ephymnion: now Herakles is in Hades and they are too old to help.

[21] Cf. above, p. 62.
[22] Compare the argument used by Aithra, *Suppl.* 314–19.

Megara and Amphitryon come out with the children, ready for
death. Megara speaks of their plans for the children ruling Greece as
Kings or wives of Kings. Amphitryon muses on the fragility of human
prosperity. Suddenly Herakles arrives. Megara tells him the situation.
He will destroy the palace and fill the whole Ismenos with corpses.
Amphitryon counsels caution because the revolution has given Lykos
many supporters (Euripides puts the whole political situation on a
fifth-century basis as in the *Supplices*). He then asks why Herakles has
been so long away, and learns that he brought back Theseus from
Hades. Herakles then takes his wife and children into the house.

The chorus sing in aeolo-choriambic of the glories of youth; those
with *arete* ought to have a double youth; they want to sing of victorious
Herakles with wine and lyre and flute. Lykos arrives to ask why Megara
and the children are not ready for death. Amphitryon refuses to fetch
them and so lures Lykos into the house;[23] he follows, to have the
satisfaction of seeing his enemy die. The chorus sing in excited dochmiacs while Lykos is murdered; they continue in aeolo-choriambic
that there will be rejoicing in Thebes; the gods are just; the whole land-
scape will celebrate Herakles; this is the proof of his divine birth.
Essentially here the technique is the same as in the *Iphigenia in Tauris*;
there extreme gloom leading up gradually to the recognition scene;
here extreme confidence and rejoicing, which is violently reversed by
the appearance of Iris and Lyssa.

Iris says that because Herakles has completed his labours Zeus has
allowed Hera to maltreat him: Lyssa expresses her unwillingness but
finally consents, telling Iris to return to Olympos. Lyssa had already
been brought on the stage by Aeschylus in the *Xantriai* and perhaps
also in the *Toxotides*, if the evidence of a vase in Boston is to be
trusted,[24] the conversation between Lyssa and Iris also recalls in
reverse the conversation between Kratos and Hephaistos in the *Prometheus Vinctus* (or on the human level the relation between Talthybios
and the Greek commanders in the *Trojan Women*). The chorus see them
as a terrifying vision over the house; if Euripides is using the *mechane*,
then the conversation between Iris and Lyssa takes place on the roof;
Lyssa gets out of the car which carries them both and at the end goes

[23] Cf. above, p. 145.
[24] Boston 00.346, *A.R.V.*[2], 1045; Pfuhl, *M.U.Z.*, fig. 515; Pickard-Cambridge, *Festivals*,
fig. 174.

down behind into the house, while Iris is swung off again on the *mechane*. The chorus' comment (880) 'she is gone in her chariot; she goads her team' is purely metaphorical and develops Lyssa's own 'I will run a race into the breast of Herakles' (863).

Lyssa marks the beginning of the madness: she describes Herakles tossing his head and rolling his eyes (867). The dochmiac commentary of the chorus is a dark contrast to their preceding commentary while Lykos was being murdered: here the stages of the action inside the house are marked by Amphitryon's cries.[25] Then the whole sequence is made clear by the messenger speech: they were sacrificing to purify the house after the death of Lykos when Herakles went mad with rolling eyes and foaming lips (932 corresponds to 867); he pretended to drive to Mycenae and threaten Eurystheus. Amphitryon puts his hand on his arm saying 'is the blood of the corpses driving you frenzied (966)?' Herakles shoved him aside and started shooting at his children and his wife, thinking they belonged to Eurystheus. This sequence corresponds to Amphitryon's cries in 887–96. Then he attacked Amphitryon, but 'there came a vision, which he seemed to see, Pallas brandishing a spear, and threw a stone at his breast, which put him to sleep': this corresponds to the end of the choral commentary (906). (The crash and its explanation anticipates the 'palace miracle' of the *Bacchae*, and may itself have been anticipated by similar miracles in the *Alkmene* and the *Cretans*.[26])

The sequence of chorus punctuated by cries off followed by messenger speech is a tremendously effective development of the normal murder scene. Here it is made more terrible by the preceding appearance of Lyssa and by the use of the *ekkyklema* immediately after the short lament[27] by the chorus to show Herakles tied to a fallen column among the corpses. Euripides clearly remembered the *Ajax* of Sophocles where Athena talks to the mad Ajax in the prologue; then Tekmessa reports the same sequence of action as seen from inside the house, and finally the *ekkyklema* shows Ajax sitting among the dead sheep. Sophocles again gave him the idea for the next scene: Amphitryon

---

[25] 906ff. should be given to the chorus, *not* to Herakles, cf. A. M. Dale, *Wiener Studien*, 69, 1956, 101.

[26] Cf. above, pp. 91, 93, 130.

[27] They quote the Danaides and Prokne as parallels, just as the chorus of the *Medea* (1282) sing of Ino after Medeia has murdered her children.

and the chorus lament antiphonally, but Amphitryon is terrified that they will wake Herakles; this recalls the scene in the *Trachiniae* where the old man, bringing in the tortured Herakles on a litter, is similarly terrified that Hyllos will wake him. Here the sequence ends with Herakles' waking and Amphitryon, his father, gradually telling him that he has murdered his wife and children.

His immediate thought of suicide is stopped by the arrival of Theseus, who had been carefully brought to the audience's attention when Herakles said that he had delayed in Hades in order to bring Theseus back. Herakles covers his head in shame, and the news is conveyed to Theseus in a long lyric dialogue by Amphitryon. Theseus is unafraid of pollution by Herakles and forces him to uncover his head. Herakles says that life is impossible; Amphitryon killed Elektryon and married Alkmene; Zeus begot him and Hera has hated him from birth; there is nowhere where he can live; let Hera dance in triumph. This is a conventional mythological account, and Theseus answers with conventional consolation: the gods commit crimes and yet live on in bliss; why should not Herakles? He can come to Athens and share Theseus' wealth, and after death Athens will honour him with sacrifices and shrines.[28] Herakles rejects the mythological consolation. These stories about the gods are the wretched figments of singers. But it would be cowardice to commit suicide. He will go to Athens. He makes arrangements for the burial of the corpses and the disposal of Kerberos. 'We have all perished by a single disaster which is Hera.' Theseus leads him off and his final word is (1425): 'Whoever wishes to possess wealth or strength rather than friends is a fool.'

This sentiment summarizes the play.[29] Wealth belongs to the tyrant, and Lykos was a tyrant. Herakles' labours and slaughter of Lykos were a manifestation of strength. Herakles is rescued, as far as he can be rescued, from his troubles by the friendship of Theseus. On this level the play has a tripartite structure somewhat like the *Andromache*; there the characters are displayed successively, Andromache, Hermione, Neoptolemos; here all three are men and embody different ideas of life: wealth and power in Lykos, strength in Herakles, friendship

[28] Possibly connected with the extension of the Theseion in the late fifth century (H. A. Thompson, *Hesperia*, 35, 1966, 47).

[29] On the play in general see H. O. Chalk, *J.H.S.*, 82, 1962, 7ff.; J. C. Kamerbeek, *Mnem.*, 19, 1966, 1.

in Theseus – a friendship, which, because it disregards the very real pollution of a madman who has killed his wife and children, is something rarer than the friendship which brings Peleus to rescue Phoinix from his father.[30] The nearest parallel is the friendship of Pylades for Orestes, which is shown in its mature beauty in the *Iphigenia in Tauris*, but there Pylades had himself assisted Orestes in killing his mother.

In the *Iphigenia in Tauris* Orestes' madness is related in a messenger speech. Earlier in the *Ino* and the *Second Phrixos* messengers told how Athamas killed Learchos while hunting and how Phrixos was thwarted by Dionysos from killing Ino. Only the madness of Athamas was disastrous and it is unlikely that he was seen again. In this play Euripides has made the madness and recovery of Herakles a major, if not the major theme of the play. What is he saying about the madness as distinct from the recovery where the operative force is clearly Theseus' friendship? Amphitryon is certainly worried at Herakles' haste in taking vengeance regardless of caution (585f.), and when Herakles starts to go mad, Amphitryon asks whether the blood of corpses is driving him frenzied (966). The messenger speaks of Athena as a 'vision which he seemed to see' (1002). Herakles' statement that he does not believe that gods commit adultery implies that his own divine birth and the enmity of Hera also belong to the 'miserable figments of singers', and therefore would imply also a purely natural cause for his madness. But he himself speaks finally 'of a single disaster which is Hera', so that Euripides does not make him draw the conclusion from the insight which he has given him, like Hekabe,[31] in his moment of greatest suffering. Lyssa is valid as an hypostatization of a psychological factor like Aphrodite in the *Hippolytus* but unlike Aphrodite she has to be set in motion by a higher agency, Hera. Lyssa is a sort of middle term between the mythological story and the naturalistic interpretation of events, and as in the *Trojan Women* Euripides seems to assert the validity of both.

3 *Andromeda, Helen, Ion, 412 B.C.*

ANDROMEDA

The *Andromeda* began with an anapaestic monody of Andromeda. The

[30] Cf. above, p. 85.
[31] Cf. above, p. 180.

note of the scholiast to Aristophanes' *Thesmophoriazusae* 1065 that 'O holy Night' (fr. 114N² = Ennius IR) is 'the beginning of the prologue' cannot be doubted. Two later night-scenes at the beginning of the *Iphigenia in Aulis* and the *Rhesus* are also in anapaests; but in the *I.A.* Agamemnon comes out of his tent and summons the old man out, and in the *Rhesus* the chorus arrive and summon Hektor from his tent; here Andromeda is already on the stage tied to her rock. This tableau-opening itself contrasts with the earlier Sophoclean *Andromeda*; four vases[32] of the middle decades of the fifth century show a version of the legend in which Andromeda in Eastern trousers is led in by negroes and tied to posts; this suggests that the Sophoclean play included (not necessarily at the beginning) a binding scene like the *Prometheus Vinctus* of Aeschylus. The Euripidean tableau was probably set on the *ekky-klema*, as Séchan[33] suggests, and so could be presented to the audience without delay; this technique also had been already used by Aeschylus in the *Niobe*.

Andromeda names herself (fr. 115N²) and may have given the exposition from her side partly in her recitative, partly in the ensuing lyric dialogue with the chorus, partly in her first scene with Perseus. Ennius fr. IIIR: *filiis propter te obiecta sum innocens Nerei*[34] shows that Euripides' story agreed in this point with Hyginus, *fab.* 64: Kassiopeia had boasted that Andromeda was more beautiful than the Nereids, and Poseidon therefore ordered Kepheus to expose her to the monster. The Ennius fragment does not necessarily imply a later scene between Andromeda and Kassiopeia (although this is a real possibility); it may come from the prologue and have followed immediately some such phrase as *crudelis mater*. This would make the line an iambic octonarius, the metre used by Ennius in the *Hecuba* (IIR) to represent lyric anapaests of the original. An alternative is to accept fr. IIIR as an iambic senarius (addressed to the absent Kassiopeia) and to use it and fr. 114aN² 'Echo answerer to my words' as evidence for an iambic speech of Andromeda between Andromeda's opening monody and her lyric dialogue with the chorus (the shape would then be parallel to the prologue of the *Iphigenia in Aulis* as preserved;) but fr. 114a may come from an iambic

[32] Cf. *B.I.C.S.*, 12, 1965, 29.
[33] *Études* 265.
[34] 'Because of you I am the innocent victim of the daughters of Nereus.'

line within the lyric dialogue, and it is doubtful whether an iambic speech is needed for the exposition.[35]

Andromeda's opening anapaests were interrupted by repetitions from Echo whom she begged to stop when the chorus appeared (fr. 118N²). Echo is an off-stage singer (unless Andromeda sings the repetitions herself): Andromeda says Echo is in a cave, which will be the central doorway behind Andromeda, and the cave is represented on several of the Andromeda vases.[36] The repetitions were naturally parodied by Aristophanes. The one repetition of which we can be fairly certain is the end of fr. 114N², where the paroemiac τοῦ σεμνοτάτου δι᾽ Ὀλύμπου is picked up by Echo with the catalectic metron δι᾽ Ὀλύμπου exactly as in *Alc.* 106f. Echo emphasizes the lonely horror of Andromeda's night chained to the rocks, and this is the romantic picture with which Euripides wanted to startle the audience.

With the dawn, presumably, the chorus enters; she addresses them as 'dear maidens' (fr. 117N²) and they are utterly sympathetic. The suggestion therefore that they are the Nereids, who were slighted by Kassiopeia, is most unlikely (the Nereids on Apulian vases, who look on while Perseus slays the monster, are probably additions of the painter unless they were mentioned in the messenger speech, and they certainly have nothing to do with the chorus). The chorus are Ethiopian maidens as illustrated on the early fourth century Attic kalyx-krater. The parodos of the Helen consists of 88 lines: brief hexameter introduction by Helen, strophe by Helen, antistrophe by the chorus, strophe by Helen, antistrophe by the chorus, epode by Helen. Here Andromeda's recitative (fr. 114–6N²), which rises to melic anapaests (fr. 121N²) was evidently much longer than Helen's introduction but the succeeding structure may have been similar. Fr. 117, 114a(?), 118N² belong to Andromeda's first strophe; fr. 119N² (shared sorrow eases the load) to the chorus' antistrophe, fr. 120N² (pitiless the father who left you to die for your country) to the chorus' second antistrophe (Andromeda had evidently complained of her parents in her second strophe). Andromeda's epode is largely preserved in fr. 122N²: 'I am not dancing

[35] Robert's suggestion (*A.Z.* 1878, 18) that fr. 114a belongs to an iambic prologue spoken by Echo before Andromeda's monody, though approved by Wilamowitz (*Kl. Schr.* V, 2, 97), is impossible because Andromeda's monody is called 'the beginning of the prologue' by the scholiast.

[36] See below, p. 304, for list of illustrations.

with my companions, but wound in chains exposed to a monster, not with a marriage hymn but with a binding song. Weep for my cruel sufferings, the lawless sufferings inflicted by my kin. Who will look upon my sufferings? Would that a thunderbolt would destroy me! I have no desire to see the sun again when the end of my journey is death.'

Perseus may arrive immediately. His winged sandals (rather than the use of the *mechane*) show that he is flying.[37] He does not know what land he has reached, and is amazed at the sight of Andromeda who is like a beautiful statue (fr. 124, 124a, 125, 125aN²). He asks who she is, and she is at first silent (126N²). When he pities her, she in turn asks who he is (127, 123N²). From this point the sequence is unclear. Fr. 136N², the famous prayer to Eros (either don't let men fall in love or help lovers in their troubles), is certainly Perseus' final speech before he goes off to slay the monster: this type of slightly quizzical prayer occurs at similar places in other late plays.[38] Before he goes, Perseus has fallen in love with Andromeda, and this stage must be later than his question 'Will you be grateful if I save you' and her answer 'take me as your servant, wife, or captive' (frs. 129, and 132N² are tied together by Diogenes Laertius who quotes them).[39] 'I have never mocked the unfortunate' (fr. 130N², Perseus) belongs in the same context, and he must have guaranteed his power to help by relating his encounter with the Gorgon; a remnant may remain in fr. 133: 'after reaching safety it is pleasant to remember one's labours'.

Müller[40] suggested that Kepheus arrived soon after Perseus and promised him Andromeda's hand if he slew the monster: his chief evidence is fr. 143N² 'I am well off for money, but my position, as you see, is far from well.' Séchan thought that this scene was implied by the inclusion of Kepheus on vases; the vases may imply that Kepheus had a part in the play; they need not imply his presence at this moment any more than the inclusion of Thoas on an Attic vase[41] of the early

---

[37] Cf. Hourmouziades, *op. cit.*, 154. The phraseology of Aristophanes, *Thesm.* 1010–16 is accounted for by the winged sandals. Pollux (IV, 128), if he is thinking of this scene, may have deduced the *mechane* from the text.

[38] Cf. above, p. 186; below, pp. 201, 209, 214.

[39] Fr. 132N² is probably elaborated in Ennius fr. IIR (cf. however Traina, *Maia*, 16, 1964, 137).

[40] *Philol.* 66, 1907, 48ff.

[41] Ferrara T 1145; *ARV²* 1440; Webster, *Greek Theatre Production*, pl. 7.

fourth century implies his presence in the letter scene of the *Iphigenia in Tauris*. It seems more natural that this very moving scene should be played without paternal interference: when Perseus confessed his love, the two must have planned the future, and in fr. 1054N[2] (Take the best of my arguments, for love is an unsure guide) Perseus seems to be asking Andromeda to help him plan. It was as the poverty-stricken lover, pale and emaciated by his passion, that Perseus impressed posterity,[42] and this is how Andromeda saw him if fr. 140N[2] (your fortunes are slender, but your words are spirited) belongs here. The plan was perhaps that Perseus should kill the monster and Andromeda plead with her parents.

A further problem is raised by fr. 128N[2]: 'Stranger, pity me in my utter misery, free me from my bonds.' If this line and a half from the *Thesmophoriazusae* is rightly attributed to the *Andromeda*, when was it spoken and when did Perseus comply with the request? In Lucian and Ovid he slays the monster before he frees Andromeda,[43] but this may not be the Euripidean version. The speech (fr. 145–7N[2], Ennius fr. IV–VIII) which reports Perseus' killing of the monster seems to have been delivered by a messenger, *not* by Perseus, and to have been addressed to Kepheus rather than to Andromeda: fr. 145N[2] 'and I see the monster speeding from the Atlantic sea to banquet on the maiden' cannot have been spoken to Andromeda and must have followed some such opening as 'I had just brought my sheep down to the sea' (cf. *Bacch.* 677–80); fr. 146N[2], describing the shepherds' efforts to refresh Perseus after the combat (perhaps fr. 147N[2] also belongs), is more naturally spoken by a messenger than by Perseus, but the matter is clinched by Ennius fr. V '*he* scans its body to see where *he* can wound it mortally'. If Andromeda is still chained to her rock, the sequence must be departure of Perseus to slay the monster, chorus, arrival of Kepheus, arrival of messenger, departure of both (?), arrival of Perseus and freeing of Andromeda. If Perseus frees Andromeda before he goes off to slay the monster, it is natural to suppose that she and the chorus depart to Kepheus' palace, when Perseus flies off over the sea. This would allow the ekkyklema to roll in so that the scene can change from the sea-shore to Kepheus' palace: the same technique was used for change of scene by Aeschylus in the *Eumenides* and by Sophocles in the *Ajax*, and

[42] Cf. Lucian and Hesychius ap. Nauck[2], p. 393.
[43] Lucian, *Mar. Dial.* 14, 3; Ovid, *Met.* IV, 663ff.

(without scene-change) the chorus leave the orchestra for a period in Euripides' *Alcestis* and *Helen*.

If this is right, the scene between the departure of the chorus with Andromeda and their re-entry would naturally belong to Kepheus, who knows nothing of what has happened. Here fr. 143N² 'I am well off for money, but my position, as you see, is far from well' is in place (also fr. 135 'every day the future frightens me'). It is not clear to whom Kepheus speaks, and perhaps a soliloquy is not impossible in spite of 'you see', since this is in fact a kind of second prologue. A wall-painting in Pompeii of the early first century A.D. has four masks: left, Perseus; centre, above, a woman with long black hair; right, Kepheus and woman. Robert identified the women as Andromeda and Kassiopeia. This is probably right, although the curious stylization of the mask which he calls Andromeda makes one think of Echo. This is the surest evidence that Kassiopeia had a part in the play, and she is the most likely partner for Kepheus in this scene. It may be that she rather than Kepheus took the lead later, but we have no evidence which of the parents was the leader. This scene was presumably followed by the re-entry of Andromeda and the chorus, and then the messenger arrived when Andromeda had gone into the palace.

Opinion has differed as to whether all the opposition to Andromeda's final departure with Perseus came from Kepheus and Kassiopeia (Müller, Séchan) or whether Andromeda's former suitor (Wecklein), who according to Hyginus conspired with Kepheus to kill Perseus, was also involved.

That Kepheus (with or without Kassiopeia) objected to Perseus as a pauper and as a bastard is proved by frs. 142, and 141N², both from a dialogue scene and possibly a dialogue with Andromeda, since 'I forbid you to have bastard children' seems to be addressed to her. This then may be the scene on Andromeda's return and have ended with her defiance.

Perseus on arrival certainly urged his own claims: his many labours have made him glorious (fr. 134N²), and the successful have the gods on their side (fr. 150N²). Kepheus refuses to have his thinking determined by Perseus (fr. 144N²) and Perseus can find no arguments to influence his barbarian mentality (fr, 139N²). The two scenes together raise the obvious points which might occur in any contemporary discussion of marriage.

The situation is not unlike the situation in the *Alexandros* when the shepherd boy has defeated Priam's sons or in the *Ion* when Ion has been accepted by Xouthos to the horror of Kreousa; in this play too an unsuccessful plot to murder Perseus is a natural sequel and Andromeda's earlier suitor the natural instrument. Müller's argument that he had no part in Euripides because he is not found in the stars would only be cogent if we knew that in the epilogue Athena arranged for all the persons in the play to be put in the stars. In fact Pseudo-Eratosthenes (*Catast.* 15–16, 37) does not quote his source for the catasterism; that his source was tragedy is a guess from the fact that he makes Athena responsible. Athena is very likely to have foretold this in a tragic epilogue, and Euripides is perhaps more likely than Sophocles to have had such an epilogue (but Aphrodite, who appears on the Attic vase, would be a very suitable epilogue speaker for this play). Nothing more can be certainly extracted for Euripides from Pseudo-Eratosthenes than that Euripides mentioned Kepheus and Andromeda. But we have a little positive evidence for Andromeda's suitor in Euripides' play. The Sicilian kalyx-krater of the mid-fourth century by the Hecate painter gives a dejected looking young man holding a spear, Andromeda at the mouth of a cave, and Perseus. The cave and the Greek costume of Andromeda agree with the other vases which illustrate Euripides, and the young man must almost be her unsuccessful suitor: this suggests that he had a part in Euripides' play. He may also perhaps be recognized in the young Oriental represented on other vases. The one fragment which it is tempting to ascribe to him (as Wecklein saw) is fr. 149N² 'I was induced by youth and rashness rather than by reason': Perseus had no cause to apologize for lack of sense, because his exploits, whether rash or not, had been successful. These words sound like Laios' apology in the *Chrysippos* (fr. 840N²) and Herakles' apology in the *Auge* (fr. 265aN²), and might have been used if after his unsuccessful attempt to murder Perseus the suitor pleaded for mercy, as Phineus does in Ovid, *Met.* V, 218: *non nos odium regnique cupido conpulit ad bellum, pro conjuge movimus arma.* Perseus may have answered that 'Justice is the daughter of Zeus and lives near to human sin' (fr. 151N²).

It is fanciful to try and reconstruct the unsuccessful plot between Andromeda's suitor and Kepheus which is attested by Hyginus, but some such sequel seems likely to make the kind of long and eventful play which Euripides was writing at this time. Perseus ultimately may have threatened to use the Gorgon's head to petrify the opposition, and this may have been the cue for Athena or Aphrodite to prophesy the future in the Epilogue.

If this reconstruction is right, the *Andromeda* consisted of the rescue in Ethiopia of a young woman from distress by a young hero, followed by an unsuccessful plot to kill the young hero. In the *Helen* a middle-aged wife is rescued in Egypt by a middle-aged husband, and the plot is a plot to escape the unwanted attentions of the local king.

HELEN

Euripides had already quoted the story in the *Electra* (1280): 'Helen is come from the house of Proteus and she never went to Troy. Zeus despatched an *eidolon* (phantom) of Helen to Ilion.' The play starts with Helen seated as a suppliant on the tomb of Proteus to avoid marriage with his son Theoklymenos (in the background is Proteus' daughter, the prophetess Theonoe). So far this is a typical asylum opening, which recalls the *Andromache*, the *Hercules*, and still more the asylum scene of the *Diktys*. Teucer enters to consult Theonoe and is horrified at the sight of a woman exactly like Helen. He tells her of the sack of Troy and the difficult return of the Greeks, the suicide of Leda and the Catasterism of the Dioskouroi. She sends him away for fear Theoklymenos may kill him.

Helen bursts into a decorated trochaic lament; the chorus (like the chorus of the *Hippolytus*) were doing the washing when they heard Helen's cry, she tells them what Teucer has said, they join her lament, she sings of Paris' fleet and the Judgment and her own exile in Egypt. She repeats the story in iambics: her beauty is responsible for all her misery. Suicide alone remains. The chorus suggests consulting Theonoe. In a lyric dialogue Helen accepts their suggestion and repeats her misery: she is more unhappy than Kallisto who was changed into a bear or the daughter of Merops who was changed into a hind. As in the *Iphigenia in Tauris* the heroine is to be shown in utter misery before the change in her fortunes.

The chorus and Helen go in to consult Theonoe so that Menelaos (like Herakles in the *Alcestis*[44]) can present himself to the audience; the illustrious general now a tattered shipwrecked sailor, who has left his

[44] See above, p. 51.

wife (the phantom Helen) in a cave while he comes to beg at the palace. An old woman tries to drive him away and tells him that Theoklymenos wants to kill all Greeks so that he can marry Helen (the sympathetic servant who received the young Kresphontes must have played the same sort of part[45]). Menelaos is in complete amazement at the news that the Spartan Helen is here, but resolves to wait for Theoklymenos.

The chorus and Helen come out with the news that Menelaos is alive but shipwrecked, and Helen runs for the tomb of Proteus when she sees the wild figure waiting for her. This recalls Elektra's fear of the unrecognized Orestes and Pylades (*El.* 215ff.), but here Menelaos and Helen turn and recognize each other. Menelaos cannot believe her story and is turning to go when an old servant arrives to say that 'Helen' has vanished from the cave (the phantom has the same apologetic dislike for the role which Hera imposed on her, as Lyssa in the *Hercules*[46]). Then the two recognize each other in a long lyric dialogue, as in the *Iphigenia in Tauris*. The old man, who had carried a torch at Helen's wedding, shares their joy but asks why Kalchas and Helenos never said anything about it; common sense is more useful than prophecy. The old man is sent back to join Menelaos' crew, and Helen tells Menelaos of his danger from Theoklymenos. They start to plan. Unless Theonoe can be persuaded to keep silence, they have no hope and they make a suicide pact (this anticipates the later *Orestes*). Theonoe enters solemnly, accompanied by a servant with a torch and a servant with an incenseburner. She knows that she can either side with Hera who wishes Menelaos' return or with Aphrodite who wants him killed. Helen begs her not to be false to her pious belief in a god who hates violence and to keep faith with Proteus who accepted Helen from Hermes. Menelaos calls on Proteus to restore his wife and on Hades, who has received so many dead in the Trojan war, to make Theonoe give back Helen, or else they will commit suicide. Theonoe says that she has a great shrine of Justice in her heart and will keep silent: they must find their own plan. The danger, which seems much more real than the danger to Orestes in the *Iphigenia in Tauris*, is over. Menelaos and Helen plan to trick Theoklymenos by pretending that Menelaos is dead and by begging for a ship and offerings so that burial

[45] Cf. above, p. 138.
[46] Cf. above, p. 189.

rites can be performed at sea. Menelaos is to sit on the tomb; Helen goes in to cut her hair and put on black mourning clothes; she leaves with a quizzical prayer to Hera and Aphrodite.[47]

At last there is a break in the action for the chorus to sing a decorated ode of Paris' voyage, the Trojan War, the wreck of the Greek fleet by Nauplios' fire-signals;[48] Helen is a demi-goddess but she is reputed to be a traitress; why cannot men decide their quarrels by arguments instead of war? Theoklymenos arrives and is astonished to see Helen in mourning. She offers him marriage if he will give her the means to perform burial rites for her husband. (This is a pretended reconciliation like that of Merope with Polyphontes.)[49] Menelaos instructs him on details. They all go in to make preparations. The chorus mark the pause with a decorated song about the great mother's distress at the loss of her daughter; the connexion seems to be at the beginning of the second antistrophe where Helen is said to have failed to reverence the great mother. Another dangerous scene follows between Helen, Theoklymenos, and Menelaos while the final arrangements are made and Menelaos prays Zeus to help him because he has suffered enough, another quizzical prayer.

The chorus sing a decorated song of the ship that will take Helen home; may she dance in Sparta with Hermione; would that they could be birds and fly to Sparta with the news; may the Dioskouroi calm the sea and dispel their sister's evil reputation. Then the messenger brings the news of the escape. The metre changes into recitative trochaics for Theoklymenos to threaten death to Theonoe. The chorus[50] try to stop him. Then the Dioskouroi appear and announce the future of Helen and Menelaos. As in the *Iphigenia in Tauris*, the cheated tyrant's fury is largely an excuse for the appearance of the god to push the story back into traditional mythology.

The *Helen* should not be taken too seriously: it is gay, often exciting, sometimes comic, always beautiful. The story of the *eidolon* makes nonsense of the Trojan War, and both the old servant and the chorus touch on this theme. No doubt Euripides believes that quarrels should be settled by argument rather than by battle, and that common sense

[47] Cf. above, p. 186, 195; below, pp. 209, 214, 273.
[48] Cf. above on *Palamedes*.
[49] Cf. above, p. 142.
[50] So the manuscripts, cf. A. M Dale, *ad loc.*

is more useful than prophecy, but he treats this very lightly, and it is no more the central issue than the distinction between Helen's name and Helen's self, which naturally arises from the story. He has simply accepted the *eidolon* story and written a very pretty play on its consequences.

ION

The *Ion* is much more a tragedy in the modern sense of the word. In the earlier *Melanippe Sophe* (we do not know about the *Erechtheus*)[51] Ion was the son of Xouthos and of the daughter of Erechtheus. Here Erechtheus' daughter, Kreousa, belongs to the tradition of women raped and deserted by the gods, like Melanippe in the *Melanippe Desmotis*. The other strain which becomes apparent is the 'stepmother' strain: when the unknown Ion is accepted by Xouthos as a son, she is easily persuaded to plot his death. In the prologue Hermes tells how Apollo raped Kreousa, she exposed the baby, Hermes brought him to Delphi, where he has grown up to be treasurer of the god, Kreousa later married Xouthos, Apollo will give the boy to Xouthos saying that he is Xouthos' son, that he may come to Athens and be recognized by Kreousa.

Ion comes out to decorate the temple and sings a long monody, which rises from recitative anapaests to lyrics and melic anapaests, as he sends the girls to fetch water, sweeps the temple steps, shoos away the birds – a lyric picture of a happy temple servant. Kreousa's attendant Athenian women[52] come in and admire the sculpture (it does not matter that the subjects were not part of the decoration of Apollo's temple at Delphi): in the last antistrophe Ion interrupts with prohibitions and instructions in recitative anapaests.

Kreousa enters, and immediately sympathy awakens between mother and son. He wants to know about Athens and her family. She wants to know about him. Then she pretends that her own story happened to a friend and that she wants to ask the oracle what has become of the baby. Ion says the question cannot be put, and Kreousa asks him not to reveal the story to Xouthos, who then enters. Kreousa has lost her baby, Ion desperately wants to know his parents; this is what makes this

[51] Cf. above, p. 130.
[52] The aeolic metre of the parodos picks up the aeolic strophe and antistrophe in the middle of Ion's anapaests.

dialogue so moving. Xouthos has been told by Trophonios that he and Kreousa will not go home childless. He will now consult Apollo and tells Kreousa to pray that he may receive an oracle that will give them children. Ion is troubled: he shrugs off his concern for Kreousa, but Apollo's rape and desertion is a bad example for men.

The chorus pray in a decorated aeolic ode to Athena to come with Artemis and beg Apollo that the ancient race of Erechtheus may have children, children who are strength in war and better than riches. At the end they sing of the cave where a girl exposed the baby she had born to Apollo. 'Neither in woven pictures nor in stories have I heard that mortals have good fortune with children from the gods.' The next scene begins in recitative trochaics: Ion enters and Xouthos comes out of the house and greets him as his son. Ion thinks he is mad; then accepts what Apollo has said. Xouthos admits that he once raped a Maenad at Delphi. The metre changes to spoken iambics for Xouthos' appeal to Ion to come to Athens. Ion urges the difficulties of a foreigner in a political society, the certain hatred of the childless Kreousa, the disadvantages of tyranny which is forced by fear to hate the good and favour the bad, the advantages of the just life lived by the temple servant. (We have already seen a comparison of lives in the *Melanippe Desmotis*; here the contrast is different, the contrast between political life and religious life.) Xouthos overrides his objections and tells the chorus to keep silent. Ion is told to prepare a feast.

The chorus sense Kreousa's distress; are they to tell her? Xouthos has deceived her; may the boy never come to Athens. Kreousa comes in with an old slave. The chorus tell her in a lyric dialogue that she is to have no children, and that Apollo has presented Xouthos with a son. The old man assumes that Ion is an illegitimate child of Xouthos brought up in Delphi so that Xouthos, not Apollo, told the lie (this is rather like the rigging of the oracle by Ino in *Phrixos B*).[53] In a monody, chiefly melic anapaests, Kreousa tells the story of her rape by Apollo; the baby has been devoured by birds but Apollo sings; the baby has been devoured by birds but Apollo's birthplace, Delos, hates him. Kreousa then remembers the drops of Gorgon's blood which she carries on her bracelet as a descendant of Erichthonios. This can be used to poison Ion at the banquet.

[53] See above, p. 133.

The chorus pray to Hekate to help the poisoner: the alternative is suicide for Kreousa; the Eleusinian mysteries could never endure Ion as king; women are more faithful than men, as Apollo and Xouthos have proved. One of Kreousa's servants reports the failure of the murder-attempt in an elaborate messenger-speech. Ion was saved because a dove drank the poisoned cup first; the old man confessed; the Delphians condemned Kreousa to death. The chorus sing briefly of the certainty of disaster. Kreousa enters trying to escape; and the chorus advise her to take refuge on the altar. The brief scene in recitative trochaics changes to iambics when Ion enters. They accuse each other, and Ion ends by saying that asylum ought to be granted only to the just. The priestess enters and tells Ion that he must enter Athens with clean hands; she gives him his recognition-tokens and tells him to seek his mother. Ion laments both his motherless boyhood and his mother's loneliness; for a moment he wishes to dedicate the tokens in case he proves a slave; then he decides to examine them. Kreousa recognizes the box and leaves the altar to try and embrace him. She describes the tokens one by one, and mother and son break into a long recognition duet in which he speaks and she sings. Now he learns that she claims that he is the son of Apollo, and decides to ask the oracle if this is true (he had refused to put a similar question for Kreousa on their first meeting). But Athena prevents him: Apollo has done all things well, he has presented his son to Xouthos, and they must preserve the fiction. In a final set of recitative trochaic tetrameters they accept the situation.

So the humans are made to pursue the official course of mythology. In the *Iphigenia* and the *Helen* it is only the local tyrant who has to be forced back into line. But here the distortion is more fundamental: Hermes announced in the prologue that Apollo's plan was for Ion to be brought to Athens and there be recognized, and Athena admits that the plan went wrong (1565). Apollo's plan went wrong because the chorus gave Xouthos away to Kreousa. On the human level one might say that Xouthos failed to trust Kreousa. What matters however is the very human people: Xouthos in his way, but particularly Ion, who grows up in the course of the play, and Kreousa, who has lost her own baby and cannot endure a substitute, particularly when the old man suggests that Xouthos has to all intents and purposes forged an oracle to secure the Athenian kingdom for his illegitimate son.

4 *Antiope, Hypsipyle, Phoenissae*

ANTIOPE

Outline of play

Prologue: ? Dionysos: Pacuvius IR; Frs. 180–2N². Amphion or neatherd: fr. 179. Amphion: 182aN² (song to lyre).

Parodos of old Athenians: fr. 911, 910N²?; Pacuvius IVR.

Debate (Pacuvius IIR): Zethos: fr. 184, 185, 186, 187, 183, 188. Amphion: 198, 196, 194, 193, 199, 200, 201–2, 190–2. Chorus: 189. End dialogue: 216, 218N².

Stasimon.

Antiope: fr. 204, 207, 203N²; Pacuvius V, VI, VII, XIV, XVR; 205, 208N²; Pacuvius XIIIR.

Zethos, Amphion: fr. 210, 941, 220, 209N².

Dirke and subsidiary chorus: Pacuvius XIIR. Seizing of Antiope.

Herdsman and twins: Pacuvius XR.

Messenger-speech.

Antiope, (Zethos), Amphion, planning: Page, *G.L.P.*, no. 10.

Lykos, Amphion.

Ekkyklema: Amphion, Lykos, (Zethos).

Epilogue: Hermes.

Bibliographical note: U. von Wilamowitz-Moellendorff, *Analecta Euripidea*, 192; *Kl. Schr.*, I, 450 n. 1; P. Frassinetti, *Antidoron H. H. Paoli*, 97f.; B. Snell, *Scenes from Greek Drama*, 70. For illustrations see below, p. 305.

The setting of the *Antiope* was before a cave in or near Eleutherai. It was the cave where Zeus disguised as a satyr had raped Antiope (this fact is given by the Homeric bowl). The cave may have been sacred to Dionysos if the corrupt fragment (203N²) 'within in the chambers . . . pillar of the cheerful god' refers to it, and this would give the reason for Dirke coming here later with her maenads, as Snell has seen. It is also the cave outside which Antiope gave birth to the twins, where they now live, and where later they punish Lykos: the last point is given by the fourth-century kalyx krater by the Dirke painter, where also the Dionysiac connexion is shown by the panther-skin in the background.

The story in Hyginus (*Fab.* 8) is expressly said to come from Euripides and is closely parallel to the story in Apollodoros (III, v, 5).

Antiope was raped by Zeus and married by Epopeus of Sikyon. Her uncle Lykos killed Epopeus and carried Antiope into captivity. On the way back to Thebes she gave birth to twins in Eleutherai, who were found by a shepherd (Apollodoros says 'neatherd') and named by him Zethos and Amphion. The play starts when the twins have grown up in the cave of the shepherd. Frs. 181, 182N² refer to the naming of the twins and agree with the etymologies given in Hyginus, *fab*. 7: both in *fab*. 7 and in *fab*. 8 he says that the shepherd (or 'neatherd' in Apollodoros) gave them their names; fr. 181N² cannot therefore be spoken by the neatherd, 'one he calls (or 'call') Zethos. For the mother had sought an easy place for childbearing'. Diodoros in his similar account says expressly that the herdsman and his wife did not know whose children the twins were. The essential past history in the prologue must have been given by a god or a nymph, and Pacuvius fragment IR '*Iovis ex Antiopa Nyctei nati duo*' will belong to it. Dionysos may well have been the speaker as his part is emphasized in all three plays of this production. On the other hand the new shape of fr. 179N² 'may you grant (prosperity?) to me and to my master, who dwells in the plains of Oinoe, which neighbours Eleutherai here' must be spoken by a man, as Snell has seen. It could conceivably have been a quotation of the neatherd's words made in the prologue speech, but there is no reason why the prologue should be confined to a single scene. (Snell combines this with a fragment of Pacuvius (347R), where Varro gives to a Pacuvian *pastor* the line *exorto iubare, noctis decurso itinere*, but this is not ascribed to any play and might equally well be a translation of E. *Bacch*. 679, since Pacuvius wrote a *Pentheus*.) The prayer could also have been made by Amphion, who must presumably have been on stage before the chorus arrives. Without more evidence the shape of the prologue remains obscure.

Eleutherai is on the borders of Boeotia and Attica, and the chorus are men of Attica, as Wilamowitz and Frassinetti have argued: they do not know Lykos by sight, which would be impossible for Boeotians. (*Attici* is therefore right in Pacuvius IVR, and the Thebans of Schol. E. *Hipp*. 58 are a miswriting for Athenians.) Pacuvius IV preserves a riddling dialogue with the chorus on Amphion's tortoise-lyre: Euripides borrowed here from Sophocles' *Ichneutai*. Presumably this was the beginning of the scene after the parodos. In that case Amphion[54] sang

---

[54] Wilamowitz, *VK*, 347, saw this as a reminiscence of Sophocles' early *Thamyras*.

a monody to the lyre before the chorus arrived or while they were
arriving. He started (at least) in hexameters: 'I sing of Ether and Earth
the mother of all things' (fr. 182aN^2). The hexameter line suits
Amphion's lyre, and the content is attested for the *Antiope* by Probus
(225N^2). Wilamowitz was surely right in suggesting that fr. 911N^2 in
dactylo-epitrites give the chorus' reaction to this their first experience of
a song sung to a lyre: 'Golden wings are about my back and the winged
sandals of the Sirens fit me, and I will go the etherial dome to visit
Zeus.'[55] I do not feel certain whether the anapaestic system, fr. 910N^2,
which has also been reasonably ascribed to this play, also belongs here,
possibly as a transition between Amphion's monody and the lyrics of
the chorus, or whether Snell is right in putting it after the debate with
Zethos; the praise of the unengaged contemplation of eternity as better
than tyranny or wealth seems to me to belong here rather than after the
debate, in which Amphion apparently yielded to Zethos.

The debate must come now: Snell has pointed out the relevance of
Horace, Ep. 1. 18, 40ff.: Horace advises his friend: 'nor when he wants
to hunt, will you write poetry. So the twin brothers, Amphion and
Zethos, quarrelled, until the lyre, suspect to the stern brother, was silent.
Amphion is thought to have yielded to his brother's discipline.' The
main lines of the debate are clear: Zethos taunts Amphion (fr. 184N^2)
with indulging in worthless *symposion* poetry (this picks up Boiotos in
the *Melanippe Desmotis*), which makes him incapable of helping his own
household or his city either in the army or in the assembly (fr. 185,[56]
186, 187N^2); he should not be entirely selfish but cultivate the higher
music of war and agriculture (183, 188N^2): Amphion answers that
happiness does not simply consist in wealth (fr. 198N^2); in the ups and
downs of life we have to live as pleasantly as we can (196N^2). The quiet
man is the best friend and the best citizen (194, 193N^2). Brain is more
useful than brawn (fr. 199, 200N^2). Snell thus accounts for most of the
fragments.[57] But fr. 201-2 (on opposite political effects of gluttony

[55] An ecstatic rephrasing of the quieter beginning in *Alc.* 963f. After quoting 911N^2 the
Life of Satyros has 'began the song' after a gap, presumably a reference to Amphion as
exarchon of the chorus.

[56] Note the addition made by Dodds, *Plato's Gorgias*, 277.

[57] Wilamowitz (*Analecta* 192) suggested that *El.* 386-90 may have been interpolated there
from the neighbourhood of fr. 199, 201; I do not feel certain that it is an interpolation.
The Auctor ad Herennium sums up the debate in Pacuvius; the beginning is about music
but the debate chiefly concerns the reasons for wisdom and the usefulness of virtue (IIR).

and poetry) probably belong here: 190–2 (on music and poetry) probably also come from Amphion's speech; 189N^2 (on debate with opposing arguments) may be a comment by the chorus. Snell gives 216, 218N^2 to the ensuing scene with Antiope, because 'we have no sign of such resignation in the other fragments of Zethos' speech and it would contradict the strength of these arguments that are concentrated on the principles of life'. It is true that the debate is a contrast of lives, but at the end (after Amphion's speech) Zethos can return to the present situation and say: 'a slave should not have a free man's thoughts and concentrate on idleness' (216N^2). According to Horace Amphion yielded to Zethos. Probably they go in rather than off, and after a stasimon Antiope arrives.

Antiope, who has spent the years being maltreated in prison by Lykos and his wife Dirke, according to Hyginus 'seized an opportunity and fled' (according to Apollodoros, her fetters were untied of their own accord).[58] She came to the steading where her sons were and asked them to receive her. According to Hyginus, Zethos thinking her a runaway refused to receive her. Nothing is said of Amphion, but it is a reasonable guess that he did not take this extreme line, and at the end of the play, where both twins are present, but only one has a speaking part, Amphion is the speaker because his view in the end triumphed.

A number of fragments survive but the order in which they should come can only be guessed. Antiope tells the chorus that there are many misfortunes in human life (fr. 204N^2). She told of her seduction by Zeus, how she was brought back here by Lykos and gave birth (fr. 207N^2) – probably she chose the place because she could see the neatherd adorning the pillar of Dionysos (fr. 203N^2). Then she described her life as a prisoner of Dirke (Pacuvius V, VI, VII, XIVR; XVR agrees in subject matter but is in trochaics and perhaps belongs to the later messenger speech). She has the misery of knowing that life need not be only misery (fr. 205N^2), but she knows only too well that she and her children may have been forgotten by the gods (fr. 208N^2). Then she greets the twins as her sons (Pacuvius XIIIR). It is not clear at what point the twins enter. Fr. 204 is spoken to the chorus, and fr. 208 sounds like the end of a speech to the chorus before she has greeted the twins as her sons, but Amphion certainly knows that she claims to have been seduced by Zeus (fr. 210N^2). Perhaps she only tells the details of her

[58] Cf. *Bacch.* 497ff.

rape and delivery when she has greeted the twins as her sons. Zethos presumably says she should be handed back to Lykos as a runaway slave. Amphion does not reject her but (like Ion when Kreousa claims that Apollo raped her)[59] refuses to believe her conventional mythology which supposes that Zeus impersonated a satyr and raped a woman (fr. 210). It would be entirely in keeping if Amphion pointed to the upper air and said that *that* was Zeus (fr. 941N^2). He may have gone on to suggest that Antiope was raped by an unknown man: fr. 220N^2 could be interpreted as the text for this, 'This happens to many. They know but refuse to follow their intellect: their souls are conquered by their friends.' Amphion also says, perhaps at the beginning of his speech, 'Punishment is not an art I know. But you should, lady, beware of excess and guard against jealousy' (fr. 209N^2). An illustration of this scene may be seen in a Lucanian hydria in Winterthur: a woman seated in the open country spinning (to show her servile condition) and on either side of her two young men, one draped and leaning on a stick, the other naked and standing erect with a spear. At the finish of the scene Antiope must be left alone because she is found here by Dirke: it would seem that Zethos does not win his point or at least that Amphion insists that they find the herdsman and consult him about her story before handing her over.

Dirke enters with her subsidiary chorus of maenads (Pacuvius XIIR) and carries Antiope off to punish her. The herdsman arrives with the twins and convinces them that Antiope is their mother (Hyginus and Schol. *Ap. Rhod.* IV, 1090). He tells them to go and rescue her (Pacuvius XR). Presumably it is arranged that he shall go and tell Lykos that Antiope is in the hut so that Lykos may fall into the trap. A messenger relates that the twins have freed Antiope and have tied Dirke to a wild bull.

The twins are on stage with Antiope when the papyrus fragment (Page, *G.L.P.*, no. 10) opens. It must be Amphion who says that the alternatives are death as a punishment for murdering Dirke or victory over Lykos, and commands Zeus to help his children (this is the nouthetetic prayer so common in these late plays).[60] The chorus see Lykos whom they do not recognize (they are Athenians, not Boeotians)

[59] Cf. above, p. 203.
[60] Cf. above, p. 186.

and warn themselves to keep silent. Lykos has come in person to capture Antiope and her accomplices and asks the chorus where they are. (Antiope and the twins have evidently gone into the cave before Lykos arrives and the chorus know and sympathize with their intentions.)

After a gap of thirty lines Lykos is talking to a second person. All editions make him the herdsman. We have no evidence for the presence of the herdsman; Thoas is tricked by Iphigeneia and Theoklymenos by Helen so that we should expect Lykos to be tricked by Amphion here. (This has the further advantage that the actor who played Antiope in the preceding scene does not have to play the herdsman before he comes on as Hermes at the end.) The story told to Lykos is not clear. It seems to me that the surviving portions of this dialogue are easiest to understand if Amphion tells him that Antiope's captors killed her guards (l. 27) but that she escaped from them and was rescued by Amphion and his friends. In l. 25 he says he is glad he has saved (*her*). In l. 31–7 he persuades Lykos to leave his spear-bearers outside to deal with the captors if they appear and try to recapture Antiope.

Lykos and Amphion go in. The chorus sing excited dochmiacs. Lykos cries out. The chorus sing 'Do you hear, do you see?', and this is the cue for the ekkyklema to roll out with Amphion and Zethos (mute) standing over Lykos. Ten lines later Hermes appears on the roof to stop the slaughter. (In the *Kresphontes* Euripides had used the ekkyklema for the attempted murder of Kresphontes.)[61] Here Hermes stops the murder, arranges that Dirke (like Siris in the *Melanippe Desmotis*) shall be honoured after death, and foretells the future of the twins, including the building of seven-gated Thebes by Amphion.

Enough remains to form some idea of this long exciting play. Clearly Euripides is writing in the tradition of the *Melanippe Desmotis*. Here the twin sons are sharply differentiated and the contrast of lives was a great showpiece which echoed down the ages. We know too little of Antiope herself to form any idea of her, and we sadly miss Dirke and her chorus of maenads. Was she a preliminary sketch for Agave in the *Bacchae*? Certainly she was a leader of maenads when she tried to murder Antiope. Her ashes are to be thrown into the spring of Ares, which will be renamed Dirke and become a familiar Theban landmark, named seven times in the *Phoenissae*.

[61] Cf. above, p. 142.

Enough remains to show that the tortured, deserted Antiope and her wild persecutor are very different from Hypsipyle and Eurydike in the next play. Of Hypsipyle's two sons Euneos was taught the lyre and Thoas was taught arms by Orpheus, but we have no evidence that the contrast was mentioned elsewhere than in the last scene (fr. 64, col. ii): the full scale opposition of the musician and the soldier had already been presented in the *Antiope*. Aeschylus' *Nemea* included the institution of the Nemean games in memory of Archemoros, son of Nemea. Euripides changed the names of mother and baby and immensely complicated the story by introducing Hypsipyle as nurse to the baby.

HYPSIPYLE

Outline of play

Prologue: Hypsipyle: fr. $752N^2$; P. Hamburg 118b; fr. 61 (Bond).
Thoas and Euneos: fr. $764N^2$; fr. 70; 96 (Bond).
Hypsipyle: fr. 1, col. i; 2 (Bond) = Page, no. 12, 1–17.
Parodos: Hypsipyle and chorus: fr. 1, cols. ii–iv (Bond) = Page, no. 12, 18–103; $856N^2$.
Amphiaraos and Hypsipyle: frs. 1, cols. iv–v = Page, no. 12, 104–52; 18–19 (Bond) = Page, no. 12, 163–7; $753N^2$.
Stasimon: fr. 6–9 = Page, no. 12, 153–62 (Tydeus and Polyneikes).
Hypsipyle and chorus fr. 10–12 (Bond) = Page, no. 12, 169–83. Arrival of paidagogos with body of child (fr. 32). Hypsipyle's monody: $754N^2$ frs. 31, 38 (Bond). Plan to escape: fr. 20–21 (Bond). Entry of Eurydike: fr. 34–5 (Bond). ? Arrival of Thoas and Euneos: fr. 33 (Bond). Trial scene: fr. 23–4 (Bond); 758, $760N^2$; 27, 28, 22, 60 (Bond) = Page, no. 12, 184–292. Arrival of Amphiaraos: fr. 60, 63 (Bond). Eurydike, Thoas, Euneos (fr. 57).
Stasimon: fr. 57, 58, 59 (Bond); $765N^2$ (Dionysos).
Messenger-speech.
Stasimon.
Amphiaraos and Eurydike.
Amphiaraos, Thoas, Euneos, Hypsipyle. Recognition, chorus: fr. 64, col. ii (Bond) = Page, no. 12, 293–304.
Recognition lyric dialogue: fr. 64, cols. ii–iii = Page, no. 12, 305–41.
Dionysos *ex machina*: fr. 64, col. iii.

Bibliographical note: D. L. Page, *Greek Literary Papyri*, no. 12; G. W.

Bond, *Euripides Hypsipyle*, Oxford 1963; A. M. Dale, *J.H.S.*, 64, 1964, 166; T. B. L. Webster, in *The Classical Tradition*; *Essays presented to Harry Caplan*, 1966, 83ff.

Illustrations, see below, p. 306. The account in the text has been cut short because the details are excellently given by Mr Bond. Where I differ from him, my reasons will be found in the article quoted above.

Hypsipyle opens the play. She starts with a genealogy, Dionysos and his sons, one of whom was Thoas, her father. (Dionysos' connexion with Thebes had already been shown in the *Antiope*.) Thoas was King of Lemnos. She must have gone on to tell how Jason came to Lemnos, stayed while she bore her twins (Euneos and the younger Thoas), and took the twins away on the Argo; she fled from Lemnos to avoid having to kill her father and is now the nurse of Opheltes, the child of Lykourgos and Eurydike of Nemea. She does not know if her sons are alive or dead; she prays they may be young and strong like the Seven against Thebes who have just arrived in Nemea. Her best hope is the gratitude of the baby Opheltes.

Hypsipyle goes in, and Euneos and Thoas arrive. The structure here is like that of the *Iphigeneia in Tauris*. They look at the painted relief on the pediment of the palace (like the chorus of the *Ion*). Perhaps Euripides imagined a decoration connected with the Argonauts to start them on their reminiscences; they must at least say that the elder Thoas gave them the golden vine and sent them to look for their mother. Hypsipyle comes out with the baby in answer to their knock. She tells them that Lykourgos is away, and it is almost certain that they refuse to enter until he has come back. Hypsipyle exclaims 'How blessed your mother, whoever she was' – the usual sympathy between unrecognized mother and sons, but the dangerous theme was evidently not developed.

The parodos is a long lyric dialogue of decorated style in aeolic and dactylic metre. Hypsipyle contrasts the songs she sang in Lemnos and the songs that she must sing now to the baby. The chorus of Nemean women ask her to forget the Argo and come to see the soldiers who are mustering against Amphion's Thebes (so the chorus invited Elektra to a festival of Hera; here the reference to Amphion's lyre playing recalls the epilogue of the *Antiope*). Hypsipyle, perhaps because of the mention of soldiers, goes back to the Argo, to Peleus and Orpheus (in the preserved part). The chorus comfort her with the examples of Europe and Io. (Europe naturally recalls Thebes to the audience and Io recalls Argos.) She counters with examples of unfortunate women who have been celebrated in song,[62] but no one will celebrate her.

Then Amphiaraos enters and asks for spring water to use in sacrifice for their journey. (This scene is illustrated in a Pompeian picture.) It is a leisurely scene in which she tells her story, and he tells her all about the expedition of the Seven and his disastrous promise to Eriphyle. He is a dignified figure who moves with composure towards his death. The exposition is very relevant if the *Phoenissae* is the next play in this production. Hypsipyle demurs at showing him the spring; it is guarded by a snake (perhaps also she knows that she should not leave the house with the baby).

The chorus sing of Tydeus and Polyneikes and their fight before the palace of Adrastos, which Polyneikes himself recalls in the *Phoenissae* (408ff.). After that only tattered fragments are preserved until the trial scene. It is at least possible that the sequence ran as follows: Hypsipyle returned distraught to sing a lyric dialogue with the chorus; the child's dead body was brought on and carried into the palace; Hypsipyle sang a long monody in her distress, and then considered flight. Eurydike, the child's mother, came out of the palace and had her bound. Before Eurydike could take any further action, Thoas and Euneos returned and still unrecognized were given hospitality by her (the papyrus Hypothesis, *P. Oxy.* 2455, frs. 14 and 15, certainly places their arrival after the death of the child, but as the narrative is very brief here it is possible that they did not arrive until after the trial scene; in either case Eurydike, like Admetos, evidently feels herself bound by the laws of hospitality to entertain them).

Eurydike then attacked Hypsipyle, apparently as a murderess plotting against the house ($758N^2$). Hypsipyle protests her love of the child and her hopes from him; in her misery she calls on the Argo, her sons, and Amphiaraos. Amphiaraos arrives in the nick of time to save her from death (the only parallel, except for gods *ex machina*, is the entry of the Pythia in the *Ion*, 1320). His reputation for modesty persuades Eurydike to hear him. He had persuaded Hypsipyle to show him the spring; the death of the child is an omen for the expedition of the

[62] Cf. *Hel.* 375f., where Helen ends her lament with the chorus by comparing herself to Kallisto etc.

Seven; for Eurydike it is a natural event which must be accepted; they will bury the child and found the Nemean games in his honour; Hypsipyle is innocent.

Eurydike apparently accepts the situation. Amphiaraos goes off. Thoas and Euneos ask to be allowed to compete in the games (either they come out of the house or only arrive now). They go off with a nouthetetic prayer to Dionysos; this is the cue for the stasimon on Dionysos which follows and covers the period of the games. Then the messenger must report that Hypsipyle's sons have been victorious in the footrace. For Eurydike the news is unwelcome, like the report in the *Alexandros* that the unknown shepherd boy has defeated the sons of Priam. Amphiaraos must have returned and persuaded her to hand over Hypsipyle to her sons. He has already achieved this when the papyrus resumes. The chorus comment in astonishment. Amphiaraos takes his leave, and Hypsipyle and Euneos (with Thoas mute) embark on a long duet in which she sings her story interrupted by his iambics and he tells their story in iambics interrupted by her lyric comments. Eighty lines after the beginning of the duet Dionysos appears to speak the epilogue.

The likeness to the *Antiope* is superficial. The sons can hardly have had a major part in the play but their exploits in the games must have been reported in an exciting messenger speech, which presumably included the athletic performances of the Seven: Euripides may have been influenced by the slightly earlier messenger speech in the Sophoclean *Electra*. The triangle of Hypsipyle, Amphiaraos, Eurydike is entirely different from the triangle Antiope, Lykos, Dirke. Hypsipyle herself recalls Ino in her name-play more than Antiope or the captive Melanippe, in so far as she did something wrong and bitterly repented it. Euripides may have explained why she put the baby down in a snake-infested meadow, but perhaps the audience is not meant to ask whether she was negligent or not: Amphiaraos' acceptance of responsibility is enough. Eurydike naturally accuses her of seeking profit by killing the baby, but what is more remarkable is her readiness to listen to Amphiaraos and her acceptance of his interpretation. Amphiaraos is a tragic figure as he moves forward unperturbed to foreseen disaster and death: with his prophetic knowledge he sees the death of the baby not as the result of his own or Hypsipyle's negligence but as part of the fabric of events called the Seven against Thebes. His part in this play is out of scale since it is Hypsipyle's play, but as preparation for the

Phoenissae it is fully justified. Amphiaraos, the just man compelled to take a wrong course of action, points forward to the *Phoenissae* just as the frequent references to Dionysos and his appearance in the epilogue are links back with the *Antiope*, where Zeus disguised himself as a satyr and Dirke led a chorus of maenads.

PHOENISSAE

The *Hypsipyle* gives an ill-omened prelude to the expedition, the *Phoenissae* starts with the attack on Thebes. The setting is Thebes so that references to Amphion, Dirke, and Dionysos are natural links back to the *Antiope*. Startlingly Iokaste speaks the prologue and tells the past history from Laios' consultation of the oracle. Oidipous blinded himself when he learnt that he had married his mother, but is still alive imprisoned by his sons, whom he cursed. Polyneikes the younger son went into voluntary exile; Eteokles refused to give up the rule after a year. Iokaste has arranged for Polyneikes to come under flag of truce and meet his brother.

She goes in and the old paidagogos, who had arranged the truce, appears on the roof, makes certain that no one is about, and in a long decorated lyric dialogue, in which Antigone sings dochmiacs and related metres and he speaks, points out to Antigone the seven champions who are attacking Thebes, including Amphiaraos. The nearest surviving parallel to this use of the roof is the watchman at the beginning of the *Agamemnon*, who also looks over the heads of the audience. Euripides has substituted this lyric dialogue for the seven messenger-speeches of the *Septem*. His feeling for visual effects (shown in quite a different way in the parodos and messenger-speech of the *Ion*) is apparent in the section on Polyneikes: 'I do not see clearly, I see the shape of a body, the likeness of a chest. Would that I could run as fast as the windswift mist to my brother. . . . How clear he is in golden arms, flaming like the rays of dawn.' We are meant to imagine that the mist between the walls and the army suddenly clears so that Polyneikes stands out in full sunlight at the end. Then with another contrasting reminiscence of the *Septem* (181) Antigone is sent in because a crowd of excited women are approaching the palace.

The women of the chorus are very unlike the frightened Theban maidens so fiercely rebuked by Eteokles in Aeschylus' *Septem*. They are Phoenicians sent via their kinsmen in Thebes as an offering to Apollo at

Delphi, where Dionysos waves his torches and has his magic vine. They are caught by the war, and fear for the fate of their kinsmen; the attack of Polyneikes is just. For them, unlike the Nemean chorus of the *Hypsipyle* (fr. i, col. ii), Io is the common ancestress of Phoenicians and Thebans, not an Argive heroine. These women are both more exotic and more detached than the Theban girls of Aeschylus.

Polyneikes enters very carefully, only half-trusting to the truce. The chorus summon Iokaste, who greets him in a long astrophic monody in dochmiacs and kindred metres – the joy of seeing him again, her tears and mourning, Oidipous' attempted suicide, Polyneikes' marriage. There follows a long and moving dialogue between mother and son, in which he speaks of his fear in coming and pities her; she asks about his life in exile and his marriage. Eteokles enters in haste; he has only come to please his mother. She tells him to calm down; Polyneikes is not a Gorgon. Polyneikes claims his share of the alternate rule, which Eteokles had sworn to give him; if he receives this, he will send the Argive army home. Eteokles answers that different people have different ideals: tyranny is his ideal, and he will not yield his tyranny to anybody. Iokaste sums up: Ambition is extremely dangerous to its possessor; Proportion is the safe basis for social and political relationships as it is the rule for the Seasons; why worship Tyranny when it may lead to defeat?[63] As for Polyneikes, victory and defeat will put him in an equally impossible position.

The metre changes to trochaic tetrameters for the final quarrel. Eteokles rejects Polyneikes' demand for alternate rule and refuses to let him see his father or his sisters. Polyneikes asks Eteokles where he will station himself so that he can kill him, and goes off calling the gods to witness that Eteokles is responsible if Thebes suffers. The chorus sing a decorated trochaic stasimon: Kadmos came to Thebes, where Dionysos was born; Kadmos killed the snake and sowed its teeth; may Epaphos, son of Io, Persephone and Demeter come and help Thebes in her troubles.

Eteokles and Kreon discuss strategy. Kreon does not question the advisability of fighting. Eteokles abandons his own plan of campaign for Kreon's suggestion of posting a company at each of the seven gates.

---

[63] Madame J. de Romilly, *R. Phil.*, 39, 1965, 28 has pointed out how much the political ideas of Eteokles and Iokaste's speech belonged to the Athenian situation when Euripides was writing.

He will not waste time reciting their names (751, an obvious criticism of the seven pairs of speeches in Aeschylus' play). He arranges Antigone's marriage to Haimon, and says he will send Kreon's son Menoikeus to lead Teiresias to Kreon, because he himself has quarrelled with Teiresias (this is Euripides' method of preparing us for the next act). He hopes he may meet Polyneikes in the battle (754). This wish picks up Polyneikes' wish in the quarrel scene (621) and should not be deleted; his final instruction that 'if my side wins, Polyneikes must never be buried in Theban soil, and even if a friend buries him he must be put to death' (775) has also been cut out; but Eteokles knows perfectly well that a Theban victory is possible even if he is killed, and he knows also that Iokaste at least loves her younger son.[64] (For the audience Sophocles' *Antigone* was part of the story.)

The chorus sing a decorated dactylic stasimon: why need Ares make a riot of war in Thebes instead of a Bacchic revel? Would that Kithairon had not reared Oidipous, nor the Sphinx come, nor the sons quarrelled; Earth bore the dragon's teeth, the gods came to the marriage of Harmonia, Thebes rose to the sound of Amphion's lyre; Thebes is now at a crisis. Then Teiresias, supported by his daughter, arrives with Menoikeus. He has arrived from Athens where he had made the Athenians victorious over Eumolpos. Those who had seen Euripides' *Erechtheus* would guess that he would demand a human sacrifice. He does not want to give his advice nor to give it in the presence of Menoikeus; but Kreon insists (like Oidipous in Sophocles' *Oedipus Tyrannus*), and hears that Menoikeus, as the last available descendant of the dragon's teeth must be killed by the snake's birthplace.[65] Teiresias goes off; Kreon tells Menoikeus to fly to Dodona. Menoikeus pretends that he must go and say good-bye to Iokaste while Kreon gets money for the journey. Kreon goes in first. Menoikeus (like a son in New Comedy) says how cleverly he has deceived his father and goes off to kill himself over the dragon's grave. Euripides certainly recalled Athamas' refusal to sacrifice Phrixos and Phrixos' voluntary acceptance of the sacrifice in the *Second Phrixos*; here he wanted the youthful heroism of Menoikeus to set against the selfishness of Eteokles and Polyneikes.

[64] Both 753–6 and 775–8 are deleted by E. D. M. Fraenkel in *S.B.B.A.*, 1963.
[65] On this passage from 915 see B. Snell, *Hermes*, 87, 1959, 7ff. = *Ges. Schr.*, 178.

The chorus sing of the Sphinx, Oidipous and his curse, their admiration for Menoikeus. The messenger reports to Iokaste that Menoikeus has committed suicide, and that the battle has gone well for the Thebans, but Eteokles has challenged Polyneikes to single combat. Iokaste calls Antigone out and says that she will either stop them or commit suicide. The chorus sing of the horrors of this duel (the metre is predominantly dochmiac). Kreon arrives to ask Iokaste to prepare Menoikeus' body for burial. The messenger meets him and tells him that the two brothers killed each other, Iokaste and Antigone arrived just before they died, Iokaste committed suicide, and Antigone is now coming back with the three bodies. Two points should be noted in passing: Antigone (1436) said that the brothers 'have betrayed her marriage', and Polyneikes (1447) asked his mother and sister to bury him and persuade the city. (Again, as in the scene between Eteokles and Kreon, Sophocles' *Antigone*, rather than his own, is in Euripides' mind.)

Antigone enters with the bodies 'as a maenad of the dead' and sings a long astrophic lament.[66] At the end she calls Oidipous out, and he joins her in lyric dialogue when he hears that his wife and sons are dead. Kreon banishes Oidipous (he quotes Teiresias as his authority, but he is interpreting rather than quoting Teiresias). Oidipous rehearses his life (this should not be cut out; Oidipous must present himself). Exile for him is murder, but he will not supplicate Kreon. Kreon then forbids the burial of Polyneikes and tells Antigone to prepare for marriage with Haimon. Antigone attacks Kreon; she begs in vain to be allowed to bury Polyneikes; she can and does kiss his lips (1671). She will never marry Haimon; that night will show her to be one of the Danaids. Kreon banishes her. She will go with Oidipous: she leads him to the bodies of his wife and sons. He quotes the oracle that he shall die in Athens. The play ends with a long lyric dialogue between the two as they move off. Oidipous remembers the Sphinx; Antigone again says that she will bury Polyneikes, and Oidipous tells her to pray with her friends to Dionysos but she says her prayers are useless.

Much in this ending has been attributed to an interpolator; in one form of the theory all passages relating to Polyneikes' burial have been ascribed to him.[67] It may, however, be doubted whether after

[66] The lament and the succeeding lyric dialogue are polymetric but dactyls dominate.
[67] E. D. M. Fraenkel, *op. cit.*; cf. review by H. Diller, *Gnomon*, 36, 1964, 641. Cf. also B. Snell, *op. cit.*

Sophocles' *Antigone* this clash could be left out of a play on Eteokles and Polyneikes, and Euripides may have seen a recent revival of Aeschylus' *Septem* with its present ending (such a revival would account for the references to the *Septem* in Gorgias and Aristophanes as well as for the obvious criticisms of the *Septem* in this play). The only difficult reference to the burial is the last one (1744): in her lyric dialogue Antigone says that she will bury Polyneikes even if she is put to death for it. Antigone is now committed to Oidipous and she cannot bury Polyneikes. It is, however, very unlikely that an interpolator would compose a further stretch of lyric and we have rather to ask whether Antigone may not (or even must not) hark back in her final monody to this theme which has moved her so deeply before. If we accept this view, then there is no reason to reject any of the references to the burial of Polyneikes, which lead up to the final clash between Antigone and Kreon.

Aeschylus' *Septem* had simple clear lines: Eteokles the sober efficient ruler suddenly becomes the frenzied son of Oidipous who insists on meeting his brother. The poet who revived it was inspired by Sophocles' *Antigone* to add the theme of Polyneikes' burial at the end. Euripides accepted the new *Septem* but rehandled it in his own way, rather as he rehandled the *Choephoroi* in his *Electra*. It is not a play about a good ruler who made a decision disastrous for himself. From the beginning it is a play about a whole family affected by the utter selfishness of a single member; hence the enormously increased cast for what is essentially the same story: Iokaste and Oidipous survive to take their considerable part; Polyneikes appears in the guise of the younger brother who has been grossly wronged, even if he takes excessive measures to right his wrong – the rightness and wrongness of the whole expedition had already been foreshadowed in the moving figure of Amphiaraos in the *Hypsipyle*. Teiresias, the family seer, points a contrast with Erechtheus' Athens and a contrast between Kreon and Erechtheus. Menoikeus' heroism shows up his father's selfishness. At the end Euripides wanted to assert again the values for which Iokaste and Menoikeus had stood. Kreon is merely vengeful against Oidipous and Polyneikes. The broken Oidipous is a heart-rending but dignified figure, and Antigone, who was shown first in the dawn excitement of seeing the Seven from the palace-roof, ends with a willing sacrifice of everything.

5 Phaethon, Meleager, Pleisthenes

PHAETHON

Outline of play

Prologue: Aphrodite: 771–2N².

Klymene and Phaethon: Cod. Clar. I, i–ii (773N²).

Parodos: Dawn song. Cod. Clar. I, ii–iii (773N²).

Merops, Phaethon, and herald: Cod. Clar. I, iii–iv (773–4N²).

Phaethon: 775, 777. Merops: 784 (exit with herald). Phaethon: 776N² (exit to visit Helios).

Stasimon: i, followed by thunder clap.

Klymene and first messenger: 779–80, 896, 971, 785–6N². Lyric dialogue.

Stasimon: ii, 783N²?

Klymene and second messenger. Merops and wedding chorus. Servant reports fire. Merops and servant into house: Cod. Clar. II, i–iii (781N²).

Chorus with Merops lamenting off: Cod. Clar. II, iii–iv (781N²).

Merops and nurse: Cod. Clar. II, iv.

Merops and Klymene.

Helios-Apollo or Okeanos *ex machina*: 778, 782N².

Bibliographical note: U. von Wilamowitz-Moellendorff, *Analecta Euripidea*, 158; *Kl. Schr.* I, 110; *Sappho und Simonides*, 38; *Griechische Verskunst*, 222; H. Von Arnim, *Supplementum Euripideum*, 67; T. Zielinski, *Tragodoumenon*, 232; H. Volmer, *De Euripidis fabula quae Phaethon inscribitur*; A. Lesky, *W.S.*, 50, 1932, 1; H. Friis-Johansen, *General Reflection*, 45; W. Ritchie, *Authenticity of the Rhesus*, 255; N. Wilson, *C.Q.* 10, 1960, 199; W. S. Barrett, *Euripides Hippolytos*, 167ff.; N. Hourmouziades, *Production and Imagination*, 22, 144.

Zielinski gives the date of the *Phaethon* as 415–409 B.C. both on the aggregate figures for resolution in the iambic trimeters and on the quality of the resolutions (of which five are characteristic of this period): if frs. 896 and 971N² belong to this play, his 22.4% can be raised to 23.3%; either figure would place the play in the group of which the earliest preserved play is the *Troades* and the latest the *Phoenissae*.[68]

[68] Wilamowitz in *Analecta Eur.* (p. 158) dated the play before 425 because of its lyric metres, but in *Gr. Verskunst* (p. 222) he says that although the metre of the parodos is

The little that survives of Aeschylus' *Heliades* (68–73N², 101–7 Mette) shows that there Phaethon was the son of Helios, that he rode his father's chariot, that Zeus hit him down with a thunderbolt, that his sisters (who presumably formed the chorus) mourned him by the Eridanos in Spain. In 428 B.C. in Euripides' *Hippolytus* (735) the chorus wish they could go to the Adriatic and the Eridanos, where the unhappy maidens weep amber tears in pity for Phaethon, which implies the same form of the story. In the *Phaethon* Euripides moved the scene to the East, introduced the marriage theme, and made Phaethon ostensibly the son of Merops and Klymene but actually the son of Helios and Klymene.

The fragmentary papyrus Hypothesis (*P. Oxy.* 2455, fr. 14, col. xiv–xvi) confirms that Klymene deceived her husband about Phaethon's father and told Phaethon himself when he grew up that he was the son of Helios; he disbelieved her and she told him to go and ask Helios for a gift. (Otherwise the hypothesis only adds that the play concluded with a prophecy.) Our chief source is two leaves of *Codex Claromontanus*; each has two columns of forty-one lines on front and back, but a strip of each leaf is lost so that each page only contains the beginning or the ends of lines in one of its two columns. The first leaf has a dialogue between Klymene and Phaethon, the parodos, the entry of Merops and his speech to Phaethon. Fr. 771 describing Klymene as the wife of Merops, King of the black Aithiopians, certainly belongs to the prologue; fr. 772, the sun burns the furthest portions of the earth as he rises, may also belong; but there is no evidence whether they were spoken by Klymene herself or by a god (to this problem I shall return later). Restoration of the first column of the dialogue between Klymene and Phaethon is impossible. Certainly there is talk of marriage, and Klymene tells Phaethon that he is the son of Helios: the Hypothesis shows that this is a revelation to Phaethon and that he disbelieves her. In the second

---

characteristic of Euripides' last period the *Phaethon* has so many unusual features that it must be regarded as a play of Euripides' youth. Kranz (*Stasimon*, 196, 306) says that the structure of the parodos – two strophes and antistrophes with an epode – places it early as also does the formal announcement of the entry of the king, but in fact (as Wilamowitz had noted) the metre of the *Phaethon* parodos is very different from the *Andromache* and *Hippolytus* with which Kranz compares it, and Hourmouziades (pp. 141, 144) has shown that at all periods entrances are formally announced when they have a special character. In subject matter the parodos is nearest to *Hel.* 1460ff. and *Ion* 82ff., 94ff. We must therefore accept the reliable evidence of the iambic trimeters for dating the play to Zielinski's Third Group.

column Phaethon proposes to go to Helios; Klymene says that if the sun grants him one wish, his divine birth will be proved. It is right here to remember both Bellerophon in his name play going to see the gods and Theseus in the *Hippolytus* with his three requests to Poseidon. Phaethon says that he will go when his old father (Merops) has got up and told him about the marriage. (Lesky well notes that this 'when' clause has purely chronological significance, and does not mean '*if* he talks about marriage'.)

The two columns together contain fifty-nine lines of prologue. The iambic prologues of the preserved plays in Group III vary greatly in length: all are over 100 lines except *Ion* and *Trojan Women*, where a long monody intervenes before the parodos. Probably we should reckon that one leaf of 160 lines preceded the preserved leaf and that the first page was occupied by title, hypothesis (which from the evidence of *P. Oxy.* 2455 ran to about seventy lines), and dramatis personae. This would give eighty-two lines for the beginning of the play and a total prologue length of 141 lines (twenty lines more than the *I.T.* and twenty lines less than the *Helen*).

At the end of the prologue Phaethon tells his mother to go in (and he goes in with her), because the women are coming out to sweep and to scent the entrance with incense. If the women are coming out of the main door, he and Klymene must, in spite of what he says, wait to go in until they have all come out and crossed into the orchestra; the difficulty is discussed by Hourmouziades (p. 22f.). My own solution would be to assume that Euripides has transferred a formula used for people seen coming from *outside* to a situation to which, as the people are supposed to be coming from *inside*, it does not logically apply. The chorus as usual come up the *parodos*; and, if pressed, Euripides would say that they were coming from the servants' quarters into the main courtyard of the palace. Similarly in the *Trojan Women* the chorus come up the *parodos* in the usual way, but they are supposed to be occupying huts adjacent to Hekabe's hut, from which she summons them. The chorus sing their lovely song of dawn occupations, and in the second antistrophe turn from the occupations of others to the royal marriage which is to happen today. Some have seen an ominous note in the song of the nightingale and the song of the swan in the dawn-song, picked up by their apprehension of danger in the second antistrophe; if this is right, then the personified Aura of the dawn-song may be meant to recall also the Aura who appears on marriage-vases bringing good health but also on funeral monuments as wafting souls to the Islands of the Blest. Primarily, however, this is what it appears, a lovely *aubade*. The tone is paralleled in Ion's dawn monody, which probably dates from 412 B.C., and in the opening anapaests of the posthumous *Iphigenia in Aulis*; and the second strophe is echoed in the *propemptikon* which the chorus sing in the *Helen* (1460ff.) in 412 B.C.

At the end they see Merops, Phaethon, and 'the holy herald' coming out of the house. The herald demands silence; the people are to assemble and pray for offspring from the marriage which father and son are ready to consummate today. This passage is elaborately composed. The chorus end their song in iambics; they announce the entrance of the three actors in recitative anapaestic dimeters; the herald sings four dactylic tetrameters each followed by a dactylic dimeter, and then ends with two iambic trimeters. It seems to me possible that Euripides remembered Aeschylus' *Semele* (355M), where, after a choral ode praying for good fortune in Semele's marriage, Hera disguised as a priestess sings in hexameters of the Nymphs as blessing marriages with increase. If the audience remembered this (and it may have been recently revived)[69] they would feel a shudder of apprehension at the herald's dactyls in the *Phaethon*.

Merops speaks about the advantages of marriage. A ship needs three anchors; a city needs more than one ruler. As the hypothesis shows, Merops has no idea that he is not the father of Phaethon. He wants to secure the succession (like Hellen and Aiolos in the *Melanippe Sophe* and Aiolos in his name play), and implies that he will make Phaethon king if he marries. Here the text breaks off. Merops' speech can be traced for about forty lines as it seems to start before the end of the third column and fills all the preserved part of the fourth column (the preserved beginnings of lines show no change of speaker). Four further fragments have been ascribed to this scene between Merops and Phaethon: 775, 'though he is free, he is a slave of his wife; he has sold his body for her dowry'; 776, 'It is a pity, but the rich are born fools etc.'; 777, 'for, wherever it may be, the land which feeds me is my country'; 784, 'I count it folly to grant authority to children – or citizens either – if they are wrong-headed'. The last is clearly Merops' reason for going ahead with marriage preparations in spite of Phaethon's objections; we know

[69] Plato quotes it in *Rep.* II, 381d5.

from the text later that he went to find a chorus to sing marriage-songs and he may, therefore, have left the stage before Phaethon. Phaethon objects to marrying a wife who brings a large dowry (Merops must, therefore, have urged the advantages of marrying a rich wife), 775. This is presumably a genuine reason; it would not be changed if he proved to be the son of Helios – although then, of course, Helios and not Merops would arrange his marriage; Lesky must be right in supposing that he is more interested in sport than marriage; after he is dead, his mother says that she hates the curved bow and she wishes there were no gymnasia (fr. 785); she therefore attributes his disaster to his love of sport. Merops may have threatened him with exile, and he answers that home is wherever the earth will feed him (fr. 777). In spite of this Merops goes out (like any father in New Comedy) to continue his preparations (fr. 784). Phaethon comments on the inborn stupidity of the wealthy; the two parallels (*Andr.* 269; *Ion* 1312) which Schade-waldt (*Monolog*, 139) quotes for the form of this fr. 776 are comments at the end of a scene or a section of a scene. So here Phaethon comments on the blindness of the wealthy after Merops has gone and before he himself takes the further action of visiting Helios. He must announce this intention, and therefore the chorus must learn at this point (not, as Wilamowitz thinks, later from the messenger speech) that Klymene claims Helios as his father. Probably he swears them to silence about his purpose.

This scene recalls various other scenes. First for the end: the young Menoikeus similarly disobeys his father in the *Phoenissae* (990f.), having sent him off contented that he is going to obey. Secondly, the marriage debate has parallels in the earlier *Aiolos*, and in the *Meleager*, *Andromeda*, and *Antigone*, which belong to this group. Merops' position is clear: he is an ordinary father recommending an advantageous marriage which will secure the succession as well as the family fortunes, and he is prepared to associate his son with him in the kingship: the subsequent arrangements would be not unlike the relationship of Hellen to Aiolos in the *Melanippe Sophe*, of Peleus to his grandson Neoptolemos in the *Andromache*, of Kadmos to his grandson Pentheus in the *Bacchae*. Thirdly, Phaethon has, as Lesky has seen, something of Hippolytos. Both Hippolytos and Ion reject political life for their careers, Hippolytos for hunting and athletics, Ion for temple service (until he is overpersuaded). We do not know (but it would make further sense of the whole situation) whether Phaethon also, like Hippolytos, Theseus in his name play, Bellerophon in the *Stheneboia*, Perseus in the *Diktys*, Boiotos (if it is he) in the *Melanippe Desmotis*, regards sexual indulgence as an impediment to his career.

Lastly, Klymene's position is now clearer: her legal husband (the phrase is used in the hypothesis) is marrying off her natural son. We remember Kreousa's anger when Xouthos accepts Ion as his son, Theano's attempt to kill the children of Ino in the *Ino*, Siris' attempt to have the sons of Melanippe murdered in the *Melanippe Desmotis*. The rule is that the mother in Euripides always sides with her own child against the child of an earlier marriage by the husband or an adopted child. The situation here is different, but on the analogy of the other women one would expect Klymene to react violently against Merops for assuming a right to dispose of Phaethon, which, according to her and in spite of her having given out that Merops was the father, he does not possess. This, I think, is why she told Phaethon the name of his true father in the prologue and encouraged him to prove it; in her view only Helios has the right to dispose of him.

The first leaf of Cod. Clar. ends with Merops still speaking. The second leaf starts with Phaethon's dead body already on stage. The gap must be a multiple of 164 lines. We can make a very rough assessment: Merops has to finish his speech, Phaethon answers refusing the marriage, he then appears to give in; on the analogy of the Ion–Xouthos scene this would take ninety lines; Phaethon then tells the chorus that he will visit Helios, perhaps twenty-five lines on the analogy of the Menoikeus scene in the *Phoenissae*. Then the chorus sing a stasimon to cover the transition and at the end they are amazed by the thunder clap which marks Phaethon's fall from the chariot. This should take at least seventy lines. Then the messenger arrives to tell the story of Phaethon's ride, and this is presumably followed by a lyric dialogue of lamentation between Klymene and the chorus: the *Andromache* gives 180 lines from the arrival of Peleus before the messenger speech about Neoptolemos' death to the end of Peleus' lament. This would fill two leaves and one column. We can then assume that three complete leaves have been lost and that the remainder of the third leaf contained a stasimon at the beginning of the scene with the second messenger: in absolute terms the first lost leaf of the play contained ll. 1–82 (see above, p. 221); the first preserved leaf contained ll. 83–245, the three lost leaves contained ll. 246–738, the last preserved leaf contained ll. 739–903. This may have some bearing on the restoration of the end of the play.

We can add a little detail for this long gap. The thunder clap, when Zeus hurls Phaethon from Helios' chariot, amazes the chorus and brings Klymene out of the house to hear the messenger speech. Thunder clap followed by a messenger-speech Euripides had already used in the *Alkmene*; the sequence here is not unlike the palace miracle followed by Dionysos' report in the *Bacchae* (591) and Athena's intervention followed by the messenger-speech in the *H.F.* (905). The messenger must be someone who can not only tell the preliminaries, how Phaethon arrived and made his request to Helios, but also the actual story of his disastrous driving. The fragments (779–80N²) give Helios' advice at the start of the drive. Helios rides behind his son on his horse Seirios, according to Lesky's certain interpretation (another horse of the Sun, Aithops, is described in fr. 896, and this fragment probably also belongs here). The disaster happens soon and only affects Phaethon; Helios gets into his chariot and drives on his normal course. Who can tell this story to Klymene? If a servant of Helios (or indeed one of the Heliades) was in the chariot, he or she could ride Seirios back and bring the news to Klymene. Iris[70] or Hermes, since Zeus is involved, could also have seen the disaster and brought the news. The messenger cannot be an ordinary mortal but must be someone closely connected either with Helios or with Zeus. One other fragment may belong to this play and place: 971, 'and he lately young and healthy was quenched like a shooting star, releasing his spirit into the upper air'. It seems a better description of Phaethon than of Meleager, to whose play some have ascribed it. Klymene's cursing of athletics (fr. 785) and her cry that her son's body is lying unwashed in a gulley (fr. 786) may be her reaction to the messenger speech. A lyric lament (and perhaps a stasimon also) intervenes before the body is brought on. Wilamowitz suggests that the description of the sun as a golden clod (fr. 783) belongs here: at this moment Euripides 'impudently' makes his chorus speak in terms of modern physics. The fragment is quoted for the influence of Anaxagoras on Euripides. Clearly someone described the sun in physical terms.[71]

In the second column of the second preserved leaf of *Cod. Clar.*

[70] Was this the origin of Iris in the *Birds* (1202ff.)? *Birds* 1239f. might be based on a warning to Klymene *not* to have the body brought home.

[71] Cf. perhaps *Orestes* 983.

Klymene describes the smoke rising from Phaethon's dead body (the obvious parallel for this is the smoking body of Kapaneus in the rather earlier *Supplices* (1017ff.)). The first column only gives the ends of lines. Clearly someone has brought the corpse; there is talk of libations to the dead and of burial before the 'I commend you' of l. 19, which should be said by Klymene. The other speaker is probably the man who brought the corpse, and the ending of the previous five lines – kingship, free men, the rich, city, law – sound like a protracted generalization at the end of his speech by someone who knows the household well.[72] Whether he is Phaethon's attendant who went out with him, or some-one sent from the household after the messenger-speech by Klymene or a friendly countryman who has found the body (like the fishermen who brought back the body of Stheneboia), we cannot tell. The account of the discovery would complete the story of the earlier messenger. There is no indication of when this second messenger goes off; if he belongs to the house, he and his party carry the body in on Klymene's orders (Col. ii, l. 3 = 781, 3N²). Klymene is only anxious to conceal the body from her husband, whom she perceives approaching at the head of a wedding-chorus of maidens. She tells the 'servants' (not the main chorus, although they were so described when they first entered, but the mutes who accompany her as a queen) to wipe up the blood and hurry.

Wilamowitz saw that the wedding-chorus was a subsidiary chorus; Vollmer[73] suggested that the main chorus, the sweepers, went in with Klymene now and rushed out again after Merops discovered the fire; Klymene by sending them in prevented their giving her story away to Merops. But in col. iii they do not say that they have come out of the house, and to do so they would have to rush past Merops as he goes in, which is impossible. Therefore they must have been in the orchestra all the time. Klymene may have told them to keep silent before, but in any case the scene plays so fast that they have no chance to speak even if they want to betray her. As far as we know, chorus and subsidiary chorus were present together in the *Alexandros* and the *Antiope* (as well as in the *Suppliants*).[74]

The wedding-song is crucial for the identification of the bride.

[72] Cf. the old man who reports the phantom's disappearance in *Helen*, 711f.
[73] Followed by Ritchie, *Authenticity of the Rhesus*, 118f.
[74] Cf. above, p. 127.

Aphrodite, a daughter of Aphrodite, Eos, and Selene have been proposed. In discussing the subsidiary chorus of the *Hippolytus* (58–60) Mr Barrett writes: 'Hippolytos must sing with them as their *exarchos* (just as in *Phaethon* fr. 781. 14–31 Merops sings as leader with the secondary chorus of girls: Klymene announces his coming (4f.), "My husband is near, singing marriage songs as he leads the maidens").' No editor, as far as I can see, has seen this point or asked what Merops sings. Two solutions are conceivable: *either* Merops and the girls sing both the strophe and the antistrophe *or* Merops sings the strophe and the girls sing the antistrophe. If Merops sings both, no person addressed in the song can refer to him; if Merops sings the strophe, no person addressed in the strophe can refer to him.

The strophe was (accepting the received text with νυμφεῖ᾽ ἀνάπτω and γεννᾶν): 'Hymen, Hymen, we sing the heavenly daughter of Zeus, queen of Erotes, Aphrodite patron of marriage for maidens. Queen, for you I kindle this wedding-torch, Kypris, fairest of gods, and for your new-yoked colt, whom you hide in the upper air to breed children from your marriage.' The antistrophe follows (accepting ᾇ sc. νυμφεῖα at the beginning) 'With this song Aphrodite weds the great king of this city, loved commander of her gold in her starry home. King, greater in happiness than the blessed ones in that you shall marry a goddess and alone of mortals be sung throughout the boundless earth as the kinsman of the immortals.'

In the mouth of Merops and the chorus the strophe can only mean that Aphrodite is marrying Phaethon; the fifth line as emended introduces the torch, which was regular in marriages (cf. *Phoen.* 344) and the difficult line at the end must pick up the herald's earlier prayer for children from the marriage. In the antistrophe, whether Merops sings or not, three arguments suggest that the 'King greater in happiness than the blessed ones' is Phaethon and not Merops. First, only violent emendation can make the 'great king of this city' refer to Merops and not to Phaethon, and the two should be the same. Secondly, the 'King, greater etc. . . .' corresponds formally to 'Queen, for you' in the strophe, and as that is addressed to Aphrodite, this should be addressed to Phaethon. Thirdly, Euripides must be recalling the possibly proverbial lines of Alkman (Page, *P.M.G.*, 1, 16) 'let none of men fly to heaven or try to marry Aphrodite', and the reminiscence points to Phaethon, not to Merops.

Phaethon then, when he marries, will be 'the great king of this city', and this picks up Merops' earlier statement (774N²) that he intends to make Phaethon king beside him or instead of him. The song is a *hymenaios* and only mentions the bride and bridegroom, like the *hymenaios* in the Aristophanes *Peace* 1334ff. But because the bride is a great goddess, this song is a preparation for taking the bridegroom to the bride instead of being sung (as in normal practice), while the bride is brought to the bridegroom; and this change of practice seems to have been made clear at the end of Merops' speech after the *hymenaios*: four lines are lost but the last line is 'to go to the precinct of the goddess from my house'. The preceding words must have been 'tell my son to get ready', and they picked up the earlier instructions which Merops had given to Phaethon after the parodos and which Phaethon had disobeyed by going to Helios.

In fact this passage throws considerable light on the earlier fragmentary scene: it was to the precinct of the goddess that Merops went to fetch the chorus of maidens who sing the marriage-song, and the 'holy herald' is presumably the herald of the precinct rather than a herald belonging to Merops as king. It seems to follow that the herald had brought with him Aphrodite's instructions for carrying out the marriage. These cannot have been first communicated in the scene with Phaethon after the parodos; both Klymene and the chorus of sweepers already know about the marriage before the parodos. The herald had therefore arrived the day before, since Merops is still asleep when the play begins (*Cod. Clar.* I, ii, 15 = 773N²).

The phrase in the strophe 'whom you hide in the upper air to breed children from your marriage' is an application to the special circumstances of the general sentiment suitable to marriage-songs: 'today bride and bridegroom are shut in the marriage-chamber.'[75] This is the sense of the words in the mouth of Merops and the wedding-chorus; but the audience have heard the messenger-speech and know (if the ascription of fr. 971 is correct) that Phaethon 'was quenched like a shooting star, releasing his spirit into the upper air'; for them in quite another sense he is being hidden in the upper air. This is a crueller play on words than Euripides usually allows himself, since the aged Merops is a more sympathetic character than, for instance, Theoklymenos in the

[75] Cf. R. Muth, *W.S.*, 67, 1954, 23ff.

Helen, but the scene is in any case cruel with Merops singing the torch-lit marriage-song while the body of the bridegroom lies in the house, the bridegroom who, as he will find, was not in fact even his son – cruel in the sense that Agave's slaughter of the lion and awakening to discover that he was Pentheus is cruel.

The major difficulty for the modern mind is the idea that a great goddess should propose to marry a mortal and then lose her bridegroom in an accident. But it may be that to phrase it like this is to phrase it wrongly. Phaethon's spirit taken into the upper air where Aphrodite has her thalamos is a union of the two in the only sense that they can be united, and the prophecy at the end of the play (attested by the Hypothesis) will have announced his appearance as a star: Helios or Apollo, whom Klymene equates with Helios (*Cod. Clar.* II, ii, 12 = 781N²), may have been the speaker. This interpretation by Wilamowitz removes part of the difficulty. But in what sense did Aphrodite propose to marry? All we know is that Merops thinks of it as a normal marriage except in so far as the bridegroom goes to the bride instead of the reverse. He thinks of it as a marriage for his mortal son which will bring security, prosperity, and stability to the régime. In Hesiod (*Theog.* 989f.) Aphrodite 'snatched Phaethon up and made him a temple-servant in her rich temple, a goodly deity'. This conception clearly coloured the phraseology of the marriage song: 'loved commander of the gold in her starry home'. Euripides has borrowed from the Hesiodic story of Phaethon, son of Eos and Kephalos, to make a new situation for Phaethon, son of Helios. Aphrodite's intentions are unclear. Does she love Phaethon? Or does she intend from the beginning to destroy him? He was the son of Helios, who had revealed her adultery to the gods, and if, as I have suggested above, he had as little interest in sexual indulgence as Hippolytos, she presumably hated him. On the mythological level the vengeful goddess destroyed her enemy; on the psychological level the single-minded careerist in flight from involvement destroyed himself. Aphrodite in Euripides' version did not do the snatching up, but somehow she set the machinery in motion. If the 'holy herald' is her herald, as I have assumed, then she used him to tell Merops to send his son to be her bridegroom. Other possibilities can be imagined, but in any case Aphrodite selfishly and ruthlessly pursued her aim (as in the *Hippolytus*), and Merops (who in this foreshadows Kadmos in the *Bacchae*) tried to use the situation for his political purposes: it would be useful to have a goddess in the family. But the audience must have been told all this, and as far as I can see, only Aphrodite could inform them of her mind and intentions; she must therefore have spoken the prologue speech before Klymene entered to reveal the truth to Phaethon about his father.

Merops has no inkling of what has happened to Phaethon when he sends his servant into the house with the girls who have sung the marriage-song. The servant comes out to say that smoke is pouring from the treasury. Merops goes in to see. The main chorus of sweepers wish for escape and are terrified for Klymene. They then hear Merops lamenting inside. The broken beginnings of lines in Columns iv, 1–22, appear to be partly lyric and partly iambic: probably therefore the lyric dialogue continues with Merops lamenting inside. Then Merops comes out and speaks with a character twice labelled *Troph.* Von Arnim takes this to be the paidagogos of Phaethon, who, according to him, had brought Phaethon's body back. The only indication that *Troph.* here is masculine, εἰδὼς, in l. 35, has been removed by Mr Wilson's new reading εἰδει; and as far as I know, *Troph.* as an indication of a character is always feminine. The *tropheus* of Agamemnon in the *Electra* (409) is called *presbys* in the list of characters and in the margins when he appears. This then is not Phaethon's paidagogos but Klymene's nurse. The beginnings of the lines (and the needs of the situation) suggest that this is an interrogation. The nurse can be supposed to have learnt the story of Phaethon's ride from Klymene, but what she knows and the paidagogos would not know is that Klymene was raped by Helios and this as well as the story of Phaethon's death must be revealed to Merops now.

Beyond this we know little. Presumably the interrogation leads not only to bitter recriminations against Aphrodite but also to a scene between Merops and Klymene. Merops had been deceived by Klymene, and it looks as if the hypothesis used the strong word 'perjured' to describe her earlier behaviour. She may therefore have had to plead for her life now and Merops may have threatened her with death.[76] The intervention of Helios-Apollo may have saved her. Alternatively her father Okeanos, to whom the chorus told her to pray, may have spoken the epilogue. Merops certainly did see his error: fr. 778 'the

[76] Cf. Athamas in the *Second Phrixos* and the king at the end of the *Melanippe Desmotis.*

congratulatory crowd threw me (*or* you) off balance' (the sense is fixed by
Plutarch who quotes it) is either a confession by Merops or a statement
by a *deus ex machina*, that ambition had led him to misinterpret
Aphrodite's intentions. Only a god can tell of Phaethon's becoming a
star and we know from the hypothesis that the play ended with a
prophecy. Fr. 782, 'refreshing trees will receive him in loving arms'
foretells or commands Phaethon's burial in a sacred grove. In the
Hippolytos (735) the sacred grove is in the West; here Euripides may
have put it in the East since the disaster occurred very early in Phaethon's
course. The 'loving arms' of the trees clearly mean that the Heliades,
who are Phaethon's half-sisters, were changed into poplars; they too
may have been moved to the East. Alternatively Helios or Okeanos
may have transported his body to the West. It is interesting that the
description of death as 'air to air and earth to earth' which Euripides
quotes several times (e.g. *Suppl.* 532ff.) here has a very special application. Phaethon's spirit becomes a star while his body is buried in the
grove of the Heliades.

On the reckoning propounded above the text fails about l. 900.
The sequence interrogation of Nurse, debate between Merops and
Klymene, epilogue must have been about 400 lines long even if this was
a short play. It is possible that a third stasimon was introduced between
the interrogation of the nurse and the scene with Klymene, but having
introduced a considerable amount of lyric dialogue and a subsidiary
chorus Euripides may have felt that two stasima were enough as in the
Electra and *Hercules*.

We have lost too much of this play to get its full flavour. The lovely
dawn parodos is a step into the world of fantasy such as Euripides loves
to take; and if my interpretation is right, contrasts violently both with
the sinister Aphrodite who opens the play and with the muddled
mortals: Merops who misinterprets the goddess, Klymene who is
jealous of him, and the one-sided young athlete Phaethon. The messenger speech must have been as effective as the *Hippolytus* messenger
speech in rousing the audience's feeling of tragic waste, which is screwed
a bit higher by the arrival of the smoking body. In this mood they take
the full irony of the very pretty wedding song and hear the recriminations of the bereaved and deceived Merops and the bereaved and
desolated Klymene until the *deus ex machina* puts them back on the rails
again.

MELEAGER

Outline of play

Prologue: ? Artemis: 515–6N², Accius IR.

Oineus and Meleager: Accius IIR; *adesp.* 188N².

Messenger: 530–1N²; new Photios; Accius IV–VR.

Marriage debate: Meleager: Accius VIIR; 518–20, 526–7N². Althaia:
   521–2, 528N², Atalante: 525N²; Accius XVR?; 517N²?.

Messenger and Oineus: Page, *G.L.P.* no. 27, Accius VIR. Althaia:
   VIII–XIR.

Arrival of Meleager dying: Accius XII–XIVR.

Nurse reports suicide of Althaia: 533N².

Epilogue: ? Athena: 537N². Chorus: 536N².

Bibliographical note: D. L. Page, *C.Q.* 31, 1937, 178; G. Murray,
Athenian Drama III, 1906, 330. Attic and Apulian vases, see p. 306.

Nothing is known of Aeschylus' *Atalante*. Sophocles' play probably
followed closely the Homeric story. Euripides' play is dated to the third
group by 26.6% resolved syllables in fifty-nine lines, and by the trochaic
tetrameter (536, perhaps from the choral exodos), but it was quoted in
Aristophanes' *Birds*, and therefore cannot have been produced later than
416 B.C. Two papyri have been added to the book fragments and the
fragments of Accius' *Meleager*. Of these *P. Oxy.* 2436 may refer to
Althaia, as Miss A. M. Dale suggested, but the address to sons of goat-
herds, shepherds, herdsmen, maenads would be very strange in a tragic
monody, and Gentili's ascription[77] to Euripides is unlikely. *P. Ashm.*
(= Page, *G.L.P.*, no. 27) mentions Atalanta and the hide of a fierce
animal, so that, although it gives very little, it probably is a dialogue
between Oineus and an old man who has reported that Meleager has
given the hide to Atalante.

The Attic vases of the Meleager painter show the heroes assembled
and Meleager conversing with Atalante: the elaborate clothing suggests
an origin in tragedy. The rather later Attic pelike gives the boar-hunt
dominated by Artemis. The Apulian vases show Meleager under the
influence of love giving the hide to Atalante and Meleager's death.

The action stretched from the preparations to hunt the Kalydonian
boar to at least the death of Meleager, but much is unclear. The prologue

[77] *Gnomon*, 33, 1961, 341.

starts with a genealogy of Oineus and describes his failure to sacrifice to Artemis and the disasters caused by the boar (515–6N², Accius IR). As it is not spoken by Oineus or Althaia, Artemis has been suggested but Meleager himself cannot be ruled out. Artemis is a very attractive suggestion because she would then dominate the action like Aphrodite in the *Hippolytus* (and perhaps in the *Phaethon*); Atalante, 'loathed by Kypris' (530N²) lives after her model like Hippolytos,[78] and (quite apart from the sins of Oineus against Artemis) Meleager tries to make Atalante his wife.

Welcker suggested that 'the practice of the singing shuttle' (523N²) implied a chorus of women. But the three preceding lines of Aristophanes' parody also seem to belong, so that the whole was in Euripides an address to women-weavers. The chorus could have addressed themselves but perhaps a lyric dialogue between Althaia and her women is more likely. But other interpretations are possible; the sentence might have come from a monody and refer to women in the palace.

Beyond the prologue speech we are in the dark until the messenger arrives to describe the heroes who took part in the boar-hunt. One hint for an earlier scene has been seen in Accius IIR, *Vagent ruspantes silvas, sectantes feras.* This may be Oineus' instructions to the hunters, and since a parade of hunters is unlikely, he may have given the instructions to Meleager (or perhaps to Meleager and Tydeus since in this play they seem to have been brothers). In any case an early scene between Oineus and Meleager is likely. Here Meleager may have prayed: 'Zeus, may it be mine to bring down the boar' (*adesp.* 188N²).

The messenger's description (530–1N²; fragment from new Photios[79]) of the hunters is in the past: 'they took such equipment'. This implies that he went on to describe their action, the boar-hunt, of which Accius IV–V preserves three lines. Atalante is mentioned in 530N² between Telamon and Ankaios, which rather suggests that she was simply one in a list of hunters, and that Euripides did not include the preliminary quarrel about whether Atalante as a woman should be allowed to join the hunt (Hyginus, *Fab.* 174, omits it; Apollodorus I, viii, 2–3 includes it).

It is not clear whether the messenger only included the boar-hunt

---

[78] Theonoe is perhaps the only feminine parallel in Euripides, *Hel.* 1006.

[79] Mentions Theseus as one of the hunters (I owe my knowledge of this to Mr K. Tsantsanoglou).

and Meleager's presentation of the hide to Atalante or whether he went on to the quarrel with the Thestiadai. This would have made the speech very long, and Hyginus implies a real break in the action: 'Meleager gave Atalante the hide, which the brothers of Althaia wanted to take. When she had begged the support of Meleager, he intervened and put love before kinship and killed his uncles.' This suggests as the Euripidean sequence: Messenger speech describing the boar-hunt, return of Meleager, arrival of Atalante to ask for help in getting the hide back, departure of Meleager (and Atalante) to kill the Thestiadai, report of the killing to Oineus.

The fragments seem to fit this sequence. Meleager returns and meets Althaia and defends his action: 'the glory is mine, but I thought fit to give the spoils to Atalante' (Accius VIIR). Then he says that he wants to marry Atalante (the whole sequence surely means that in Euripides he was not already married). Marrying a good wife is the one guarantee of good children (518, 520, probably 526-7; perhaps 519N², which Ribbeck referred to the quarrel with the Thestiadai).[80] Althaia answers that women's place is in the home (521) and if wives take to war they will themselves be inefficient and will in addition make the men effeminate (522). Mother and son are hopelessly estranged. Perhaps the debate ends with the arrival of Atalante (525): 'if I were to marry (and may that never happen!) my children would be better than the children of women who spend all day in the house', and perhaps Althaia answers 'I hate all women who combine fair words with evil deeds, and you most of all' (528). Althaia's feelings can reasonably be described as jealousy, Phthonos, which is inscribed on the Eros on the Apulian vase with the death of Meleager.

According to this view Atalante has come to ask Meleager's help in getting back the boar's hide from his uncles. Accius XV, 'Who will not despise, scorn, abuse me and publish my ill-fame?', has been given to Atalante but might belong to Althaia's repentance later. Meleager, still in love even if hopelessly in love, agrees to help her. The next scene is the arrival of the messenger to report to Oineus that Meleager has killed his uncles and given back the hide to Atalante; Page combines the

---

[80] I do not feel certain that, as Murray suggested, *Hipp.* 634-7 also belong here; it sounds more like a father arguing against marriage but it must come from some marriage debate. The punning fragment (517N²), 'Meleager, your hunt is a wretched thing' (μελέαν ἀγράν) perhaps belongs in this context.

papyrus (*G.L.P.*, no. 27) with Accius VI, 'he gave the hide and the crown to this virgin' (but the original presentation must have been mentioned in the earlier messenger-speech), and suggests that Oineus' 'I will go' at the end means that he is going to break the news to Althaia. But Althaia has guessed the truth: Accius VIII 'I came out in terror as soon as the shouting reached my ears.' She breaks into a mad frenzy (Accius IX). The fates prophesied that Meleager would die when the torch was extinguished (Accius X). 'If only I could feel the kindly sympathy of a mother!' (Accius XI). She goes into the house and extinguishes the torch. Meleager is led or carried on dying (Accius XII–XIV) by Tydeus, if we may trust the Apulian vase.[81] Althaia in repentance rushes into the house to commit suicide and her suicide is reported by her nurse: the evidence for this is fr. 533N² where an old woman says how much she hates the idea of death in spite of her age:[82] this is clearly a comment on a death; Althaia would hardly comment like this on Meleager's death, so that it should be an old nurse commenting on Althaia's death.

A god speaks the epilogue (537N²) and prophesies that Tydeus will eat the head of Melanippos, cannibalism by which we know he forfeited his immortality. Tydeus was also a son of Oineus; and as the Apulian vase makes him assist at Meleager's death, he was probably also Althaia's son in this play and he may have gone out with Meleager to hunt the boar. The god (perhaps Athena, as she promised Tydeus immortality) evidently prophesies complete disaster for the house of Oineus, and the chorus comments (536N²) 'how quickly god reverses prosperity'.

PLEISTHENES

The large amount of resolution (25%) coupled with quotation in the *Birds* place this play like the *Meleager* at the beginning of Group III. Wilamowitz'[83] strictures on the language do not appear to be justified. The story may be given by Hyginus, *Fab.* 86. Thyestes in exile sent Pleisthenes, Atreus' son whom he had adopted, to kill Atreus. Atreus instead killed him, believing him to be Thyestes' son. Fr. 625 could be said by Atreus to the youth whom he believed to be the son of

[81] Compare *Alc.* 19, which gives the phraseology.
[82] For the idea cf. Admetos' parents, *Alc.* 669f., 691f.; Hekabe, *Tro.* 632–3.
[83] *Kl. Schr.* I, 205; IV, 186.

Thyestes. Fr. 629 refers perhaps to Pleisthenes when he had taken refuge on an altar.

If the collocation *Phaethon, Meleager, Pleisthenes* is right (and it is only a conjecture), Euripides was already experimenting with the strophe, antistrophe, epode form of trilogy. Meleager and Phaethon have really something in common; both are young and perform a great deed with disastrous consequences to themselves; both take part in a marriage debate with a parent. But the plays, like the later antistrophic pairs, are also very different. The father urges the marriage on an unwilling Phaethon, Meleager wants the marriage which his mother rejects. The celibate athleticism which may be detected in Phaethon is in the *Meleager* a strong characteristic of Atalante, and the contrast is emphasized if her patron Artemis spoke the prologue of this play, whereas Aphrodite, patron of sex-desire and herself the intended 'bride' spoke the prologue of the *Phaethon*. The collocation cannot be proved but it would give a complementary pair of plays in the same sense that the *Andromeda* and *Helen* in 412 B.C. are complementary.

V

Euripides' Last Plays

The certain dates in the last group of Euripides' plays are *Orestes* 408 B.C.; *Archelaos* produced at the court of Archelaos of Macedon and therefore probably in 407 B.C.; *Iphigenia in Aulis*, *Alkmaion in Corinth*, *Bacchae* produced by Euripides' son after his death, which was known in Athens by March 406 B.C. Zielinski's statistics for resolution in the iambic trimeter show a marked increase in the preserved plays over the highest figures for the preceding group, and the fragments of *Archelaos* and *Alkmaion in Corinth* agree. The other lost plays with figures which suit this group are *Auge*, *Oidipous*, and *Temenidai*. Zielinski[1] suggested that *Temenos*, *Temenidai*, and *Archelaos* were produced together in Macedonia; the six trimeters preserved in four fragments of the *Temenos* show no resolution, but Zielinski suggested that fr. 1083N², describing the lands for which the Herakleidai drew lots came from the *Temenos*; its metre is certainly too free for the *Kresphontes*, which is the only other likely play. If this is accepted, the *Auge* and *Oidipous* remain as the two plays produced with the *Orestes* in 408 B.C.

1 *Auge, Oidipous, Orestes*

AUGE

According to Strabo (XIII, 615) Euripides said that Auge was put in a chest with her child Telephos by her father Aleos, but Athena arranged for the chest to be cast up at the mouth of the Kaikos, and Teuthras found them and 'made Auge his wife and Telephos his son'. This must depend on the *Auge* rather than the *Telephos* because in the papyrus version of the prologue of the *Telephos* (Page, *G.L.P.*, no. 17) Telephos says that he came to Mysia *and there found* his mother. Moses Chorenensis, whom Wilamowitz[2] used for the plot, after describing the rape

---

[1] *Mnem.* 50, 1922, 305, cf. *Tragodoumenon* 236.
[2] *Analecta Euripidea*, 186ff. The text is given in N², p. 436.

of Auge by Herakles, who left her a ring, the birth and exposure of
Telephos (whose name here came from being suckled by a deer –
Wilamowitz gives many parallels in late Euripides for punning etymology) and the condemnation of Auge, says that Herakles arrived and
recognized the ring, then saved the child and freed the mother from
imminent death: 'Teuthras is said then in accordance with an oracle of
Apollo to have married Auge and adopted Telephos.' The end coincides
with Strabo, who is only interested in what happened in Teuthrania.
Herakles therefore saved his wife and child from death but not from
being cast adrift (like Danae); a god must have foretold the future.

The prologue began 'This is the house of rich Aleos' (264aN²). He
was a rich man and is later described as a tyrant (275N²). The prologue
must have told the story of Herakles' rape of Auge. (*P. Hamburg* 119,
col. iii, has a fragment of a prologue, which from the number and
quality of its resolutions must come from some late play of Euripides,
telling the story of Alkmene's marriage, and presumably going on to
the birth of Herakles; it is possible that it belongs here; if so, the speaker
may have been a god rather than either Herakles or Auge herself.) As
Herakles later finds the baby being suckled by a deer (fr. 278 with τῆς
νεβροῦ for ἡ νευρά, as Wilamowitz suggested) the baby had either
already been exposed when the play begins or was exposed early in the
play. Aristophanes speaks of Euripidean women giving birth in temples
(*Frogs* 1080), and the scholiast refers this to the *Auge* but does not imply
necessarily that she gave birth to Telephos during the play rather than
before the play. The play probably starts after the birth of Telephos
and when Aleos has discovered the truth.

Auge herself complains that Athena has no objection to trophies won
in war or dead bodies but finds her having given birth a terrible thing
(266N²). Three points can be made here. First, this by itself could provide the text for Aristophanes. Secondly, someone (presumably a
soothsayer consulted by Aleos) must have said that Athena took this
view, and with fr. 267N² 'a city sick is very good at discovering complaints', this rather suggests that as in Apollodoros (II, vii, 4) the country
was struck by a plague after the birth of the baby. Thirdly, Auge herself, the priestess, like Iphigeneia when she refuses to believe that
Artemis commanded human sacrifice (*I.T.* 380ff.), probably does not
take this view but prays to Athena to bring up '*this* baby' worthily of
Herakles and herself (*adesp.* 399N²). If this belongs here, probably Auge

now sends the nurse to expose the baby, and Aleos has ordered this and the punishment of Auge in an earlier scene.

For the moment Auge herself is in desperate need, and it looks as if the nurse, when she returns after a choral ode, recommends finding a friend who will search out Herakles. 'We are women. Sometimes we are overcome by fear; sometimes no one could surpass us in daring' ($276N^2$). Then Auge: 'To what end? How will you escape detection? What faithful friend have we?' Nurse: 'Let us look for one. Opinions are often misleading.' Auge: 'Yes, but action leads to disaster' ($277N^2$), 'It is better to let things go' (Diogenes Laertius ascribed this line, *El.* 379, to this play; it is easier to suppose that Euripides quoted himself than with Wilamowitz to transpose *El.* 373-9 here). At this point, if we follow Moses Chorenensis, Herakles arrives and discovers from Auge, who shows him his ring, that the baby has been exposed and goes off to find it.

After a stasimon Herakles comes back with the baby on his arms: 'I am playing with him. I like a change from my labours' (fr. $864N^2$, perhaps also $272N^2$, 'Who does not rejoice in childish toys?'). He finds Aleos and says that, after Aleos had feasted him ($268N^2$), love and wine led him to abandon reason and rape Auge; it was an act of violence, not persuasion; but nature has no respect for conventions; it was an injustice but an involuntary injustice (269, omitting l. 2, as Wilamo-witz[3] saw; *adesp.* 402 (Aleos); *adesp.* 570; 265a; $265N^2$). What Herakles achieved seems to have been not the restoration of Auge and the establishment of Telephos but a change of punishment; instead of death Auge was now to be cast adrift with Telephos in a chest. Aleos points out here probably that the city is very quick to complain when it is suffering from a plague ($267N^2$), and Herakles burst out against tyrants ($275N^2$). Strabo's statement that the forethought of Athena caused the chest to be cast up where Teuthras could find it implies that Athena spoke the epilogue; Herakles can hardly have submitted tamely to Aleos. Possibly he was stopped from shooting him by Athena who promised a great future for Telephos in Mysia.

It is difficult to get much of the flavour of this play. Auge is the last of the line of 'women with irregular babies' and like many of her pre-decessors suffered for her conduct. Minos threatening Pasiphae, Hellen and Aiolos threatening Melanippe, Aiolos threatening Kanake are the

[3] *Kl. Schr.*, I, 203.

obvious earlier parallels. Her 'taking issue with Athena', as Clement calls it (266N²), is like the nouthetetic prayer of Menelaos in the *Helen*.[4] Aleos seems to be the weak tyrant who is not prepared to withstand public opinion (267, 275N², a theme we shall find developed in the *Orestes* and the *Iphigenia in Aulis*).

It is this cowardice which makes him condemn Auge in the first place and then only commute her punishment when Herakles admitted his responsibility. The terminology of their discussion is the terminology of sophistic debate: violence/persuasion, voluntary/involuntary, passion/reason, nature/convention. The contrasts are not used here, as earlier,[5] to portray a conflict in the soul but to establish Auge's innocence and the extent of Herakles' guilt.

OIDIPOUS

The first line of the *Oidipous* was 'Against Phoibos' command (Laios) begat children' (539aN²). The speaker might be a god or Iokaste or Kreon, but could hardly be Oidipous. The possibilities can be limited if the description of the sphinx belongs to the prologue. The papyrus fragment (*P. Oxy.* 2459), which includes two book fragments (540 and *ades.* 541N²) is badly preserved. The speech certainly gave a description of the Sphinx alighting and displaying her wings in the sun. Here again Euripides shows his interest in light effects as in Antigone's vision of Polyneikes in the *Phoenissae* (161ff.). This was followed by the sphinx reciting her riddle in hexameters and calling for interpreters. Just before the sphinx starts her riddle, the speaker says '*we* left'. He was therefore not one of the interpreters; in the next line '*they* stood' must refer to the interpreters. Before the discovery of the papyrus Robert[6] thought of Kreon as the prologue-speaker; according to Hyginus (*Fab.* 67)[7] he made a general proclamation that the successful interpreter should have the kingdom and Iokaste's hand; a newly published Apulian 'phlyax'-oinochoe[8] gives Kreon (inscribed) seated in front

---

[4] Cf. above, p. 201.
[5] Cf. above, p. 96.
[6] *Ödipus*, I, 305ff.; Séchan, *Études*, 434ff. Cf. also the careful article of J. Vaio, G.R.B.S., 5, 1964, 43.
[7] Hyginus certainly used other sources here besides Euripides' *Oidipous*, but this play seems to have been one of his sources, see below.
[8] See p. 307, below.

of the Sphinx and talking to Oidipous; it may illustrate Euboulos'
Oidipous, which in this may derive from Euripides. The speech cannot
have been a messenger speech about events that happened during the
action of the play because Oidipous was established in Thebes before
the play began (this is, I think, a fair deduction from 543–6, 551N²).
The prologue is, therefore, the natural place for this narrative, Kreon
the natural speaker. Kreon starts with Laios' oracle, then tells that the
baby was exposed, that after some sixteen years Laios was killed, that
the sphinx came, that Oidipous solved her riddle, received the kingdom,
and married Iokaste. Alternatively Hermes may have told the story up
to the death of Laios including the very individual account of the
exposing of the baby which Euripides seems to have adopted (see
below). Then Kreon in a second scene will have told the back history
from when he took over power and presumably also showed which
way the story was going to develop, whether by voicing his discontent
with Oidipous or by saying that the killer of Laios must be found.

The only event which the fragments certainly attest is the blinding
of Oidipous (541N²). In the *Phoenissae* (61) Euripides makes Oidipous
blind himself when he discovers the truth as in Sophocles. The scholiast
then says 'But in the *Oidipous* the servants of Laios blinded him: "We
thrust the son of Polybos on the ground, blind him and destroy his
eyes".' At first one naturally thinks of the death of Laios as the occasion, but this would mean that Oidipous was blinded before he solved
the riddle, and that Kreon extracted this story from the survivors of the
death of Laios during the course of the play. This is, of course, possible
but Robert found a better solution in an Etruscan urn [9] which gives
a scene of three soldiers blinding a young man; to the left an older man
directs the operation; to the right two small boys lament, and a woman
rushes up but is held back by an old man. Robert convincingly interpreted this as Kreon directing the servants of Laios to blind Oidipous,
Polyneikes and Eteokles lamenting, and Iokaste attempting to intervene. Then fr. 541N² comes from a messenger speech in which a
servant of Laios related the blinding of Oidipous in the palace. Two
further facts are implied, first that Kreon has discovered that Oidipous
killed Laios, and secondly that, as Oidipous is called the son of Polybos,
he has *not* yet been recognized as the son of Laios. This may have been

[9] See p. 307, below

the speech which Nero sang (Suetonius, *Nero*, 21)[10] since *Oedipodem excaecatum* could hardly refer to self-blinding.

A fragment (551N²), 'Envy, which corrupts the mind of many, destroyed him and has destroyed me with him' has been reasonably given to Iokaste and referred to the jealous desire of Kreon for Oidipous' power; it cannot have been spoken until the whole truth came out. What the Sophoclean Oidipous believed of Kreon (*O.T.* 532ff.) was true of the Euripidean Kreon (who is thus much more like the Kreon of the *Antigone* and *O.C.*); and there are fragments which suggest a contrast between a ruthless efficient Kreon and a contemplative Oidipous who has ideals. 'White silver and gold are not the only currency; excellence is also a universal currency which should be used' (542N²); 'Desire is one, but not pleasure. Some desire the bad, and some the good' (547N²); 'Which is it better to be? Intelligent and unenterprising or bold and unintelligent? One is a fool but fights, but quietness is idleness. Both have faults' (552N²). The last fragment has been compared to the debate in the *Antiope*, and it is possible that someone, perhaps Iokaste after the blinding, summed up the contrast between Kreon and Oidipous like this. Robert's suggestion that this was the survivor of Laios describing his own hesitation is less likely. If so, Oidipous is intelligent but has his period of activity behind him. Kreon is active but has the wrong values. And in Euripides it is Oidipous who conceals his misfortunes (553N², said according to Robert in self-defence to Iokaste for keeping silent about the death of Laios) and Kreon who reveals them. Was it Oidipous who spoke of the 'songful reed which the river Melas grows, poetic nightingale of sweet-breathing flutes' (556N²)[11] and was the symposion one of his pleasures? Kreon on the other hand must say that he would not fear the gods in moving a criminal from an altar to punish him (554aN²), a step which Ion under extreme provocation is not prepared to take (*Ion* 1310). We cannot be certain where these fragments belong but they establish a contrast between the characters of Kreon and Oidipous.

What set Kreon on the track of Laios' killer is unknown. Euripides may have used the Sophoclean framework of the plague and oracle: given the demand, Kreon had only to interrogate the survivors. Alternatively the survivor may have only now volunteered the information.

[10] Cf. above, p. 158, on *Aiolos*.
[11] For the text see *P. Oxy.* 2536.

When Kreon had established the truth, he arranged with the survivors to collect assistants and blind Oidipous, and the result was reported. Why Kreon should punish Oidipous in the same way as Amyntor punished Phoinix for supposedly seducing the queen we do not know, but the blinding was in any case part of the story.

Robert supposes that Oidipous also lost his power and his children to Kreon and was being sent into exile but that Iokaste remained loyal to him, when he had explained that he killed Laios in self-defence ($553-4N^2$ are attributed to his defence). The reconstruction is attractive: in $543N^2$ Oidipous seems to be saying that to lose a good wife is a worse disaster than losing children, fatherland and money. The only question here is whether the loss of children, etc. may not be hypothetical; if the threat is real, Oidipous, who at this stage still thinks of himself as a Corinthian, could not speak of losing his fatherland. This fragment is, therefore, evidence for the loyalty of Iokaste but not for Kreon depriving Oidipous of his children and sending him out of the country. If the loss of children is hypothetical, then the first line 'Children and wife have great power over a man' need not be moved to another scene, although some lines may have fallen out after it. The loyalty of Iokaste is also attested by $544N^2$: 'a wife is the hardest thing of all to fight against' (whether said by Kreon or by Iokaste of herself) and by the trochaic fragment ($545N^2$) 'The modest wife is the slave of her husband; the immodest wife in her folly despises her consort'; the anapaestic fragment ($546N^2$) 'a wife is always less than her husband even if the basest man marries a noble woman' may be a choral comment.

Hermann put the trochaic fragment in the middle of the long trochaic passage which has been reconstructed from Clement ($909N^2$). Clement, without naming the play, quotes the lines out of order as Euripides' description of a loving wife. Fr. $545N^2$ fits well into the sequence of thought of $909N^2$: not beauty but excellence is the standard; the good woman who is in love with her husband knows modesty; she will believe him beautiful if he is ugly, etc.; *the modest wife is the slave of her husband* ($545N^2$); 'But *I* will endure sharing *your* sickness.' This line marks the transition from the general and hypothetical to the particular. The speaker of this fragment has a sick husband with whom she is prepared to share bad times as well as good (the words recall Theseus' loyalty to Herakles at the end of the *H.F.* 1220f.). This long run of trochaics must belong to Group III or IV; none of the plays in Group III has or admits a wife comforting a husband in distress; in Group IV we perhaps know too little of the *Temenos* to rule that play out. But the neatness with which the *Oidipous* fragment fits in is a strong argument in favour of the ascription of 909N^2 to *Oidipous*, and Clement also quotes frs. 542, 545 and 546N^2 (all according to Stobaeus from the *Oidipous*) without naming the play. It is true Ino professes her love of Athamas when she is carrying out her plot to get Phrixos sacrificed.[12] The evidence that Iokaste is genuine in her sympathy is partly the close similarity of Theseus' words in the *H.F.*, partly the Etruscan urn which shows her trying to stop the blinding, partly the fragment about jealousy (551N^2) which must be attributed to her.

We cannot be certain how these fragments should be distributed. Oidipous' iambic statement of the power of wife and children (543N^2) may belong to an earlier scene with Kreon. The recognition that Iokaste will fight for Oidipous (544N^2) and the anapaestic comment (546N^2) may belong to the scene in which Kreon plots Oidipous' blinding. But the trochaic passage (545 + 909N^2) must belong to a scene in which Oidipous is already deeply involved in disaster, but has not yet been recognized as Iokaste's son.

The discovery that Oidipous killed Laios must have been followed by the discovery that he was Laios' son. Here Robert followed Pottier in finding the clue in Hyginus (*Fab.* 66 and 67) and the illustration on a Homeric bowl in the Louvre.[13] The Homeric bowls have illustrations from Aeschylus, Sophocles, and Euripides (as well as epic) so that the probability that this is Euripides' version is considerable. The bowl illustrates and amplifies Hyginus *Fab.* 66: Periboia, wife of Polybos of Corinth, found the exposed baby (which had been cast up on the shore) when she went to the sea to wash clothes; they brought it up as their own. In Hyginus *Fab.* 67 Oidipous hears of the death of Polybos and is grieved because he thinks that he has lost his father; Periboia makes it clear that he was a supposititious child. The contention is that Euripides made Periboia come from Corinth to bring Oidipous home to succeed his adoptive father. This is perhaps no more improbable than making Klytemnestra journey from Argos to Aulis in the *Iphigenia in Aulis* (and has the further advantage of giving a name for

[12] Cf. above, p. 134.
[13] See below, p. 307.

the woman who is seated on the left of the blinding scene of the Etrus-can urn). Robert takes fr. 550N² 'The joy which shines out unex-pectedly is greater than what is expected' as said by Oidipous in his joy at finding that he has a refuge in Corinth; this goes against Hyginus where Oidipous is concerned for his father's death. It may rather be Periboia's description of her joy at finding the baby.

Hyginus continues that Menoetes, the old man who had exposed him, recognized that he was the son of Laios by the scars on his feet and ankles. Robert thinks that Menoetes is unnecessary in Euripides' play because the point of introducing Periboia's story was to enable Iokaste to make the recognition; she knew that she had ordered the baby to be put into a chest and cast into the sea. Hyginus only says that she ordered the baby to be exposed, and the scholiast to *Phoen.* 26, who has the story of the chest coming ashore in Sikyon, does not say who gave the orders. Euripides may have wanted to clinch the recognition in another scene; it may even have given Kreon another chance to force a revelation 'Justice sees even through the dark' (555N²), and the fragment about jealousy taken literally should belong here since Iokaste is only now destroyed (551N²). Presumably Periboia went home in horror. Robert assumes that Iokaste committed suicide, but we have no evidence that she did not live on with Oidipous as in the *Phoenissae*.

Where so much is unclear, we can at least say that Euripides loosened the intertwined structure of the Sophoclean play so that the death of Laios was dealt with first before the problem of Oidipous' birth arose, and that the driving force was not the inquisitive energy of Oidipous but partly chance and partly the jealousy of Kreon. This intelligent and perhaps easygoing Oidipous does not act; he only suffers, and Iokaste, whom Sophocles treats so cavalierly, is developed into a full-scale figure of great sympathy and power. The metrical evidence places this play after the *Phoenissae* (and it is difficult in any case to accommodate it in Group III). In the *Phoenissae* Euripides had accepted the back history from Sophocles but he made Iokaste live on as the wise and dignified mother of her younger sons; Oidipous bitterly repents the curse he put on his sons, and as we see him is gentle and dignified. It looks as if Euripides wrote this play to provide his own back history for Iokaste and Oidipous as he had presented them in the *Phoenissae*. Sophocles then reasserted the old angry Oidipous of heroic stature in the *Oedipus Coloneus*.

ORESTES

The *Orestes* starts with an ekkyklema scene, like the *Andromeda*. Here Orestes is in bed asleep. The scene is the palace of Agamemnon five days after the funeral of Klytemnestra. At the end of the Euripidean *Electra* (1249ff.) the Dioskouroi told Orestes to betroth Elektra to Pylades, to escape the Furies by going to Athens, and to leave Klytemnestra to Menelaos and Helen to bury. Sophocles cut the story short after the murders and asked none of the uncomfortable questions. Euripides, like Gilbert Murray, must have disliked this 'combination of matricide and high spirits'. He forgets his own *Electra*, accepts from Sophocles Apollo's command to Orestes to kill his mother, though he calls it injustice (28), the existence of Chrysothemis (23) though he does not use her, and the palace as the scene of the murders. Then he asks what happened next. As in the *Phoenissae* he asks how far was the rest of the family involved and how did they behave.

Elektra speaks the prologue. Orestes has fits of madness; he is starving but for the moment asleep. The city will decide today whether they are to die by stoning. Their one hope is Menelaos; he is in Nauplia and has already sent Helen into the palace by night (the Egyptian Helen is forgotten). Hermione has been there for the duration of the Trojan War. Helen enters; she is afraid to take offerings to Klytemnestra's tomb, and with superb tactlessness asks Elektra to do it for her; Elektra suggests that Hermione should be sent; Hermione is called out and goes; Elektra wryly notes that Helen has only cut the tips of her hair for offering (the audience would remember that the Egyptian Helen did not spare her hair in feigned mourning for Menelaos, *Hel.* 1187, 1224). Euripides needed Hermione outside and not far away so that she could be captured later: he solved the problem by this brief brilliant appearance of Helen.

The chorus of Argive women enter, fearful of waking Orestes, to ask for news. Elektra begs them to keep quiet. We have noticed this theme in the *Hercules*,[14] where Euripides was following the Sophoclean *Trachiniae*; here also he had a Sophoclean parallel. Someone in the Sophoclean *Epigonoi* (fr. 197P) said 'Go away, you are disturbing sleep, doctor of sickness', where evidently Alkmaion had fallen asleep after a fit of madness. The parodos is a lyric dialogue largely in excited dochmiacs with the earlier part of each stanza divided between Elektra

[14] Cf. above, p. 191.

and the chorus and the later part given to Elektra alone. Elektra again sings of the injustice of Apollo's command. Phoibos has sacrificed them. Klytemnestra has killed them.

During all this Orestes is gradually waking. Then he wakes up and Elektra tends him in his weakness. Suddenly Elektra sees him going mad; he thinks he is being attacked by the Furies and that Elektra is one of them. Then the fit leaves him, and he recognizes Elektra's affection. He doubts whether Agamemnon himself would have allowed him to kill his mother. Now brother and sister have only each other. He sends Elektra in to wash and change, and she tells him to rest on the bed. This is the first mad scene that Euripides actually put on the stage (as distinct from narrating). It is a visual presentation of the mad scene in the first messenger-speech of the *Iphigenia in Tauris* (281ff.), and here too perhaps the chief point is not the mad scene itself, though that is good theatre, but the sympathy between the two characters before and after.

In a stasimon, largely in dochmiacs, the chorus pray to the Erinyes to allow Orestes to forget; what terrible vengeance he is suffering and yet what house is more glorious? Menelaos enters: 'his luxurious appearance shows him to be a Tantalid' (later Orestes speaks of Menelaos' golden locks tossing on his shoulders, 1532). He is shattered by the ghostlike appearance of Orestes, destroyed by grief and madness. Orestes tells him his story: Apollo promises help but does not give it. The city spurred on by Oiax (the brother of Palamedes – a reference back to the second play of the Trojan trilogy in 415 B.C.) and led by the friends of Aigisthos hates him. He begs Menelaos to help him. He is interrupted by the arrival of his grandfather Tyndareos, who brought him up when he was small. The old man is in black with shorn head. He quarrels with Menelaos for speaking to Orestes. Orestes ought to have gone to law with Klytemnestra. Now let him be stoned by the people. Orestes defends himself by pleading his love for his father, Klytemnestra's treachery with Aigisthos, her bad example to other women, his fear of his father's furies, the command of Apollo. Tyndareos answers that he will go to the assembly and persuade the city to condemn Orestes and Elektra (who is even more guilty) to death by stoning. Tyndareos goes, and Orestes appeals to Menelaos to repay the debt he owes to Agamemnon for the Trojan expedition and the sacrifice of Iphigeneia. Menelaos says that he will wait until the people have calmed down and then try to put in a word for Orestes (he does not appear at the trial at all, 1058). After this display by the older generation Pylades appears, and the metre changes to recitative trochaic tetrameters. Pylades has been banished by his father for his part in the murder of Klytemnestra. He persuades Orestes to go and speak at the trial, and the scene ends with Pylades supporting Orestes off the stage, undisturbed either by his own difficulties or his friend's fear of madness – a demonstration of friendship which knows no bounds, like that of Theseus in the *Hercules Furens* and of Iokaste in the *Oidipous*.

The chorus sing in aeolo-choriambics of the great prosperity and virtue of the family which has suffered disaster since the time of the golden lamb, and now the just matricide is in fact the crime of a madman. Elektra comes out to ask for Orestes and receives the messenger, who reports the trial. So far we have had the reactions of the family; now we have the reactions of the town. Talthybios, Agamemnon's herald, sided with the friends of Aigisthos; Diomede suggested exile instead of death; a popular orator with doubtful credentials urged death by stoning in a speech inspired by Tyndareos; an honest farmer said Orestes ought to be rewarded for killing a bad woman (Euripides surely meant the audience to recall the farmer of the *Electra* here). Orestes pleaded the danger to all husbands if Klytemnestra had been allowed to escape, but all he could achieve was permission for himself and Elektra to die at their own hands. Elektra breaks into a long lamentation for the house of Pelops, destroyed by the jealousy of the gods and the hostility of the court. She wishes she could fly up and lament with Tantalos, the father of Pelops, who killed Myrtilos – whence the golden lamb, the feast of Thyestes, the adultery of Aerope and her present troubles.

Orestes and Pylades return. Orestes begs Elektra to spare him feminine lamentations. They must nobly die together. Pylades refuses to leave them and will die with them, but they can make Menelaos suffer first. They can kill Helen, who deserves to die anyway. Elektra adds that they can seize Hermione as a hostage, and then Menelaos, who is a coward, will save them. The three pray to Agamemnon to help them; then Orestes and Pylades go in to murder Helen.

Euripides means the audience to remember Aeschylus. In the *Electra* (671) he reduced the great Kommos of the *Choephori* to thirteen lines of iambic prayer before Orestes went off to murder Aigisthos;

here we have fifteen lines of prayer before the murder of the unfortunate Helen. Again, if they remember Aeschylus, the audience will contrast the solemn establishment of the first murder court and the acquittal of Orestes by Athena and her jury, with the realistic family quarrel of the first act and the give and take of a democratic assembly reported by the messenger.

Orestes, who in his deep but sane depression believed that Agamemnon would have begged him not to kill his mother, now counts on Agamemnon's aid because he has killed his mother. Elektra remains outside singing an excited lyric dialogue (in dochmiacs and associable metres), with the chorus, who are divided to watch for anyone coming from left or right. Helen cries out from inside. Elektra sings encouragement in pizzicato polymetric lyric. Then the tone sinks to spoken iambics as Hermione arrives and Elektra takes her in to Orestes. The chorus sing a dochmiac strophe – noise to cover the murder, wonder whether Helen is dead, nemesis from the gods. Then they see one of Helen's Phrygian slaves (who have already been described by Orestes when the plan was made) coming out of the door.[15] He sings 130 lines of free polymetric lyric[16] punctuated by iambic lines from the chorus leader and tells of his escape, of the miseries that Helen caused to Troy, of the entry of Orestes and Pylades and their feigned supplication of Helen, of their attack on Helen, of the rally of the Phrygian slaves and finally of the arrival of Hermione and the miraculous disappearance of Helen. His report follows the sequence of events planned by Orestes and Pylades and therefore is intelligible to the audience. An iambic messenger speech would not have suited the frenzied sequence as well as this brilliant aria. Orestes comes out and in a brief trochaic scene drives the Phrygian eunuch in again. The chorus round off this section with the antistrophe to the earlier dochmiac strophe: a new struggle; the smoke means they are firing the house; a long tale of ruin starting with the fall of Myrtilos.

Menelaos arrives having heard the news.[17] He tells his attendants

[15] Cf. A. M. Dale, *Wiener Studien*, 69, 1956, 103.

[16] Cf. above, p. 19.

[17] How he knows is unclear, unless we adopt Wecklein's drastic remedy of cutting out the trochaic scene, 1503–36, so that the Phrygian can escape and tell him; it is true that in the trochaic scene Orestes also speaks as if he had killed Helen. But an interpolator is unlikely to have composed a trochaic scene, and it fits admirably into the whole polymetric sequence.

to break open the doors. This diverts the audience' attention so that the tableau can be set on the roof: Elektra and Pylades brandishing torches, Orestes with his sword at Hermione's throat. Menelaos then looks up and sees them. Orestes threatens to kill Hermione and burn down the house. Orestes' terms are that Menelaos shall persuade the Argives not to put them to death. Menelaos admits that he is caught. But then Orestes calls on Elektra and Pylades to set fire to the house, and Menelaos calls on the Argives to come in force to his help. This inconsistency cannot be solved either by excision or, I think, by the assumption that Orestes is mad, although this is tempting when we consider his delusion in the trochaic scene (1512, 1536) that he has killed Helen. Rather Euripides wanted to show the cowardice of Menelaos and therefore Menelaos had to give in, but he also wanted the appearance of Apollo. In the *Ion* (1546) Ion naturally wishes to put his impossible question to the oracle, and in the *Helen* (1624f.) Theoklymenos naturally wishes to take vengeance on Theonoe, so that in both plays the occasion for the *deus ex machina* is convincingly provided. In the *Iphigenia in Tauris* (1394) a highly improbable storm is invented to wash Orestes' ship back so that Thoas has a chance of capturing him, and this makes Athena's intervention necessary. So here Euripides makes Orestes give his mad order, after Menelaos has given in, because he wants to finish with the appearance of Apollo on the *mechane* with Helen beside him.

Apollo stops Menelaos and Orestes. Helen will live in heaven with Kastor and Polydeukes. Orestes will be purified in Athens and marry Hermione (Neoptolemos will be killed in Delphi). Elektra will marry Pylades. The mortals accept their instructions: Orestes is ready to marry Hermione; Menelaos betroths her to him and wishes for a happy future for all three. The contrast between this future given by traditional mythology and the actual situation which the very naturally conceived characters, starting from the murder of Klytemnestra, have produced is so startling that it compels us to ask why Euripides forces it on our attention. Having got the story to a point where Menelaos was giving in, why could he not have ended with Menelaos' surrender? He is surely not saying, as has recently been suggested,[18] that Apollo brings order into the chaos. This would be to deny all the powers of self-determination with which he so richly endows his characters. Nor can

[18] A. Spira, *Untersuchungen zum deus ex machina*, 140ff.

we suppose that he is ending his play with nonsense, to show up Apollo and deny the truth of the legend. In the *Hercules* he both gave a naturalistic interpretation of Herakles' madness and stated that Hera's enmity was responsible for it. There the human story and the mythological story do not conflict because Herakles goes mad whatever the reason. Here, as at the end of the *Electra*, the characters have to be pulled back on to the mythological tramlines. We can only say that Euripides wanted to assert both stories: the human story of a young neurotic with a devoted sister and friend, a selfish uncle and aunt, a disapproving grandfather, living in a town which showed varied reactions to his crime, and the traditional story of mythology.

Elektra begins the prologue with examples of human endurance, Tantalos, Atreus and Thyestes. The chorus in the first stasimon speak of the glory of the house of Tantalos; in the second stasimon the chain of murder starts with the golden lamb and the feast of Thyestes; Elektra in her lament sings of Pelops' winged chariot and the murder of Myrtilos as the reason for the birth of the golden lamb, the change of the sun's course, and the feast of Thyestes. The murder of Klytemnestra is the beginning of the human story. The back history from Tantalos to Thyestes, like the future foretold by Apollo, is traditional mythology. The human story starts from it but it has no direct bearing on the human story, whereas in the *Oresteia* the feast of Thyestes is part of the fabric of causation which leads to the murder of Klytemnestra. Here Euripides reserves traditional mythology for prologue, lyric, and epilogue.

2 *Temenos, Temenidai, Archelaos*

Zielinski suggested that these three plays formed a trilogy. The *Archelaos* was produced in honour of Archelaos, King of Macedon. The metrical figures for *Temenidai* would permit a late date. The ascription of fr. 1083, which describes Messenia, Lakonia, and Elis, to the *Temenos* (and it is difficult to see from what other play it could come) would make it late too. Siegmann, in his very careful treatment of the problems arising out of the Hamburg papyrus (*P. Hamburg* 118) finds the trilogy unlikely because of the very long genealogical prologue in the *Archelaos*. A possible answer is that for performance in the Macedonian capital the pedigree had to be given in this play just because this play gave the ancestry of the king. The section of the prologue preserved by the papyrus gives the line Lynkeus, Abas, Akrisios, Danae, Perseus, Elektryon, Alkmene, Herakles, Hyllos, Temenos. With Lynkeus we cannot be far from the beginning. Unfortunately, Alexandrian scholars were unclear about the beginning and suggested that fr. 228N² was Euripides' later substitution for fr. 846N², which Aristophanes quotes in the *Frogs* (1206). The prologue surely started with Danaos (fr. 228) and brought him to Argos, but Euripides must also have brought the sons of Aigyptos to Argos since the papyrus starts with Lynkeus and Hypermnestra. Stoessl's suggestion (*R.E.s.v.* Prologos) that 846N² followed soon after 228N² may be the easiest solution.

Siegmann argues that in this play Archelaos was the eldest son of Temenos and this is the obvious interpretation of l. 43 of the papyrus 'my father being childless' went to Dodona 'in his desire for children'. But it raises the question of how his, on this theory, younger brothers managed to drive Archelaos into exile (*a fratribus ejectus*, Hyginus, *Fab.* 219) while he was himself still a young man (237N²). What is more difficult is that the prologue implies that Temenos was in Argos before he consulted Dodona about a child, and a papyrus Hypothesis (*P. Oxy.* 2455, fr. 9), after telling the story of Oxylos and his one-eyed ass, goes on to say that Oxylos divided up the Peloponnese and Temenos drew the Argolid, then in two corrupt lines the words 'production of children' and 'Archelaos' appear, which again places the birth of Archelaos after the arrival of Temenos in Argos. Professor Turner has ascribed this Hypothesis to the *Archelaos* itself.

The tripartition of the Peloponnese is described also in *P. Oxy.* 2455 fr. 10 which gives us no further help. (The fragment seems to belong to the Hypothesis of the *Temenos*, of which an earlier fragment preserves the end of the first line, fr. 741a). But *P. Oxy.* 2455 fr. 11, which conceivably precedes fr. 10, begins with the son of Agamemnon (Teisamenos) and continues with the sons of Temenos; it looks therefore as if it described the defeat and death of Teisamenos at the hands of the Herakleidai, which preceded the tripartition of the land. The mention of the sons of Temenos in this context suggests that they were grown up and fighting. In that case we must suppose that Temenos had married again and desired a child from his new wife. Then it is probable that the *Archelaos* was the third play and that Archelaos was his youngest son.

The *Temenos* dates to the time soon after the battles in the Peloponnese. 'Different land is useful for different products' (742N²) is naturally referred to the Argolid, Lakonia, and Messenia; and fr. 1083N² which describes Sparta, Messenia, and Elis, has been connected with it. Temenos spoke of the allocated lands in the prologue. The only other significant fragments describe the good general (743-4N²) and this is compatible with the suggestion that in this play Temenos chose or had chosen Deiphontes, the husband of his daughter Hyrnetho, as his chief officer in preference to his sons. The action may therefore have developed to the stage when in their fear that Temenos might make Deiphontes his successor they decided to murder their father. In Apollodoros (II, viii, 5) one of the sons passed over is Agelaos, who has a name remarkably like Archelaos. It may not be chance that the word 'counsellor', used by Pausanias (II, 19, 1) in telling this story, occurs also in *P. Oxy.* 2455 ft. 11 and may be used of Deiphontes there.

If the *Temenidai* dealt with the story of Hyrnetho, then the background (whether given in the *Temenos* or not) was the murder of Temenos. The scanty fragments are not incompatible with this. The story has obvious tragic possibilities and Dioskorides' unfortunate poem,[19] written in the late third century, may well have been based on Euripides. The story (Pausanias II, 28) is that the sons of Temenos (except for the youngest Agraios who refused) wanted to get their sister Hyrnetho away from Deiphontes, who was established in Epidauros. They accused Deiphontes of all sorts of crimes and begged her to come back to Argos and marry a braver and richer husband. Hyrnetho said that Deiphontes was a good husband and a blameless son-in-law, but they should be called Temenos' murderers rather than his sons. They then carried her off in their chariot; Deiphontes heard of this and pursued them. In the battle Hyrnetho as well as the brothers was killed. Her body was brought back and she was given special honours in a Heroon.

The scholiast to *Frogs* 1338 says that the lyric lines 'But, servants, light a lamp, heat water, that I may wash away the heaven-sent dream' are a parody of the *Temenidai* (741N²). Hyrnetho may therefore have told of an ominous dream in the prologue, and the parodos may have been a lyric dialogue with her handmaids. The fragments about war

[19] Gow-Page, XXXVI, cf. my *Hellenistic Poetry and Art*, 143.

killing good young men and the immortality of courage (728, 734N²) may have been, as Murray[20] suggests, a reference to the young brother Agraios; he had disagreed and the others may have killed him and told Hyrnetho that he died in war; they echo passages in the Sophoclean *Philoctetes* (446f., 1443f.) which was produced in 409 B.C. Murray is undecided whether the fragment (736N²) about the ingratitude of the dead man's friends is Hyrnetho's accusation of her brothers or a slander against Deiphontes. 'A rare thing are firm friends to the dead, even if they are of the same family' suggests that the reference is to the sons, but Deiphontes was a son-in-law and also a relative because he also was descended from Herakles, and the beginning 'how stupid the man is, how inhospitable, how forgetful of all a friend's duties' must refer to a single man, not to the two sons; therefore the fragment is best regarded as the sons' false accusation against Deiphontes. All that we can say is, however, that the fragments can be fitted into the Hyrnetho story. The sequence – carrying off of Hyrnetho, pursuit of Deiphontes – differs from the sequences at the end of the *I.T.* and *Helen* because Hyrnetho goes against her will; it is echoed by Sophocles in the *O.C.* 821ff., where Kreon seizes Antigone and Theseus is summoned to pursue them. But this pursuit had an unhappy ending.

Can we trace Archelaos in this play? It is of course possible that the fragments about good young men being killed in war (728, 734N²) may not refer to Agraios but to Archelaos, and that the brothers had sent him into exile and covered this act of violence by telling Hyrnetho that he had been killed in war. Another fragment (739N²) which speaks of the pride and honour of a noble father's son, even if he is himself poor, rather points in this direction, and one would expect to find him mentioned in both the earlier plays.

In the *Archelaos* itself the hero spoke the prologue tracing his descent from Danaos.[21] It is presumably a monologue spoken on his arrival in Thrace, like the opening monologue of the *Telephos*. The anapaestic address to Kisseus by the chorus (229N²) show that in fact Kisseus is the king and that therefore Hyginus *Fab.* 219 is based on Euripides. These choral anapaests complaining of the war probably come at the end of the parodos or of a stasimon, which rather suggests that Kisseus did not appear until after the parodos. Kisseus greets Archelaos: 'What

[20] *Athenian Drama*, III, 1906, 348.
[21] See above, p. 253.

need have you of us? Your noble parentage augurs well' (231N²). According to Hyginus Kisseus promised Archelaos kingdom and wife if he defeated the enemy, and this is the next clear point in the action. In 254N² Kisseus seems to be excusing his failure in war, and Archelaos answers that it is easy to put the blame on the gods. 'Children must obey their father's word' (234N²) perhaps suggests that Kisseus has to persuade his daughter when Archelaos has set out, and she may object to marrying a poor man (248N², 'there is no shrine of poverty, the ugliest of gods'); to which Kisseus answers in words which recall *Temenidai* fr. 739N²: 'In their children the virtues of the noble shine forth, and breed is better than a rich marriage. The poor man does not lose the nobility of his father' (232N²).

Archelaos' victory is reported by a messenger to Kisseus, who is persuaded by his friends to break faith with him and kill him by making him walk into concealed fire (as Ixion killed Eioneus in Aeschylus' *Perrhaibides*). A scene of intrigue therefore followed the messenger-speech. Some fragments clearly advise removing Archelaos: 'youth, poverty, and wits combined give cause for worry' (246N²), 'Don't make him rich. If he is poor, he'll be humble' (249N²), 'Royal power has everything except immortality' (250N²), 'To keep in the house a slave or free-man stronger than you is unsafe' (251N²). Someone answers 'Do you think that you are more clever than the gods? . . . Justice is near; and, though unseen, sees and knows who to punish' (255, perhaps also 256–9N² on the advantages of piety). This must then be a scene with three actors, one proposing the plot (conceivably this friend of Kisseus was in league with Kisseus' daughter),[22] the other urging Archelaos' just claims, and Kisseus giving his decision and arranging the murder. There is one clue to the identity of the speaker who tries to protect Archelaos: Agatharchides in a Photius manuscript (N², p. 426) writes 'I do not condemn Euripides for giving Archelaos the actions of Temenos or for introducing Teiresias when he would have to have lived more than five generations.' If Teiresias too came into this play, no one could have more convincingly threatened Kisseus with the punishment of the gods.

As in the *Second Phrixos*, a royal slave is not prepared to carry loyalty to the extent of seeing a brave young man killed, but gives the plot

[22] Perhaps a suitor, as in the plot against Perseus assumed for the *Andromeda*, see above, p. 198.

away to Archelaos when he returns. Kisseus comes out ostensibly to celebrate Archelaos' victory, 'I want to wreathe your head' (241N²). Archelaos persuades him to come to a secret conference (a variant of the temptation scene in *Antiope*) and Kisseus is caught in his own trap (like Dirke in the *Antiope*). This must be reported whether by Archelaos or by another, and a fragment of lyric lament (263N²), perhaps sung by the daughter, survives, and the chorus comment on the retribution which falls on the unjust (264N²); finally Archelaos is told by Apollo to follow the goats which will lead him to Aigai, where he will establish the Macedonian dynasty (Hyginus; Dio Chrys., 4, 71).

A number of fragments seem to be incitements to action: 'I tell you, my son, to seek your fortune by hard toil' (233 cf. 236N²); 'a young man must always be daring' (237N²; the longer version of 1052N² may be the original); 'desire for the pleasant life never brought fame' (238 cf. 239N²). And Archelaos accepts the challenge: 'is it not right that I should toil?' (240N²). It is possible that all this is self-exhortation, and that Archelaos quotes the words of Temenos in fr. 233, and then it may have come anywhere in the play. The trochaic fragment (245 with *P. Oxy.* 419) seems to come from a dialogue taking the same line: 'die as a free man rather than live as a slave', but here Apollo is probably the speaker,[23] and it is possible that as in the *Ion* the *deus ex machina* first speaks in iambics, prophesying the future and giving his exhortation, and then changes into trochaics for the end of the play.

3 *The posthumous plays*

'The records say that after the death of Euripides his son produced at the City Dionysia under the same name *Iphigenia in Aulis, Alkmaion, Bacchae*' (Schol. to Aristophanes' *Frogs* 67). Euripides' death was known in Athens before the Dionysia of 406, because at the preliminary announcement of the plays for that festival Sophocles, hearing that Euripides was dead, appeared in mourning (*Vit. Eur.* 45). The phrasing suggests that the news was recent, and therefore the younger Euripides probably did not produce the posthumous plays before the Dionysia of 405 B.C. We have no reason to doubt the order of the plays. In other productions the most tragic play seems to have come at the end, and

[23] In a line preceding the quotation (245N²) Φοῖβ' ἄναξ is the obvious completion of βαναξ, so that in that line Archelaos addresses Apollo.

here the *Bacchae* is tragedy in a different sense from either the *Iphigenia*, which ends with a miracle, or the *Alkmaion in Corinth*, which ends happily at least for Alkmaion and his children.

IPHIGENIA IN AULIS

In all these plays, as in the *Phoenissae* and *Orestes*, the story affects the whole family; the Iphigeneia story had already been dramatized by Aeschylus and Sophocles, and the Pentheus story by Aeschylus, but this formula, which is peculiarly characteristic of Euripides in his later plays, is unlikely to have been used by his predecessors. Unfortunately, nothing is known of either of Aeschylus' plays; Sophocles' *Iphigeneia* certainly had Klytemnestra and Odysseus as characters (305P), and two fragments (306–7P) suggest that Achilles advised telling her the truth and Odysseus told Achilles to play the false part of bridegroom. The mere fact that the intrigue was part of the play shows that the emphases were quite different. (It is not clear that the scene was Aulis rather than Argos.)

Euripides' play begins with recitative anapaests, continues with an iambic speech, then moves into lyric anapaests before the chorus enter. The sequence is an experiment. The opening anapaests create the atmosphere: night and stars; Agamemnon outside his tent, complaining of the cares of generalship; the old man, who is Klytemnestra's dower-slave, telling him to accept human troubles; why is he tying and untying the tablet and weeping? The atmosphere is evoked as surely as by Ion's dawn-song and the parodos of the *Phaethon*, but the nearest parallel is the opening anapaestic monody of Andromeda alone on her rock. Then Agamemnon launches into a normal iambic prologue speech starting with the marriage of Helen and ending with his message to Klytemnestra to send Iphigeneia to Aulis to marry Achilles (an intrigue only known to Menelaos, Kalchas, and Odysseus) and the metre changes to lyric anapaests as he dictates a message cancelling this summons and sends the old man off with the letter and his seal. (Both the anapaests and the iambics have been attributed to the younger Euripides or another, and various theories have been proposed to account for the present shape of the prologue. Of course the formal speech is unnatural in between the two anapaestic dialogues but the high percentage and advanced character of its resolved syllables are characteristic of late Euripides, and we cannot be certain that Euripides did not also have an iambic speech after the anapaest monody in the *Andromeda*.)[24]

In contrast to the night doubts of Agamemnon the chorus of Chalkidian women arrive cheerfully to see the army and the fleet. They sing in pretty decorated aeolics: they have seen a group of heroes playing draughts and Achilles racing in full armour beside Eumelos' chariot. This fills a strophe, antistrophe, and epode. It is followed by an excessively dull catalogue of ships in short trochaic lines grouped in two pairs of strophe and antistrophe and a long epode. Professor Page[25] has noted both its relevance as pointing up Agamemnon's fear of the army's reactions and the improbability of a large choral composition long after 400 B.C.; he concluded nevertheless, that the writer was not Euripides.

After the light heroic picture of the Greek heroes at play, Menelaos enters dragging the old man, from whom he has snatched the tablet. The metre changes to recitative trochaic tetrameters when Agamemnon enters. The brothers quarrel as they quarrelled in the *Telephos*, and one line (331) recalls that quarrel (723N²). Menelaos says that Agamemnon had canvassed shamelessly to get the command and had then become unapproachable; (Agamemnon is painted as a modern Athenian politician-soldier). He was much afraid that the bad weather would lose him his glory and gladly promised to sacrifice Iphigeneia, and now he has changed his mind again. Agamemnon answers that Menelaos only wants a pretty woman and is mad to try and get Helen back; Iphigeneia shall not be sacrificed for that.

The metre changes to iambics and Menelaos is going away to stir up his other friends, when a messenger appears to announce that Iphigeneia, Klytemnestra, and Orestes are arriving: they are resting in a meadow, and the army is excited by their appearance. The whole family (except Elektra, whom, to make the scene complete, a Hellenistic artist added, when illustrating the arrival)[26] is coming: in describing the sacrifice in the *Iphigenia in Tauris* Euripides wanted the loneliness of Iphigeneia, and Orestes and Klytemnestra were left at home

---

[24] See above, p. 193. On textual problems of the *I.A.* see D. L. Page, *Actor-Interpolations*, 122ff. E. Fraenkel, *Studi U. E. Paoli*, 1955, 298ff. accepts the anapaests but rejects the iambics. On the anapaests see also A. Rome, *Misc. Mercati*, IV.

[25] *Op. cit.* 145. For a defence see Kranz, *Stasimon*, 257.

[26] Cf. *Hellenistic Poetry and Art*, 150.

(25, 235). Here he wants the whole family to be faced with the situation, as the whole family is faced with the matricide in the *Orestes* and the fratricide in the *Phoenissae*. Agamemnon had summoned Iphigeneia alone; now he has to meet the whole family; to emphasize this surprise Euripides makes the messenger burst in, dividing the line with Menelaos.[27] The news reverses the position of the brothers: Menelaos cannot stand Agamemnon's tears, he can find another wife, he was a young fool not to consider what it meant to kill a daughter; Agamemnon is afraid that Kalchas and Odysseus will rouse the army against him.

The chorus sing a pretty decorated aeolic stasimon: the blessings of Aphrodite and Eros if they come in moderation; the wisdom of respect (aidos); Paris was driven mad by the Judgment, and in the madness of love stole Helen. The antistrophe, which comes between the strophe on moderation in love and the epode on Paris, comes very near to the Socratic equation of virtue and knowledge: 'Different the natures of men, different their manners. But the truly good is always clear, and education greatly helps towards excellence. For to feel respect is wisdom and has the abounding grace of seeing with the eyes of judgment the right, in which reputation brings ageless glory. To pursue excellence is a great thing, for women particularly when Kypris comes secretly, but for men too discipline in countless numbers increases the city's might.' The immediate allusion is to Helen, but one remembers also the bad women of Euripides' early plays culminating in Phaidra, who knew what was right but did not pursue it.

The entry of Klytemnestra with Iphigeneia and Orestes on a carriage is clearly modelled on her entrance in the *Electra* (988ff.). Euripides wanted to create the same effect, the arrival of a rich and rather fussy woman; she is Helen's sister, and we have seen a similar Helen in the *Orestes* (71f.). (The difficulty here is the anapaests, 590–606: as in the *Electra*, the chorus greet Klytemnestra but the Chalkidian girls should not call Iphigeneia 'my queen'; the easiest explanation is that Euripides forgot that they were not an ordinary chorus of confidantes, but then they cannot call themselves 'foreign growth of Chalkis' in l. 598; the answer probably is that 598–606, which are strange in

---

[27] Page's strictures on 404–440, *op. cit.* 151ff., seem to me to be outweighed by (a) the necessity of the news here, (b) the Euripidean metrical technique shown in these lines, (c) the parallel for the *antilabe* in 1368, where Iphigeneia bursts into the conversation.

language and include three unmetrical lines, are a Byzantine addition.)[28]

The dialogue with Iphigeneia, who loves him, is agony for Agamemnon, and he finally sends her inside to avoid breaking down; the other double-edged dialogues (e.g. Helen and Theoklymenos) cause no such pain to the deceiver. Klytemnestra, like any Athenian mother, asks for the pedigree of the bridegroom and the details of the wedding. Agamemnon makes a last hopeless attempt to send her back to Argos, but she goes in to make preparations and he says that he will do his duty, wishing that he had a better wife.

The chorus sing a decorated aeolic stasimon: the army will go to Troy where Kassandra prophesies. The Trojans will fight when the Greek fleet comes to fetch Helen. The city will be sacked and the rich wives will wonder who will carry them off – because of you, child of the swan, if that story is true. (The doubt is more gently expressed than in the *Electra*, 736, where the Mycenaean ladies, equally out of character, say that they do not believe that the sun changed its course because of mortal crime, but terrifying stories encourage men to worship the gods.) Achilles enters to ask Agamemnon why the fleet is delayed, and is met by Klytemnestra, who greets him as her prospective son-in-law. Achilles chafes at the delay as in the *Telephos* (Page, G.L.P., no. 3), and the scene of misunderstanding has a parallel in the *Ion* (517ff.) where Ion is incredulous when Xouthos greets him as his son. In Sophocles' *Iphigeneia* Achilles certainly knew of the intrigue and may have taken part in it; here Euripides delightfully confronts the very correct young man with the great lady who is mistaken.

Both are going in, Klytemnestra to escape, Achilles to question Agamemnon, when the old dower-slave comes out and stops them; the metre changes to excited recitative tetrameters. Euripides has to get the conversation on the stage; obviously the old man wants Klytemnestra alone, but the scene has to be played on the stage and Euripides makes it all the more effective by keeping Achilles there to overhear.[29] The old man betrays his master to his mistress in the attempt to save her daughter just as in the *Second Phrixos* the old man betrays his

[28] Page, *op. cit.*, 161.
[29] Scenic necessity and dramatic convenience lead to the difficulties which Hourmouziades rightly notices, *Production and Imagination*, 21.

mistress to his master to save his son.[30] Both Klytemnestra and
Achilles now learn the truth: the marriage story was concocted to get
Iphigeneia to Aulis for sacrifice. Klytemnestra throws herself at
Achilles. He is the son of a goddess, so she can cast her pride away. She
is a woman among undisciplined soldiers. The metre changes back to
spoken iambics for Achilles' answer. This Achilles has already surprised us by the calmness with which he took Klytemnestra's assumption that he was going to marry Iphigeneia (845ff.). Now he is furious,
but from the beginning he knows that he must control himself and
act reasonably, in a world which conflicts with the ideals of a simple
soldier. Much of this first speech is pity for Klytemnestra, and more is
fury with Agamemnon, Menelaos, and Kalchas. Klytemnestra asks if
she shall call Iphigeneia to appeal to him, but he refuses; the army loves
scandal. Then his control shows itself and he advises them to appeal to
Agamemnon, and only if they fail to throw themselves on him.

The chorus sing in decorated style of the marriage of Peleus and
Thetis attended by the gods and by Ganymede, when the Centaurs
sang of the future glory of Achilles. In the epode they sing that Iphigeneia will be slaughtered like a calf: where is the strength of Honour
(*Aidos*) and Excellence, when Lawlessness conquers law and the Jealousy
of the Gods is no longer feared? This is an outright condemnation of
Agamemnon in Hesiodic and traditional-religious terms. Agamemnon
returns, still apparently hoping to get Iphigeneia to the sacrifice without Klytemnestra's knowledge, and has to face Klytemnestra and
Iphigeneia, who holds the infant Orestes. Formally this scene is like the
appeal of Helen and Menelaos to Theonoe. Klytemnestra tears Agamemnon's pretence to pieces: you killed my former husband and my
baby,[31] but I have been a good wife to you. What sort of a return
home do you think you are making for yourself? If you want to sacrifice
a daughter, kill Hermione. Iphigeneia says that she has no eloquence
but tears, and begs Orestes to join in supplication: 'life in misery is
better than a noble death'. Agamemnon answers that the army has a
mad passion for the expedition; they will kill the whole family if he
does not sacrifice Iphigeneia; she must die for Hellas and Hellas must
be free. Agamemnon goes off and Iphigeneia breaks into a long polymetric lament: Priam exposed the baby; would that Paris had never

[30] Cf. above, p. 134. *I.A.* 868 is a reminiscence of fr. 830N².
[31] The story is unknown but Jacobs' emendation must be right here.

grown up to judge the goddesses and bring death to me; would that the fleet had never come to Aulis nor Zeus sent a contrary wind to Euripos. Then she sees Achilles coming and shrinks back for shame into the doorway. The scene is again in recitative trochaic tetrameters. Achilles reports that the whole army, even his Myrmidons, are intent on the sacrifice, but he and his few loyal men will defend Iphigeneia when Odysseus comes to fetch her. Iphigeneia breaks in (in the middle of a line like the first messenger):[32] it is no good being angry with Agamemnon, and we cannot allow Achilles to be killed; the eyes of Hellas are on me, and I must allow Hellas to be free. The tone sinks to spoken iambics as the chorus comment on the nobility of Iphigeneia and the 'sickness' of events and the goddess. Achilles protests his devotion: he will be at the temple in arms in case she changes her mind. She begs Klytemnestra not to hate Agamemnon and calls on the chorus to sing a paean to Artemis and asks for the sacrifice to be prepared, while one of Agamemnon's servants escorts her to the meadow of Artemis.

The rest of the play is full of difficulties. As we have it, Iphigeneia sings a dialogue in lyric iambics with the chorus: she ends 'farewell, beloved light' (1508). The chorus continue, picking up the words of her song and ending with a prayer to Artemis.[33] The messenger, who has conducted Iphigeneia to the meadow, enters and reports the sacrifice to Klytemnestra. After the description of Achilles' prayer to Artemis (1578) the text has evidently been rewritten by a Byzantine scribe round isolated lines which were still visible, but the story is clear. At the moment when Iphigeneia was to be killed she vanished and a deer was seen on the ground. The sacrifice was made and the fleet is ready to sail. Then Agamemnon enters and tells Klytemnestra to take Orestes home and goes off himself to his ship.

We must suppose that Iphigeneia goes off when she says 'farewell, beloved light' (1508). The twenty lines of chorus (1509–31) are less than one expects to cover the gap between her exit and the entry of the messenger, and, as far as we can see, the messenger only reported what he saw – the girl vanished and a deer on the ground – nor does Kalchas say that Artemis appeared and wafted Iphigeneia away to Tauris. Just this information could be given by Artemis herself, and Aelian (H.A.

[32] Cf. above, p. 260.
[33] Though 1510–31 is repetitious and parts are obviously corrupt, I am not entirely convinced that this is not by Euripides. Contrast D. L. Page, op. cit., 192.

7, 39) preserves two and a half lines which he attributes to 'Euripides in the *Iphigenia*': 'I will put into the hands of the Achaeans a horned deer, which they will sacrifice and boast that they are sacrificing your daughter.' This is Artemis speaking to Klytemnestra, and she must have appeared *before* the messenger speech (but our manuscripts have omitted the whole scene). Euripides changed the normal order for a special occasion: it is worth remembering that Iris and Lyssa appear before the messenger-speech in the *Hercules Furens*, and Artemis appears before Hippolytos is carried on in the *Hippolytus*. A god always announces the future, and Artemis therefore must have appeared here before the messenger-speech. The human messenger only tells what could be seen, rather as the messenger of the *Heraclidae* (849) carefully distinguishes between what he has seen and the miraculous rejuvenation of Iolaos which he has heard from others.[34] The scene between Artemis and Klytemnestra lengthened the gap before the appearance of the messenger.

As in the Trojan plays – *Andromache, Hecuba, Trojan Women* – the traditional story from the marriage of Peleus and Thetis to the sack of Troy is told in a series of extraordinarily beautiful lyrics and Artemis' speech was the completion of this series. On the human level the formula is the same as in the *Orestes*: given the situation – Kalchas' announcement that the expedition can only sail if Iphigeneia is sacrificed – how does an ordinary fifth-century family react to it? Agamemnon wobbles between his pride in office and his affection for his daughter, Menelaos wobbles between his desire to get back Helen and his unwillingness to accept so great a crime, the snobbish fussy Klytemnestra introduces herself to Achilles, the old dower-slave gives his master away, Achilles advises an appeal to Agamemnon, finally it is clear that the army insists on the sacrifice (the army here has even more importance than the assembly in the *Orestes*), and Iphigeneia, who is too unselfish to let Achilles risk death in trying to save her, plays the heroine. Thus, though the action wavers this way and that, it does not end up like the *Orestes* with a situation incompatible with the traditional story. The god does not need to pull the characters back on to the rails again, but still the contrast remains clear between modern human muddle and epic heroism.

[34] For another view of the ending see D. L. Page, *op. cit.*, 196ff.

ALKMAION IN CORINTH

The second play of this production was the *Alkmaion in Corinth*. In discussing the early *Alkmaion in Psophis*[35] we have seen that frs. 67, 73a, 74, 75, 76, 77, 80, 84N² belong to the later play and that Tatian's description of the mad and ragged Alkmaion (N², p. 380) in conjunction with the fragments of Ennius' *Alcimeo* (II–IVR) make it likely that fr. 68, 78aN²[36] and the fragments of Ennius also belong. The outline is given by Apollodoros (III, vii, 7), who says that Alkmaion had two children by Manto – Amphilochos and Tisiphone, and left them in Corinth with Kreon to bring up; Kreon's wife sold the girl, because she was afraid that Kreon would marry her; Alkmaion bought her without recognizing her; he arrived at Corinth to ask for his children and also got his son back, and Amphilochos in obedience to Apollo's oracle founded Amphilochian Argos.

The play cannot have begun until Alkmaion returned to Corinth. Apollo is telling the past history in fr. 73aN² which must belong to the prologue: 'I had no child from her (Manto) but she bore twins to Alkmaion unwed.' (It is not necessary for Apollo also to speak the epilogue; Hermes or Athena could have told Amphilochos the oracle; the *Bacchae* does not provide a parallel for the same god speaking prologue and epilogue, in so far as Dionysos speaks the prologue in mortal form and the epilogue in divine majesty.)

The parodos begins with fr. 74N². The Corinthian women call each other on; a stranger has arrived. As this is quoted as an instance of a parodos, defined as a song sung by the chorus on entrance, these must be the first lines and they imply almost certainly that Alkmaion (with Tisiphone) is already on stage. Euripides had used this form already in the *Heraclidae* (and probably even earlier in the *Aigeus*). Wilamowitz[37] associated with this fr. 1084N² 'I am come leaving seagirt Akrokorinth, holy hill, city of Aprodite.' He argued that only this play and the *Medea* were set in Corinth. We should have to assume that the chorus became calmer before they uttered this long aeolo-choriambic (rather than ionic) line; in Sophocles' *Oedipus Coloneus* the second strophe of the similarly arranged parodos opens with a long aeolo-choriambic

[35] See above, p. 39.
[36] Both the emendations proposed for the beginning of fr. 78a would be metrically unlikely as early as 438 B.C.
[37] *Kl. Schr.*, I, 186.

line (176). The parallel between fr. 74N² and the beginning of the parodos of the *Oedipus Coloneus* has been explained by Van Looy[38] as imitation by Sophocles, and by Zielinski[39] as imitation by Euripides based on a reading of the *Oedipus Coloneus* long before its production, which seems most unlikely. Perhaps the parallel should not be over-stressed: both poets shape the parodos as a lyric dialogue in their late plays, and Euripides had used a lyric dialogue parodos for suppliant plays long before this.

Whether fr. 1084N² belongs to this play or not, 'advance' in fr. 74 shows that the chorus are visitors coming to Kreon's palace. As they are women, they will not have been summoned to deal with the strangers, like the chorus of the *Oedipus Coloneus*, but have come on some normal occasion and find the strangers unexpectedly. It is possible that they arrive at the same time as the strangers, who are on stage in the sense that they issue from one parodos while the chorus file up the other. Or Alkmaion may have already arrived with Tisiphone but not yet been admitted to the palace: this would then be the second part of the prologue, whether it included a dialogue with a porter or not.

It is difficult to see how the other elements of this play fit together: the mad-scene attested by Tatian and Ennius, Alkmaion's defence of his life (67, 68N²), Kreon's discomfiture and exile (76N²). The main lines have been made out with great probability by Zielinski: what follows only varies in some details from his interpretation. If the chorus of women is unlikely to interrogate Alkmaion far, the only likely interrogator is Amphilochos, whom we must suppose to be ignorant of his father's identity and his own. It is possible therefore that the interrogation passed from the chorus to Amphilochos, and that the interrogation led straight into the mad-scene (it is uncertain whether 68N², 'In a word, I killed my mother'; 'With her will and yours or against the will of both?' belongs here). Alkmaion said he was ill, exiled, and poor; fear takes his wits away; his mother threatens him with torture and death; he is drained white with fear (Ennius IIR, he repeats his fear when Kreon later attacks him, 67N²). Then he sees flames; the Furies are on him, he begs Tisiphone to help him, to drive away the flaming horror; the Furies are attacking him with snakes and torches; then he sees Apollo and Artemis shooting at them (IIIR). The fit is

[38] *Zes Tragedien*, 78ff.
[39] *Mnem.* 50, 1922, 305.

abating and his fears no longer agree with what he sees (IVR). This was clearly a brilliant mad-scene, but, as in the *Orestes* the chief point is the intimacy of brother and sister, so here we have Tisiphone's loving care and Amphilochos' concern for the unkempt stranger, a trio of father, daughter, and son, none of whom knew either of the other's identity. Amphilochos looks with pity on Alkmaion's rags (78aN^2). Here fr. 75N^2 must belong: 'Son of Kreon, how true it was that good parents have good children and that the children of the bad reproduce the character of their father.' This is Alkmaion's gratitude to the unrecognized Amphilochos, an irony usually confined to mothers and sons. Hartung supposed that Amphilochos purified Alkmaion, Zielinski[40] supposed that Amphilochos advised Alkmaion to take refuge on the altar because everyone in Corinth was against a matricide. In any case this was a preliminary to the serious clash between Alkmaion and Kreon; whether there Amphilochos pleaded for Alkmaion we have no evidence, but he must have told his supposed father that a matricide had arrived with a girl and this was enough to identify Alkmaion to Kreon before he saw him.

Zielinski is clearly right in suggesting that Kreon wants Alkmaion out of the way so that he can both keep Amphilochos as his son and get hold of Tisiphone again, whom he naturally recognizes as soon as he sees her. His wife on the other hand has every reason to bring about the recognition so as to be rid of Tisiphone (and if she is like other Euripidean queens she will not want an adopted son to succeed). Alkmaion's fear at having to plead for his life (fr. 67N^2) is a preparation for a debate with Kreon, which presumably ends with his being condemned to death by Kreon. The mechanics of the recognition are unclear. Zielinski is probably right in supposing that from the beginning the children were separated: Amphilochos was brought up by Kreon as his son; Tisiphone was brought up by the Queen as a slave. Otherwise Amphilochos would have recognized Tisiphone as soon as he saw her, and this would have been an additional complication. The final recognition needs all three actors. The two children cannot speak

---

[40] Zielinsky found an illustration in an early Apulian vase in the Vatican, where he saw Amphilochos on the left, Tisiphone and Alkmaion on the altar, and Kreon arriving. The difficulty of this or any identification so far proposed, as Trendall has pointed out (*Vasi Dipinti del Vaticano*, II, pl. 52a–c, no. AA2), is that the very carefully painted date-palm between Amphilochos and the altar should suggest a site outside Greece.

with a single voice in the recognition scene, as in the *Hypsipyle*, because here they are recognizing each other as well as their father. Alkmaion has been condemned and Tisiphone is his slave: the free agent is Amphilochos: however this was worked in detail, the first step must have been for the Queen to prove to Amphilochos that he and Tisiphone were the children of Alkmaion. Then after the actual recognition, Alkmaion and his children plan vengeance on Kreon. 'What is the good of children, father, if we do not help in danger' (84N²) clearly belongs here: the same sentiment is expressed by Theseus when he takes Aithra home in the *Suppliants* (361–4) and by Perseus in the *Diktys* (345N²), probably when he plans vengeance on Polydektes. The vengeance is perhaps stopped, as in the *Antiope*, by the appearance of a god who sends Kreon, and presumably his wife, into exile (76N²), 'you see the tyrant: he goes into exile, a childless old man. A mortal should not be proud', and commands Amphilochos to found Amphilochian Argos (as we know from Apollodoros). Fr. 80N² 'great crimes meet with great punishment' is presumably a comment of the chorus on Kreon's fate.

This gives the following outline:

Prologue: Apollo, fr. 73aN². Alkmaion and Tisiphone arrive.
Parodos: Corinthian women interested in the strangers, fr. 74; 1084N².
Interrogation of Alkmaion by Amphilochos, fr. 68(?), 78a, 75N².
Mad-scene, Tatian (N², p. 380), Ennius II–IVR.
Debate scene of Alkmaion and Kreon: fr. 67N². Condemnation of Alkmaion.
Pre-recognition: Queen and Amphilochos.
Recognition: Alkmaion, Amphilochos, Tisiphone.
Plan to take vengeance on Kreon: fr. 84N².
Execution and *deus ex machina*: fr. 76, 80N².

BACCHAE

In the *Iphigenia in Aulis* Euripides treated a traditional story in his new way, making it a family tragedy; for the story of the *Alkmaion in Corinth* we have no evidence before Euripides, and the formula is the same. For the third play he used a traditional story again and we should like to know how much he innovated. The Hypothesis ascribed to

Aristophanes of Byzantion says that the story is found in the *Pentheus* of Aeschylus, but it would be rash to conclude more from this than that Aeschylus included the resistance and rending of Pentheus. The earliest vases[41] which take the story back beyond Aeschylus and possibly to Thespis show Pentheus being torn to pieces by maenads, and on the Boston psykter (about 520 B.C.) the maenad who has hold of Pentheus' head is called Galene, which seems to exclude Agave. In the *Eumenides*, which is later than the *Pentheus*, Dionysos was commander of the maenads, contriving a hare's death for Pentheus (26), and no word is said of Agave. In fact we have no positive evidence for Agave's part in the rending before Euripides. Dodds[42] shows that Aeschylus probably had a scene in which Dionysos lured Pentheus to spy on the maenads (183N², 365M, with *Bacch*. 837) and that Euripides may have borrowed the palace miracle, the imprisonment of Dionysos, the raid on the farms, and the effeminate Dionysos from Aeschylus' *Lykourgeia*: we do not of course know whether Aeschylus also used these themes in his *Pentheus*. If we cannot be sure of the details, we can be sure that stories of mortal opponents of Dionysos had been in the repertoire from the beginning of tragedy and were peculiarly suited to Dionysos' festival. Pentheus' attack on Dionysos and the tearing to pieces of Pentheus are the essentials of the story. Euripides may have been the first to make the leading maenad Pentheus' mother; that he was the first to add Kadmos (Agave's father and Pentheus' grandfather) and Teiresias the family seer is almost certain; thus it became a family tragedy, and Agave after murdering her son could be nursed back to sanity like Herakles in the *Hercules Furens*, but here the end of her madness also is shown on the stage.

The play opens with Dionysos. He is in mortal form (Pentheus describes him later as a beautiful young man with long hair, 453); at the end he appears as a god and probably then wears a bearded mask: the two types exist side by side in late fifth-century art. He has come from the East to establish his worship in Thebes before any other city in

[41] Cf. E. R. Dodds, *Euripides Bacchae*, xxxii; J. D. Beazley, *Attic Vase paintings in Boston*, II, 2; *A.R.V.*² 16, 133, and probably 208. I cannot see that on the Villa Giulia cup (quoted by Dodds) the maenad who carries the head is in any way distinguished as Agave, nor is she on the Meidias painter's hydria (*Deltion*, 18B1, 1963, 27, pl. 24–5).

[42] *Op. cit.*, xxviiif. On the *Bacchae* in general cf. also R. P. Winnington-Ingram, *Euripides and Dionysus*, 1948; H. Diller, *Abh. Ak. Mainz*, 1955, no. 5; J. de Romilly, *R.E.G.*, 76, 1963, 361ff.

Greece. Semele's sisters had denied Dionysos' divine birth; now he has driven them and the women of Thebes to run mad on the mountains as maenads. Pentheus, the grandson of Kadmos, is now King and because he denies Dionysos must be shown that Dionysos is a god. Dionysos then calls on the Lydian maenads, who have accompanied him, to lift their drums and sing in front of the house of Pentheus, while he joins the dances of the maenads on Kithairon.

The parallel with Aphrodite in the *Hippolytus* is obvious. On one level Dionysos operates as a vengeful deity because his mother has been wronged; on another level, like Aphrodite and Artemis, he is a force in the human mind, something like ecstasy. He ruins his mother's sisters by this ecstasy, as Aphrodite ruins Phaidra by making her fall in love; he ruins Pentheus, as Aphrodite ruins Hippolytos, because he denies him. What distinguishes him from Aphrodite in the *Hippolytus* is that he appears in mortal form and can act visibly among the humans.

The chorus of maenads is traditional: we can trace it back to the time of Aeschylus, if not to that of Thespis.[43] Here they have the new drums which Euripides had already mentioned in the *Palamedes* (586N^2) of 415 B.C. and in the *Helen* (1347) of 412 B.C., and which appear on vases from 440 B.C. held by single maenads, but from 420 B.C. onwards are with the thyrsos their normal attribute. They ask for holy silence, and sing of the joys of Dionysiac ecstasy and the miracle of Dionysos' birth; Thebes must wear ivy and fawn-skins and dance on the mountains; the Korybantes discovered the drum and gave it to Rhea, but the satyrs brought it to Dionysos. They end with the joy of the maenad's life on the mountains. This is a ritual song emphasizing the ecstasy of maenad dancing. The style is decorated, and the structure is elaborate; prologue, strophe and antistrophe in ionics; strophe and antistrophe in mixed ionic and aeolic; long epode in mixed metres. The ionic is probably intentionally reminiscent of cult.[44]

With a reasonable disregard for chronology Euripides introduces Teiresias who, wearing ivy-wreath and fawn-skin and holding the thyrsos, has come to fetch Kadmos to join the mountain dance in honour of Dionysos. The old man is sufficiently rejuvenated to forget

[43] Cf. my *Monuments of Tragedy and Satyr-play*, nos. AV 9, 10, 15; Pickard-Cambridge, *Dithyramb etc.*^{2}, pl. 6a.

[44] A. M. Dale, *Greek Lyric Metres*, 121. Cf. also A. J. Festugière, *Eranos*, 54, 1956, 72.

his age and his blindness: this kind of ancient rite, he says, shows the nothingness of human cleverness (200ff.).[45] Their enthusiasm is real, but Teiresias remains still a modernist churchman and Kadmos a family politician. Pentheus enters 'greatly disturbed' (the same word is used of Agave in her madness, 1268). He has come back to find that the women have gone to the mountains in pursuit of sex. He has caught some and he will catch the others, including Ino, Agave his mother, and Autonoe the mother of Aktaion,[46] and he will kill the impostor who claims to be Dionysos. Then he turns on the old men and accuses Teiresias of introducing the new religion as a new source of money for himself. Sex and money are the only things that he understands; if we want to classify him, the class would include Eteokles in the *Phoenissae*, Aigisthos in the *Electra*, and the portraits of the tyrant in the *Supplices* (450-5) and *Erechtheus* (fr. 362, 24N^2). Teiresias answers first: Dionysos is the god of the wet principle (a true modernist theory); the thigh story is to be explained by etymology (falsely); Dionysos is a prophet and can cause panic fear; he has a great future; sexual indulgence has nothing to do with Dionysos, but depends on character (the Phaidra problem again and, in fact, terribly relevant to Pentheus himself). Kadmos argues (as we have supposed Merops argued in the *Phaethon*)[47] that, whatever the truth, it is a good thing to have a god in the family. Pentheus gives orders for the destruction of Teiresias' augural seat and the capture of Dionysos. Teiresias tells Kadmos to come and pray for Pentheus: again we remember the old man's prayer to Aphrodite in the *Hippolytus* (114ff.).

The chorus sing in decorated ionics with an admixture of aeolic in the second strophe and antistrophe. Holiness, queen of the gods, must hear Pentheus' violence against Dionysos, god of dance, music, and wine. The end of madness is misery. Human cleverness is not wisdom; superhuman thoughts have a short life. May I go to Cyprus and Olympos; there the bacchants may dance. Dionysos loves Peace. He gave wine to rich and poor. I would accept the beliefs and customs of the

[45] To excise these lines because Dionysos' religion is new is no remedy because the chorus use similar terms in 71 and 893ff.; Teiresias universalizes the new religion. On the idea cf. above, p. 24.

[46] These lines should not be excised. Agave's name has not yet been pronounced. Aktaion's fate is a warning to Pentheus (337). Ino is ominous as the heroine of the *Ino* and *Phrixos B*. They are the three who tear Pentheus to pieces (1129ff.).

[47] Cf. above, p. 230.

simple. (Like Teiresias before, the chorus recognize the ordinary man's religion as superior to human invention.) A servant of Pentheus enters with Dionysos whom he has captured: the maenads whom Pentheus had imprisoned have escaped because their fetters fell apart and the doors opened.[48] This is the first duel between Dionysos and Pentheus, who only reiterates that the rites encourage sexual indulgence and threatens imprisonment. Finally Dionysos goads him into ordering his imprisonment and threatening to sell or enslave the Lydian maenads (threats to punish the chorus are never realized).

The chorus sing another decorated stasimon in ionics: Dirke received the infant Dionysos, why does Dirke deny us now? (The maenad Dirke of the *Antiope* is forgotten here.) Pentheus is like a giant fighting against the gods. Dionysos, wherever you are, come and help your followers. Their prayer is immediately answered. Dionysos (the god) is heard calling them. A wild lyric dialogue follows as they answer him. He asks for an earthquake. They see the house shaking. He asks for lightning, and they see fire on the tomb of Semele. They fall to the ground in fear. Dionysos (in mortal form) comes out and reports in recitative trochaic tetrameters: Pentheus found a bull and thought he was Dionysos and bound him; then the earthquake and the fire; then a fight with a phantom in the courtyard. Formally this sequence is like that in the *Hercules Furens* (875ff.): lyric dialogue between chorus and singer off stage (there Amphitryon, and at the end the chorus); earthquake; messenger-speech. Here the brief excited trochaic recital of Dionysos is substituted for the full messenger-speech because Pentheus is coming out to face a new problem. His two illusions – in the first he mistakes a bull for a man, like Ajax; in the second a phantom, like Helen, is provided for him to fight – may be attributed to Dionysos, just as Herakles' madness is caused by Lyssa and Hera; but, just as Amphitryon suggested that Herakles was maddened by shedding blood, we should remember here that on his first appearance Kadmos described him as 'greatly disturbed'.

A messenger arrives, a herdsman from Kithairon. He has seen the three companies of maenads led by Autonoe, Agave, and Ino in their chaste sleep; then their waking, their play with wild animals, the miraculous springs of water, wine, and milk. The herdsman and

[48] Cf. the escape of Antiope above, p. 208.

shepherds conferred; a persuasive townsman suggested capturing Agave for Pentheus (he is the successor of the 'bold unbeliever' who suggested the capture of Orestes and Pylades in the *Iphigenia in Tauris*, 275, and of the glib orator who proposed stoning Orestes and Elektra in the *Orestes*, 903). Agave turned the maenads on them and defeated them; then the maenads tore the herds to pieces and raided the neighbouring villages. Pentheus orders out the army. There then follows a deception scene of a peculiarly horrible kind: the simple sequence is seen in the *Helen*; Theoklymenos arrives, Helen (in mourning with her hair cut short) deceives him, all go into the house while the chorus sing a decorated stasimon, they come out with Menelaos dressed for his new part and Theoklymenos speeds them on their way (in the earlier *Iphigenia in Tauris* the two scenes are run together). There all our sympathy is with the deceivers; here the dice are too heavily loaded against Pentheus and the stake is his life. Dionysos first offers to bring the women from the mountains without the use of force. Pentheus suspects this and calls again for arms. Dionysos stops him: 'Do you want to see them sitting on the mountain?' 'Yes, I would give an enormous weight of gold.' So Pentheus accepts the proposal that he shall be dressed as a maenad and excuses the performance as a military reconnaissance. Dionysos (in mortal form) prays to Dionysos (the god) to make Pentheus slightly mad so that he may put on female clothing and be the laughing-stock of Thebes: when he dies at his mother's hands he will know that Dionysos is in rank a god most terrible but to men most kind. Here again the concluding prayer which Euripides[49] normally introduces when the intrigue is to be launched is turned into something infinitely more sinister.

The chorus sing in decorated aeolics. Shall I ever dance again by night, like a fawn which has escaped the hunters? What is *their* wisdom? What is a better gift from heaven than vengeance? The gods punish the impious at length; it is easy to believe that god is strong and that age-old belief is as valid as Nature. What is *their* wisdom, etc.? In the difficult and competitive sea of life with its hopes fulfilled and unfulfilled, I count him happy who is happy today. Again the chorus insist on the superior reality of popular belief, as they have in the stasimon before (430) and as Teiresias had earlier (201–2), and couple with it not

[49] Cf. above, pp. 186, 195, 201, 207, 214.

only a belief in divine punishment of crime but an equation of this belief (*nomos*) with Nature (*physis*). The simple belief in divine power is naturally expressed in a play in which divine power is manifested: long before, a chorus had drawn the same lesson from the birth of Herakles.[50] Here it is phrased in the terminology of the *physis-nomos* contrast: *nomos* which has been believed long enough comes to have the validity of *physis*. This is up-to-date phraseology like the reminiscence of Socrates in the *Iphigenia in Aulis* (558ff.), but the belief itself is right for the Lydian maenads and they add to it their personal pleasure in vengeance, the ugly side of ecstasy exemplified by the Theban maenads when they raid the villages.

Pentheus comes out dressed as a maenad. He sees Thebes double and thinks Dionysos is a bull; he has the strength to carry Kithairon and the maenads on his shoulders. This is his ultimate degradation; at the end of the scene five lines split at the caesura between Dionysos and Pentheus make a sort of ritual chant. Dionysos cries to Agave and her sisters to stretch out their hands – not in appeal (*Ion* 961) nor in farewell (*Alc.* 738) but to catch him as he falls into their grasp (*Hec.* 439). The chorus in excited dochmiacs call on Lyssa (personified Madness, who entered Pentheus in a light form (851) and who made Herakles kill his wife and children and who appeared on the stage in the *Xantriai* to drive the women mad) to enter the daughters of Kadmos: let Justice come clear to see; Pentheus is a sinner; Piety is the only safe way of life; let Dionysos appear as bull or snake or lion. The change of metre from ritual ionics to wild dochmiacs marks the change in them from devotees to destroyers.

The messenger who had gone out with Pentheus comes to tell his story and is greeted with wild joy by the chorus. He starts with the picture of the Theban maenads at peace. Then Dionysos put Pentheus on a pine-tree and vanished: a voice was heard urging the maenads to kill Pentheus. They pulled the tree up and tore Pentheus to pieces (the rending is the scene that appears on vases back to Thespis' time). Agave is bringing his head fixed on her thyrsos; she thinks it is a lion's head. This is a grim reminiscence of Orestes bringing Aigisthos' head back to Elektra.[51] I believe that when Euripides departs from the traditional story his departure often takes a shape which has been successful in an

[50] Cf. above, p. 93.
[51] Cf. above, p. 145.

earlier play, and I am very inclined to see the reminiscence of the *Electra* as evidence of such a departure. Earlier Dionysiac plays, I suspect, ended with the destruction of the Resister.

The chorus sing for joy at Pentheus' disaster, but go on to say that the Theban maenads' victory has ended in tears. Agave enters and they sing with her a dochmiac lyric dialogue, which wavers between joy and horror, horror at least when she asks them to share her feast (the lion has become a calf) and when they tell her to show her prey to Thebes. In spoken iambics she describes her triumph and asks for the approval of Kadmos and Pentheus. Kadmos enters followed by servants with Pentheus' remains. Agave gives him the head and asks for congratulation. Kadmos expresses his horror, and she says that old men are naturally peevish and her son only knows how to fight against gods. He nurses her back to sanity. She recognizes Pentheus' head which is still in her arms but she has no idea how she and her sisters came to be on the mountains: 'Dionysos destroyed us. Now I understand' (echoing Admetos' words when he discovered that life was not worth living).[52]

There remain lamentations and the appearance of Dionysos in divine form to speak the epilogue. Mr Willink[53] has suggested that when Agave asks where Pentheus' body is (1298) Kadmos tells her to add the head to the torn limbs on the bier. Agave, as we are told by a late rhetorician, accused herself and raised pity by touching the different parts of Pentheus' body (we should perhaps remember here Hekabe's description of the dead Astyanax and of Hektor's shield in the *Trojan Women*, particularly 1173–1179, 1196ff.). Kadmos follows: Pentheus was the protector of his old age. This is a different Pentheus, but we have no reason to disbelieve Kadmos, who states clearly that Pentheus, like Agave and her sisters, had failed to worship Dionysos. The eulogy puts the good side of Pentheus (which the audience has not seen) just as Adrastos in the *Supplices*[54] praised the five warriors who had been involved in the ill-omened and ill-advised expedition against Thebes. After Kadmos' eulogy Dionysos[55] appears on the *mechane* to justify the punishment of Pentheus and state the future for Agave, her sisters,

[52] *Alc.* 940. Cf. above, p. 52.
[53] *C.Q.* 16, 1966, 44ff. with detailed discussion and restitution of the text.
[54] *Suppl.* 857ff. contrasted with 132ff., particularly 145, 157, 160f., 219ff.
[55] On this speech see C. W. Willink, *C.Q.* 16, 1966, 47.

and Kadmos and Harmonia, who are to become snakes and migrate to
Illyria (thus apparently giving a reason for a modern cult in Euripidean manner and introducing one more member of the family). Kadmos
admits their sin but utters the bitter and unanswerable reproach that
gods should not behave like mortals. The play ends in anapaests: father
and daughter part in utter misery.[56]

The last play ends with complete devastation and no hope, not even
such hope as Herakles has at the end of the *Hercules Furens* or Oidipous
and Antigone at the end of the *Phoenissae*. The force that has been
released is more destructive even than the forces released in those plays
or in the *Hippolytus*. Euripides says so many things in this play. On the
mythological level Dionysos, like Aphrodite in the *Hippolytus*, avenges
a wrong. On another level Euripides asserts, for some people at any
rate, the validity of worship as a guide in living. On another level
Dionysos is ecstasy, a force for good and evil, just as Aphrodite is sex,
a force for good and evil. Here, much more than in the *Hippolytus*,
where even the nurse praises the power rather than the beauty of
Aphrodite (447ff.), the beauty of the force is emphasized by the chorus,
by the servant who captured Dionysos, by the first messenger from
Kithairon, and by the second messenger who describes the maenads
at play before Pentheus is put on the fir-tree. In both the messenger-
speeches it is interference which turns beauty into hideous destruction;
in the first case the persuasive townsman bent on gain, in the second case
Pentheus. Euripides probably took from Aeschylus the idea of Pentheus going to spy on the maenads, but he developed it into the two
cruel scenes which show the degradation of Pentheus. They are immensely effective but they only make horribly clear the streak in
Pentheus' mind which causes his disastrous interference. In the *Ion*
(550f.) Xouthos was invited to join[57] the maenads above Delphi and
being drunk raped one of them, like a young man in New Comedy, but
this, though exactly what Pentheus deplores in the rites (222f.), is not
an interference which turns ecstasy into destruction: it is irrelevant, as
Teiresias implies (314ff.). Xouthos is simple; the text for Pentheus is in

[56] Lines have gone after 1371 and Dionysos' instructions to Agave are lost. She is to go
to the (house) of Aristaios, the father of Aktaion. Had he already in this version migrated
to Keos?

[57] The phrase is very strange: does it mean that he was their leader like the Lydian
(Dionysos in mortal form) of the *Bacchae*.

the *Hippolytus* (445): 'Aphrodite is gentle to him who yields to her, but whomsoever she finds scornful and arrogant, she takes and destroys.' The first is Xouthos; the second Pentheus. His scorn is in fact a craving which makes him yield to the suggestion that he should go and see for himself, but because he comes as a spy, when he is revealed it is the kind of interference which turns the ecstasy to destruction. As in the *Phoenissae* the disastrous streak in one young man ruins the entire family: here it meets the peculiarly inflammable material provided by ecstasy, and it is the portraying of ecstasy which gives the play its tremendous power.

VI
Conclusion

Even on our inadequate evidence Euripides' work appears bewilderingly various, and any generalization invites contradiction. To say, however, that his production is various is to say something about Euripides – something that would not be said about Aeschylus or Sophocles on the smaller amount of evidence we possess (which may, of course, be misleading). It is a variety both of types of play and of incidents within the single play, a variety between plays produced at the same time and a variety between plays produced at different times, a variety also of metrical and, therefore, of musical texture.

The tragic poet chooses a story from mythology and casts it into the traditional pattern of spoken scenes, choral odes, lyric dialogues, and monodies for presentation on the stage. The story might have been recently presented by another poet or might be new for the stage. In the former case Euripides may more or less overtly criticize his predecessor's play: the most interesting sequence is the sequence, revival of Aeschylus' *Choephoroi* – Euripides' *Electra* – Sophocles' *Electra* – Euripides' *Orestes*, where we can see Euripides criticizing Aeschylus, then being himself criticized by Sophocles, and finally answering Sophocles from his own realistic position.[1]

Where a story is new, we can very often see Euripides casting it into shapes which he or others had used before.[2] The *Kresphontes* was a new story for the stage. One of the plays in Euripides' mind when he wrote it was the *Choephoroi*; Orestes also returned from exile and gained admittance with a false story of his own death, Orestes' mother also attacked him with an axe. But having made his new play, Euripides then drew on it for his own remodelling of the *Choephoroi* in his *Electra*.

[1] But cf. also the sequence *Hippolytos I*, *Phaidra*, *Hippolytus II* and *Septem*, *Phoenissae*, *O.C.*
[2] Cf. particularly, besides the *Kresphontes*, the *Melanippe Desmotis* and the *Archelaos*.

Starting from an incident in another play or using a traditional type of scene, Euripides nevertheless sometimes produces a brilliant new piece of theatre. The Aeschylean Klytemnestra asks vainly for an axe to use against her son, in Sophocles' *Mysians* the messenger relates that Auge was only prevented from slaying her son by the appearance of a snake, but the audience of Euripides' *Kresphontes* saw Merope with the axe raised above her sleeping son, a startling new use of the *ekkyklema*. The appearance of Medeia in her snaky chariot above the palace while Jason battered on the gates was a brilliant use of the *mechane*.

Instances could be multiplied of Euripides' use of theatrical machinery,[3] but also without machinery Euripides sometimes achieved a quite new theatrical effect. Scenes of voluntary self-sacrifice are obviously good theatre and may have been invented by Euripides. Besides the *Heraclidae*, *Hecuba*, *Erechtheus*, *Phrixos B*, *Phoenissae*, where this theatrical scene may almost be termed a standard interlude, and the *Iphigenia in Aulis*, where Iphigeneia's triumphant exit is the climax of the whole play, he has a startling variation in the final speech of Kassandra in the *Trojan Women* (444): she changes to recitative trochaics as she throws away Apollo's garlands and demands to be taken as a death-bride to Agamemnon.[4] This is a bitter parody on the self-sacrifice of Makaria and her like.

Rather in the same way Agamemnon's deception of Iphigeneia in the *Iphigenia in Aulis* and Dionysos' deception of Pentheus in the *Bacchae* are cruel variations on the light-hearted but exciting deceptions of the local ruler in the *Iphigenia in Tauris* and the *Helen*. Euripides is a master of the theatre both in the single scene and in the sequence leading up to a climax, of which perhaps the most theatrical is the sequence in the *Orestes*; it starts with the lyric dialogue of Elektra and the chorus, when Orestes and Pylades have gone into the palace to murder Helen, continues with the luring of Hermione and the lyric messenger-speech of the Phrygian, the arrival of Menelaos and his soldiers, the appearance on the roof of Orestes with his sword at Hermione's throat while Elektra and Pylades brandish torches, and ends with the appearance of

[3] Cf. above on *mechane* in *Stheneboia*, *Bellerophon*, *ekkyklema* in *Supplices*, *Hercules Furens*, *Andromeda*.

[4] Cf. J. de Romilly, *L'Évolution du pathétique*, 95.

Apollo with Helen on the *mechane*.[5] This sequence exploits all the
Greek theatre's resources of staging, metre, and music.

The man who knew so well how to use stage-effects chose particularly in his early period stories containing deeds of horror and unusual
events – on the one hand the boiling of Pelias, the feast of Thyestes,
the blinding of Phoinix, Medeia's murder of her children (and later
Herakles' madness and the rending of Pentheus) and on the other hand
Deidameia, Pasiphae, Alkmene, and their fellows down to Auge in the
last period, Bellerophon storming heaven (and later Phaethon driving
the chariot of the Sun and the phantom Helen).

But however horrible or strange the events, the people are ordinary
modern people and the connexion of events is naturalistic. Medeia is a
ruthless young woman, Pelias is a fussy old man, Stheneboia behaves
like a prostitute, Pasiphae has a spirited and probably dishonest defence
of her action, Odysseus is a clever careerist, Hippolytos prefers athletics
to women. More endearingly Peleus rescues Phoinix in his disaster,
an old retainer betrays Alkmaion to Phegeus and Arsinoe remains
loyal to him. Here in the *Alkmaion in Psophis*, if the reconstruction is
correct, we see also what I have called the naturalistic connexion of
events. The action turns in an entirely new direction because of the
independence of the old retainer,[6] and he has a long line of successors
of which the nearest in kind are the *satelles* of *Phrixos B* and the servant
of Kisseus in the *Archelaos*. Because of Arsinoe's loyalty the play ends
with her recrimination and perhaps her punishment instead of with
the successful ambush of Alkmaion. For this unexpected turn at the
end of the play the switch from Deidameia's seduction to Achilles' call
to Troy in the *Skyrioi*, from Pasiphae and the Minotaur to Daidalos
and Ikaros in the *Cretans*, from Iolaos to Eurystheus in the *Heraclidae*
are parallels. Very often the new direction is given by a new character
whose arrival has not been prepared but is well motivated. This kind of
structure with its variations – the successive treatment of Andromache,
Hermione, and Neoptolemos in the *Andromache* or the three successive
actions in the *Hercules* – is characteristic of Euripides.

---

[5] Cf. N. Hourmouziades, *op. cit.*, 168. A. Lesky in his excellent discussion of the play says
Theologeion (*W.S.*, 53, 1935, 37ff.); in any case Apollo and Helen are *higher* than Orestes
and Elektra. I assume that the *theologeion* is the roof (*Greek Theatre Production*, 11ff.).

[6] Probably the slave in the *Alcestis* who gives away his mistress' death to Herakles should
be included.

In the late thirties and the early twenties Euripides wrote a number of plays which show a character wavering between the promptings of reason and passion, a Socratic problem which Sophocles reflected in quite a different way.[7] The simplest instances are Medeia in her name play, Phaidra in the *Hippolytus*, and Laios in the *Chrysippos*. Ino's tremendous attempt to dissuade Themisto, her switching of the children's clothing when she fails, and her later bitter repentance should surely be added. Hermione in the *Andromache* is a slighter study of the same kind. Here we can point to an ancestor in Admetos in the *Alcestis*, particularly his late speech of realization (940). Something like this sequence must have been shown on a grand scale in the *Bellerophon* if the hero who was so incensed by the injustice of the world that he flew up to heaven to question the gods finally accepted his fate with courage and dignity.

But there are two quite different kinds of 'split character' which start late in the first period and are repeated later. One is the woman brutalized by her sufferings: in this period Alkmene in the *Heraclidae*, in the next Hekabe and Elektra in the plays named after them and probably Merope in the *Kresphontes*, and in the third period Althaia in the *Meleager*, and to a certain extent, Iphigeneia in the *Iphigenia in Tauris*, Kreousa in the *Ion*. But in these late plays[8] it is perhaps better to speak of unpredicted but (in spite of Aristotle) intelligible reactions to circumstances that have arisen in the course of the play. It is the appreciation of what dangers Achilles is prepared to run for her that changes Iphigeneia in the *Iphigenia in Aulis* from a suppliant into a heroine. This formula also suits the other kind of 'split character': Ion's change from temple-boy to man of action in the *Ion*, and Orestes' similar change in the *Iphigenia in Tauris* and still more strikingly in the *Orestes*. The ancestor of these changes may be seen (in so far as it is not the result of a miracle) in the rejuvenation of Iolaos in the *Heraclidae*.

It is tempting to suppose that some relation exists between the new

[7] Cf. above, p. 76. A. Rivier, *Entretiens Hardt*, VI, 1960, 54f. on 'l'élément démonique' seems to me to underrate the differences between Euripides and Sophocles. E. Schlesinger in his study of the *Medea*, *Hermes*, 94, 1966, 52, also equates Euripides with the other tragic poets in the representation of human existence in its complete dependency on a super-human and supra-rational power. Euripides seems to me to be doing something new, but he gives his characters traditional language.

[8] On the new 'lability' of late Euripidean characters, cf. A. Lesky, *Entretiens Hardt*, VI, 1960, 146ff.

less stable and more emotional characters and the development of Euripides' metrical technique. If we exclude the *Kresphontes* in case the figures for the smaller number of lines are misleading, the first break with the classical norm for the spoken iambic trimeter comes with the *Andromache*, which has 12 resolved longs per 100 iambics as against 5.6 in the *Hippolytos*. This is a small but noticeable increase and means that the steady rhythm is by that much less insistent; the hard lines are beginning to be slightly blurred.

For other metres only preserved plays can be used, and phenomena which appear new may in fact have ancestors in plays which are lost. With this reservation I should quote the following as probably significant: the elaborate gradation of metre in the parodos of the *Medea* with recitative anapaests from the nurse, sung anapaests from Medeia, and lyrics from the chorus; the long opening monody of Hekabe in the *Hecuba* which rises and falls between recitative anapaests, sung anapaests, and lyric dactyls, Evadne's strange aeolo-choriambic strophe and antistrophe when poised above Kapaneus' pyre in the *Supplices* (990–1030); and Electra's opening monody with her hydria, moving from sung anapaests into aeolics with sung anapaests again between the second strophe and antistrophe, followed by an aeolic lyric dialogue with the chorus, a sequence which sets the style for many succeeding parodoi. None of these are technically laments, where a lyric outpouring of emotion by actors as well as chorus is expected. All of them are emotional. In all of them an actor sings. Euripides is blurring the contrast between what is normally reserved for actors and what is normally reserved for chorus.

Only the preserved plays show their total structure. Various instances have been noted where Euripides seems to achieve a kind of symmetry by balancing an earlier against a later scene. This is a dangerous subject;[9] it is too easy to chase out subtle symmetries in every play, and Euripides' liking for the unexpected on the whole makes against formal balance. In the *Medea* the Kreon scene and the first Jason scene are balanced after the central Aigeus scene by the second Jason scene and the report of Kreon's disaster. In the *Hippolytus* the appearance of Aphrodite at the beginning followed by the prayer to Artemis is balanced at the end by the hymn to Aphrodite and the

---

[9] My analysis of the *Medea* differs from E. Schlesinger, *Hermes*, 94, 1966, 36 and of the *Trojan Women* from O. H. Friedrich, *Euripides und Diphilos*, 73ff.

appearance of Artemis, and on the stage the second use of the *ekkyklema* to show Phaidra's body would recall her first entrance on a couch on the *ekkyklema*. In the *Andromache* the three lyric dialogues underline the three lowest points of misery for Andromache, Hermione, and Peleus. In the *Electra* when the audience see Klytemnestra arriving on a carriage with her servants, they naturally remember and contrast Elektra's entry with a waterpot on her head. But the nerve of the *Electra*, as of the later *Iphigenia in Tauris*, *Helen*, and *Ion*, and *Orestes*, is the plot.

I still think that the patterns which I noted in the *Trojan Women* and the *Bacchae* are valid.[10] In the *Trojan Women* the Kassandra scene and the Helen scene are elaborated into independent display pieces; before and after the Kassandra scene the interest centres on Polyxena; before and after the Helen scene the interest centres on Astyanax. Thus between the dialogue parodos and the final great lament the form of the whole play runs (a) Talthybios with misunderstood news of Polyxene, (b) *Kassandra*, (a¹) Andromache with news of Polyxene's death, (c) Talthybios with orders for Astyanax' death, (b¹) *Helen*, (c¹) Talthybios with Astyanax' body. In the *Bacchae* the sequence runs Dionysos (in human form) – Kadmos – *Pentheus* – Dionysos is defeated by Pentheus – *Persuasion of Pentheus* – Pentheus is defeated by Dionysos – *Agave* – Kadmos – Dionysos (in divine form). Here the early jubilant entry of Kadmos contrasts with his late heartbroken entry, and this technique of picking up and contrasting an earlier and a later entry of the same character is seen again with Antigone in the *Phoenissae* and Hermione in the *Orestes*.

So far only patterns involving actors have been mentioned, but there is a further question whether any pattern can be seen in the odes sung by the chorus. In the *Medea* the odes are all strictly relevant to the particular situation; four stasima (410, 627, 824, 976) are metrically and musically akin with each other and with the dactyls ending in single-short clausula sung by the chorus in the parodos; but just before the murder of the children they sing shocked dochmiacs (1251). Here we can speak of metrical-musical pattern and contrast. In style the lovely first strophe and antistrophe of the third stasimon (824) is quite different from the rest: the chorus sing of Athens, Muses, Harmonia, Kypris, Erotes, and Wisdom in a decorated style with many adjectives and

[10] *Greek Art and Literature, 500–430 B.C.*, 159.

compound adjectives, and beautiful phrase added to beautiful phrase until the thread of the sentence almost or quite breaks under the strain. This decorated style is recognizable in many later choruses. In the *Hippolytus* it is used to describe washing-day in the parodos and the places to which the chorus wish to escape when Phaidra has announced her intention to commit suicide – escape to a world of mythological fantasy, 'the apple-tree, the singing and the gold'. Hippolytos' hymn to Artemis, the parodos, and the three stasima (525, 732, 1102) are akin metrically and musically with variants of aeolic, but the strophe sung by the chorus after Phaidra's confession is pure dochmiac (Phaidra herself sings the antistrophe when she has overheard Hippolytos' tirade against women) and the late hymn to Aphrodite is largely dochmiac. Here too we see metrical-musical pattern and contrast.

For us the *Andromache* is the first play in which Euripides uses decorated odes giving relevant traditional mythology as a foil to the story which he is representing realistically. Andromache is back in Troy in her elegiac lament before the parodos, the first stasimon describes the judgment of Paris and his birth, the third stasimon ends with the glorious deeds of Peleus, the fourth stasimon describes the Trojan War and the Greek return, and Peleus goes back to Trojan War themes in his dactylic lament for Neoptolemos. The large dactylic element in the 'Trojan' odes links them to Andromache's elegiacs as well as to Peleus' lament. This technique of linking choral odes by kindred subject matter-traditional mythology relevant to the play – as well as by kindred metre is common also in later Euripides. Trojan mythology occupies all three stasima of the *Hecuba* and *Trojan Women*, the first stasimon of the *Electra*, the parodos of the *Iphigenia in Tauris*, the parodos and second stasimon of the *Helen*, the parodos and all three stasima of the *Iphigenia in Aulis*. So also Theban mythology dominates the stasima of the *Phoenissae* and the mythology of Dionysos the choral odes of the *Bacchae*. Very occasionally the mythology is only marginally relevant – the Apollo chorus in the *Iphigenia in Tauris* (1234) and the Magna Mater chorus in the *Helen* (1301). In the late plays traditional mythology also provides material for monodies: Antigone sings of the Seven in the *Phoenissae*, Elektra sings Pelopid mythology in the *Orestes* (982), and Iphigeneia sings of the Judgment of Paris in the *Iphigenia in Aulis* (1284). Here the actor is absorbed completely into the style and the subject matter evolved for the chorus, even where singing free monodies and not leading the chorus as in the parodoi. In the dialogue-parodoi of the late plays there is naturally no distinction of style between the actor and the chorus, and here mythology and everyday are transmuted into the same decorated fantasy: Helen sings of her troubles, the chorus sing of washing day, Helen sings of the sack of Troy and the death of Leda and the Dioskouroi, the chorus sing of Zeus raping Leda as a swan, Helen ends with Paris' voyage to Sparta and her removal by Hermes.[11] The same style is used for the dawn parodos of the *Phaethon*, Ion's dawn monody, and the Phrygian's narration of the attack on Helen in the *Orestes*.

The Phrygian's narration is a masterpiece of the new musical and metrical technique which probably shows the influence of Timotheos. It is first seen in the recognition duet of the *Iphigenia in Tauris* but a similar duet may well have occurred in the *Alexandros* of 415 B.C. Essentially the new actor-music is free of the bonds of strophic correspondence (astrophic) and exhibits considerable variety of metre within a single song (polymetric). Ion's lovely dawn song, however surprising in its subject matter for an audience which associated monody with lamentation, is metrically traditional. He starts in recitative anapaests, then sings an aeolic strophe and antistrophe, and ends with a long epode in sung anapaests. Kreousa's monody, sung in the depths of her misery and contrasting with the joy of the unawakened Ion, is entirely in sung anapaests with occasional dochmiacs, but this mixture is already found in the *Hecuba* (177ff.) in the lyric dialogue between Hekabe and Polyxene. For us the great polymetric astrophic songs start with Antigone, Iokaste, and Oidipous in the *Phoenissae*. Perhaps Amphion's monody in the same year developed from its hexameter beginning (1023N²) to a long astrophic polymetric monody, which made the chorus feel that they were in heaven (911N²). The *Orestes* has, besides the Phrygian's narrative, the long polymetric epode in which Elektra takes refuge in the past mythology of her family (982ff.).

In dialogue Euripides reintroduced the recitative trochaic tetrameter[12] at the beginning of Group III (the *Meleager* fragment, 536N², probably belongs to the first production of Group III, perhaps 416 B.C.). He goes back to the practice of Aeschylus' *Persae* in having a second

[11] *Hel.* 164ff. cf. particularly *I.T.*, *Hyps.*, *Andromeda*. The earliest preserved is *Electra*.
[12] Cf. most recently M.Imhof, *Mus. Helv.* 13, 1956, 125ff.

metre for dialogue scenes, a recitative metre instead of spoken iambic trimeters. (The *Persae* has four passages amounting to 117 lines.) The only other trochaic tetrameters before the *Meleager* are 28 in the *Agamemnon* and the 16 doubtful lines at the end of the *Oedipus Tyrannus*. For us Euripides starts with Kassandra's final speech (*Tro.* 444–461) where she demands to be taken as a death-bride to Agamemnon's ship. Every later preserved play and the fragments of *Oidipous* and *Archelaos* show this metre in varying quantities. The most striking examples are *Ion* with 84 lines in three scenes – the meeting between Xouthos and Ion, Kreousa's hurried arrival to take refuge on the altar, and the final move-off of Ion, Kreousa, and Athena; *Orestes* with 114 lines in three scenes – Pylades' arrival and his persuasion of Orestes to attend his trial, Orestes driving the Phrygian back into the palace, and the chorus' announcement of Menelaos' arrival; *Iphigenia in Aulis* with 210 lines in three scenes – Agamemnon's quarrel with Menelaos, the old man's intervention with Achilles and Klytemnestra, and the last scene between Iphigeneia, Klytemnestra, and Achilles. What is more, internally the trochaic tetrameter is developed in exactly the same way as the iambic trimeter: the number of long syllables resolved into two shorts per 100 lines is 16.7 in the *Trojan Women*, 22.5 in the *Iphigenia in Tauris*, 26 in the *Ion*, 36 in the *Orestes*, and 49 in the *Iphigenia in Aulis*.

So that from the time of the Trojan trilogy of 415 B.C. we not only have characters singing the new astrophic polymetric monodies, but also using the recitative trochaic tetrameter for dialogue scenes, as a kind of utterance somewhere between spoken iambics and lyrics, and the steady rhythm of the trochaic tetrameters becomes blurred and unstable in the latest plays in just the same way as the rhythm of the iambic trimeters (the figures for resolved long syllables in iambics are *Trojan Women* 21.2%, *Iphigenia in Tauris* 23.4%, *Ion* 25.8%, *Orestes* 39.4%, *Iphigenia in Aulis* 34.7%).[13]

The question is how far these metrical developments reflect a new approach to the story. Certainly they obscure the clear contrast between spoken and sung which marked classical tragedy. Recitative (previously confined to anapaests of characters and chorus) is reintroduced for dialogue so as to make a new level between spoken and sung. The great increase of resolved syllables in spoken and recitative and the abandon-

[13] Cf. above, p. 2.

ment of strophic correspondence and dominant metres for astrophic, polymetric songs is something like the substitution of plastic shading for line drawing.[14]

I have suggested already[15] that there may be some relation between the new metrical form and the new unstable characters or, to put it perhaps more safely, between the new metrical-musical form and the reaction of the characters to a very varied sequence of situations. This formulation fits Hekabe in the *Trojan Women*, Herakles in the *Hercules Furens*, Pentheus in the *Bacchae* as well as Ion, Kreousa, Iphigeneia, and Orestes, who were mentioned above.

We can at least ask what other new elements can be seen in late Euripidean tragedy and whether any of them are relevant to this development. The clearest mark of late Euripides is the increase in the number of people who affect the action, people both in the family circle and beyond it. This is a further development of the naturalistic construction noted early in Euripides.[16] Broadly speaking, the action in the early plays is directed by a few strong characters and in the late plays is pushed this way and that by a larger number of less decisive characters. This statement is applicable to all the preserved late plays except the *Iphigenia in Tauris* (where the foreign setting and the insignificance of Thoas have kept the lines simple) but most obviously to the *Electra*, *Phoenissae*, *Orestes*, *Iphigenia in Aulis*, and *Bacchae*, where we either know or can easily imagine how Aeschylus and Sophocles represented or would have represented the story.

Euripides saw the story as the resultant of a number of forces which might be of unequal power but were none of them negligible. The slave, loyal or disloyal, may have the minimum authority but in the early *Alkmaion in Psophis*, *Alcestis*, *Hippolytus*, as well as in the later

[14] Cf. above, p. 54.
[15] Cf. above, p. 281.
[16] Cf. above, p. 280. I have avoided using the word Tyche, who is usually invoked in describing late Euripidean tragedy as a superhuman director of human events, Unreason or Chance (Schadewaldt, *Monolog*, 256f.; Solmsen, *Hermes*, 69, 1934, 400). Dr G. Busch (*Untersuchungen zum Wesen der Tyche*, Heidelberg, 1937, 55) says roundly that the epoch of Euripidean creation in which Tyche directs the action does not exist. When Ion after the recognition scene apostrophizes Tyche (1512) as the cause of disaster and success, he of course emphasizes the suddenness with which things have happened (*tyche*), but the things that have happened are that Kreousa attempted to murder Ion, Ion attempted to murder Kreousa, and the Pythia intervened, three human beings reacting quickly to the situations which confronted them.

Phrixos B, Ion, Archelaos and *Iphigenia in Aulis*, a slave gives a decisive push to the action. Slaves are included in the family; Teiresias in the *Phoenissae* is the family prophet; the Pythia stands *in loco parentis* to Ion. But an even wider circle may be called in.[17] In the political passages of the second group of plays, particularly the *Supplices*, Euripides makes us aware of crowd action. In the *Iphigenia in Tauris* the capture of Orestes and Pylades is due to a 'fool, bold in disbelief' (275) and in the *Bacchae* (717) 'a town orator' persuades the herdsman to try and capture the Theban maenads, thus provoking the violence which causes Pentheus to call out the army and lays him open to the persuasion of Dionysos. A similar character, suborned by Tyndareos, persuaded the Argive assembly to stone Orestes and Elektra, thereby setting in motion the whole later development of the *Orestes*. In the *Iphigenia in Aulis* the army is always in the background. Agamemnon dare not save Iphigeneia because of the army (514), and Iphigeneia finally accepts death because she knows what the army will do to Achilles (1348f., 1372f.).

For us the introduction of Menelaos, Peleus, and Orestes in the *Andromache* appears as the first step towards the developed family tragedy of the later years. The next step is the very individual *Electra* with the addition of the farmer and the old man and with Aigisthos much more positively conceived than in Aeschylus. Marriage debates obviously belong to family tragedy: not one is preserved but we know enough of the stories to see the different issues involved in the *Aiolos, Phaethon, Meleager, Antigone, Andromeda,* and *Archelaos*. Another common element in the late plays is the 'contest of lives'. In the early period Hippolytos and his fellows stand for one sort of life, Phaidra and hers for another. This sort of active clash between ideals can be seen later in the *Polyidos* and the *Palamedes*, in the *Phaethon* and the *Ion*, and in the *Bacchae*. The *Melanippe Desmotis*, if the reconstruction suggested is correct,[18] is the first instance of two brothers standing for different ideals, and this contrast is found again in *Antiope, Hypsipyle,* and *Phoenissae*. In all these cases the clash shows a diversity of temperaments within the family. It is only disastrous in the *Phoenissae*, where, it has to be admitted, Polyneikes, though far more sympathetic than Eteokles, also backs his claim by force. In the *Antiope* one suspects that

[17] Cf. H. Diller, *Entretiens Hardt*, VI, 1960, 88ff.
[18] See above, p. 154.

Euripides' sympathies lie with the artistic rather than with the military brother, as also with Polyidos and Palamedes; but Amphion, like Ion, has become a man of action before the end of the play.

Loyalty between members of the family and friends is a positive value which Euripides wants to assert, like the heroism of Makaria and Menoikeus and the disinterestedness of Phaethon and Ion. Here he does not distinguish between wife and husband, brother and sister, friend and friend. The loyalty of Alkestis to Admetos and of Peleus to Phoinix in the early period is essentially the same as the loyalty of Iokaste to Oidipous in the late *Oidipous* and the loyalty of Theseus to Herakles in the *Hercules*, but Oidipous and Herakles are involved in worse and more contagious disasters than Admetos or Phoinix. In the later plays Euripides is fascinated with the affinities between brother and sister (particularly *I.T.* and *Orestes*), friends (the same two plays), husband and wife (*Helen, Oidipous*). It may be felt even where parents and children have not yet recognized each other (perhaps *Melanippe Desmotis*, certainly *Ion* and *Hypsipyle*, and most movingly *Alkmaion in Corinth*). In the young this affinity may be perceived across the sexes and may burst into love, Perseus and Andromeda, Haimon and Antigone, Achilles and Iphigeneia. It may even appear in elderly muddlers who have quarrelled desperately, and they may then be reconciled like Agamemnon and Menelaos in the *Iphigenia in Aulis*.

Youthful heroism and idealism but occasionally villainy, elderly muddle or self-seeking or fear but occasionally wisdom and affection, slaves loyal or treacherous, family likeness and family diversity, awareness of a larger community outside the family, all phrased in the terms of fifth century discussion, these are the realistic elements in Euripidean tragedy. But they are clothed in the traditional forms of fifth-century tragedy, which, however much Euripides altered them, however much he increased the range of expression between spoken, recitative, and sung, could not but remain conventional, far more conventional than the prose of modern drama (although we are too apt to forget that this also has its own conventions).[19]

[19] I have spoken all through this book of Euripides' characters as people about whom judgments can be made, and I believe that he so conceived them. One major reservation must be made. What they say is conditioned by the context in which they say it and therefore must not be taken out of context as an expression of their personality. Context includes not only the particular situation or the particular person or persons who are addressed but also the dramatic form used: prologue, monologue, debate, stichomyth,

✣ In addition to having to use traditional forms Euripides has to use traditional stories, stories about gods and heroes, which had never been treated so realistically before. Aeschylus so represents the traditional story that the human characters show the operation of divine law, and his plays essentially exemplify the view of Hesiod and Solon that Zeus is just. Sophocles is more concerned to show what kind of characters make the traditional story come true, but his religious position is not far from Aeschylus and he has no doubt that oracles are always proved right. It is far more difficult to define Euripides' religious position, and here, if anywhere, what one is tempted to say on the basis of one play will be found contradicted in another. We can only look carefully and always ask in whose mouth and in what context the words are put.

Among Greek attitudes to gods and heroes we can distinguish the attitude of the ordinary man who takes part in cult, the attitude of the believer towards oracles (the truth of which may be regarded as proving the existence of gods), the attitude of epic poetry (in which the gods intervene directly in human affairs), the Hesiodic-Aeschylean view that divine government is just, if slow to operate, the scientific and philosophical attitudes touched upon in the first chapter, and two views derived from epic poetry but still alive, one that human conduct can be justified by divine or heroic examples (I shall call this the paradeigmatic theory) and the other that the heroic world was a superior world to which the poets gave the only certain immortality.

In all the surviving plays except the *Iphigenia in Aulis* (where we have lost the end)[20] and at least eleven of the lost plays the story was tied, generally by the *deus ex machina* at the end, to a holy place or a cult. This was quite unnecessary (Sophocles only does it explicitly in the *Oedipus Coloneus*) and much more incidental than the establishment of the Erinyes as Eumenides at the end of the *Oresteia*. Euripides is certainly

---

lament, lyric dialogue, monody, have each their own rhetoric which affects the words used and the views expressed. All this has to be taken into account, but when this is done the characters still remain different, recognizable, and individual. See particularly W. Zürcher, *Darstellung des Menschen im Drama des Euripides*, Basel, 1947; A. M. Dale, *Euripides Alcestis*, xxii; *A.U.M.L.A.*, 11, 1959, 3ff.; A. Lesky, *Entretiens Hardt*, VI, 1960, 125ff. On the dramatic forms themselves and their use in Euripides see particularly H. Strohm, *Euripides*, Munich, 1957; W. Ludwig, *Sapheneia*, Tübingen, 1954.

[20] Artemis must surely have prophesied that Iphigeneia would return and found the Brauron cult.

not saying that the hero or heroine so honoured is a model for men to follow. Neither Dirke in the *Antiope* nor Siris in the *Melanippe Desmotis* can possibly be fitted into the paradeigmatic theory but arrangements are made for cults in their honour. Artemis says that she will give Hippolytos 'very great honours in Troizene in return for this disaster' (1423); so for the hero the cult may be seen as a recompense for suffering. But Euripides must have felt that cult had some value for ordinary men or he would not have called attention to it. So the chorus of the *Electra* (171) invite Elektra to come to a festival of Hera as a normal part of Greek life. However much Euripides hated the violence and excesses of the maenads, when he makes them say 'What the ordinary crowd believe and practise I accept' (*Bacch.* 430), he probably agrees with them.[21] Protagoras regarded worship as a distinctively human activity, and Euripides repeatedly affirms its existence.

Besides the immortality given by cult there is the immortality given by poetry, and the other function of the *deus ex machina* is to reinsert the characters in the traditional story, which has preserved their exploits. This again was not necessary. Sophocles could end his *Electra* with no mention of the Furies and his *Trachiniae* with no mention of the apotheosis of Herakles. So Hekabe probably speaks with the voice of Euripides when she says (*Tro.* 1242f.) 'if god had not destroyed us, we should have been unknown; we should not have given songs to the Muses of posterity'. The stories are immortal, and by reasserting them the *deux ex machina* gives the characters back their immortality. Apollo at the end of the *Orestes* when he tells Orestes to marry Hermione whose throat Orestes is about to cut (or the Dioskouroi at the end of the *Electra*, or Hermes at the end of the *Antiope*) does not restore order, moral or cosmic; he merely reasserts the traditional story.

The traditional sequel to the *Orestes* is untrue in the sense that the Euripidean characters could not conceivably have taken their places in it. Poetic stories may be untrue. The chorus of the *Iphigenia in Aulis* (793) suggest that the story of Leda and the swan may be an inappropriate poetic fiction. The chorus in the *Electra* (737) do not believe that the sun changed its course because of mortal crime, but horror stories may make men serve the gods, which Klytemnestra forgot. Here

[21] I think Euripides is simply affirming *fortunatus et ille deos qui novit agrestes*, not celebrating his own ideal, 'la vraie paix du coeur' (A. J. Festugière, *Eranos*, 55, 1957, 144).

Euripides glances at the paradeigmatic theory. In the *Hercules Furens* (1314f.) Theseus puts forward the paradeigmatic theory: 'if what the singers say is true, the gods make illegal marriages, imprison their fathers to win tyranny, and yet live on Olympus; why should not Herakles a mortal bear his misfortunes?' Herakles answers (1341) 'I will never believe any of this. These are the miserable tales of the poets.' The stories are untrue (including, by implication, the divine birth of Herakles), but though Euripides, as we have seen, provides a modern psychological account of Herakles' madness,[22] he cannot cut completely adrift from his material and Herakles ends 'we are all destroyed by a single blow of Hera' (1932). Hekabe similarly demolishes Helen's defence by refusing to believe that Athena and Hera had a beauty contest or that Aphrodite came in person to Sparta, but to accept this insight is to demolish also the whole presupposition of the trilogy. For the moment, however, let us note that Euripides makes Hekabe and Herakles at a moment of great suffering reject the Homeric notion of divine intervention in human affairs.

The traditional stories may be untrue, they may or may not be paradeigmatic, but they are immortal and they may be beautiful. Euripides is too good a poet to abandon them, and so far from abandoning them he uses them as a foil of fantasy to the realistic action not only in the decorated choruses but also in some of the monodies. And everyday events are translated into the same style and transplanted into the same visual world: washing-day in the *Hippolytus*, dawn-song in the *Ion* and *Phaethon*, a starry night at the beginning of the *Iphigenia in Aulis*, as well as Antigone's description of the Seven in the *Phoenissae* and the Sphinx with the sun on its wings in the *Oidipous*. This last example is from an iambic prologue and so it is justifiable to add the messenger's description of the tent with its mythological tapestries in the *Ion*. There is a beautiful world of fantasy which may be enjoyed if you do not look below the surface. It is in some such sense that Euripides would have accepted the proposition that the heroic world was a superior world.[23]

The possibility of foretelling the future is one of the foundations of

[22] Cf. J. de Romilly, *L'Évolution du pathétique*, 103, cf. 97f. on Euripides' 'clinical' account of Orestes.

[23] On the whole question of the relation of myth and reality in Euripides see J. C. Kamerbeek, *Entretiens Hardt*, VI, 1960, 1ff.

Greek belief in the gods. In Theseus' account of the development of human civilization foretelling the future has its place (*Suppl.* 211f.), and in fact Euripides seems to have believed in the possibility of prophecy and Apollo's responsibility for it. An oracle can be rigged by an unscrupulous woman like Ino, and the old man in the *Ion* (825) believes that Xouthos has planted his illegitimate son in Apollo's temple. A prophet may be disbelieved – probably the prophet in the early *Likymnios* (920aN²), certainly Polymestor in the *Hecuba* (1280), Kassandra in the *Alexandros* and *Trojan Women* – but they are all proved right by events or by the known sequel to the acted story. Apollo himself is disbelieved by Orestes in the *Iphigenia in Tauris* (711), but is magnificently justified by the recognition and escape. And Theonoe, Polyidos, and Amphiaraos are represented as noble and respected figures.

But there are some difficult cases which need examination. The old man in the *Helen* (744f.) naturally complains that neither Kalchas nor Helenos ever suggested that Greeks or Trojans were dying for a phantom, but his reaction is entirely conditioned by the strange story which Euripides adopted for this play.

In the *Ion* (69f.) Hermes tells us in the prologue that Apollo will give his child to Xouthos and say that he is Xouthos' son so that when he gets back to Athens he may be recognized by Kreousa. This plan is wrecked by the old man and Kreousa, who attempt to murder the boy, and Athena has to patch up the situation at the end. Is it not justifiable to say that it is not Apollo's power of foreseeing the future that goes wrong but his method of dealing with mortals to bring the future to pass? So in the *Andromache* (1161) Apollo is criticized for remembering old scores against Neoptolemos, and in the *Electra* (both by Orestes (971) and by the Dioskouroi (1302)) and in the *Orestes* (29) it is the rightness of Apollo's command to kill Klytemnestra that is questioned, not his power to foresee the future.

So whereas there is no reason to doubt Euripides' belief in the possibility of prophecy, Apollo's intervention in human affairs may be criticized; in the same spirit Hekabe disbelieves that Athena and Hera submitted to the Judgment of Paris, and Herakles implies that his divine birth is an unfortunate poetic fiction. Perhaps one could say that where divine intervention is an essential part of the traditional story Euripides also provides a human explanation. Orestes plays a bigger part than

Apollo in the murder of Neoptolemos;[24] Elektra dispels Orestes' doubts about murdering his mother. It is at least suggested that Ion may have been a love-child (either of Xouthos or of Kreousa), and Amphion cannot believe that Antiope was raped by Zeus. But where a character accepts the fact of divine intervention, he is allowed to criticize: 'you are either a fool or unjust' says Amphitryon of Zeus, when the death of Herakles' children seems certain (*H.F.*, 340ff.). After Kreousa's story of her friend who was raped by Apollo, Ion attacks Apollo (436ff.) 'Do not do such things. As you are a ruler, you must pursue virtue. If a man is base, the gods punish him . . . if we imitate the gods' standards, it is not men who should be abused but their teachers.'[25]

Ion rejects such divine intervention as a bad example (the reverse of the paradeigmatic theory). He assumes that gods punish men for their sins. This Hesiodic-Aeschylean theory is a common assumption of Euripidean characters and choruses particularly when they think that criminals are being or will be punished.[26] But it does not go very deep; and Melanippe, trying to save her children, tears the assumption to shreds (506N²).[27] Here we desperately need the *Bellerophon*.[28] He seems to have held the Hesiodic-Aeschylean theory, but the facts of experience suggested that the gods either condoned crime or did not exist. He flew to heaven to find out. His disastrous fall certainly implied the existence of the gods, probably also that they do not punish vice at any rate in the way in which he conceived it happening, but he also drew the conclusion that man must live out his life according to his own standards of piety and friendship. Herakles also, when he has recovered his sanity and perceives that god if he is truly god has no human lusts or needs, decides to endure to the end (*H.F.*, 1341–50).

[24] Cf. above, p. 120. A. Lesky (*AAW*, 84, 1947, 99 = *Ges. Schr.*, 144f.) discusses very convincingly the part played by Orestes. My remaining doubt is whether Euripides thought of the voice (1147f.) as Apollo's or a fake. The messenger concludes that it was Apollo but the actual phrasing 'someone' leaves the other interpretation open. The Apulian volute-krater (Séchan, *Études*, 253, fig. 75; Pickard-Cambridge, *Theatre*, 90, fig. 18; Watzinger, *F.R.*, III, 349; Trendall, *Frühitaliotische*, 29, n. 46) illustrates the messenger speech: Orestes is sneaking away and looking back, i.e. he had concocted the plot which his accomplice carries out.

[25] Milder examples are the quizzical prayers noted above, pp. 186, 201, 214.

[26] E.g. Hekabe, when she thinks Menelaos will put Helen to death (*Tro.* 884f.).

[27] Cf. F. Solmsen, *C.Q.*, 38, 1944, 27ff.

[28] Cf. above, p. 110.

The god who needs nothing is clearly derived from Xenophanes, and Iphigeneia in the depths of misery quotes Xenophanes when she says that the Taurians, being themselves murderers, assume that their goddess likes human sacrifice (*I.T.*, 389ff.). Euripides gives his characters modern views of the gods at moments of crisis. This formula covers Hekabe's statement that Nomos is the master of the gods. 'For by Nomos we believe in the gods and determine right and wrong' (*Hec.*, 798ff.). She hopes to get Agamemnon's help in punishing Polymestor for the murder of Polydoros, and she asserts that the whole fabric of civilized life including law and religion depends on the conduct of those in authority. Civilized men have civilized customs and beliefs (just as the uncivilized Taurians in the *Iphigenia in Tauris* have uncivilized laws and beliefs). In the *Supplices* (201f.) Theseus ascribes the growth of civilization to divine providence, and this is clearly the background to the sane democracy which he advocates and which is shown in action in this play. Hekabe and Theseus give the kind of theory which the modernist can accept as a substitute for the Hesiodic-Aeschylean theory of divine punishment.

Theseus in the *Supplices* stands for Athens, and one would gladly suppose that he also stands for Euripides. Another modern theory (in no way incompatible with this) can more certainly be ascribed to Euripides himself. Hekabe, when she destroys Helen's claim that Aphrodite came with Paris to Sparta, says 'Your mind seeing him turned into Kypris' (*Tro.* 988). 'Aphrodite' in the *Iphigenia in Aulis* (1284ff.) is the desire of the Greeks to sail to Troy; Aphrodite in Hekabe's interpretation is the projection of Helen's desire. But this is also a reasonable description of Aphrodite in the *Hippolytus*, the projection of Phaidra's desire, and she is certainly a creation of Euripides, not a view which he gives for a moment to a character.[29] Euripides is saying that sexual passion is an influence on man's mind as strong as the influence attributed by Homer and ordinary men to the gods. So Artemis in the *Hippolytus* is the devotion to athletics, and Dionysos in the *Bacchae* is ecstasy, both delightful and destructive. In each case the identification of god and psychological state is easy; traditionally Aphrodite is the goddess of love, Artemis the goddess of hunting, and Dionysos the god of the maenads. But because they are gods, they can also appear as figures in

[29] Cf. A. Lesky, *Entretiens Hardt*, VI, 1960, 129ff.

mythology: Aphrodite hates Hippolytos, Artemis loves Hippolytos and will take vengeance on Aphrodite's favourite Adonis, Dionysos avenges the wrong done to his mother. And because they are gods, their cults may also be mentioned – Hippolytos' very individual reverence for Artemis, and the maenads' dances with their leader in honour of Dionysos.

Even in these cases where it is fairly certain that the modern view is held by Euripides himself, he also draws a traditional deity. Probably Hekabe in both plays, Herakles, Iphigeneia, and Theseus are given Euripides' own beliefs to utter, but this is not a 'message'. In so far as Euripides has a message, it is the play in its totality with all its metrical and musical varieties and gradations, all its range from beautiful fantasy to modern reality, all its differences of interpretation and behaviour, all its differences between characters and within single characters, a flux of events and emotions in which nevertheless certain human qualities are always condemned and certain human qualities are praised without qualification, but except for them 'the lights are dim and the very stars wander'.

Selected illustrations of lost
plays by Euripides[1]

GROUP I

AIGEUS

The vases are listed by B. B. Shefton, *A.J.A.*, 60, 1956, 159ff. (from which a selection is included here). I have discussed the interpretation in *Ant. Class.*, 34, 1965, 519. Dr Von Bothmer has told me of another early example, Paris Market, *Vente Hôtel Drouot, 28 juin 1966*, pl. 1, no. 101. N. Alfieri has published a fourth-century skyphos from Spina, Tomb 238c, not unlike the skyphos from Populonia below, *Mélanges Piganiol*, I, 613.

Attic kalyx-krater. New York 56.171.48. *A.R.V.*², 1057 (not far from Polygnotos). Shefton no. 3; *Ant. Class.* 34, 1965, 519, 450–25 B.C. Aigeus, Theseus and the bull, woman (Medea) with jug and phiale.

Attic skyphos. Florence, from Populonia, no. 80. Shefton, *loc. cit.*, 162, pl. 61, about 430 B.C. A. Theseus brings the bull. B. Medeia holding a box, and Aegeus.

Attic bell-krater. Madrid (red 217). *A.R.V.*², 1163, ptr. of Munich 2335. Shefton, *op. cit.*, 161, pl. 60, 2–3. 430–20 B.C. Aigeus, Theseus, Marathon greeting, bull, Medea with phiale.

Attic kalyx-krater. Adolphseck, 78. *A.R.V.*², 1346, Kekrops ptr. Brommer, *C.V.*, I, pl. 49–52; *Charites Langlotz*, 159; Shefton, *op. cit.*, 162. 420–400 B.C. Medea with phiale and jug. Aigeus. Theseus and the bull. Athena.

[1] Abbreviations are mostly standard: *A.R.V.* = J. D. Beazley, Attic Red-figure *Vase-painters*; *M.T.S.* = Webster, *Monuments illustrating Tragedy and Satyr-play*, B.I.C.S. Supplt. no. 14, 1962; *LCS* = A. D. Trendall, *Red-figure vases of Lucania, Campania, and Sicily*.

Apulian bell-krater. Adolphseck 179. Shefton, *loc. cit.*, 162, n. 25; *C.V.*, 2, pl. 80; Trendall and Cambitoglou, *Apulian of the plain style*, 19, Adolphseck painter. 400–380 B.C. Theseus pouring a libation on an altar; Aigeus holds his sword and hat; Medea drops her oenochoe. Attic bell-krater. Sydney 49.04. Pryce, *J.H.S.*, 56, 1936, 77, pl. 5; Metzger, *Réprésentations*, 319f.; Trendall, *J.H.S.*, 71, 1951, 192. 400–375 B.C. Theseus seated on a rock by an altar, Athena, Poseidon. Attic bell-krater. Ancona. *A.R.V.*², 1453; Shefton, no. 7; 375–50 B.C. Aigeus, Theseus and the bull, Medea with jug and phiale.

ALKMENE

Apulian kalyx-krater by Dionysiac painter. Taranto 4600. *Archaeological Reports*, 67, 1956, 62, pl. 5c. Above, Zeus, Eros, Hermes; Alkmene on pyre, thunderbolt, Amphitryon.

Paestan bell-krater by Python. British Museum F 149. Séchan, 242, pl. V; Trendall, *Paestan Pottery*, 56, no. 107 pl. 15. 350–25 B.C. Alkmene seated on an altar surrounded by golden rain. Antenor and Amphitryon light wood in front of the altar. Zeus causes Clouds to pour water on Alkmene. Eos looks on.

Campanian neck amphora, Andromeda group, British Museum F 193. Séchan, 244, fig. 73. Trendall, *Jb. Berl. Mus.*, 2, 1960, 18, fig. 9; *LCS*, 231, no. 36. 360–50 B.C. The same scene reduced to Amphitryon with torches, Alkmene, and the two Clouds.

CHRYSIPPOS

Attic red-figure krater. Pulzky Collection. Séchan, 315, fig. 90, dates 420–400 B.C. Laios carries off Chrysippos; Nymph (?) in the background urging him on.

Apulian amphora. Berlin 3239. Séchan, fig. 91. 350–25 B.C. Laios carries off Chrysippos. Youth tries to stop horses; Peleus pursues.

Apulian amphora. Naples H 1769. Séchan, fig. 92; Schmidt, Dareiosmaler, pl. 14a, 15a. 350–25 B.C. Laios carries off Chrysippos. Pedagogue pursues.

Praenestine bronze chest. Rome, Villa Giulia. Early third century B.C. Robert, *Ödipus*, fig. 54; Mansuelli, *Etruria and Early Rome*, 150, fig. 58. Laios carries off Chrysippos. Pedagogue pursues. Ionic column (limit of hippodrome).

KRETES

Fragment of South Italian red-figured kotyle. Oxford 1922. 208. About 415 B.C. J. D. Beazley, *J.H.S.*, 47, 1927, 226, pl. 21, 2; A. Cambitoglou and A. D. Trendall, *Apulian r.f. vases of the plain style*, 11, suggests a date soon after 420 (Sisyphos group). Daidalos affixes the wings on Ikaros.

Fragment of Apulian red-figure kalyx-krater. Amsterdam, Allard Pierson Stichting, 2572. *Allgemeine Gids*, no. 1398; J. D. Beazley, *J.H.S.*, 47, 1927, 223, pl. 21, 1; R. Cantarella, *Euripide: I Cretesi*, 38, pl. I. 350–40 B.C. Daidalos (and Ikaros?) supplicate Minos and Pasiphae. Above, tripod Apollo and Hermes.

Apulian Volute krater. Naples 1767. J. D. Beazley, *J.H.S.*, 47, 1927, 228, fig. 5. 350–25 B.C. Athena; Daidalos affixes wings on Ikaros; nymph, Krete (?).

Etruscan urns, Brunn-Körte, II, 79, pl. 28–30. Hellenistic.

Pl. 28, 1–2: Cantarella, pl. 3. Daidalos and his workmen make the bull. Daidalos (young) talks with Pasiphae.

Pl. 28, 3: Cantarella, pl. 5. Pasiphae takes refuge on an altar. Daidalos (young). Woman with baby Minotaur (cf. J. D. Beazley, *Etruscan Vase-painting*, 54f.). Man fleeing in astonishment at Minotaur baby.

Pl. 29, 4: Cantarella, pl. 6. Daidalos (old) seated bound. Pasiphae, nurse with Minotaur baby. Half-naked woman beseeching Minos. Attendant. Fury.

Pl. 29, 5: Cantarella, pl. 7. Man and woman. Woman with small Minotaur. Half-naked woman beseeching Minos. Daidalos with Ikaros seated between two attendants, one with spear, one with axe. Youth with cow.

Pl. 30, 6: Cantarella, pl. 8. Woman with little Minotaur. Woman running towards her. Half-naked woman beseeching Minos with sword.

Roman Sarcophagus. Louvre. Robert, *Sarkophag-reliefs*, III, 1 fig. 35. Daidalos and Pasiphae. The making of the bull. The short side: Minos and woman with fruits.

OINEUS

Paestan hydria, by Python. London, British Museum, F155. Séchan, fig. 125; Trendall, *Paestan pottery*, pl. 16b, no. 154. 350–25 B.C. King and woman advancing past young man holding sword towards man crouching on altar with his hands tied (AGRIOS). The inscription (previously doubted) has, as Professor A. D. Trendall informs me, been confirmed by an infra-red photograph.

PELIADES

Attic kalyx-krater, Tarquinia 685, *ARV²* 864 (manner of Pistoxenos ptr.). *Annali*, 1876, pl. F. 470–50 B.C. A. Alkandra in Attic peplos with sword, leading Pelias. B. Woman in chiton and himation welcoming them (acc. to Beazley another Peliad). Perhaps too early for Euripides.

Attic hydria. Cambridge 12.17. *ARV²* 623 (Villa Giulia ptr.), *C.V.*, pl. 40, 8; Séchan, fig. 138. G. Neumann, *Gesten u. Gebärden*, fig. 65 (innerer Kampf). 450 B.C. Woman in chiton and himation with sword. Woman in Attic peplos with right hand to her mouth and phiale in left hand. Woman starting back in horror.

Attic pyxis. Louvre CA 636. *ARV²* 1289 (Painter of Heidelberg 209). Séchan, fig. 137. 430 B.C. Pelias with stick. Peliades in Attic peploi: one with phiale and tainia (?), one with sword, one with both hands raised; between 1 and 2 cauldron, between 2 and 3 ram.

Attic cup. Vatican. *AZ* 1846 pl. 40; Séchan, fig. 136; G. Neumann, *Gesten u. Gebärden*, fig. 64 (besorgtes Nachdenken); 430 B.C. I, Pelias seated and Medea. A. Medeia with ram, 3 girls with coffers and phiale. B. Pelias led to cauldron. Woman with chiton, himation, and sword. Woman with hand on chin.

Marble relief. Rome, Lateran etc. G. M. A. Richter, *Sculpture and Sculptors*, fig. 308; H. A. Thompson, *Hesperia*, 21, 1952, 46ff.; E. B. Harrison, *Hesperia*, 33, 1964, 76. Copy of Attic original of about 420 B.C. Medeia in Persian headdress with box of herbs; girl bringing cauldron; girl with head resting on hand and sword.

Attic hydria. British Museum E224. *ARV²* 1313 (Meidias painter); *C.V.*, pll. 91–2. 420 B.C. Medeia between Arniope and Elera.

Fresco, Pompeii VI, 13, 2. 1st cent. A.D. Phot. Anderson 23445; Curtius, *Wandmalerei*, fig. 170; Reinach, *R.P.* 195, 1; *A.Z.* 1874, 134, pl. 13; Wilamowitz, *Kl. Schr.* I, 21; Weitzmann, *Hesperia*, 18, 1949, 176; Maiuri, *Roman Painting*, 45. Before a palace: right, Medeia holding a statue of Artemis, greeted by a Peliad. Centre, a figure seated with a girl beside; left, Medeia and the ram miracle; two Peliads impressed, the third sits back dissociating herself (Alkestis).

SKYRIOI

Attic Volute krater by Niobid ptr. Boston 33.56. About 450 B.C. Interpreted by E. Simon, *A.J.A.*, 67, 1963, 57, as Achilles leaving Deidameia, Lykomedes, and his other daughters, as distinct from the vases with Neoptolemos' departure: *ARV²* 536, Boreas ptr.; 633, Methyse ptr; 1044, Lykaon ptr. The first two are unlikely to be later than the Niobid painter.

Picture by Polygnotos, *S.Q.* 1060 ὁμοῦ ταῖς παρθένοις Ἀχιλλέα ἔχειν ἐν Σκύρῳ δίαιταν.

Picture by Athenion, *S.Q.* 1975 pinxit . . . Achillem virginis habitu occultatum Ulixe deprehendente.

Roman Sarcophagus. Cambridge, Fitzwilliam GR 45.1850. L. Budde and R. Nicholls, *Catalogue*, no. 162. Lykomedes in tragic costume. Daughters of Lykomedes. Deidameia kneeling to Achilles. Odysseus with trumpet.

STHENEBOIA

(Pictures of Bellerophon killing the Chimaira are not included.)

South Italian pseudo-panathenaic amphora (Amykos ptr.). Naples 2418. Séchan, 499, fig. 146; A. D. Trendall, *Frühitaliotische Vasen*, 177; *LCS*, 44, no. 218; Schauenburg, *J.D.A.I.*, 71, 1956, 82, fig. 24. About 400 B.C. Stheneboia; Proitos leaning on stick; Bellerophon with letter; Pegasos.

South Italian bell-krater. Naples 1891. Séchan, 500, fig. 147; A. D. Trendall, *Frühitaliotische Vasen*, 217; Schauenburg, *op. cit.*, 83 fig. 25. 400/375 B.C. Stheneboia in doorway with mirror and dish of fruit; Bellerophon and Pegasos.

South Italian stamnos (Ariadne ptr.). Boston 00.349. A. D. Trendall, *op. cit.*, pl. 23; *Plain Style*, 16. 400/375 B.C. Stheneboia coming out of door with bridal gesture, Proitos with sceptre giving letter to Bellerophon with Pegasos behind him. (On the other side, Theseus and Ariadne, see below, p. 303.)

Apulian volute krater. Ruvo 1499. Séchan, 498, fig. 145; Pickard-Cambridge, *New Chapters³*, 134, fig. 10. 350/25 B.C. Proitos leaning on stick gives letter to Bellerophon with Pegasos behind. Stheneboia seated, girl with fan.

Campanian hydria (Caivano group) Capua. A. D. Trendall, *Paestan Pottery*, 87, no. 273, fig. 54; *P.P.S.*, no. 367; *LCS*, 308, no. 571. 325 B.C. Bellerophon leaving Proitos.

TELEPHOS

Attic kalyx-krater. Berlin 3974. Metzger, *Représentations*, 287, pl. 39/1. Early fourth century. Telephos with his knee on the altar, sword in right hand and young Orestes on his right arm. Above left, Apollo seated; behind the altar a tree with pinakes, to the right a laurel spray and a basket. On the right, a woman runs away; Agamemnon rushes up with a spear. On the left, a woman runs away; a young man, dressed in a chlamys, with two spears in his left hand and his right arm extended, watches (Achilles?).

Campanian hydria (Ixion painter). Naples, RC141. Séchan, 509, fig. 149; Beazley, *J.H.S.*, 63, 1943, 95; Trendall, *Atti del Settimo Congresso*, 134; *LCS*, 338. 350–25 B.C. Telephos with Orestes on altar. Agamemnon rushes up from right with spear and is restrained by Klytemnestra; woman arrives from right tearing her hair. On right, bust of woman.

Apulian Vase. Lost. Séchan, 510, fig. 150; Tischbein, II, pl. 6. 350–25 B.C. Telephos on altar with Orestes. Woman rushes up from right to take child. On left, woman stops Agamemnon who holds spear.

Campanian bell krater. Naples 2293. Séchan, 511, fig. 151; Beazley, *J.H.S.*, 63, 73 (compares floral ornament with Parrish painter); *LCS*, 340, no. 804. 350–25 B.C. Telephos on altar with infant Orestes. Agamemnon approaches. Laurel sprays on either side of altar.

Etruscan column-krater. Berlin inv. 30042. Beazley, *Etruscan Vasepainting*, 66. 350–25 B.C. Like the Campanian bell-krater.

Attic relief. Squat lekythos. New York, Metropolitan Museum 28.57.9. G. M. A. Richter, *Handbook of the Greek Collection*, 1953, 116, pl. 95d. Late fourth century B.C. Telephos and Orestes on the altar, a woman extends both arms to the child.

Attic Pelike. Thessaloniki 34.263. *A.R.V.*² 1473. D. M. Robinson, *Olynthus*, XIII, 100, pl. 62, no. 48. 375–50 B.C. Telephos in pilos with baby; two bearded men conversing (Agamemnon and Odysseus?); man with chlamys (Achilles?).

THESEUS

Attic rf. kalyx krater. Syracuse 17427. *A.R.V.*² 1184/4. Kadmos ptr. E. Simon, *Antike Kunst*, 6, 1963, 14, pl. 5/2; C. Dugas, *R.E.G.*, 56, 1943, 19, fig. 13; Webster, *Greece and Rome*, 13, 1966, 27, pl. 2. 430/20 B.C. Aphrodite sends Eros to crown Ariadne whom Dionysos approaches. Athena crowns Theseus with olive and sends him to the ship where two of the fourteen are already. Poseidon looks on from above.

South Italian Stamnos (Ariadne ptr.). Boston 00.349. A. D. Trendall, *Frühitaliotische Vasen*, pl. 23; *Greece and Rome*, 13, 1966, 28, pl. 3. 400/375 B.C. Theseus returning to his ship, Athena, Ariadne asleep (on the other side of this vase Stheneboia, Proitos and Bellerophon, see above, p. 301).

GROUP II

AIOLOS

Lucanian hydria. Bari 1535. Séchan 236, fig. 71; *LCS*, 45, no. 221; Kalkmann, *A.Z.* 41, 1883, pl. 7, 1. 420–10 B.C. Kanake on couch with sword. Makareus bound, left; right, Aiolos with stick. Nurse, wife of Aiolos, other sons and daughters.

IXION

Campanian neck-amphorae (Ixion painter). Berlin 3023. Séchan, fig. 116; Neugebauer, *Führer*, pl. 73; Beazley, *J.H.S.*, 63, 1943, 94; Trendall, *Atti del VII⁰ Congresso*, 134; *LCS*, 338 nos. 787–8. Capua 7336. Beazley, Trendall, *loc. cit.*; *C.V.* IV Er, pl. 18–20. 350/25 B.C. Ixion tied to his wheel; Furies.

PHRIXOS

Attic neck amphora (Ptr. of Munich 2335). Naples, Stg. 270. *ARV*² 1161; *Annali*, 1867, pl. C; Roscher III, 2467, 8. 440/30 B.C. Woman holding axe (perhaps maenad rather than Ino) pursuing Phrixos who is mounting ram.

Paestan kalyx krater (Assteas). Naples 3412. Trendall, *P.P.*, no. 34; *PPS*, no. 40; Roscher III, 2467, 7. 360/40 B.C. Nephele holding out her cloak; Ram with Phrixos and Helle; Dionysos on Panther; Papposilenos behind; Triton and Scylla on sea-monsters.

Lucanian hydriae (Choephoroi painter). Naples 2858, Berlin F3144, Naples 1988, Paris market. Bock, *A.A.* 50, 1935, 508; Trendall, *LCS*, 120; *Robinson Studies*, 123. 360/30 B.C. Phrixos sacrificing the ram at the altar in the presence of Aietes, Chalkiope, and a young Oriental.

GROUP III

ANDROMEDA

Attic kalyx-krater. Berlin 3237. Séchan, A, fig. 76; Bieber, *History²*, fig. 110–1; Pickard-Cambridge, *Festivals*, fig. 164; *M.T.S.*, no. 34. Early fourth century. Andromeda (in Greek dress as in all Euripidean vases) standing on a rock with her arms stretched out. Above, right, Aphrodite and altar; left, Hermes and Aithiopian woman. Below, right, Perseus; left, Kepheus. Vegetation and chests (funeral offerings).

Apulian barrel amphora. Naples 3225. Séchan, B, pl. 6; Schauenburg, *Perseus*, pl. 24/12. 350–25 B.C. Kassiopeia seated; Andromeda between trees; Kepheus conducted by young Asiatic. Below, Perseus fighting sea-monster, Eros, Nereids.

Apulian pelike. Naples S.A.708. Séchan, C, fig. 77; Schauenburg, *Perseus*, pl. 23. 350–25 B.C. Above, Aphrodite and young Asiatic soldiers. Main zone, seated Kassiopeia; Andromeda between trees; Kepheus (restored as old woman) and young Asiatic. Below, Perseus and Monster between Nereid and Skylla.

Apulian fragments. Halle 214. Séchan, E, fig. 79; Bielefeld, *Wiss. Ztg.*, *Halle-Wittenberg*, 11, 1952/2, 100, pl. 16. 350–25 B.C. Kassiopeia seated with two women; Andromeda in a cave. Perhaps from another zone, soldiers and a woman seated on an altar.

Apulian vase. Naples S.A. 318. Séchan, I, fig. 83; Schauenburg, 58, much restored and overpainted. 375–50 B.C. Left, Kepheus kneeling to Perseus. Andromeda. Young man with wreath. Kassiopeia seated.

Apulian fragments. Würzburg. Langlotz, pl. 242, 855; Schauenburg, 59. 350/25 B.C. Nereids; Andromeda in cave.

Apulian plate. Taranto 8928. Schauenburg, 61, pl. 25/1. 350/25 B.C. Andromeda between trees with nimbus; Perseus to whom Kepheus kneels, supported by young Asiatic.

Apulian cylindrical amphora. Bari 5591. Schauenburg, 63, pl. 24/1, 25/2. 350/25 B.C. Perseus; Andromeda in cave; Kepheus.

Campanian hydria (Andromeda group). Berlin 3238. Séchan, D, fig. 78; Trendall, *Jb. der Berl. Mus.*, II, 1960, 11, *LCS*, 227, no. 8. 360/50 B.C. Andromeda in cave. Kepheus to left; Kassiopeia seated to right. Perseus (with winged sandals) and monster.

Apulian hydria. British Museum F185. Séchan, G, fig. 81. 350/40 B.C. Andromeda between two columns. Woman with hydria; Perseus (with winged sandals) and Kepheus seated.

Sicilian kalyx-krater (Lentini group). Caltagirone. Arias, *Dioniso*, 20, 1962, 50; Trendall, *Arch. Reports*, 1963–4, 46, *LCS*, 540, no. 29. 350–25 B.C. Andromeda in cave; left, dejected young man holding spear; right, Perseus (with winged sandals).

Wall-painting. Pompeii, I, ii, 6, east wall. Bieber, *History*[2], fig. 571; Robert, *A.Z.*, 1878, 13, pl. 3/1; Pickard-Cambridge, *Festivals*, fig. 71; *M.T.S.*, no. NP5, 1st cent. A.D. Mask of Perseus, young woman with fair hair (Andromeda?), Kepheus, woman with dark hair (Kassiopeia?).

ANTIOPE

Lucanian hydria (Painter of Naples 1959), Winterthur. H. Bloesch, *Antike Kleinkunst in Winterthur*, no. 34; *LCS*, 145, no. 792. 350–40 B.C. Woman seated in the open country spinning, two young men, one draped and leaning on a stick, one naked and standing erect with a spear.

Sicilian kalyx-krater (Dirce painter). Berlin 3296. Séchan, 306, fig. 88; Trendall, *Paestan Pottery*, 7, pls. 2a, 3a; *LCS*, 203, no. 27. 400–380 B.C. The bull with Dirke; Hermes outside the cave; cave with panther skin in the background, Zethos and Amphion about to kill Lykos, Antiope.

'Homeric' bowl. Athens 11798 Mid-2nd cent. B.C. U. Hausmann, *M.D.A.I.*(A), 73, 1958, 50, interprets Zeus as satyr raping Antiope in a cave; Amphion, Zethos, and shepherd; Bacchant (chorus), Dirke, Antiope.

HYPSIPYLE

Apulian amphora. Naples, M.N. 3255. Séchan, 360, fig. 3; Pickard-Cambridge, *Theatre of Dionysus*, fig. 20; Webster, *C.Q.*, 42, 1948, 17; *M.T.S.*, TV8. 330/20 B.C. Stage-building with Hypsipyle, Eurydike, Amphiaraos. Left, Thoas and Euneos. Right, Parthenopaios and Kapaneus. Above, left, Dionysos; right, Zeus and Nemea. Below, Archemoros lying on a couch and Paidagogos (holding lyre) leading soldiers with offerings.

Wall painting. Naples, M.N. 9039, from Pompeii, VI, ix, 6. Bieber, *History*², fig. 773; Pickard-Cambridge, *Festivals*, fig. 77; L. Richardson, *M.A.A.R.*, 23, 1955, 153, pl. 51, 1; Webster, *M.T.S.*, NP9. 1st cent. A.D. Amphiaraos with jug; Hypsipyle with baby.

MELEAGER

Attic vases by Meleager painter, Metzger, *Représentations*, 312ff.; *A.R.V.*², 1408–12, very early fourth century B.C., show Heroes assembled for the Kalydonian boar-hunt. On all Meleager is talking to Atalante. On the hydria in Ruvo, Jatta 1418 (*Bull. Nap.*, N.S. V, pl. 1) and on the kalyx-krater; Würzburg 522 (Metzger pl. 39/2), Eros also appears but is not actively engaged in the scene. On the krater, Vienna 158 (*Mon.* 4, pl. 43) one of the men is bearded and looks older than the rest, perhaps Oineus? On the amphora, Athens, N.M. 15113 (Metzger, pl. 40/4) the young hunter with an ivy-spray may be Telamon, who wore a vine-wreath for the boar-hunt (Euripides, fr. 530).

Attic pelike. Leningrad, Hermitage B4528, Metzger, pl. 41/4; Webster, *Athenian Art and Literature*, 81, pl. 11. 370–60 B.C. The boar-hunt. Artemis presides in the background. Atalante, Meleager, and Theseus on the left. Ankaios behind the boar.

Apulian amphora. Bari, Séchan, fig. 122. 350–25 B.C. Meleager gives Atalante the hide in the presence of Eros, Aphrodite, a bearded man leaning on a stick, and a fury.

Apulian volute krater. Naples, Santangelo 11. Séchan, fig. 123; Pickard-Cambridge, *Theatre*, fig. 22; F.R., iii, 200, n. 124; *C.Q.*, 42, 1948, 16; *M.T.S.*, TV 10. 350–30 B.C. Meleager helped to a couch in a building by Deianeira and Tydeus. Althaia(?) rushing out. Outside, mourning Peleus, Theseus, Oineus. Above, Aphrodite and Phthonos.

GROUP IV

OIDIPOUS

Apulian oinochoe. Ragusa collection. Lo Porto, *Bollettino d'Arte* (forthcoming), 350 B.C. Kreon (inscribed) seated in front of Sphinx (inscribed). Kreon is talking to Oidipous, who stands behind him: Oidipous' swollen feet are clearly marked. Perhaps illustrates, like A. D. Trendall, *Phlyax Vases*, no. 124, Euboulos' *Oidipous*, which may derive from Euripides.

Etruscan Urn. Florence. Brunn-Körte, II, 21, pl. 7, 1; Robert, *Ödipus*, I, 307, fig. 48. Seated woman with girl (Periboia?); man with staff directing action; three soldiers blind young kneeling Oidipous; two small boys lament; Iokaste rushes up held back by old man.

Homeric bowl. Louvre. Séchan, 438, fig. 124; Hausmann, *Hellenistische Reliefbecher*, no. 24; Webster, *H.P.A.*, 150. From right to left a woman seated on a dolphin; Hermes (inscr.) turns towards Periboia (inscr.) who picks up baby, letting fall a basket; Periboia puts the child Oidipous (inscr.) on the knees of Polybos (inscr.).

Index

I PLAYS AND FRAGMENTS OF EURIPIDES

(chief passages in italics)

II GENERAL INDEX